SACRA DOCTRINA

Christian Theology for a Postmodern Age

D1519344

www.ctrf.info

SACRA DOCTRINA

Christian Theology for a Postmodern Age

CREATION SET FREE

The Spirit as Liberator of Nature

SIGURD BERGMANN

With a Foreword by
JÜRGEN MOLTMANN

Translated by
DOUGLAS STOTT

WILLIAM B. EERDMANS PUBLISHING COMPANY
GRAND RAPIDS, MICHIGAN / CAMBRIDGE, U.K.

First published in German under the title
Geist der Natur befreit. Die trinitarische Kosmologie Gregors von Nazianz
im Horizont einer ökologischen Theologie der Befreiung.
© 1995 Matthias-Grünewald Verlag

English edition © 2005 Wm. B. Eerdmans Publishing Co.

Wm. B. Eerdmans Publishing Co.
255 Jefferson Ave. S.E., Grand Rapids, Michigan 49503 /
P.O. Box 163, Cambridge CB3 9PU U.K.

Printed in the United States of America

10 09 08 07 06 05   7 6 5 4 3 2 1

Library of Congress Cataloging-in-Publication Data

Bergmann, Sigurd, 1956-
[Geist, der Natur befreit. English]
Creation set free: the Spirit as liberator of nature / Sigurd Bergmann;
foreword by Jürgen Moltmann; translated by Douglas Stott.
p.   cm.
ISBN-10: 0-8028-2224-X / ISBN-13: 978-0-8028-2224-6 (pbk.: alk. paper)
1. Human ecology — Religious aspects — Christianity.
2. Gregory, of Nazianzus, Saint. 3. Liberation theology.   I. Title.

BT695.5.B46313   2005

261.8'8 — dc22

2005054130

www.eerdmans.com

Contents

I: The Altered Understanding
of Nature in Modernity: The Situation

II: The Trinitarian Cosmology
of Gregory of Nazianzus: A Tradition

III: Cosmology as Soteriology —
a Constructive Correlation

Foreword

A foreword is not a review. Its purpose is not to discuss or dispute a book, but to introduce it, to open it up and draw attention to its wealth and to the new material it contains. A foreword should also be brief so that the reader can quickly get to the matter at hand. My purpose here is accordingly to open the door and roll out an introductory carpet.

With his book *Creation Set Free: The Spirit as Liberator of Nature*, the author presents an extraordinarily expansive work whose wealth of material links quite disparate fields and whose surprising associations open up completely new vistas. Those who allow this book to exert its influence on them will quickly generate new ideas of their own. Indeed, the most flattering thing one can say about any book — and something for which one should always doubtless be grateful to the author — is that it creatively inspires its readers. This book does that.

Although Western theologians and philosophers from Augustine to Calvin and from Descartes to Jaspers have long been familiar with the correlation between the understanding of God and the understanding of self, this exclusive concentration on "God and the soul" has always also included the potential for degrading, subjugating, and otherwise destroying nature. What we now know as the "ecological crisis" of the present first brought this danger to public consciousness. If human beings are themselves "part of nature," as maintained by the United Nations' Earth Charter, then any destruction of nature necessarily also includes an element of human self-destruction. Hence, not only are our understandings of God and of human beings intimately connected, but with them our understanding of nature as well, either positively or negatively.

Sigurd Bergmann accomplishes at least two things in this book. First, he critically and constructively summarizes the previous initiatives toward an ecological theology, and second, he reflects on these initiatives in connection with Gregory of Nazianzus's trinitarian theology. Although this undertaking initially takes us somewhat by surprise because of its seemingly illogical nature, it ultimately yields a wealth of insights as the author develops an ecologically relevant doctrine of creation and redemption. Whatever else may link late antiquity to our own situation in late modernity, this Eastern church father can indeed free us from the one-sidedness of the Western church father.

In referring to his own vision as an "ecological theology of liberation," Bergmann is alluding to the same freedom for which "groaning creation" yearns according to Paul (Rom. 8:19ff.). Here Bergmann positions himself on the bridge between the social revolution of Latin American "liberation theology," on the one hand, and the doctrine of "physical redemption" as articulated by early church and Orthodox theology, on the other. New associations flash into view together with correspondences that have previously occurred to hardly anyone, least of all to contemporary Orthodox theologians. Although the bridge on which Bergmann stands looks down upon the groaning of nature amid increasing exploitation and destruction, above that bridge one can sense together with Bergmann the turbulent life forces of the "Spirit that liberates." For what better describes the preeminent task of God's Spirit on behalf of all creatures than to create, liberate, and redeem life?

I admire the ingenuousness with which the author develops his "ecological theology of the liberation of nature" against the background of Gregory's trinitarian cosmology. It is precisely against this theological background that Bergmann's theology acquires its own luminosity. Bergmann manages to understand not only the sociality of creation, but its movement as well. While theologians have indeed already presented various initiatives concerning the concept of time against a trinitarian background and concerning the attendant concept of space, to my knowledge no one has yet proposed any comparable understanding of the concept of movement that includes God's inner-trinitarian movement as well as God's movement in connection with both creation and redemptive history.

The author is concerned with "cosmology and soteriology," that is, with redemption that encompasses the entire cosmos rather than merely human salvation. He is concerned with understanding the cosmos as something that is itself involved in redemption rather than as the mere material or stage of the human salvific drama. Because he establishes connections in this regard by drawing on the concept of correspondence, the reader frequently encounters references, for example, to how the communal God corresponds to the communality of creation or to how God's movement corresponds to the movement of the liberation of creation, and so on. Although he adheres here to the Chalcedonian notion of "unmixed and unseparated," one might ask whether the concept of correspondence — like the concept of analogy — does not emphasize the notion of distance more than that of transition. With regard to the philosophy of nature, Friedrich Cramer's theory of "world resonance" (*Symphonie des Lebendigen: Versuch einer allgemeinen Resonanztheorie* [Frankfurt, 1996]) might be helpful here. Perhaps perichoretic thinking might also help bridge the distance inhering within the concept of correspondence.

Alongside the enormous wealth of material, one can certainly also praise this book's exemplary structural clarity. Although the reader is led through a myriad of discussions and details, the table of contents always provides sure orientation. Gregory of Nazianzus's own writings provide the thematic topics in part II: (1) sociality, (2) movement, (3) suffering, (4) Spirit. Part III then incorporates these topics into its thematic summary and discussion of the contemporary initiatives toward an ecological theology from John Cobb, Günter Altner, Jürgen Moltmann, Christian Link, Gerhard Liedke, Sallie McFague, and Rosemary Ruether. Although this thematic cross section does not do justice to the larger vision of these authors' theologies, it does help the author develop his own "ecological theology of liberation." The "methodological considerations" (chap. 6) are helpful insofar as they demonstrate to the reader the work's overall methodological soundness.

In this book, Sigurd Bergmann manages to survey, summarize, and assess a thirty-year theological discussion and then to move it a considerable distance forward. Rather than moving about in the uncontested theological mainstream, he delights in transgressing boundaries. Rather than searching for comforting answers, he looks for disturbing questions. Rather than thinking in an anxious mono-causal fashion, he delights in free association. Whereas the original version of this book represented his doctoral dissertation at Lund (1995), his second work (1997) draws from the aesthetics of nature, the cultural sciences, architecture, urban ecology, and landscape painting. By engaging in theology in the midst of the larger world, he becomes the dialogue partner for many outside the church as well. Indeed, he engages in theology not as the doctrine of faith or as church dogmatics, but as theology of the kingdom of God, to use my own expression. Although such theology is still a rarity today, it may well become the future of Christian theology.

JÜRGEN MOLTMANN
Tübingen, February 6, 2003

Preface to the English Edition

When I began this study in 1988, I was only intuitively conscious of the creative complexity of the project. The emphatic objections I received early on from provoked opponents, that it was academically unacceptable to use a contemporary problem formulation as a hermeneutical tool for the investigation of an older source, made me quickly aware of the challenge. It seemed to be necessary to describe the issue explicitly — not in a veiled manner, as is common — and to examine transparently whether the antique text could offer, if not answers, then perspectives, contrasts, and fresh lenses on the contemporary ecological challenge to theology.

I hope the reader will agree that this is actually what happens if one takes seriously the task of understanding Gregory in the context of both his *and* our place and time. I still often wonder why so many academic studies do not develop a similar openness of sharing and using the presuppositions of the interpreter in developing correlation studies.

Only two of the many international reviews of the original edition of this work have made explicit use of a normative formulation as a hermeneutic tool to postulate the historical uselessness of this study. The majority of academic responses, from many countries and disciplines, have shared the astonishingly sweet fruits of such an approach. Pastoral theologians in churches were more eager and able to transform their readings into practical flourishing projects, for example, in post-Soviet eastern Germany and northwest Russia as well as in Brazil, Costa Rica, and South Africa.

One can learn much from Gregory the Theologian. His work unfortunately and undeservedly has lain dormant for a long time in the shadows of Western theology, in spite of his first-rung position in the East, together with

John the Evangelist and Symeon the New Theologian.[1] In much the same way that the renewed reading of Maximus the Confessor in the West has radically fertilized patristic and ecumenical discourses,[2] a reappraisal of the Cappadocians offers many rich fruits that should be shared by different confessional Christian traditions. Today, a study of Gregory's trinitarian theology seems to be crucial for the explosive challenge to revision pneumatology in the transcultural spaces of globalization and new spiritualities.[3]

"That what God has begun he also fulfils." With an eloquent and clear pen, so typical for him, Gregory thus describes the cosmic horizon in which nature's and humanity's drama of salvation takes place.

Creation and salvation, although often placed in destructive opposition to each other in the history of Christianity, indissolubly rest in each other here. If God is the Creator of all, everything necessarily appears in God's loving eye and is touched by his/her artistic, liberative hands. How else could it be?

Every religious interpretation of life develops particular and local, as well as universal and global, claims of validity. Believing in God, who has begun the creation of this world, also includes longing for the perfection of God's work, to be realized in synergy with his/her creatures of all levels of the crying earth.

"For the creation was subjected to futility — not willingly but because of God who subjected it — in hope that the creation itself will also be set free from the bondage of decay into the glorious freedom of God's children. For we know that the whole creation groans and suffers together until now" (Rom. 8:20-22).

I regard Gregory's desire to express his experiences with the living "God in context" as the driving force behind his highly creative and constructive formulations about the Spirit's *inhabitation* in creation. Reflection about God's ongoing revelation and the still open-ended drama of salvation fuels Gregory's powerful constructions. His consequent emphasis on the earthly and historical dimension of God's acting in this world leads him and the whole *communio sanctorum* to the mature doctrine of the triune God, salvation, and creation.

"Only that which he has assumed can actually be redeemed." Thus reads another of Gregory's strikingly well-formulated insights that deepens the in-

1. Cf. Anestis G. Keselopoulos, *Man and the Environment: A Study of St. Symeon the New Theologian* (Crestwood, N.Y., 2001).

2. See Lars Thunberg, *Microcosm and Mediator: The Theological Anthropology of Maximus the Confessor,* 2nd ed. (Chicago, 1995).

3. Cf. Sturla St. Salsett and Berge Furre, eds., *Spirits of Globalisation: The Growth of Pentecostalism and Experiential Spiritualities in a Global Age* (forthcoming), and my contribution to this volume, "Revisioning Pneumatology in Transcultural Spaces."

tegration of salvation in creation even more. The salvation of creation necessarily needs to be developed from the inside of life. For Gregory and Christianity God has chosen to share the poor conditions of bodily life, and to heal and liberate that which she/he bodily assumes.

The *ecumenical* significance of the study of Gregory is obvious, both in a historical and a geographical perspective, through its location between late antiquity and late modernity and between Eastern and Western spheres in Europe. The broad reception of the original German edition of this work (1995), and its translation into Russian (Arkhangelsk University Press, 1999) and extensive use in many different regions and contexts, and now an English translation, fill the author with humility and strengthen his vision of a reconciled diversity of natures and cultures.

The book is also significant in an *interdisciplinary* way. While some have interpreted it as an enriching contribution from the humanities to an emerging, broad environmental science characterized by methodological pluralism with regard to explosive sociocultural problems, others have regarded it from a certain distance and preferred to continue their ontological projects in the field of science and theology, unaware of the scientific commodification of nature. Georg Picht's famous question still seems very applicable in this context: How can science be true if its application destroys its own object (nature)?

One of the aims of this book is to manifest the critical difference between natural science and technology (commodifying and ruling over nature) and environmental science (furthering nature's flourishing on its own terms). It is my hope that the book's proposals and language games inspire the deepening of the interaction of religious studies/theology, on the one hand, and environmental science and technology on the other—not for the sake of humanity alone, but for the development of the best of life and "our common good."[4]

Research in European countries, the European Union, and the USA has still not invested adequately in transdisciplinary studies of *the human dimension* of nature and environment, although even a child can recognize that the solution to man-made problems on the planet requires reflection about and a change of human beings. It would please me greatly if Saint Gregory's under-

---

4. John Cobb's and Herman Daly's work in this area still represents one of the few successful models for such a coreflection about nature, religion, environment, and God. Herman E. Daly and John B. Cobb, *For the Common Good: Redirecting the Economy toward Community, the Environment, and a Sustainable Future,* with contributions by Clifford W. Cobb, 2nd ed., updated and expanded (Boston, 1994).

standing of life could be used to challenge and change the borders of academic power and money sharing for establishing a truly transdisciplinary environmental science.

Two impulses fueled this study. Firstly, I wanted to build a bridge between the growing environmental movement and the Christian interpretation of life, influenced by the ecumenical movement's clear confession in Uppsala 1968 that it is the world that offers the agenda for the church, and by Moltmann's likewise clear insight into the whole Trinity's suffering in *The Crucified God.*

Secondly, I had by chance come across a small volume of Gregory of Nazianzus's two homilies "On the Love to the Poor" and "On Peace." What started as a casual reading of these sermons, without any particular focus, turned into a dizzy adventure, which is still going on, that challenged me to satisfy my curiosity about how it could be possible that such an old text — in my tradition quite unknown and strange — could express and address so many clarifying, problematizing, exciting, and creative perspectives inside me, and be relevant for others as well.

Gregory's central thesis in the first of these two homilies is that love for the poor is the best criterion for the believer's love for God, for his/her neighbor, and for himself/herself. Love for the poor simply offers the most visible evidence for being a Christian and reveals the God who acts.

The Cappadocian's claim coincided so clearly with Gustavo Gutiérrez's famous approach representing not only the modern Latin American liberation theology but also the classical biblical and patristic tradition where love for the poor is at the heart not only of ethics but also of theology and anthropology in general.

It was easy to widen this insight from the human person not only to nature in general but also to the suffering creatures in the so-called global environmental crisis, which affects all life-forms and ecoprocesses on the planet in a widespread globalization process that has no apparent goal other than the accumulation of finance capital.[5] Gregory's text and his emphasis of the bodily being of the poor firmly pushed me to formulate what in the subtitle of the German edition was called "The Trinitarian Cosmology of Gregory of Nazianzus in the Horizon of an Ecological Theology of Liberation."

I am glad to belong to the first generation of theologians[6] to investigate

5. Cf. Ulrich Duchrow and Franz J. Hinkelammert, *Property for People, Not for Profit: Alternatives to the Global Tyranny of Capital* (London, 2004).

6. The original version was published at the same time as Leonardo Boff's *Ecology and Liberation: A New Paradigm* (Maryknoll, N.Y., 1995), while Sallie McFague describes "ecological theology" as a North American liberation theology. *Life Abundant: Rethinking Theology and Economy for a Planet in Peril* (Minneapolis, 2001), 33f.

this path of an *ecotheology of liberation* for interpreting God in what has been called "the millennium of the environment, challenging peoples and nations."[7] Ecotheology is not, as many still misunderstand it to be, just another trendy approach totally dependent on modern social flows and movements. Ecotheology is the experiential and historic-systematically revisioning of theology in general in the horizon of God's mystery of creation and salvation. Ecotheology of liberation is — and this might be the only real conclusion from this book — in full accordance with classical theology, and it might even be the central continuation of classical theology in the globally changing world of today and tomorrow.[8]

This edition offers a shortened and, in language style, heavily revised version of the original German edition (1995). During the last ten years discourse about the relation of the image of God and the view of nature has developed and expanded its interfaces with other discourses. Had I written the book today, other themes would have naturally been highlighted. Here I can point to only some of them, such as globalization,[9] the many-faceted ecofeminist approaches, the ecological spirituality inside and outside of established religious traditions, and the conflict between ecomanagement and ecojustice ideologies and practices in politics and ethics.

Not least should the rich sources of a theologically reflected environmental aesthetics be mentioned, representing a colorful garden that I have started to dig in a bit since 1999 in projects about "Spirit, space, and atmospheres." Also, the linkages between geography, architecture, and religious studies have kept me busy, after I discovered the formulation of "the topology of the Spirit" in a section of this book.[10]

Colleagues sometimes do not understand how one can finish this book in 1994 and walk straight into a long-term study of indigenous visual arts in the Arctic north, even if it once more entailed the reciprocal interactions of religion and nature. That work is now completed, in which also were addressed the interactions of arts and ethnicity. These four corners (religion, nature, arts, ethnicity) represent the thematic rectangle of my study about

---

7. Ernst Ulrich von Weizsäcker, *Erdpolitik: Ökologische Realpolitik an der Schwelle zum Jahrhundert der Umwelt*, 4th ed. (Darmstadt, 1994 [1989]), 8; in English, *Earth Politics*, London, 1994.

8. The transnational academic discourse is clearly and widely developed in the volumes of *Ecotheology — the Journal of Religion, Nature and the Environment*.

9. Cf. Mary C. Grey, *Sacred Longings: Ecofeminist Theology and Globalization* (London, 2003).

10. Cf. S. Bergmann, ed., *Architecture, Aesth/Ethics, and Religion* (Frankfurt am Main, 2005), and my contribution, "Space and Spirit: Towards a Theology of Inhabitation."

world arts and spirituality in the margins, focusing on the visual arts of Sápmi in the contrasts of Australia and Peru.

Nature offers us a blank screen, reflecting the worst or the best of human ways of being and acting. Therefore it is so necessary to reflect and deepen our modes of *perceiving nature*. Nature, as one of God's two "books" of revelation, should be approached with open senses and minds and the artistic thinking eye. According to insights like this, my reflection on Gregory and the ecotheologians led me naturally to a study of visual arts and their aesthetic modes of bodily being in and with nature.[11] In the horizon of the insights from the study of motion and movement in Gregory, my present responsibility for the transdisciplinary university program "Technical Mobilities in Trnasition," which unites scholars from psychology, engineering, transport sociology, ethics, architecture, and theology, seems to be more in continuit than in discontinuity with the investigations of this book.

Having learned the radical wisdom from the Cappadocians' apophatic theory of knowledge offering the main criterion for classical theology, I was further pushed into the ongoing struggle about the challenge to negotiate the change of paradigm for theology. All theology is contextual, so also Gregory's work, but not every theologian is conscious of the contextuality of his/her reflection.

I might be naive with regard to the power-sharing struggles in faith congregations, but for me it seems very consistent and easy to walk directly from the insights of apophatic (positive as well as negative) theology, where one can interpret only the "God who acts" and never fully the "God who is," into the paradigm of contextual theology, where the interpretation of God, who acts, takes place necessarily as a contextualized praxis on earth. The triune God of the Bible and the apophatic classical tradition can be reflected only as a "God in context," as a liberating God of the here and now.[12]

Therefore also theology needs to be changed from a tool of elites into the instrument of the many in nature and culture who in their daily lives convert Christianity. The church and theology is — alluding to Gustav Aulén — nothing more and nothing less than a tool of God for the expansion of his reign in the whole of creation. In spite of Aulén and Moltmann, I prefer the metaphor "garden" to "reign." The flourishing of God's garden is achieved by reconciled synergy, liberating love, and artistic creativity. What God has

---

11. See my monograph *I begynnelsen är bilden: En befriande bild-konst-kultur-teologi* (In the beginning is the icon: A liberating theology of images, arts, and culture) (Stockholm, 2003).

12. Cf. my *God in Context: A Survey of Contextual Theology* (Aldershot, 2003).

started she/he also fulfills and perfects in a creative synergy of the creatures and the Spirit who gives life.

Finally, my acknowledgments to all who have shared the sweat and joy of work behind the editing: Robert J. Schreiter, Chicago, for taking the German edition over the northern Atlantic; Alan Padgett, St. Paul, for the long and faithful power behind the editing; Douglas Stott, Atlanta, for his sensitive translation of a sometimes not easy German text; Jon Pott, Grand Rapids, and his staff for the professional publishing, which is unfortunately not any longer usual these days; the Norwegian Research Council in Oslo for financial support; my three former *Doktorväter* (supervisors), Per Erik Persson (Lund), Lars Thunberg (Sigtuna), and Per Frostin († 1992), as well as my teacher in "matristics," Kari Børresen (Oslo), for their long-term support. A strong source and a fruitful context for rewriting this book was offered by the increasing development of exchanges and reciprocal empowerments in the academic networks Nordic Forum of Contextual Theology (founded 1991), Northern Forum of Nature, Worldview and Religion (founded 1998), and the Network of "Religion and Environment in Europe" (founded 2003), which I had the pleasure to initiate and organize with a growing number of committed scholars and friends. Also my participation as an assistant editor of the *Encyclopedia of Religion and Nature* (2005), edited by Bron Taylor, Florida, offered me a great source for learning and inspiration. Using the painter Paul Klee's famous notion, I would like to thank "The Thinking Eye" behind my work, Ingela, and our children Lovisa and Fabian for offering a life-enhancing space inside the global ecumenical communion, where we help keep alive the vision of "the Spirit's world to come" (Nicea-Constantinople, 391) in the context of "the Cry of the Earth and the suffering of its people."[13]

Sigurd Bergmann
Trondheim, October 2004

---

13. The formulation was used in 2004 in the World Council of Churches' working group Alternative Globalization Addressing Peoples and Earth, as they prepared a draft for an ecumenical consensus document on the response of the Christian churches to the present globalization and their proposals for alternatives.

Abbreviations

Carm.	*Carmina* (poems)
Ep.	*Epistles*
ET	English Translation
FC	Fathers of the Church
LCC 3	Library of Christian Classics, vol 3: *Christology of the Later Fathers*
NPNF2/7	Nicene and Post-Nicene Fathers, 2nd ser., vol. 7 (S. Gregory Nazianzen)
Or.	*Orations*
PG	Patrologiae Cursus Completus, Series Graeca, ed. J. P. Migne
SC	Sources Chrétiennes

Sources for English Quotations

Sources used for English quotations from Gregory's works:

LCC 3	*Or.* 27-31 (the "theological orations"), *Ep.* 101, 102, 202
FC 107	*Or.* 6, 9-11, 13-15, 17, 19-20, 22-26, 32, 35-36, 44
NCNF2/7	*Or.* 1-3, 7-8, 12, 16, 18, 21, 33-34, 37-43, 45, and various epistles

The editor would like to thank Luther Seminary, and especially his research assistant Chelsea DeArmond, for the essential support and hard work which helped make this American edition a reality.

Introduction

1. Point of Departure

Theology cannot avoid the questions raised by the way human beings interact with nature today. One of the fundamental challenges to civilization and to the Christian faith involves not only the crisis of survival experienced today in so many quarters by the world's ecosystems and by the world's poor, but also the economic injustice inhering in the *kairos* of the global system and the crisis of perception, reason, and morality in late modernity. The task of Christianity in the face of this challenge is less that of trying to discover the "historical roots of our ecological crisis"[1] than of offering constructive ways to overcome the ecological destruction generated by that crisis. In that sense, we urgently need a theology that both examines and overcomes the ecological crisis.

On the one hand, pastoral theology and academic theology lose social credibility if they avoid the community of discourse that is already addressing the ecological challenge. On the other, if ecological discourse itself does not take note of the contributions of theology, it loses sight of the significance that the understanding of God has for the interplay of organisms and their

---

1. So the title of an essay by Lynn White, who by provocatively assigning to Christianity historical responsibility for the ecological crisis, also prompted Christian theologians to enter the ecological discussion more quickly than they otherwise might have. White's one-sided thesis does however overlook the dynamics of the process of secular modernization and the fact that since the Enlightenment, Christianity has largely lost its former capacity for influencing society. Groh and Groh's cultural-historical analysis of the metaphysics implied in the optimism of the modern worldview offers a more differentiated response to White's question.

surroundings. The question then becomes what theology and ecology can expect from one another. My intention in this book is to deepen and expand the encounter between theology and ecology. My point of departure is the conviction that in a pluralistic context, it is only in dialogue with others that the unique contribution of systematic theology can come to fruition.

There is an indissoluble connection between one's vision of human beings and one's vision of the cosmos, between one's understanding of nature, society, human beings, and God. A shift in the understanding of any one of these entities invariably causes the others to appear in a different light as well. Accordingly, any *change in the modern understanding of nature* simultaneously calls into question the understanding of God inhering within Christian life and Christian faith.

What about our understanding of the world? Is the world to be viewed as a commodity? As a household? A metaphor? As the body of God? What does it mean in an ecological context if a person believes in God as the one who creates, liberates, and perfects heaven and earth?

What is the connection between the promise of God's universality, on the one hand, and the gospel of the liberation of all creatures, on the other? And what about the places where people and other creatures struggle for survival? How does one talk in such places about the God who is "turned toward the world and made visible in suffering and the cross" (Martin Luther)?

My intention in this book is to examine the correspondence between our understanding of God and nature in a way that ultimately offers theology new possibilities for integrating and relating its views on creation and liberation.

The *epistemological revolution* accompanying liberation theology found that the poor, on the underbelly of history and society, are in a particularly advantageous position to perceive and reflect upon reality, and that one of the necessary conditions for the development of theology is that it be mindful to include the poor in its considerations.

The question now is whether this view is meaningful *only* in connection with human society. That is, can it not also apply to a consideration of other creatures and their surroundings? Can one meaningfully speak about creatures themselves perceiving the creation and its Creator? What does reference to "love of the poor" (Gregory of Nazianzus) mean in connection with love of the poor among *other* creatures, creatures whose garden human beings — as the "image of God" — are to "till and keep" (Gen. 1:27; 2:15)?

Is it possible to redress the injustices attending the social construction of the female gender and the social construction of nature? What is the relationship between the discourse of the theology of liberation and that of ecological theology? Can an ecological theology of liberation also articulate the hope that "the creation itself will be set free" (Rom. 8:21)?

Here I invite the reader to examine the extent to which one genuinely can link liberation theology with ecological theology. I hope to contribute to the development of a new paradigm for contextual theology by emphasizing how enormously fruitful it can be to reexamine tradition, to carry on a dialogue with those human beings and other creatures who are victims of cultural-ecological violence, and to reassess our doctrine of the Spirit.

"Pneumatology is a neglected field of systematic theology."[2] An ecological theology can expect great things if it will but *rediscover* how to speak about the Holy Spirit.[3] Although environmentalists and adherents of the new religiosity are constantly searching for new sources of spirituality, and although scientific theory increasingly requires an element of wisdom, few people speak about the Spirit *itself* today.

Word is getting around that "spirit" and "nature" are no longer antitheses. Yet despite numerous proposals regarding precisely this topic, still no one quite seems to know how we are to understand the encounter between the two concepts. Is "spirit" a function of nature? Is "nature" a function of spirit? Or are they perhaps identical? Or are "spirit" and "nature" both different *and* somehow connected?

In late modernity theology has a difficult time remembering that the hermeneutical question actually depends on the doctrine of the Spirit. How are we to understand the tradition that the Spirit that bestows biological life is the same Spirit that, instead of "killing like the letter," gives new life to both the word *and* the body? Is it possible that the same Spirit is composing and interpreting both the holy book of scripture *and* that of nature?

What is the relationship between pneumatology and the cosmological deficit? How are we today to speak about the same Spirit that in 381 the Nicene Creed said would summon the "life of the world to come" to enter into its presence? Is it possible for an ecological pneumatology to come to terms with the hermeneutical task of the theologian as a "critical service to the church"?[4]

2. Berkhof's 1968 statement (p. 10) is still valid today.

3. See the statement of the WCC in 1991, "Come Holy Spirit, Renew All Creation."

4. Cf. Jeanrond 1994, 181: "Thus hermeneutics has proven to be . . . a vital necessity for any theologian who understands his or her task as a critical service to the church, the world and to the pursuit of truth." Rather than understanding "church" and "world" as antitheses, one should rather follow the tradition of the Confessing Church in combining them such that, in Bonhoeffer's words, the "being of the Church as Church" emerges in its "being for the world." See Lange 1981, 59.

This book also hopes to help rediscover ways to speak about the Holy Spirit and to understand its mission and the way it indwells both history and nature (cf. Ps. 104:30). What we are really seeking is a path that can lead us out of the present emptiness in which we have forgotten both the Spirit and nature; we can find that path by recalling the path God traveled from the incarnation of the Son to the indwelling of the Spirit.

The title of this book also points in this direction by combining the words "spirit," "nature," and "liberator." Because the triune God is always at work in the Holy Spirit, God always creates and perfects the nature of his creation in the Spirit. The colorful refraction of this assertion offers the thread of Ariadne which in the labyrinth of problems constantly accompanies the question of how ecological theology can speak about the Spirit that "liberates" (J. Sobrino) as "the Spirit as liberator of nature."[5]

The presuppositions for answering this question can be found in a reflection on the history and present status of trinitarian theology, a theology that speaks about the Spirit in connection with the dynamic God as encountered in the community of Christians.[6] Here we are tying the reconstruction of pneumatology to a reconstruction of the doctrine of the Trinity. Reflection on the *social experience of God* (J. Moltmann) in connection with the historical and systematic doctrine of the Trinity dovetails into reflection on the *ecological experience of God* in connection with the trinitarian doctrine of the Spirit.

One sensitive issue in modernity is its relationship to *tradition*. Did the Enlightenment *really* neutralize the dogma of tradition? Or did it merely pass on in a disguised form the insights and aporiae of Greek ontology and metaphysics? What "present power" does history really exercise today?[7] Has postmodernity itself really jettisoned the baggage of its *modern* tradition? Or is it in fact merely hovering — as "late modernity" — between past modernity and a new modernity?

Within late modernity Christianity finds it difficult to drink from its

---

5. The Spanish title of Sobrino's book *Spirituality of Liberation* is *Liberación con espíritu.*

6. "Reflection" here refers to something quite distinct from "laying or establishing foundations." I understand the task of systematic theology to be to reflect critically and constructively on our knowledge of, and the various modes of expression we use when articulating our experiences of, God in life and in the world. Understood in this way, such reflections, rather than preceding experience (something suggested by the metaphor "establishing foundations"), reflect on them retrospectively and in so doing generate new presuppositions for yet additional experiences, modes of expression, and insights.

7. Cf. Picht 1989, 9.

own springs. If theology is serious about not forgetting the lessons it has learned from modernity, it cannot allow itself to comprehend its own tradition as some normative, a priori argument, that is, as a dogma of tradition; instead it must view it hermeneutically as a recollection of something past for the sake of constructively addressing the present and the future. In this context the challenge facing theology is to transmit its past in a manner allowing it to correlate that past constructively with the present situation, that is, to fashion a contextual theology as a theory that is at once both rational *and* historical (C. Baudelaire).

In this book I will venture to articulate such a correlation with respect to four problem areas that not only faced theology during late antiquity, but are also facing contemporary theology and ecological discourse today. One particular question I would like to address is whether the dogma of tradition can be transformed into a source of insights — into *traditio* as a substantive gift — for the problems facing ecological theology.

Unfortunately, conditions in late modernity have resulted in an increasing lack of epistemological clarity, raising the question whether holistically knowledge of "everything" is really possible or whether instead knowledge of "a little" in a relative sense must suffice. How is one to deal with things about which ultimately one is supposed to be silent? Indeed, can one even distinguish with any consistency between those things about which one knows nothing and those about which one does not *yet* know anything? Is a theory of knowledge even possible in the first place? In any event, does the discourse concerning knowledge not already represent the central, substantive issue — an issue of power — of science in the larger sense? How can theology, which purports to say something about our knowledge of God, respond to the quite justifiable suspicion that the real goal of its discourse is in fact merely to justify metaphysically certain issues and claims of *physical* power?

Those hoping that this book will offer a completely new answer to this question or will even confirm their own, previous answer should probably read a different book. I have no intention of adding yet another opinion to the current plethora of responses to the question of whether the conditions for the possibility of knowledge obtain or are a priori impossible. Any answer making claims to finality in this sense too easily shifts its identity and becomes a prophecy followed all too quickly by practical self-fulfillment.

The intention of this book is as little to contribute to the proliferation of "social atomism" (Bonhoeffer) as it is to engage in an uncritical holistic enterprise. My premise is rather that the conditions for the possibility of establishing a consensus in "theoretical and practical discourse" (J. Habermas) do indeed exist and can indeed be creatively engaged. By exploiting precisely this possibility, I intend to engage in and contribute to the praxis of a "philosophy of dialogue" within the larger project of "transmodernity" (E. Dussel).

On the other hand, I will indeed try to establish a measure of clarity within contemporary discourse concerning the possibility of knowledge by examining whether and, if so, how one can best employ the classic apophatic principle in the service of an ecological theology of liberation. Specifically, can this principle aid our understanding of the *boundaries* of our knowledge of God and nature as a necessary presupposition of constructive knowledge in the larger sense? A creative apophatic application of the knowledge of that about which we are knowingly silent can help express ecologically and theologically our understanding of the holiness of God's Spirit and the holiness of nature, and help articulate the movement of liberation shared by both.

2. Organization

In the following discussion I will first identify those particular texts that provide the actual material for my later discussion and then describe the task and organizational principles guiding the examination of those texts. In conclusion I will describe more precisely the method guiding my procedures and the concepts providing hermeneutical access to the texts.

The Material

Two basic groups of texts provide the primary materials for this study: first, the written legacy of the early church Cappadocian theologian Gregory of Nazianzus, and second, certain monographs published in the field of systematic theology between 1972 and 2003. Secondary material includes various theological, patristic, and ancient historical texts as well as texts from broader ecological discourse. My choice of monographs from systematic theology has been guided by two questions, namely, whether they understand and accept the ecological challenge as a theological challenge, and whether their acceptance of this challenge prompts a systematic reassessment and reconstruction of the doctrinal understanding of faith in the larger sense.

One chronological note is of significance in this respect. Because the concept of ecology as such did not really enter the general social debate of the First World until the early 1970s, it is only since that period that one encounters studies concerning this topic within systematic theology. Theologians meeting the criteria listed in the preceding paragraph include (in chronologi-

6

cal order) John B. Cobb, Jr.; Günter Altner; Gerhard Liedke and Ulrich Duchrow; Christian Link; Jürgen Moltmann; Sallie McFague; and Rosemary Radford Ruether.

It is worth noting that the monographs attributing *theological* significance to the ecological problem during this period emerged exclusively within the northern cultural horizon of the First World, specifically in the context of academic theology of the wealthier countries of western Europe and North America and within the specifically Protestant interpretation of Christianity. In that sense one can understand the selections in this book as representing historically an *initial stage* in the development of ecological theology. Following the publication of the first edition of this book in German, a *second stage* in this development became clearly discernible as a dialogue on ecological theology in other cultural regions in the world as well, regions including Christianity as well as other, non-Christian religions, and even dialogue between different religions.[8]

The material for the patristic discussion comes from the writings of Gregory of Nazianzus. My systematic analysis concentrates on those texts among Gregory's orations and theological letters and poems containing material relevant to the issues addressed here, with the Cappadocian's letters being integrated into my analysis of the context of his theology.

The Task

The task of this study is to examine the correspondence between our understanding of God and our understanding of nature, and to do so while giving special consideration to the doctrine of redemption and to the relationship between two different historical contexts.

The study encompasses three parts. Chapter 1 examines the conditions within our current *initial stage* that present ecological challenges to theology. Chapters 2 and 3 examine contextually the *tradition* of the theology of Greg-

---

8. Concerning the variety of voices in the Christian-ecumenical discussion, see Hallmann 1994. Bakken 1995 provides a bibliographical survey with commentary. Concerning the dynamics of the development of ecofeminism in philosophical and theological studies, see Mies and Shiva 1993, Warren 1996, Warren and Erkal 1997, Mellor 1998, MacKinnon and McIntyre 1995, and Ruether 1996. Concerning ecological studies in other religions, see Holm 1994, Khalid and O'Brian 1992, Tucker and Grim 1994, McCagney 1998, Bernstein 1998, and Cooper and Palmer 1998. Concerning the relationship between religion and ecology in the (sub)arctic polar region, see Irimoto and Yamada 1994; concerning the Amazon, see Descola 1994.

ory of Nazianzus. In part III, three additional chapters try to determine how one can constructively *correlate* one's understanding and description of the *situation,* on the one hand, and *tradition,* on the other.

In part I, I examine in detail how our understanding of nature has shifted during the period of modernity; I then describe the form that shift in understanding takes in connection with the concept of "ecology" and what this shift means for theology. I then address the question of just how theologians in late modernity must deal with this shift in our understanding of nature. Finally I show how an interpretation of the theology of Gregory of Nazianzus can help us with that shift.

Part II specifically examines the theology of Gregory, looking first at the context of late antiquity itself providing the backdrop to that theology and then thoroughly examining how Gregory's theology articulates the correspondence between an understanding of God and an understanding of nature from the perspective of four specific problems.

Part III is itself subdivided into three sections. Chapter 4 examines whether and how studies from late antiquity and late modernity are related to the problems of ecological discourse — and indeed to each other — in the first place. Chapter 5 examines how the understanding of God and nature in late antiquity and late modernity relates to the paradigm of the contextual theology of liberation.

In conclusion, chapter 6 engages in various methodological reflections. First, I discuss theoretically how one is to understand and assess the limitations and possibilities of the method of correlation actually employed in chapter 4. I then examine the significance of the criterion of tradition for contextual theology. Finally, I show the considerable success with which the classic principle of apophatic knowledge can be applied to ecological theology.

The Method

The method I employ in this study is *systematic* insofar as I focus on understanding various relationships and connections. The systematic method here is also *hermeneutical* insofar as it approaches texts in order to understand them within the horizon of interpretive query. I inquire concerning the relationship between the *interpretation* of theological texts from late antiquity and late modernity by applying the method of historical-hermeneutical correlation.

Yet another question involves the problem of how exactly to integrate the different *discourses* of ecology and theology, on the one hand, and those of ecological theology and liberation theology, on the other. Finally, and certainly of no less importance, I try to establish a connection with the larger context of the Christian faith today.

In this context it is important to articulate clearly for the reader what one might call the *preunderstanding* of the contemporary interpreter that conceals the hermeneutical keys for interpreting the texts of the past. This is why I examine the ecological challenge as such *before* examining the theology of Gregory of Nazianzus; the hermeneutical keys emerging from an examination of the situation of contemporary authors and readers then aid in interpreting the texts of Gregory from late antiquity.

In this whole undertaking I respect the *internal, systematic integrity of the texts,* texts written by a specific person in a specific time and place.[9] With this in mind I provide a great many textual citations in the book so that readers can engage their own interpretation and also compare the texts with the interpretation I have myself presented.

Throughout the book I also apply various other methods deriving from the historical disciplines of social history, philosophy, the humanities, and other sciences. All these disciplines combine to provide diverse contextual perspectives on theological texts from both late modernity and late antiquity, and in so doing expand the horizon of understanding of the text and the reader alike.

While the first four chapters engage in systematic examination, the last two develop normative lines of thought. Chapter 5 proceeds argumentatively, and chapter 6 engages in a methodological reflection on three different problem areas emerging within the overall study.

The Concepts

Certain concepts facilitate our hermeneutical assessment of the texts.

When I refer to the "spirit," I am referring to what Lessing calls "das Sein des einen in oder bei einem anderen," essentially: the being of the one in or with the other.[10] In the Christian doctrine of the Spirit, this definition refers more specifically to the being of the Holy Spirit in or with the hypostases

---

9. Cf. Frostin 1988, 21, who insists that one of the most important criteria for textual interpretation is to accept the "internal logic" of a text.

10. Lessing 1984, 218; cf. chaps. 3 and 4.

of the triune God as well as to the being of the Holy Spirit in or with the creation and its creatures.

When I refer to "natures," I am referring in a general sense to that which exists or "is" taken as a whole, understood further as the flow of becoming and passing away or decaying.[11] Although *natura* is the Latin translation of the Greek word *physis,* the term *natura* refers more specifically to the genesis and birth of living things, while *physis* refers both to such genesis as well as to its passing away or decaying, the "reconcealment" of what has appeared *(phthora).*[12] Because this whole process of genesis and decay takes place within time, the concept of *physis* is accordingly closely associated with the concept of time. In Greek thinking it referred to growth and was related synonymously to the notion of "this All here" *(tode to pan)* as a reference to the All and to the totality of being. My definition of the concept of nature invokes this broader understanding of the word *physis* in Greek thought.

When I refer to the "cosmos," I am referring to the "beautiful order of nature and the world." By "world" I mean — synonymous with the concept of nature — the totality of being conceived as an all-encompassing space.[13] By "creation" I mean nature and the world in the sense that they cannot be conceived independent of the Creator.

The third term in my title qualifies the action of the Spirit as a liberation of nature. By "liberation" I understand in a general sense that particular dialectic of existence involving human beings and other creatures that experience an absence of a different reality as well as an absence of any hope for that reality; that dialectic also includes a movement from the reality of a lack of freedom to one of freedom.[14]

11. Cf. Picht 1989, 89f., 160ff.

12. Picht 1989, 162.

13. Although I use the terms "nature" and "world" synonymously, the term "nature" does more clearly invoke the concept of time, while the term "world" evokes more the concept of space. Whereas the English term "cosmology" encompasses an extremely wide semantic field, the German word *Weltbild* is a bit broader than *Kosmologie.* The word "cosmology" *(Kosmologie)* as a technical term, which was unknown in antiquity, derives from Christian Wolff, who distinguished between rational and empirical cosmology. Today the disciplines of astronomy and physics carry on the tradition of empirical cosmology, whereas the tradition of rational cosmologies has receded in the disciplines of philosophy and theology. Indeed, since Kant, modern thinkers generally dispute the possibility of a rational cosmology, and as a result every cosmology claiming sole validity is viewed as being unenlightened and unscientific. Cosmologies may not be absolutized for ideological purposes. Cf. Jaspers 1974, 59-62.

14. Cf. Gutiérrez 1976, 42, who defines liberation as the demand for "the unfolding of all man's dimensions" (36, ET) and freedom as a process and as historical conquest (29, ET).

The *movement* of liberation passes through three different stages:[15]

1. from the reality of a situation in need of liberation (liberation *from* something),
2. to the reality of a situation of liberation (liberation *to* something),
3. proceeding by way of mediated liberation (liberation *by* something).

In this sense the "Spirit as liberator of nature" is referring to an activity of the Spirit in or with nature that sets into motion a movement involving the totality of being, a movement proceeding from the reality of a lack of freedom to the reality of freedom. Here the concept of liberation also qualifies the concept of nature insofar as it describes the growth or development of being associated with nature as a movement of liberation from evil to freedom in the Spirit.

By "initial stage" I understand in a general sense the totality of circumstances in which an entity is found. This "entity" can be an object in the physical, social, or intellectual world. The "circumstances" include all the various factors constituting this particular situation in time and space; the totality of these "circumstances" then naturally defines the *particularity* of any given situation compared to other possible situations. In this sense a "situation" refers to that which appears in a certain way (and not otherwise) here and now.

By "tradition" I understand in a general sense that which is passed down, mediated, or transmitted in time from one person to another. We will have occasion later to examine the rather broad semantic spectrum of that which is actually transmitted. The concept of tradition is closely related to the concept of time insofar as it refers to that which is transferred from one situation to another within the irreversible course of time. One must remember that in this sense "tradition" refers not merely to that which is *actively* transmitted or mediated, but also to that which remains constant over time and is passed down, as it were, *against* otherwise disruptive forces present within an age and *with* those forces that are "flowing forward" within the current of time itself. I will examine the theological concept of tradition in the final chapter (chap. 6). The concept of tradition can also however include the concept of space insofar as it refers to that which is mediated from one particular situation at one particular place to a different situation at a different place.

The term "correlation" refers in a general sense to the interplay or relationship in which one entity necessarily and mutually relates to another. When one "correlates tradition and situation," one reflects on the relation-

---

15. Concerning the schema of redemption, cf. Thunberg 1977, 12-18.

ship between that which is passed down to us from the situation of late antiquity and that which constitutes the specifics of our situation in late modernity.

Finally, let me say a few words regarding the material content of this work, "the trinitarian cosmology of Gregory of Nazianzus within the horizon of an ecological theology of liberation."[16] A "horizon" designates the "boundaries of our field of view."[17] The notion of a "horizon" as a "field of view" necessarily relates the concept to the perspective or particular location of an observer. If observers rotate within their own position, things appear to be within the boundaries of their field of view. If they move from one position to a different one, phenomena also shift according to the boundaries of that field of view. It is a mistake, however, to believe that the boundaries of that horizon can themselves be discerned; only what appears *within* the horizon is visible, never the horizon itself.[18]

When I say that I examine Gregory's trinitarian cosmology "within the horizon of an ecological theology of liberation," I am merely saying that my interpretation of the two modes of thought will indeed fall within the field of view of the reader in one and the same book. I will be expanding the *boundaries* of the observer's hermeneutical field of view such that Gregory's trinitarian cosmology will be visible to the reader in the present situation *in* that field of view.[19]

I will effect this "expansion" by shifting the reader's position and horizon on several different occasions. Beginning with the present position and perspective of ecological challenge *(situation)*, I will shift the field of view to that of the ancient church *tradition*. A reflection on the experiences within these two perspectives will in its own turn generate yet a third field of view, that of *correlation*. From the perspective of this third field, I will then shift our position yet again, this time into the *horizon of correlation*. Only by moving through all four fields of view — situation, tradition, correlation, and liberation theology — can we examine trinitarian cosmology within the horizon of an ecological theology of liberation.

16. This phrase constitutes the subtitle of the first German edition of this book.

17. Picht 1989, 219.

18. Picht 1989, 220.

19. That is, I do not intend to combine the one *and* the other, the old *and* the new; rather, I intend to articulate the one *in* the other, the old *in* the new. Whereas in his own essay *"und"* (1927) Kandinsky described the task of the twentieth century to be to focus on the "and" in moving beyond the "either-or" of the nineteenth century, I believe the task of the future at the beginning of the new millennium is to come to terms with the problems of the "in."

3. The Present Study and Patristics Research

One can legitimately ask how the present study relates to the more comprehensive field of research on Gregory of Nazianzus.[20] Let me first address one problem that has hitherto not really attracted much attention. The designation "trinitarian cosmology" implies that the study will focus primarily on the relationship between God and world. What is the relationship between the two in Gregory's writings? How do Gregory's texts deal with the understanding of God's nature and work, on the one hand, and the understanding of nature, the world, and life, on the other?[21]

By examining Gregory's theological interpretation of the world as creation, the present study will throw light on what is presently a rather obscure area of research. My hypothesis is that Gregory's trinitarian understanding of God is closely related to his understanding of creation. My examination of his writings will show the extent to which this assumption applies to the correspondence between Gregory's understanding of God and world from four different perspectives; in this examination the idea of movement will play a particularly important role, an idea that Gregory was the first theologian to emphasize positively both in his understanding of God and in his understanding of the world.

My study also shows that Gregory is to be understood as an original Christian theologian who accorded primacy to biblical theology and to the Christian tradition. Here the Cappadocian proves to be remarkably open to the presuppositions of his context, for example, in his sensitivity to the situation of the poor. Understanding his theological originality also requires that one recognize his positive reception of philosophical presuppositions, something also discernible in his interpretation of the world as creation.[22]

---

20. The German edition of this book (pp. 31-46) provides a comprehensive examination of the status of scholarship in the lexicographical, historical, philological, and systematic-theological fields, and a critical discussion from gender-specific, denominational, and geographical perspectives.

21. Pelikan 1993, 248, has described this relationship quite clearly: "The trinitarian doctrine and the cosmological doctrine of the Cappadocians were based upon Nicaea and then contributed to Constantinople, and each of these two doctrines was used to clarify the other. Trinity and cosmology were therefore intimately related, and in some sense correlative, doctrines." Pelikan does not, however, address the relationship between these two doctrines and soteriology as I do in the present study.

22. Norris 1991, 25, interprets Gregory as a "philosophical rhetorician." Norris views the active use of Aristotelian dialectics as one of the key weapons the Cappadocians employed in their debate with the neo-Arians. Norris (36) shows how Gregory, rather than seek-

In Gregory's theology the universal dimension functions as a foundation of soteriology, not merely as an appendix for the doctrine of redemption. Because he understands creation and redemption not as two different aspects of the divine economy but as two wholly intertwined spheres, he also understands the redemption of all created things to include not only corporeality but also all *non*human living beings. My thesis is that the doctrine of redemption, rather than being *complemented* by the universal dimension, is rather wholly embedded within that dimension.

These considerations also throw one's understanding of the antithetical relationship between "body/evil" and "spirit/good" into a completely different light insofar as the anthropological dualism characterizing the Platonic understanding of salvation in late antiquity does *not* emerge in Gregory's interpretation of soteriology.[23] Quite to the contrary, because Gregory understands that which is created to be "good," he is able to include the element of the physical — corporeality — in the redemptive process.

Moreover, in this study I will be employing a hermeneutical method that has not yet been applied to Gregory's writings. My interpretation of these historical texts employs hermeneutical keys developed under the presuppositions of the current situation. The key question concerning the elimination of nature from the interpretive theological horizon emerging in our current situation can be applied such that it allows previously more obscure material to reemerge from Gregory's texts. Indeed, my suspicion is confirmed that previous interpretations of Gregory's theology have avoided the issue of nature; what I find instead is that the redemption of nature does indeed represent an important theme in Gregory's thought.

Because my method of interpretation clearly presents its presuppositions to the reader while simultaneously employing these presuppositions as

---

ing a neutral basis for his theology, in fact managed to transform the notion of Greek reason into an instrument of faith, a situation refuting the thesis of so-called Christian Platonism. Norris presents Gregory's position in a way making it possible to engage it as an argument in the earlier North American debate between David Tracy and George Lindbeck regarding the doctrinal foundations of faith.

23. Ruether insinuates the following equation to Gregory's thought: corporeal = evil, incorporeal = good. She then transfers this antithesis onto Gregory's worldview, arguing that Gregory basically agrees with the traditional cosmological piety otherwise characterizing antiquity. She also maintains that for God the creation is something foreign, and as such "virtually an evil thing" (1969, 133). Ruether accommodates her own interpretation completely to the traditional schema according to which Gregory does not really contribute anything new to the Greek philosophical model: "Greek Christian christology was modeled on Platonic anthropology" (136).

an interpretive instrument, it is in a position to create presuppositions allowing the results of that interpretation to be engaged or applied in the *present* situation as well.

My goal in the present study, then, is to contribute to the development of a contextual methodology that can be applied to the interpretation of a historical text within the framework of a model of correlation between tradition and situation. Let me emphasize that I can hope to offer only a contribution, certainly not a "final solution." I do, however, intend to emphasize the necessity of addressing the criterion of tradition within the methodology of contextual theology.

Finally this study will also try to contribute to the understanding of the originality of this Cappadocian theologian. Several such contributions have already been presented that address Gregory's doctrine of peace, his sensitivity to the plight of the poor, his metaphorical language, his pneumatology, his dynamic soteriology, and his theological reception of Aristotelian philosophy. The present study will add an examination of the originality of Gregory's thought in his understanding of the relationship between God and world, a relationship I would describe with the conceptual figure of active synergy. Gregory's identity as a Christian theologian within the flow of tradition is attested by the significance he attaches to the notion of the redemption of creation.

PART I

The Altered Understanding
of Nature in Modernity:
The Situation

CHAPTER 1

The Ecological Challenge to Theology

1. Fluid and Fixed Elements in the Understanding of Nature

Ever since Charles Darwin came to understand living forms as evolving beings (1859), the understanding of nature itself has been in flux. In the twentieth century natural scientists also discovered that not only had the understanding of nature shifted, but nature itself had slipped into what could only
be described as a disastrous line of development. A geopolitical consensus of
the United Nations in Stockholm (1972) and Rio de Janeiro (1992) determined that modern culture itself had come to pose a significant threat to nature and consequently also to itself.

Public debate generally refers to modern civilization's threat to nature
as an "ecological crisis"; in its own turn, this crisis presupposes that certain
conditions contributed to its emergence as well as to the possibility of recognizing and understanding it.

Critical philosophy has had good reason to identify modern instrumental rationality as the ultimate initiator of the global devastation of ecological
and cultural systems. Within the history of modernity itself, however, a
counterdiscussion has also emerged that has examined possibilities for liberating modernity from the seemingly inexorable vortex of this devastation of
nature.[1]

Within the flow of change, however, certain elements are also at work

1. In late modernity this counterdiscussion is represented by environmentalist groups
and by scientists in alliance with the women's movement and with movements concerned
with social justice in impoverished countries. Today movements in the First World are increasingly seeking alliances with those in the Third and Fourth World.

making this understanding of nature more fixed. The concept of ecology itself is involved in such a process. In coining the word "ecology" in 1866, Ernst Haeckel articulated a new biological subdiscipline. Since then, other disciplines have been picking up this term with almost missionary zeal; although the word quite naturally thereby acquires enhanced significance, at the same time it begins to lose semantic precision.

In the following discussion I examine the changing understanding of nature from six perspectives within "ecological discourse."

1. From the perspective of *cultural history*, one can inquire regarding the presuppositions of continuity and change in the historical interpretation of ecological perspectives and applicability.
2. From the perspective of the *natural sciences*, one can inquire regarding the laws or the consistency and predictability inhering in our model of relationships between living beings and their surroundings.
3. From the perspective of *philosophy*, one can inquire regarding the conditions for the possibility of ecological thinking and knowledge.
4. From the perspective of *aesthetics*, one can inquire regarding presuppositions for perceiving ecological relationships and for articulating and shaping experience according to those models.
5. From the perspective of *sociopolitical considerations*, one can inquire regarding conditions for developing new social behavior based on ecological insights.
6. From the perspective of *ethics*, one can inquire in practical discourse regarding the normative correctness of both individual and collective dealings with the ecosystems in which human beings live and on which they depend.

The seventh perspective of inquiry concealed in ecological discourse, namely, *metaphysics*, is rarely addressed. And yet the history of the change in our understanding of nature clearly shows that the notion of a Creator who has arranged everything for human use or for human benefit represents a constant, consistent element in the Western understanding of the world. The metaphysical understanding of the Creator may not however be identified without further qualification with the understanding of God in Christianity.

What his teacher Carl von Linné had already articulated as the economy of nature on the foundation of the metaphysical optimism of physico-theology, Adam Smith applied to the economy of society, creating thus — with the help of Francis Bacon's organization of the sciences for controlling nature through technology — the presuppositions for the current ecological crisis. This domination of nature was given legitimacy by sciences that were never quite able to answer the question of how their knowledge of nature could be true if the use or application of precisely that knowledge simultaneously destroyed nature.

At the same time, the integrity of this knowledge was made more plausible precisely by its industrial applicability and certainly also by the underlying metaphysical justification, namely, that the Creator had indeed done a good job creating and arranging nature in a way making it useful to human beings, who were themselves created in the image of the Creator. No one, however, ever inquired how the Creator, too, might be active within that very nature.

Although the hard experiences and subsequent interpretation of the ecological crisis have by no means stifled the metaphysical optimism of the technological and industrial age, they have called that optimism into question with increasing forcefulness. Metaphysically anchored faith in progress has recently been replaced by acute anxiety regarding the future and by an eschatological mood, an ecological "end-time" mood. Growing cultural pessimism and an ideologically based biologism have seriously called into question the optimism of technological reason and its application on behalf of profit making.

This diagnosis of the ecological crisis as a crisis of culture and of its metaphysics simultaneously raises not only the question concerning appropriate environmental ethics, but also the theological question regarding how our understanding of God functions within our understanding of ourselves, nature, and the world. Our perception of how nature suffers under the violence inflicted on it by our culture leads to the question regarding the essence of nature and the appropriate mode of behavior within the world, and then on to the question of God. Ecological discourse challenges us theologically to articulate just what is actually functioning as God in modernity's understanding of nature and in modernity's attitude and behavior toward nature.

This chapter addresses three questions:

1. How is the ecological challenge articulated in the six problem areas of ecological discourse?
2. How is theology responding to the ecological challenge?
3. How can an examination of the writings of Gregory of Nazianzus serve theology in the face of this ecological challenge?

2. Problem Areas of Ecological Discourse

The Change and Dialectics of Modernity's Understanding of Nature as the Presupposition of Ecological Discourse

Scholars occasionally maintain that ecological issues have been present throughout the history of Western civilization, from the pre-Socratics to modernity, that is, even before Haeckel coined the phrase in 1866.[2] Although this hypothesis of a "prehistory" of ecology can indeed throw new light on the philosophical understanding of nature in the past, if conducted too one-sidedly it obscures what is unique about the modern understanding of nature. There is no real concept of "ecology" before 1866 because modernity itself generated the *need* for such a concept.

What can the emergence of ecological discourse tell us from the perspective of cultural history about the shift in modernity's understanding of nature?

At the turn from the eighteenth to the nineteenth century, one discerns a change from a hierarchical understanding of nature to an egalitarian one corresponding to the Enlightenment shift from a hierarchical understanding of society based on class to an egalitarian one. At this time, it also became increasingly more difficult to maintain a unified understanding of nature as a whole. The emancipation of the various subdisciplines of science from the traditional primacy claims of philosophy resulted in more specialized concepts of nature, and despite intensive efforts, modernity has still — even today — not managed to establish any comprehensive theory of nature.[3]

Wolf Lepenies suggests that around 1800 the understanding of both the inner nature of human beings themselves and their natural environment was "dynamized" and "historicized."[4] Here it becomes disturbingly clear how the development of technological dominion over external nature emerges hand in hand with a repression of inner human nature. Lepenies explains how this far-reaching contradiction can be traced back to the close association between the concept of development in the natural sciences and the concept of progress as entertained by the philosophy of history.[5] One characteristic feature of this development is that scientific biology now displaces the older notion of a history of nature.

2. Schramm 1984, 15f.; cf. in this regard the criticism of Trepl 1987, 31.
3. Schäfer 1982, 34.
4. Lepenies 1982, 285.
5. Lepenies 1982, 299.

A change in the consciousness of time is also discernible after 1800. The past loses its authority, and the modern concept of history emerges. Whereas human beings were earlier understood to be part of a chain of living beings, now their function in history determines and defines their position and identity. Following the lead of Michel Foucault, Ludwig Trepl shows how the historization of our understanding of human beings also changed our understanding of life: "'Life' is no longer a characterizing feature . . . but rather a mode of being: an existence as an organization in an ongoing, systematic relationship with its surroundings."[6]

One must point out, however, that the historization of the understanding of nature in the nineteenth century had already been anticipated by the surrender or deliverance of natural objects over to technological and scientific appropriation during the time of Galileo. Dietrich Böhler describes this earlier period — the "genesis of the Copernican world"[7] — as a "scientific-constructivist reinterpretation of the topos of the 'book of nature.'"[8] The "book" becomes a "machine." Nicholas of Cusa theologically justifies the investigation and construction of nature as *machina mundi*: "[M]an is a second god. For just as God is the Creator of real beings and of natural forms, so man is the creator of conceptual beings and of artificial forms that are only likenesses of his intellect, even as God's creatures are likenesses of the Divine Intellect."[9]

This process of justifying scientific constructivism is also accompanied by a change in metaphysics from the classical ontology of substance to a system-functional ontology of relation. Nicholas of Cusa lends theological legitimacy to this shift by reserving "substantial being" exclusively for God, thus removing the concept of substance from ontology altogether.[10] The birth of the Copernican world releases nature for human appropriation and control, albeit without substantively revising the ancient Pythagorean notion of an inherent harmony in nature. Kant then strengthens this notion of the appropriation of nature by universalizing the concept of object underlying the natural sciences and thus "elevating the constructive-

---

6. Trepl 1987, 93f.

7. Blumenberg 1989.

8. Böhler 1981, 81.

9. Nicholas of Cusa, *De Beryllo* §7, in *Metaphysical Speculations,* trans. Jasper Hopkins (Minneapolis: Arthur J. Banning Pr., 1998), 794. See also Böhler 1981, 82. The metaphor of the "world machine" derives from Lucretius (*De rerum natura* 5.96). Cf. also Gregory of Nyssa, *De hominis opificio* 3, PG 44:134C. Up to the time of Copernicus, this metaphor could be piously interpreted within an organic world model. Cf. Mittelstrass 1981, 51.

10. Böhler 1981, 83.

causal experience of physics to a paradigm of every possible reliable experience."[11]

Yet another presupposition of the understanding of nature that emerged and asserted itself around 1800 was the change in the tradition of natural history. Donald Worster identifies two different traditions in the prehistory of ecology during the eighteenth century: an Arcadian line and an imperial line.[12] Inspired by the ancient notion of "peaceful nature" (Virgil), the goal of the Arcadian tradition's examination of nature is for spiritual, intellectual human beings to attain community with nature; by contrast, the goal of the imperial tradition is "to establish, through the exercise of reason and by hard work, man's dominion over nature."[13] Whereas the Arcadian tradition was influenced by ancient pagan thinking, the imperial tradition was borne forward by "Christian pastoralism,"[14] in whose view human beings function as the shepherds guarding and protecting nature from hostile forces. Precisely this thinking, however, resulted in an emotional separation of human beings and nature, since understanding the human being as a shepherd in this sense made it impossible to understand the same human being also as part of the flock, that is, of nature.

As Trepl insightfully points out, Worster's typology obscures the fact that originally the Enlightenment's unified notion of the utopia of nature prevented the Arcadian and imperial lines from contradicting one another.[15] It was only after the shift around 1800 that the two came into contradiction and the tradition of a unified, teleologically oriented history of nature[16] — one in which human beings played a part — collapsed.

One can also describe this change in modernity's understanding of nature with metaphors. Carolyn Merchant has shown how between 1500 and 1700 the metaphor of the world as "machine" replaced the previously regnant metaphor of the world as "cosmos and organism" deriving from the religious tradition in which the earth was revered as mother.[17] Susan Griffin brought to our attention the analogous identification and mechanisms of the appropriation of nature and women in exploitative patriarchal thinking.[18] Finally

---

11. Böhler 1981, 88.

12. Worster 1992, 2. Worster mentions Gilbert White as a representative of the Arcadian line and Carl von Linné as a representative of the imperial line. Cf. Sörlin 1991, 104-7.

13. Worster 1992, 2.

14. Worster 1992, 26.

15. Trepl 1987, 86ff.

16. Concerning the history of nature, see Trepl 1987, 43ff., 46ff.

17. Merchant 1987, 18, 54.

18. S. Griffin 1987, 19ff.

Hans Blumenberg has shown how the metaphor of the "book of nature" begins to be absolutized at the beginning of modernity.[19]

One additional characteristic of this change is discernible in the aesthetic transformation of the understanding of nature in the eighteenth century; as a result of this transformation, science and art began to develop conflicting understandings of nature that remain unreconciled even today. Romanticism saw the development of the utopian notion of a qualitatively different kind of science[20] picking up on earlier, in part hermetic[21] metaphysical traditions. In this sense, within the philosophy of nature Goethe can be understood as representing the opposing position to that of Newton and Kant.[22]

Ideologically the aesthetic understanding of nature gave expression to both regressive and progressive tendencies — regressive in the art of the idyll as a dream leading back to lost nature and as a "secularization of the myth of the Fall,"[23] and progressive in portraying the antithesis between mute and speaking nature, dead and living nature as a contrast between repression and freedom, that is, as a "metaphysically disguised protest against the increasing instrumentalization of the human relationship with nature."[24] The writings of the poet and mining engineer Novalis (Friedrich von Hardenberg) show with exemplary clarity how closely related were romantic nature poetry and the early stages of industrialization.[25]

One discovery of particular significance for modernity's understanding of nature was its insight into the variety and uniqueness of language. In articulating this insight in 1822 following the lead of J. G. Herder, Humboldt managed to overcome the notion that all languages shape the reality external to them in a semantically unified fashion.[26] In its own turn, this insight now also revealed the particular or unique nature of the various understandings of the world.

What can the interpretations of historians contribute to our understanding of the concept of ecology?

Ecology was established as a scientific discipline beginning in 1866

19. Cf. Blumenberg 1993, 267-99, concerning Schlegel and Humboldt.

20. Zimmermann 1982, 130.

21. Cf. H. Böhme 1988, 200.

22. Concerning Goethe's science, see Weizsäcker 1976, 222-43; Picht 1989, 37-46; Altner 1987, 105-13; 1988, 156-64.

23. Zimmermann 1982, 141.

24. Zimmermann 1982, 142.

25. H. Böhme 1988, 97-100, 204-9.

26. Coseriu 1982, 264.

within the discussion surrounding the modern understanding of nature. As discussed above, that understanding is characterized by its separation from the traditional understanding of natural history, which in its own turn was replaced by an imperial constructivism, by dominion over nature and the subject, by a traditionally optimistic understanding of metaphysics, and by a relational ontology. At the same time, however, an opposing understanding of nature emerges within modernity deriving from the tradition of the history of nature; from romanticism's alternative association of nature, deity, and subject; and from the Arcadian line of research into nature.

In summary I would suggest that ecology has incorporated the dialectic of the modern understanding of nature into its own discipline, and that its unique identity is its effort to maintain this tension between the hermeneutical mode of understanding and a precise mode of understanding oriented toward explanation and application. It was precisely the tension inhering in the various elements constituting the modern understanding of nature that provided the setting in which ecological discourse could emerge in the mid–nineteenth century and continue even today as a focus on the "relationships between the organism and its external surroundings" (Haeckel).

Ontologically the question regarding these "relationships" still begs discussion. Biologically the question regarding the identity of living beings is now addressed relationally instead of substantially. Anthropologically the disposition of the naturalistic observer in research constitutes a counterweight to the disciplining of the modern subject — even in the case of precise, exact research. Haeckel's expression "external surroundings" (*umgebende Aussenwelt;* literally, surrounding external world) is both adequately obscure and theoretically stimulating, since it can disclose new approaches to an otherwise unknown sphere.[27] The expression can thus also serve as a metaphysical cipher including both the notion of pantheism, which emerged since the period of romanticism, and the earlier, optimistic notion of a creation organized for the general good *(summum bonum).* It can be noted that the discipline of ecology, too, has not yet really adequately addressed the question of evil within nature, a question that has remained unresolved since physico-theology.

27. The original lack of clarity in the expression "external surroundings" *(umgebende Aussenwelt)* has been rendered differently in different languages. Whereas German refers to *Umgebung* (surroundings), *Umwelt* (surrounding world/environment), and more recently *Mitwelt* ("co-world," "companion world"), English and French prefer the term "environment"; by contrast, Swedish exclusively uses the term *miljö,* a term inspired by French *milieu.*

The Tension between Observation, Law, and Social Function in the Discipline of Ecology

Ecological discourse originally began within the scientific discipline of biology. Haeckel's view was that ecological discourse focused on the "relationships between the organism and its external surroundings, which in the broader sense include all of the 'conditions of its existence.'"[28] One can view Thomas Malthus, Alexander von Humboldt, and Charles Darwin as precursors of Haeckel. Malthus recognized the connection between population increase and the production of food. Humboldt's physiognomic understanding of geography enabled him to develop the notion of "biogeography" as a precursor to ecological geography or landscape ecology. Finally, in 1862/63 Haeckel himself entered into an intensive discussion with Darwin's *Origin of Species*.[29] In the United States of America, Gilbert White, Ralph Waldo Emerson, and Henry David Thoreau are often viewed as the fathers of ecology; indeed, Thoreau has even been called a "theological ecologist."[30]

Until 1972 ecological discussion was restricted largely to the scientific discipline of biology. In 1972 Heinz-Ulrich Nennen brought about the "ecological turn," that is, the expansion of the discussion to other disciplines, including the earlier movement of nature conservation and more recent social movements, the political arena, and even the public media.[31] The introduction of the following terms — some newly coined, others adopted from earlier discourse — provides a rough chronology of the history of ecology as an independent discipline.[32]

1877 "biocenosis" (Möbius)

1887 "microcosm" (of a lake; Forbes)

1895 "community" (in relation to plant geography; Warming)

1896 "autecology" (individual organism or species in relation to its environment; Schröter)

28. Haeckel 1866, 286f.

29. Cf. Nennen 1991, 70ff.

30. Sörlin 1991, 107-17.

31. Nennen 1991, 81f., associates the turn in 1972 with Meadows et al.'s publication of the report of the Club of Rome, *The Limits of Growth*. The actual expansion of the discussion, of course, did not just commence in 1972, since ecology had ceased to be an issue exclusive to the discipline of biology at latest with the publication of Rachel Carson's book *Silent Spring* in 1962.

32. Concerning the chronology, see Nennen 1991, 74-76; Trepl 1987, 122, 134-38, 168ff., 197, 200; Sörlin 1991, 138f., 213; Kinzelbach 1989, 49f., 58-60, 76.

1902 "synecology" (relations between entire natural communities of
living beings and their environments; Schröter)

1917 "ecological niche" (Grinnell)

1928 "Gestalt system" (Woltereck)

1935 "ecosystem" (Tansley) and *Umwelt* (Uexküll)[33]

1936 "human ecology" (Renner)

1939 "geographical ecology," "landscape ecology" (Troll)

1948 "cybernetics" (Wiener)

1949 "information theory" (Shannon)

1970 "environmental protection," *Umweltschutz* (Graul)

1971 "medical environmentology" (Graul), "system dynamics/world
model" (Forrester)

The history of ecology has largely taken place within the field of tension between exact nomothetic methodology and observational methodology.

Over the course of this history, opposing poles gradually emerged between organic and individualistic conceptions, the initially predominant organic concept (Clements) eventually being eclipsed by the individualistic approach (Gleason).[34] Other polar opposites involved holistic and mechanistic conceptions.[35] It was only Eugene Odum's synthesis in the concept of the "ecosystem" that managed to overcome the dispute surrounding holism.[36]

A more rigorous specialization as a scientific discipline was in store for ecology after 1945. Not only did its various subdisciplines undergo a quantitative revolution, it also developed a theoretical, nomothetically exact methodology modeled on that of physics. Moreover, it also began adopting and incorporating various theoretical elements from disciplines outside biology, including the concept of system, cybernetics, energetics, and information theory.[37]

More recently the discipline of ecology has considerably expanded its interdisciplinary presence by entering into fruitful discussions with the disciplines of economics, sociology, psychology, the technical sciences, and medi-

33. The German term *Umwelt* was not received well at first, and has only recently been reintroduced into the discussion. Concerning J. von Uexküll's understanding of *Umwelt*, see J. von Uexküll and Kriszat 1983, 15f., 114-17.

34. Trepl 1987, 139-58.

35. Concerning holism, see Trepl 1987, 148, 183ff.; Meyer-Abich 1988, 89-103; 1989b.

36. Trepl 1987, 190ff.

37. Trepl 1987, 202. The differing definitions of "ecology" in contemporary instructional texts show that the controversy between the understanding of ecology from the perspectives of natural history and physics is still unresolved.

cine, and has also addressed — albeit to a lesser degree — common problem areas with philosophy, the legal sciences, and theology. The challenges posed by environmental protection and rehabilitation as well as issues of social planning have been particularly significant in revealing new areas of concern. The result has been the emergence of a more comprehensive interdisciplinary field of environmental sciences in which ecology now plays an important role.

Like every other scientific discipline, so also must ecology be subject to criticism. For ecology such criticism is even more urgent insofar as during the course of its disciplinary specialization, it has slipped into the vortex of quantitative and reductionist methodologies.

The methodological transition from an analysis of individual causes to the analysis of several different variables has brought phenomena into view that previously were neither observed nor manipulated. Hence, although our understanding and perspective on the horizon of the "whole" — to take one example — has doubtless expanded, we now also see that such a "whole" will in each instance naturally appear different to the observer, depending on the particular organizational disposition of the research itself. Any subsequent application of the instrumental aspects as well as the interpretation of results themselves depend on the perspective of the actual observer, while the pattern or model as such always remains hidden to the ecologist.

The discernment of new relationships and connections invariably significantly enhances the possibilities for the social applications of the technology emerging from research. Human beings can acquire the ability to manipulate parts of the ecosystem, and indeed, one of the tendencies inhering in the multifunctional method has been critically referred to as the "economization of nature." One result of a rigorous system-analytical examination of the economy of energy and information is that the researcher loses sight of the qualitative elements and phenomena constituting their uniqueness.

It seems likely that if the discipline of ecology develops primarily as a quantitative science, it will inevitably expose itself to the perils of reductionism and objectivization of the sort already sufficiently evident in the "hard" natural sciences. The application of "quantitative" ecology in this sense justifiably prompts the suspicion of an underlying ecological economization of nature according to the conditions of technological exploitation by regnant or at least sufficiently powerful entities within society. Beyond even these considerations, any quantitative natural science invariably also tends to explain human and cultural phenomena from a reductionist position. For all these reasons, the discipline of ecology should constantly be subjected to ideological criticism lest it fall prey to epistemological, technological, and anthropological reductionism.

From a critical historical perspective, one can certainly raise the question whether Linné's and Smith's model of the economy of nature and society is not experiencing a kind of renaissance today in the association of quantitative ecology with ideological economics. Does the uncritical association of economy and ecology not pose just as serious a threat to the ongoing integrity of the environment as does the phenomenon of industrialization, a phenomenon it is indeed able to alter but not overcome?

Unfortunately, these economic and constructivist problems seem to represent the unavoidable inheritance of the scientific discipline of ecology. At the same time, however, this criticism should not obscure the fact that within the discipline of ecology itself, *non*utilitarian and *non*-system-functional principles have also always managed to survive, principles that do emphasize and acknowledge the otherness of nature in all its uniqueness. If ecology is not to become constricted into a biotechnical discipline oriented on the model of physics, it must undertake a rigorous examination of the attendant philosophical problems and considerations within the field of tension between qualitative observation, quantitative analysis, and social relevance.

The Conditions of the Possibility of an Ecological Philosophy

Whereas ecological discourse in the sense of a natural science focuses on the patterns and laws of natural relationships, the philosophical discussion of ecology focuses on the conditions of ecological thinking in the larger sense. In what follows I will describe two of the more influential positions in ecological philosophy.[38]

38. Additional fundamental philosophical discussions of ecological thought can be found in Picht 1979; 1989; Meyer-Abich 1979; 1988; and Hösle 1991; 1992, 166-97. Des Jardins provides a thorough presentation of the ethical issues of environmental philosophy. Concerning the philosophy of ecofeminism, see Warren 1996. Although Whitehead's process philosophy provides an important philosophical discussion of the foundations of ecological thought, I will not discuss his system here because his successors (especially in theology) were the ones who provided the link between process philosophy and ecology. Concerning the process-theological interpretation of Whitehead, see Link 1991, 434ff. D. Griffin interprets Whitehead from the perspective of depth ecology (Næss 1989).

Gregory Bateson's Ecology of Mind

In 1972 Bateson's book *Ecology of Mind* opened up common ground for ecology and philosophy, his most important contribution being a disclosure of the depth of the epistemological and theoretical problem facing ecological thought. Bateson did, however, take the methodologically risky path of examining synoptically socioanthropological, psychological, biological, and epistemological research in ultimately establishing a "sacred unity of the biosphere"[39] and an "ecology of mind/ideas."[40]

One of his fundamental theses is that thinking resembles evolution and that both can be understood as "stochastic processes," that is, as an interplay between chance and selection.[41] Bateson begins with Russell's hierarchy of logical typology, replacing it with "grouping."[42] He relates the processes of evolution and thinking by emphasizing the process of the naming of names and of names of names.

One can, it must be noted, misunderstand Bateson as a biologist who is subordinating thinking to the biological process. One can do better justice to his socioanthropological position, however, by recognizing the capacity of his epistemology of the ecology of mind to articulate the unique elements of the human mind's capacity to discern the intellectual or spiritual pattern uniting all living things.[43]

One critical question is whether Bateson has not slipped into circular argumentation insofar as it is, after all, only human thought itself that can discern that which he is calling the model or pattern.[44] Bateson maintains that the capacity of the mind to discern the ecological pattern resides in the empirical but largely hypothetical analogy of substance and process in thinking and natural evolution. It is difficult to see how Bateson can persuasively demonstrate that the mind really can discern — in thought — not only itself, but also the "mental model" of all living entities. Does this assertion not also require some sort of metaphysical axiom such as the assumption of what might be called an "ecological world soul"?

39. Bateson 1990a, 31.
40. Bateson 1990b, 15.
41. Bateson 1990a, 31, 113f.
42. Bateson 1990a, 232f.
43. Hoffmeyer 1988, 19f.
44. Bateson 1990a, 15.

Ecosophy T: Arne Næss

The Norwegian philosopher Arne Næss offers yet another explication and grounding of ecological thought. Ever since the publication of his book *Ecology, Community, and Lifestyle: Outline of an Ecosophy* in 1973 (ET, rev.), his "ecosophy" has exerted considerable influence especially on the social ecological movement specifically but also on the broader discipline of ecology. Næss's point of departure is the ecological crisis of modernity, which he believes provides opportunities for developing new criteria for and perspectives on our understanding of progress and rationality.[45]

Although Næss's understanding of "ecosophy" employs the tools of specialized philosophical inquiry, it has also been inspired by biological ecology without really deriving from the latter (37-40). His basic line of thinking picks up on the natural derivation of ethics following from Spinoza's anti-Cartesian philosophy of nature.[46]

In contrast to Bateson, Næss is not interested in establishing a comprehensive synthesis of biology, anthropology, and epistemology. Instead, he develops his system as one among many possible systems, giving it the designation "ecosophy T," T being the abbreviation for Tseringma, which in the language of the Himalayan Sherpa means both "mountain" and "princess" (61). Næss emphasizes the necessity of establishing a philosophical basis for ecology that prevents the latter from being misunderstood as a universal science: "Without an ecosophy, ecology can provide no principles for acting, no motive for political and individual efforts" (41).

At the risk of oversimplifying, let me summarize Næss's position in the following six theses:

1. As a phenomenon, life is basically one or unified (164).
2. All living things have inherent value; the right of life to develop itself is unified and the same for all and cannot be quantified (164f.).
3. The ecological assessment of the significance of symbioses reveals a tendency toward solidarity that in its own turn presupposes identification (168).

---

45. Næss 1989, 26. Page numbers in the following text refer to Næss 1989.

46. In contrast to Descartes, who posited the dualism of mind and nature, Spinoza begins with the unity of the divine substance constituting both nature *and* mind. He understands the phenomenal forms of nature as "modes," nature itself as the "sum of all modes," and the deity as infinite and all-inclusive "substance."

4. Identification implies the overcoming of alienation and a rediscovery of community (171ff.).

5. Although human beings are characterized by the capacity for assessment and valuation (176f.), the anthropocentrism resulting from relating all values to human beings is philosophically untenable (177).

6. Ecosophy T combines the principles of self-realization, a philosophy of unity (deriving from identification), and nonviolence (after the model of Gandhi) (207, 193-96).

Næss constructs his system in the form of a pyramid such that the integral unity of the individual and whole prevents the individual's self-realization from generating conflict; quite the contrary, with the aid of nonviolent conflict resolution the individual's self-realization enhances the diversity, variety, and overall potential for self-realization within the whole and as such also enhances the chances for survival.[47]

Næss has emphasized in an extremely comprehensive fashion the necessity of grounding ecology philosophically in the face of current global ethical challenges; in so doing, he has also allowed the classic questions of the philosophy of nature to receive a hearing in the new situation.

Just as for Spinoza, however, one can question the extent to which such an understanding and interpretation of the totality of all phenomenal forms of biological life *necessarily* leads to behavioral norms that best serve both nature *and* human beings.

Spinoza's ethics led to the maxim according to which one accepts the divinely given situation in nature. Næss intends for his own ethics to lead to new, responsible ecopolitics. What is the philosophical reasoning behind this leap from the symbiotic unity of being as articulated by ecology, on the one hand, to the establishment of norms for correct behavior in the case of conflicts, on the other? That is, how can behavioral norms aimed at altering existing situations be derived from the unity of being?

Whereas the application of Spinoza's system led to fatalism, the application of ecosophy seems to lead to philosophically unsupported activism on behalf of the potential realizational possibilities of all.

Let me stress that I do not intend to diminish the potential of Næss's ecosophy with my objections. Quite the contrary, in the face of the regnant ontological-atomistic justification and inclination of the natural sciences to-

---

47. Næss 1989, 201, interprets Spinoza such that this "variety" encompasses an infinite number of expressions of an infinite number of modes of nature and thus of God. Cf. Spinoza 1989, I, Theorem 16, 25.

day, which acknowledge in nature only that which can be made into a manip-ulable object of natural sciences' operations, Næss provides an extremely valuable perspective that tries to take into account all the attendant problem-atical issues.

I do not see how one can reconcile the Christian understanding of a God who subjects himself as a sacrifice even to the evil forces of nature — even to the point of death for the sake of subjugating those forces — with Spinoza's understanding of a God who ontologically encompasses the sum of all natural entities. For Næss God remains a necessary axiom, whereas the God of the He-brew and Greek Bible is active even *in* the history of nature. At the same time, however, I do think that any philosophical construction of a Christian theol-ogy of creation should remain ever mindful of Spinoza's thesis that because nature is ultimately grounded in the divine itself, it is also unified.[48]

Problems of Ecological Philosophy

In summary, we can now identify several basic problems in the philosophical discussion of ecological discourse.

First, the ontological question recurs regarding the being and essence of nature. Are we to understand the being of nature ontologically as all-encompassing substance (Næss), as process (Whitehead), or as the unity of phenomena in time (Picht)? Questions regarding natural ethics, biological anthropology, and epistemology also need to be addressed.

Other questions involve the conditions for articulating our understand-ing of unity, uniformity, diversity, and changeability in nature. Does nature include only that which is accessible as an object to empirical, logically de-ductive natural science? Or can it also include the "perspectival deformation of phenomena by the *logos*"?[49] How are we to understand the interplay be-tween thinking and evolution, mind and nature? Can "scientific integrity" be ascribed to a science of nature that ignores its metaphysical axioms and in so doing basically resists rational grounding? What is the relationship between the unique elements in human beings, on the one hand, and the diversity of other living beings among which they live and which vivify them, on the other? What is the relationship between our evaluation of nature and our knowledge of its modes of being? Can one even speak in a meaningful fashion about the intrinsic value of being? And if so, what is the relationship between

48. Spinoza 1989, I, Theorem 15.
49. Picht 1979, 21.

this intrinsic value and the values of society? Is all power or force value-neutral, or does evil exist in and against nature?

Aesthetics and Ecology — a New Form of Knowledge?

There has always been a fundamental difference between the scientific and aesthetic observation of nature. Science in the narrower sense explains its sensory perceptions of nature through reference to natural laws with the aid of quantitative measurement. By contrast, the aesthetic observation of nature lingers with its object and "endows the individual entity with a discrete meaning."[50] Aesthetic judgment is always directed toward the object itself. In contrast to the object of science, the aesthetic object is not characterized by an assessment of its utilitarian value. For the beautiful: "Its purpose and object are immanent in it."[51]

I would like to address the relationship between aesthetics and ecology even though these two areas have not traditionally received much attention.

Gernot Böhme and Martin Seel have provided initial points of departure for establishing an aesthetics of nature within philosophical studies, with Böhme providing pieces of a mosaic that might contribute to an "ecological aesthetics of nature,"[52] while Seel delimits his eudaemonistic "aesthetics of nature" over against the ecological concept of nature.[53] The discipline of art history has also made important contributions through its studies of landscape painting throughout history and into the present.[54]

Let me enumerate five reasons why I believe aesthetic-ecological discourse can enhance our understanding of ecological problems and even provide insights for their solution; such discussion can also contribute to the development of new practical and theoretical forms of knowledge.

1. For the scientific discipline of ecology to remain true to its tradition in natural history, it must ultimately also reflect aesthetically on the conditions underlying human observation of nature.
2. If it is to speak persuasively about its capacity for discerning the intrinsic value of natural forms of life, ecological ethics as grounded in moral

50. Nelson 1949 (ET), 48.
51. Nelson 1949 (ET), 52.
52. G. Böhme 1989.
53. Seel 1991, 29-31. Lesch and Bergmann (1998) also move in the direction of a theologically qualified aesthetics of nature.
54. Bätschmann 1989; Ellenius 1992; Boehm 1986.

philosophy cannot avoid addressing issues of aesthetics. Whereas the rationality of the natural sciences excludes any acknowledgment of the intrinsic value of nature, it is precisely that intrinsic value that constitutes the presupposition for observing nature aesthetically.

3. Art history has shown how artistic media have always anticipated discoveries in the natural sciences. The work of Claude Monet, to take one example, shows how painting, rather than merely "illustrating" the insights of the natural sciences, creates the pictorial or representational presuppositions for "discoveries" in the natural sciences.[55]

4. In overcoming the technological imperative of genuinely having to implement everything that is technologically possible, the artistic sector in the community of sciences and scholarship can provide insights of enormous value to the kind of ecologically inspired alteration of technology that is *not* oriented exclusively toward the principle of "technology for technology's sake," but rather toward the principle that technology can be employed for the sake of nature and art.

5. The aesthetic reflection on human and cultural perceptions, interpretations, and shaping of nature can function as a corrective to an excessively *instrumental* rationality. In 1750 Alexander Baumgarten, the founder of modern aesthetics, fashioned an "aestheticological" understanding of truth that synthesized aesthetic truth and logical truth.[56] Can we today effectively adopt this earlier notion from the Enlightenment envisioning a unified totality of perception, analysis, and action?

The Conditions of New Social Action

In 1972 findings in the discipline of ecology began to be applied to debate regarding society and to social theories, and what might be called a public "ecological consciousness" emerged in which the new understanding of the connection between social growth and biological environment prompted a demand for new concepts of political action and new models of production and consumption.

Seven groups of actors can be distinguished in the sphere of social action:

1. the many less prominent people of ordinary daily life;

55. Cf. Bergmann 1997b, 40f.
56. Baumgarten 1973, 440.

2. social movements emerging from earlier nature conservation movements and also from more recent movements focusing on sociocultural and biological problems both locally and globally and arising since 1970 especially in urban areas. The methods of more recent movements largely employ the tools of the electronic public media in civilian society, while earlier movements tended to be organized more conventionally in associations;

3. the political organization of the Greens, active in parliamentary democracies;

4. national political institutions active at the national, bilateral, and international level;

5. academicians focusing analytically and normatively on the problems of environmental science in all areas of research;

6. praxis-oriented institutions outside academia with various networks of interest;

7. entrepreneurs whose production is affected by environmental demands and laws, and transnational profit-making organizations.

In First World countries the ecological understanding of nature has become a necessary, stable part of our understanding of society. Persuasive ecological findings have led us to believe we are indeed capable of countering what we see as increasing biological devastation with enormous risks for human cultures. The conference of the United Nations in Rio de Janeiro in 1992 produced a geopolitical consensus regarding the global challenge posed by biological environmental problems and by the problems generated by cultural development.[57]

To mention but three of the many strategies for action:

1. Those favoring an acknowledgment of the "rights of nature" analogous to human rights suggest taking decisive steps toward altering society itself.[58]

2. Others are developing far-reaching strategies for technological social planning and for adjusting financial planning and national economies to be less inimical to nature.[59]

3. Representatives of the ecologically, economically, and culturally impov-

---

57. *Vår gemensamma framtid (Our Common Future).*

58. Goethe 1989a, 772; Stone 1992; Moltmann 1989, 69ff.; Vischer 1990; Altner 1991, 101-11; Link 1991, 485f.; Bergmann 1992.

59. E.g., Binswanger 1991.

erished South advocate a policy by which the North might readjust its technological identity in combination with a redistribution of power to local communities for developing and accessing resources.[60]

The Necessity of Comprehensive Bioethics

One of the most basic questions of ethics regards the relationship between the good and nature.

The change in modernity's understanding of nature, however, has made it impossible to answer this question with conceptions oriented toward the tradition of natural law or traditional humanistic values. More specifically, the change in the social constructions of society and nature has rendered both these conceptions incapable of addressing the issue.

First, the being of nature can no longer be viewed as the norm for human ethical action. Second, human beings can no longer be viewed as the center of the universe for whose utilitarian sake alone life has evolved. Third, our experiences with the science of ecology and with new sociopolitical concepts have generated previously unknown normative problems. Fourth, the consequences of technology have become so comprehensive that they now require global ethics. Ecological discourse cannot avoid the ethical question concerning nature and concerning the normative actions of human beings in and with nature.

Three typological metaethical positions can be observed in the interplay between ethics and ecology. (1) Ecological problems continue to be addressed as exclusively individual ethical problems within the framework of traditional ethical conceptions (individualistic traditionalism).[61] (2) New moral problems are acknowledged and addressed with the aid of conventional or pragmatic conceptions (social pragmatism).[62] (3) Basic metaethical principles are developed in dialogue with those affected by bioethical problems and with the help of previous ethical traditions and then carefully exam-

60. Shiva 1993, 40f.

61. So, e.g., Nozick, who advocates a "minimalist state," a kind of night-watchman state in which citizens themselves organize institutions of learning, care, and pension. Apel 1992a, 29f., shows why individualist ethical conceptions cannot adequately address the ecological challenge.

62. Birnbacher (1979; 1986) and Singer (1990) represent a utilitarian position. Jonas (1979) offers a principled ethical position based on earlier conservative positions (*altkonservativ*, so Habermas). Irrgang stays with a humanistic grounding of ethics within the Catholic tradition of social ethics.

ined in light of the contributions of the ecological sciences, philosophy, and the various social movements (ecological constructivism).[63]

Because normative ethics is focusing with increasing intensity on precisely these issues, and because such questions are also now affecting the discussion of metaethics, in what follows I will discuss several of the core problems of theoretical ethical-ecological discourse.

Are Human Beings the Only Ethical Subjects?

General consensus holds that human beings are ethical subjects, that is, capable of moral action.

Representatives of the anthropocentric position maintain that nature becomes involved in the enterprise of establishing ethical principles only to the extent that it fulfills a function for human beings. The result is that human interest in nature becomes an ethical object and nonhuman forms of life appear as ethical objects only insofar as they fulfill a function for human beings.[64] By contrast, representatives of an ecocentric position maintain that it is not just human beings but also animals, plants, and ecosystems that have intrinsic value and must thus be viewed as autonomous ethical objects.[65]

Anthropocentrists subordinate moral obligation toward other ethical objects (nonhuman life-forms) to the obligation toward ethical subjects (fellow human beings and sentient animals). By contrast, ecocentrists subordinate moral obligation toward ethical subjects — which are, after all, also part of a whole — to the obligation toward the ethical object of precisely that whole, namely, the ecosystem.[66]

Can Values Be Discerned? Can One Speak Meaningfully about the Intrinsic Value and Rights of Nature?

Because the value-nihilistic, emotivist position acknowledges the values attaching to nature and human beings *only* as exclusively subjective values, it contributes little to ecological ethics.

63. Næss 1989; Apel 1992b; Nennen 1991, 12; Altner 1991.
64. Irrgang 1992, 70.
65. Meyer-Abich 1989a, 260-64; Næss 1989, 166ff.; Rolston 1988, 2. Bloch 1977, 802-7, has developed the most comprehensive understanding of a "natural subject," that is, of nature as a subject. Concerning the ecocentric expansion of biocentrism, see Des Jardins 1997, 147f.
66. Rolston 1988, 190f.

Although the noncognitivist position does acknowledge that human beings do posit values, it concludes from this insight that there are no values without human input.[67] As far as ecological ethics is concerned, this position at most leads to solutions based on social contracts determined exclusively by the relationships of power and interest represented by the respective contractual parties.

A third position begins with the cognitive assumption that values can indeed be discerned. Subscribing to the presuppositions of such a position seems to be unavoidable if ecological ethics intends to speak meaningfully about the intrinsic value and rights of nature. The goal in this sense is to articulate as precisely as possible what we understand to be the intrinsic value of living beings. Intrinsic value is ascribed to all beings — including human beings — as the basic value underlying their existence and their right to development.[68] The assumption of this intrinsic value of nature now also provides the basis for postulating the rights of nature, since at a deeper level the thesis of intrinsic value also involves the thesis that diversity and value (valence) are inseparable.[69]

Can We Discern Hierarchies of Values in Nature?

Advocates of the anthropocentric position who acknowledge other living beings, for example, animals, as ethical objects also maintain the existence of value hierarchies. In conflict situations they then adduce as their normative argument the notion of status or rank within such hierarchies, axiomatically ascribing the highest rank to human beings. Although ecosophical ethics rejects the existence of such ontologically determined value hierarchies in favor of the view that nonquantifiable values attach to existence, they do maintain that human beings are obligated to their conspecifics and to other related living beings to an even *greater* degree.[70] An ecosophical position based on an ethics of reverence or respect views every living being as of equal value and assumes that every living being inherently strives for self-realization (Næss). Conflicts arising from this inherent striving are to be resolved based on a consideration of *all* involved living beings,[71] a position that ontologically based value hierarchies reject.

67. Irrgang 1992, 98.
68. Næss 1989, 164ff.
69. Shiva 1993, 38; Næss 1989, 200f.
70. Næss 1989, 170.
71. Altner 1991, 288.

Other issues of metaethics involve how to employ our ecological findings in establishing normative principles of action,[72] how our understanding of "utopia" is to function in ecological ethics,[73] how best to act on what we recognize as the necessity of metaphysical reflection and grounding,[74] and how to develop metaphysical pluralism amid the enormous complexity of environmental ethical problems.[75]

3. How Can Theology Respond to the Ecological Challenge?

We have examined the ecological challenge from several perspectives. From the perspective of cultural history, it appears as the provocative change in the modern understanding of nature. In the natural sciences, it involves the development of a new, more comprehensive biological theory. In philosophy we see the return of metaphysics and ontology. Sociopolitically it has generated a new understanding of human beings and a new conception of human action in response to a crisis situation. And finally, in ethics it involves a reassessment of the intrinsic value of nature in our metaethical and normative-ethical considerations. But how can theology respond to this challenge?

Three Paths

In what follows I describe the three paths theologians have taken in recent decades.[76] The first draws a fundamental distinction between the object of theology and that of the interpretation of nature; it then tries to integrate the in-

---

72. Næss 1989, 40f.; Wandén 1992, 156ff.

73. Nennen 1991, 201-5. Cf. Apel's (1986) criticism of Jonas's anti-utopianism and Bergmann 1997b, 209-12. I believe it imperative to include ethical visions in the ecological discussion of ethics if we are to develop viable normative principles for action.

74. For all practical purposes, Wandén 1992, 102ff., and Irrgang 1992, 69-172, avoid the problem whereas Rolston 1988, 335, does acknowledge it. By contrast, Seel 1991, 16, eudaemonistically postulates the "postmetaphysical" age. Apel 1992b, 242-57, offers a well-considered transcendental-pragmatic solution.

75. Des Jardins 1997, 250-54.

76. I am not including contributions from the dialogue between the natural sciences and theology, since they focus largely on the relationship between newer scientific theories and creation dogmas. Concerning the dialogue between creation theology and the natural sciences, see Peacocke 1990 and Pannenberg 1994, 59-136.

terpretations of both according to the tenets of the doctrine of faith. The second removes the boundary between the interpretations of faith and life and combines the two. The third responds to the ecological challenge by synthesizing our understandings of God and nature in a critical but integrative fashion.

1. Conjunction

The first way of responding to these challenges makes a fundamental distinction between the interpretation of faith and various other interpretations of life.

Oswald Bayer describes the path of theological "reorientation" as an "essay in translation": "Life in the larger sense and, with it, *theology* is possible *only in translation,* that is, in freely listening and responding to what is said to us."[77] Bayer engages his theological reflections methodologically as an "orientation toward primary texts" from the Christian tradition. Theology is to reflect on the "concrete truth in these primary texts" and then translate these truths amid the "conflict of interpretations."[78] Although such an understanding of theology does indeed emphasize the capacity for dialogue with its attendant background theories, it implies that the interests and concerns of theology are in fact unique to theology itself and must be asserted in conflict situations.[79]

This position rejects any integration of theological and ecological interpretations. Instead of including non-Christian views of nature in their theological presuppositions, advocates of this position reduce the ecological challenge to a problem of language. The historic sphere of "global technological language" or the "language necessary for dealing successfully with the political sphere"[80] is of theological interest *only* because it is in precisely these spheres that the truth of the primary texts is, after all, to be proclaimed.

---

77. Bayer 1990, 7. The North American Mennonite theologian Thomas N. Finger has attempted a similar "conjunction." Finger begins with the phenomenon of human alienation and seeks traditional Christian responses to it. Although he presents his study as a "'critical conversation' with current culture" (1997, 11), he merely offers the postulated answers of faith to the questions of a generalized situation, and although he promises a "trinitarian transformation," that transformation does not get beyond its own Jesus-centered and kerygmatic point of departure.

78. Bayer 1990, 8.

79. Bayer 1990, 1.

80. Bayer 1990, 7.

What we find, of course, is that the "ecological crisis" is merely taken as the occasion for reformulating basic Christian creation doctrines. As secular statements, however, the reinterpretation of nature prompted by this crisis has no genuinely integral connection with the Christian confession, and for that reason also fails to acquire any genuine relevance for the interpretation of faith.

I refer to this type of response to the ecological challenge as *conjunction*. Ideally the Christian interpretation of faith is combined with secular interpretations of life; in other instances it can be wholly severed from them. In any event, the theologian first makes a fundamental distinction between faith and life, God and nature, before then reconnecting them.

By making such fundamental distinctions, of course, this method reflects the historical separation of the natural sciences and the humanities according to which objects of nature are "explained" while those of the humanities are "understood." As one of the traditional disciplines in the humanities, theology takes as its object the human understanding of faith, whereas ecological theories address the question of external nature.

The question one would like to put to advocates of this position is whether God's revelation and reflection on it are reserved *exclusively* for confessing Christians and their representatives in church and theology; that is, might one also expect revelatory knowledge and insight to come to expression in *other* religions and *other* interpretations of life? Might such revelation also come to expression, for example, in an ecological interpretation of nature? Because the hermeneutical method of such theology is so exclusive, one wonders whether that method does not inevitably reduce theology to biblical philology and denominational homiletics. Indeed, does not the thesis of the exclusive or unique "interests and concerns" of theology not expand the field of purview of theology so excessively as to make it virtually impossible to reach any reasonable understanding with others regarding precisely these "interests and concerns"?

2. Syncretism

The second response to the ecological challenge eliminates the boundary between the interpretation of faith and of life. Matthew Fox, enthusiastically shifting the focus of Christology from the historical Jesus to the cosmic Christ, has tried to develop a new, "mystical cosmology" by assembling an eclectic and imposing number of passages from the Old and New Testaments, from the writings of Christian creation mystics, from the New Age movement, and from depth psychology. Only the insights gathered from these sources, says Fox, can save the planet. Although Fox accuses the Enlightenment of having thwarted the emergence of such a cosmology,[81] he fails to consider that the concept of "cosmology" ultimately derives from the Enlightenment itself. In any event, by cosmology he understands (a) the scientific history of the origin of our universe, (b) mysticism as an answer for the soul, and (c) art as a portrait of our development.[82]

I refer to this second response as *syncretism* since it treats statements deriving from an ecological understanding of nature uncritically as statements of faith without first critically examining the truth claims of scientific and theological theories. Instead it employs the concept of "spirituality" as an eclectic collective term without first mediating its newly developed theological statements with the Christian tradition of the Holy Spirit.[83]

3. Critical Integration

John B. Cobb, Jr., describes theology as "self-conscious Christian reflection about important matters."[84] Because one of these "important matters" is the ecological challenge, that challenge naturally represents an object of theological reflection. By describing theology thus, Cobb also provides a convenient common denominator for all those authors who are the subject of the present study.[85] When these authors reflect on the content and form of the Christian faith, they are actually reflecting on the shift in modernity's understanding of nature. In so doing, they articulate the theological interpretation of faith as a specifically Christian interpretation of life and nature, and in that sense the ecological challenge ultimately prompts them to reconstruct the Christian interpretation of life.

---

81. Fox 1991, 10.

82. Fox 1991, 11.

83. Burns (1994, 79f.) criticizes Fox for having weakened the incarnational theology of the Gospel of John, and for having allowed the intended panentheism to collapse into "functional pantheism" because of his refusal to ascribe divine transcendence to it (81). Burns (82) believes that Fox has reduced both the divine and the human to the cosmos. Santmire (1994, 18ff.) objects that Fox's position (1994) has nothing to say to the urban poor of America, and that Fox's doctrine of reconciliation — which Santmire examines typologically from the perspective of the Swedish theologian Gustaf Aulén (1983) — excessively restricts the classical type Abelard developed as Christ our example and teacher.

84. Cobb 1990, 262.

85. Cobb, D. Griffin, Birch, Altner, Liedke, Duchrow, Link, Moltmann, McFague, and Ruether.

This reconstruction of the Christian interpretation of life proceeds methodologically by first recognizing how important it is to integrate "background theories"[86] into its theological premises for the sake of facilitating dialogue. These "background theories" of the Christian interpretation of life emerge from the various problem areas of ecological discourse discussed above.

One of the issues facing the ecumenical movement has been to address in an integrated fashion the problems of the church *and* the world, and in 1968 the movement articulated this challenge by saying that one should let the *world* determine what the ecumenical agenda should be.[87] The theologians I will be discussing here have applied this suggestion to their theology, the result being, of course, that the problems of the world end up determining the agenda of theological reflection.

I refer to this third response to the ecological challenge as *critical integration,* the term "integration" referring to the conviction that theological knowledge need not contradict or stand in an antithetical relationship to ecological knowledge. Quite the contrary, one should be able to reconcile the two. The term "critical" refers to theology's capacity for functioning as a "corrective" to the truth claims of the ecological sciences, something it is able to do because of its history and tradition of rigorous scholarship and its particular methodology and mode of inquiry.

As ideal types, conjunction and syncretism represent antithetical positions. The one clings desperately to its "own" truth and to the particular concerns of the Christian faith, while the other broadly incorporates the "spiritual" at large into Christianity. The one responds to the ecological challenge with exclusive references to revelation in scripture, while the other advocates a kind of natural cosmological theology under the banner of Christianity. By developing theological discourse as part of ecological discourse, critical integration chooses a third path, albeit without subordinating the totality of theological discourse to the conditions of ecological discourse as do the syncretists and without merely translating one discourse into another.

Just as the relevant problems of theological discourse can and should be discussed within an interdisciplinary dialogue, so also can theological problems be addressed as ecological problems.[88]

86. The expression "background theory" refers to "those implied theories that impact upon considered hypotheses and judgments" (F. Schüssler Fiorenza 1991, 74).

87. Slenczka 1988, 537.

88. The critically integrative position also includes the variety of perspectives found in ecofeminist theology emerging from the discourses surrounding feminism, ecology, and feminist theology. Concerning the connection between ecology and perspectives in the Third

Whatever is an *important matter* in ecological discourse, whether as a theoretical problem of truth or as a practical problem of normative behavior, is also an important matter for theology. It is *not* theologians, however, who determine which matters are to be viewed as "important," but rather the partners in the various public spheres that theology enters into dialogue with as well as, within the paradigm of liberation theology, the victims and those affected by ecological problems.

Advocates of critical integration begin with the common problems confronting theology and the church, on the one hand, and representatives of the ecological understanding of nature in the sciences, daily life, culture at large, and popular movements, on the other. Such integration has been taking place since 1970 in many churches and in the ecumenical movement,[89] and it is these experiences within the larger community of church theology and ecology that constitute the presuppositions for my examination of selected theologians below. In their attempts to find and implement new solutions, these theologians reflect the new presuppositions influencing the Christian interpretation of life.

Two Directions: Creation Dogmatics and Theological Ecology

Authors responding to the ecological challenge generally fall in one of two methodologically polar positions that can be described as "ecological creation dogmatics" and "theological ecology"/"theology of nature."

Creation dogmatics begins with an interpretation of the Christian confessions and the question of God, while the theology of nature begins with the problems and proposed solutions of ecology and then examines these within a theological context.[90] Creation dogmatics comes at the question of

---

World, see Ruether 1996 and Riley 1995. Green 1994, 53-57, discusses the tensions emerging for ecofeminist theology from within these cross-disciplinary discussions, namely, the tensions between cosmocentrism in the understanding of nature and anthropocentrism in the understanding of human beings; Green also proposes a trinitarian solution.

89. Evidence of this copious emergence of comprehensive discourse between ecology and theology can be found in six areas: (1) local pastoral engagement and publications; (2) church commitment; (3) interdenominational conferences and ecumenical movements; cf. WCC 1983; WCC 1991a; cf. Duchrow 1989; WCC 1991b; "Fred genom rättvisa" 1989 (Peace with justice); WCC 1990 (Seoul); (4) interdisciplinary exchanges and studies; (5) ecological perspectives on problems in practical theology (cf. Bergant 1998; Mick 1997; Fragomeni and Pawlikowski 1994); (6) geopolitical developments. Fowler's detailed study of Protestantism in the USA, 1970-1990, clearly reveals a "greening of Protestant thought," especially as regards environmental ethics and biblical interpretation.

90. Cf. the thorough discussion in Link 1991, 473f.

nature from the question of God, while theological ecology comes at the question of God from the question of nature. As might be expected, theological ecology is also more strongly oriented toward praxis and can even view itself as a "practical theology of nature."[91]

It is important, however, not to view these two positions precipitately as antitheses. In the following discussion I often examine them in a complementary fashion that enables the conflicts between their respective dogmatic and ecological findings to help articulate possible points of criticism and deepen our understanding of the underlying problems.

It is only in connection with the conjunctive model that one can speak of genuine antithesis between dogmatics and contextual ecological theology. Otherwise the increasing inclination of theologians today to engage in qualitatively and quantitatively enhanced dialogue[92] encourages those who hope for a more comprehensive integration of the Christian interpretation of nature.[93]

4. Why Gregory of Nazianzus?

How can an interpretation of the writings of Gregory of Nazianzus help theology respond to the ecological challenge? Taking note of possible objections against this choice, I will examine my choice from the perspectives of history, Gregory's later influence, philosophical issues, and systematic theology. In chapter 3 I then offer my interpretation of Gregory's theological understanding of the world, and in chapter 4 examine *how* this interpretation of his writings can correlatively serve ecology theology.

The "Present Power" of History

Obvious differences between the context of late modernity and the context of late antiquity naturally militate against choosing a "premodern" theologian from the ancient church. The preeminent ecological question of survival con-

91. Daecke 1979. Cf. Meyer-Abich 1979, 237.

92. Cf. the surveys of scholarship in Frey 1988; Stolz 1992; and Bakken 1995.

93. One should not forget to mention Joseph Sittler as one of the pioneers of ecological theology in the USA. In 1961 his book *The Ecology of Faith* was already clearly viewing the discipline of ecology as well as the challenge to preserve ecologically threatened life-forms as a "new situation" confronting the proclamation of faith. Concerning Sittler's cosmic Christology, see Bouma-Prediger 1995, 61-101. Altner's 1974 book *Schöpfung am Abgrund* marks the beginning of the ecological theological discussion in German-speaking countries.

fronting late twentieth-century culture was an utterly unknown issue to Gregory's fourth-century contemporaries. Although, as we will see, his contemporaries were indeed coming to view the phenomenon of increasing social impoverishment as a challenge, even as one to be addressed theologically, human cultural dealings with nature in the larger sense were not yet an issue.

The term "ecology" or even the "concept" of nature would have meant absolutely nothing to those living in late antiquity, for whom the word *oikos* referred to the notion of "keeping house" or of maintaining a certain arrangement in the familial, local, and also regional-political sense. By contrast, the terms *physis, kosmos,* and *ta panta* referred to being as such and the order attaching to it, an order characterized by the complexity and changeability that by definition accompany the phenomena of growth and dying away. *Oikonomia* refers to the laws or regularity inhering in such "housekeeping." One should point out that antiquity did indeed recognize what modernity calls an "ecological" problem. Aristotle notes quite early that the economic mechanism of commerce (money) and surplus was threatening to outstrip that of the general economy — "housekeeping."[94]

Gregory's understanding of the *oikos* contains surprising parallels to the modern understanding of ecology. Whereas the Stoic term *oikumene* included the entirety of global culture and as such contributed to the Christian understanding of humankind within the context of creation theology, Gregory's understanding of *oikonomia* acquires central significance as a reference to the *oikos* as God's "housekeeping" or economy and its history. For the Cappadocian, the divine "economy" in this sense is the history of the Creator with the entirety of creation.

But can the writing of an unequivocally "premodern" theologian contribute to articulating a response to the contemporary problems attaching to modernity's understanding of nature? Are the questions facing that period of antiquity not too far removed from those of the twenty-first century? Can an understanding of questions and answers from a distant historical period possibly contribute to solving modern problems?

One is certainly justified in objecting that the distance between the two contexts is indeed considerable. The conclusion to be drawn from this objection for the method of correlation, however, is that establishing a connection between the interpretations of tradition and of the contemporary situation is possible *only* if one can identify and persuasively articulate a *common* or *shared* problem in the two sets of writings.

General consensus actually tends to reject this objection because the ba-

94. Aristotle, *Politics* 1257a.

sic conceptual modes of modernity have of course been shaped by those in antiquity. The aporiae of ancient philosophy continue to exert their influence on the present, an influence Georg Picht calls a "present power."[95] In this sense, despite or perhaps even *because* of his location in antiquity, Gregory can enter into fruitful dialogue with us in pursuing a common history of philosophy whose modes of thinking and querying continue to demand more precise understanding.

Gregory's theological understanding of the world, of course, was subject to a completely different set of technological and cultural presuppositions than those obtaining in the Copernican understanding. As such, however, the manner in which the Cappadocian theologically interprets and transforms the understanding of the world entertained during his *own* age can serve as both a contrast to and an inspiration for our theology. Indeed, what we will ultimately find is that the theological understanding of the world in late antiquity can function as a critical lens through which to view the various models of modernity.

Hence my first reason for choosing Gregory's "premodern" theology is the "present power" of ancient modes of query in today's intellectual landscape, the historical continuity of certain modes of thought despite enormous contextual differences, and the possibility of interpreting Gregory's patristic system as a contrast and corrective to modern theologies.

The Influence of Gregory's Theological Construction in Context and in Subsequent History

A second objection might question whether the influence Gregory's theology exerted on his contemporaries justifies ascribing such significance to it today. Anytime a text is examined hermeneutically, it exerts additional influence by way of precisely that interpretation itself, and by interpreting a text, every interpreter grants a certain status to it, a status that is in part also normative. What justifies choosing Gregory's writings?

Every hermeneutical investigation must articulate the criteria prompting the text to be chosen in the first place. As a matter of fact, I do *not* believe that Gregory's historical influence on subsequent thinkers alone is sufficient to justify subjecting his writings to systematic theological interpretation. My choice was prompted rather by considerations of *content*, though such is really possible only hypothetically and can only be demonstrated later by the method of correlation (chap. 4).

95. Picht 1989, 9.

49

Nonetheless, an examination of the influence of the Cappadocian's theology in context and of the history of its subsequent influence is also of interest in explaining my choice. What we find is that Gregory's theology enjoyed a rather comprehensive reception even during his life, a reception continuing in the Eastern tradition even today and confirming thus my suspicion that the content of his theology is certainly capable of relating to the content of theologies during other periods.

During the time of the three Cappadocians, their theology exerted considerable influence on the missiologically and ecclesiologically important synthesis between asceticism and the acceptance of social responsibility, and on the development of the ecumenical council in Constantinople. The maturing of the doctrine of the Trinity toward the end of the century owes much to Gregory's rigorous thesis concerning the divinity of the Spirit; indeed, his famous fifth theological oration on the Holy Spirit may possibly have been addressed directly to the council participants themselves.[96]

Not only did a reinterpretation of this confession by the Faith and Order Commission of the World Council of Churches serve as the basic document of the ecumenical movement in 1992, it has also been used liturgically without interruption in both Eastern and Western churches. Hence, even into the present, Christian churches have ascribed normative function to the theology of this council as expressed in this confession. Viewed from another angle, the reception of this creed also constitutes an element in the reception of Cappadocian theology, prompting the suspicion that an examination of Gregory's writings and especially of his trinitarian doctrine of the Spirit might indeed have something to say to ecumenical theology today.

The reception of Gregory's theology among Orthodox theologians offers yet another reason to take notice of his writings. Over the course of the history of interpretation, Gregory acquired the honorific title "Theologian," a title otherwise bestowed only on the evangelist John and on Symeon, the latter being called the "New Theologian," though just when, how, and why Gregory acquired this title is not known.[97] What is certain is that the relatively numerous manuscripts that were passed down do show quite early that Gregory's theology exerted considerable influence. Maximus Confessor, who views Gregory as a theological authority, comments on the more difficult pas-

---

96. One can no longer determine with any certainty whether the oration was delivered just prior to the council in 381.

97. Neither in secondary literature nor in private communication have I found even the slightest trace of the history of this title.

sages in Gregory's writings[98] and explicitly adduces Gregory's third theological oration in developing his own understanding of the Trinity.[99]

Current ecumenical studies concerning the "integrity of creation" have also turned to Gregory's theology; here the consensus document of Orthodoxy adduces Gregory's writings with regard to issues of both anthropology and universal soteriology.[100]

In the construction of his Orthodox understanding of nature, Paulos Gregorios has referred primarily to Gregory of Nyssa, citing him as the founder of classical Christian cosmology.[101] While Gregory of Nyssa doubtless differs from Gregory of Nazianzus on several key issues, Gregorios's thesis concerning the constructive influence of Gregory of Nyssa certainly suggests that a similar situation might also apply to Gregory of Nazianzus.

As for the interdenominational ecumenical dialogue, yet another reason for considering Gregory's theology is that in the broader sense, studies of the Cappadocian Fathers have hitherto hardly touched at all on the burning ecological issues currently on the table in ecumenical discussions. Protestant theologians have been particularly inclined to treat Gregory rather like a stepchild, probably because of the widespread notion that he was a largely unoriginal, unsystematic, and excessively rhetorical theologian. This disproportionate denominational assessment of Gregory thus offers yet another reason to ask whether his theology might have something to say after all regarding the pressing ecological issues currently confronting ecumenical theology.

In summary, then, the second reason for choosing Gregory derives from the influence his theology exerted not only on his contemporaries, but also on subsequent theologians even into the present.

The Systematic Originality of the Cappadocian's Theology

A third objection derives from Gregory's presumed conventionalism. Whereas the understanding of Gregory among Western scholars has largely been influenced by philological studies emphasizing his considerable linguistic capabilities, theologically he is generally viewed as being rather conventional, rhetorically bombastic, unoriginal, and lacking in systematic rigor.

---

98. Thunberg 1985, 22.

99. Maximus Confessor 1860-65, *Ambiguorum Liber I,* second epistle to Thomas. Cf. Thunberg 1985, 36-39.

100. "Skapelsens förvandling" 1987, par. 2, 76; par. 11, 797; par. 15, 80f.

101. Gregorios 1988, 54.

From the perspective of cosmology, scholars have generally portrayed him as a dualist who distinguishes in a Platonist fashion between the corporeal and evil, on the one hand, and the spiritual and the good, on the other. From the perspective of systematic theology, then, much seems to militate *against* focusing on his theology.

Against the assertion that Gregory merely clothed old thoughts in a new literary garb, one can certainly adduce the originality of the Cappadocian's metaphorical language, something Kertsch has persuasively demonstrated.[102] One can also adduce his considerable knowledge of ancient philosophy, especially of Aristotelian logic and rhetoric, and his compelling incorporation of this knowledge into his theological argumentation against the Eunomians, of which Norris provides an especially persuasive presentation.[103]

Against the assertion that Gregory lacked originality, one can adduce Maximus Confessor's emphasis on his positive application of the idea of movement in the understanding of the Trinity (I will examine this issue in greater detail in chap. 3). Gregory's controversy with Basil concerning the divinity of the Spirit also attests his theological independence, since here Gregory argues unrelentingly against his hesitant friend in favor of the full divinity of the Holy Spirit.

Gregory of Nazianzus differs from Gregory of Nyssa by remaining more aloof from philosophical speculation and by maintaining a more critical position toward the Origenian doctrine of the double creation, which Gregory of Nyssa adopts and modifies.[104] Gregory may also be viewed as the initiator of the historical doctrine of the Trinity.

Later I will have occasion to correct the understanding of Gregory as a theologian who juxtaposes body and spirit antithetically. Although I can present my position only as a hypothesis at this point, albeit one whose integrity I will demonstrate later in this study, I intend to treat Gregory not as a dualistic Platonist but rather as a theologian who by ascribing priority to biblical interpretation and to the Christian understanding of incarnation is able to transform the philosophical premises of the Christian theology of his age.

I can, however, demonstrate at least the cogency of my hypothesis here by making the following points. In his writings Gregory critically transforms the doctrine concerning the four elements he finds in the tradition of the philosophy of nature.[105] He argues as a "patristic feminist" (Børresen) in his

102. Kertsch 1976, 1980.
103. See preface by Norris to Kertsch 1976; 1980, 3.
104. Cf. Thunberg 1974, 37f.
105. Bergmann 1993a.

derivation of the being of women by introducing the doctrine that because human beings were created in the image and likeness of God, women, too, should enjoy the same rights as men.[106] He epistemologically structures his interpretation of the physical suffering of the poor such that the wealthy and the healthy are able to learn something about creation and indeed even about the Creator from the suffering of their fellow human beings.[107] He explicitly associates the ancient philosophical understanding of the spirit *(nous)* with the biblical and Christian understanding of and experience with the Holy Spirit *(pneuma),* and takes the Holy Spirit itself as the criterion for adopting or incorporating various philosophical understandings of the spirit.[108]

In summary, I think sound systematic theological considerations suggest viewing Gregory hypothetically as an original systematic theologian and examining his theology from this perspective. This consideration also suggests that one might confirm from the perspective of content the influence Gregory has exerted throughout theological history.

It was in the doctrine of the Trinity and Spirit that the Cappadocian contributed to the development of the understanding of God. By understanding God's being as both community *and* movement, Gregory anticipates cosmologically and ontologically the doctrine of being as "relation," a doctrine whose problems and advantages are still being discussed today. Rather than juxtaposing body and spirit antithetically, Gregory subordinates the corporeal to the spiritual anthropologically and cosmologically in a fashion following the lead of the Stoic philosophy of nature. Finally, the key soteriological feature of Gregory's theology is his conscious and rigorous incorporation of the *entirety* of creation into salvation history, which the Spirit itself perfects. From the perspective of aesthetics, Gregory was the first thinker to show how the genre of poetry could be incorporated into Christian theology.

On philosophical constructions and understanding of nature of his age, Gregory proceeds neither "syncretistically" nor "conjunctively." Instead, he is one of the first theologians who consciously exploits the possibility of critically integrating missiologically and theologically in the manner described above the various philosophical positions of his context.[109] Indeed, from the

106. E. Schüssler Fiorenza 1995, 276f., 284.

107. *Or.* 14.36.

108. *Or.* 31.5.

109. Concerning mission in late antiquity in general, see Brox 1982; 1988. Concerning the significance of Gregory's theology for missiology and mission praxis, see Bergmann 1994e.

perspective of the three ideal types discussed above, Gregory and the other two Cappadocians as well as Augustine fall within the same model as the contemporary theologians I discuss below, namely, that of critical integration. With regard to the conditions obtaining in his age, Gregory can certainly be viewed as a "contextual" theologian.

PART II

The Trinitarian Cosmology of Gregory of Nazianzus: A Tradition

CHAPTER 2

The Context of Cappadocian Theology

In this section I describe the situation in which the Cappadocian theologian Gregory of Nazianzus lived and wrote. What do we know about Gregory's reality? Every situation is actually composed of a multiplicity of dimensions. So also that of Gregory of Nazianzus. Because a conventional description of his life in Cappadocia from 329/30 to 389/90 cannot do justice to this dimensional multiplicity, I will instead synthetically sketch in the contours of several different political, social, economic, ecological, ecclesiastical, and cultural dimensions known about the period and examine possible connections.[1]

Because the situation of late antiquity was characterized to such a great extent by crisis, change, new awakenings and departures, and thus also by an enormous diversity of perspectives, I will not attempt to harmonize those perspectives artificially. What the small farmer viewed as a catastrophe might have meant increased wealth for the coastal merchant; what the powerful classes in Rome viewed as provocative degeneracy might have provided the hope of liberation for world-weary Eastern Christians; what neo-Arians viewed as sound theological praxis in imperial politics might have seemed like theologically sanctioned violence to the community of believers; what male heads of household viewed as moral degeneracy might have meant emancipation for female ascetics; what prompted some to flee the land might have opened up the opportunity for land acquisition to others; and what the

---

1. Not much is known about the dates of Gregory's birth and death. See Mossay 1985, 165; Norris 1991, 1; and Hanson 1988, 701. Concerning Gregory's biography, cf. his *De vita sua*, and among several different studies of his life, especially Gallay 1943; Hanson 1988, 699-707; Norris 1991, 1-12; Otis 1961; and Ullmann 1867. Studies of ancient history to which I am indebted include Brown 1971; 1988; Ehrhardt 1959a; 1959b; 1969; Jones 1981; Kippenberg 1977; Landels 1980; Momigliano 1963; Schluchter 1985; Ste. Croix 1981; and K. White 1981.

emperor understood as self-evident imperial ideology may have seemed like idolatry to others. Life in Cappadocia in late antiquity, not least also under the conditions of a coercive state, is ambiguous and characterized above all by an extremely high degree of social change. What do we know about conditions during the period?

1. Political Considerations

In the fourth century Cappadocia was a province within the eastern prefecture of the Roman Empire, and as such exhibited a social structure comparable to that in other parts of the empire.[2] Because it bordered Persian territory on the east, the province was of particular strategic significance for imperial politics. Imperial workshops, weapons manufacture, and the stationing of troops attest the military function of the capital, Caesarea.[3] Although Persian cultural influence did play a role in Cappadocia's prehistory, it is doubtful such was still the case in the fourth century.[4]

During Gregory's lifetime the eastern empire was ruled by emperors Constantine I (d. 337) and Constantius II (d. 361), by Julian the Apostate (d. 363), the Arian Valens (d. 378), and by the Christian Theodosius I (d. 395). Given the discontinuity characterizing the political reasoning of the various emperors during this period, one quickly sees that the period represented neither a "turn" to Christianity as the state church nor a Christianizing of the state.[5]

The extent to which Constantine fused theological and political considerations in his conversion after his vision of the cross is still not entirely clear. Through a Hellenistic program of restoration Julian tried to enlist the gods of Greece in the service of his throne (for which the Renaissance still revered him).[6] Valens again picked up the thread of past tradition in Eunomian

---

2. Concerning the divisional structure of the empire and the consequences of the division of Cappadocia for Gregory, see Treucker 1961, 107-12.

3. Kirsten 1954, 867f. Gregory mentions the rebelliousness of the workers in the weapons workshops and imperial weaving mills (*Or.* 43.57). In *Ep.* 225 he petitions that the cleric Mamas be excused from military service, and in *Ep.* 86 he mentions the prohibition against wearing a military uniform when taking the Lord's Supper.

4. Although Kirsten, 865f., argues that the upper classes had a Persian cultural identity in the fourth century, Kopecek 1972, 255f., and Treucker 1961, 19-21, justifiably question this assertion.

5. Cf. Andresen 1975, 42-57.

6. Although Gregory believed that Julian revived the tradition of Christian persecution, this seems unlikely. Sozomen (*Historia ecclesiastica* 5.15) recounts that although Julian

Arianism and revived the program of a naive, Christian-theological theocracy.[7] It was only the pragmatist Theodosius who then managed to reestablish what Constantine had done before him, namely, to fuse the unity of the political empire with the unity of the religious empire of faith and the church. Although one might argue that he learned a bit too much from Julian regarding the form of this synthesis, the principles of Julian's Neoplatonic "political philosophy" lived on in Theodosius's Christian imperial politics.[8]

Clearly, then, Cappadocia was characterized by enormous change in political systems and in their accompanying symbolic-theological underpinnings. These same changes, however, also generated a whole series of opportunities for creative social reorientation and reorganization. Changes in political-theocratic institutions, for example, enabled educated Christians to compete with educated "pagans" in entering state offices and the nobility; amid the new political signals, educated pagans now also had to fear for their status. It is here that one also finds the social background of the Christianization of the Hellenistic *paideia* insofar as the converted Hellenist could now count on social advancement.[9]

2. Economic Considerations

In the fourth century, however, the development of the Roman state and its centralized, bureaucratic hierarchy reached its limit. The tax reform introduced by Diocletian continued on its own power, despite ideological changes, and ultimately led to overtaxation, which in its own turn hindered the production of foodstuffs and made state offices considerably more unattractive because of the increasing brutality required by their fiscal functions.[10]

---

did not persecute Christians, the latter did indeed flee the cities and villages. See in this regard Trombley 1993, 274. Pelikan 1993, 11f., is probably correct in understanding Julian's goal as breaking the alliance between Christianity and classical culture.

7. Campenhausen 1973, 291, interprets the Arian controversy as a "crisis of this naive state ecclesiology" and as a "protest of faith" against the state peace policies that meant to coerce the unity of the church, a protest that quickly changed into the Arianism of a largely political theology of legitimation.

8. Ehrhardt 1969, 9. Norderval 1988, 109, shows how in contrast to Gregory's model of an open cultural exchange, Theodosius actually made Christianity into the only religion in the empire.

9. The setting of the dispute surrounding the inheritance of the true *paideia* is found in this struggle for social survival among intellectuals. The struggle itself focused on the privilege of defining *paideia*. Cf. Brown 1971, 32, and Momigliano 1963, 37.

10. Cf. Jones 1981; Ritter 1981, 423; Treucker 1961, 64-97; and Momigliano 1963, 22. This

The lower pillars of the Roman state were the urban metropolises, which were supported by their surrounding districts.[11] The wealth of the aristocracy, which represented the state to the lower classes, was based primarily on real estate. Although there was an enormous cultural and educational gap between the urban and rural populations, Cappadocia seems to have developed an organized infrastructure of colonus villages in which Christianity was able to develop its communities at a relatively early period.[12]

As is already well known, during late antiquity agricultural yield steadily declined, resulting in regional famine and increasing social injustice between the rich and the poor.[13] Especially for small farmers, whose possessions were overtaxed in any event, this situation often meant economic catastrophe. With an ever diminishing labor force, the economic decimation of small farmers, and the accompanying expansion of ever larger estates that ultimately were unable to use the land efficiently, Cappadocia along with other parts of the empire became characterized by increasing social differentiation and social tension between the various population groups. Increasingly more small farmers — whose numbers were already quite large — came under the control of increasingly fewer large estate holders.[14] While the working rural population lost more and more of its possessions and became increasingly impoverished and vulnerable to famine,[15] merchants and the upper classes became ever wealthier.[16] The result, of course, was that an increasing number of farmers became dependent on patronage. The social differences between urban and rural populations widened, as did those between state officials and subjects. Indeed, amid the excruciating economic pressures, the sale of children increased during this period.[17] Because the money economy spurred

---

entire development apparently went hand in hand with the corruption of state officials, who, as Gregory tells us in *Or.* 18.6, greedily coveted public property and sought illegitimate wealth.

11. Ste. Croix 1981, 10f., cites Lynn White: "Cities were atolls of civilization (etymologically 'citification') on an ocean of rural primitivism."

12. Kirsten 1954, 882.

13. Jones 1981, 102ff. Gregory speaks quite often about the threat of famine.

14. In his poem on greed, Gregory mentions this limitless lust for ever more real estate acquisition as well as the slandering and extortion of small farmers (*Carm.* 1.2.28.21-31, 32-54).

15. The mortality rate among the rural population was abnormally high, so Jones 1981, 106f.

16. Gregory often laments the acquisition of wealth without work: *Or.* 16.18; 22.15; 43.34; 40.13; *Carm.* 1.2.28.185. Concerning Gregory's understanding of acquiring earthly wealth, see Beuckmann 1988, 16f.

17. Finley 1977, 193.

commerce in commodities and goods, and because such commerce was also carried on over the sea-lanes, coastal cities often became quite wealthy. Indeed, commerce and provisioning by way of an economy of money and barter increasingly came to compete with manual and agricultural labor; such was the case especially in the interior of the country, which because of poor transport and distribution routes could not compete with maritime commerce.[18]

3. Ecological Considerations

One additional consideration is that an increasing amount of agricultural land became marshland, resulting in significantly diminishing agricultural yield.[19] It was not until the nineteenth century that scholars came to understand the connection between overwatering and the increasing salinization of agricultural fields that took place in antiquity.[20] It seems quite likely that a disastrous interrelationship obtained between the brutal imperial taxation policies, the increasingly unjust distribution of land, and the accompanying inefficient land use and ultimate salinization from overwatering, though this entire nexus probably also included the less than prudent use of excessively large tracts of land, for example, for pasturing the famous Cappadocian horses.

My own hypothesis — to be understood as a modest contribution to the understanding of this admittedly complex situation — is that a connection did indeed exist between overtaxation (especially of land), the physical ecological devastation of the ground and soil itself, and increasing social injustice. The result was that the ecologically and economically viable use of land by small farmers was gradually replaced by a predominantly money-oriented economy of large, aristocratic estate owners who had clearly abandoned faith in the values of emperor, the future of the empire, and God.

18. Concerning the significance of inferior inland transportation routes with regard to the expanding market, see K. White 1981, 116ff.

19. Kreeb 1979, 30. Jones 1981, 103f., traces this development back to an insufficient labor force, rejecting the hypothesis that the ground itself was exhausted.

20. Kreeb 1979, 22-31, shows how this salinization of the ground from overwatering began in about 500 B.C.E. and continued escalating into late antiquity throughout the Mediterranean region.

4. Theological Considerations

One indicator of this social crisis with its ecological, political, and economic dimensions is that a great many members of the aristocracy began refusing to serve the state, while a smaller number chose the ascetic alternative of renouncing land possession entirely or of distributing property to the monasteries.[21] Basil's "social work" can be understood in this context. On the one hand, he managed to articulate a new path by transforming into an ascetic reality *within* the world the original flight *from* the world on the Egyptian model chosen by earlier ascetics and their successors.[22] On the other hand, he managed to address the increasing injustice with a symbolically viable model by using believers' tithes to support the poor rather than investing those tithes in land that would itself merely be excessively taxed. The poor also benefited from the yield of the communal land of propertyless monks. "Here Basil develops the basic notion of a new economic ethics."[23] His doctrine of the "portion of the soul" stipulates that at least part of the inheritance of believers should benefit the poor, a notion underscoring the theory and praxis of a theologically justified redistribution of surplus to the poor and one obviously of use in strengthening the economic circumstances of the church, monasteries, and church communities.[24]

Here one can clearly see how the understanding of the church's economic circumstances, rather than following the kind of economic rationality characterizing much of late antiquity as described above (investment in trading capital or real estate), takes as its foundation the idea of a redistribution of surplus to the poor. The church actualizes this idea by first creating surpluses through congregational tithes, monastic labor, and inheritance, and then distributing them through regionally organized, autarchic ecclesiastical administrative bodies. This conception operates at an obvious critical distance from the organizational forms of the state and is justified theoretically through a theological criticism of surplus wealth and through pastoral admonition to practice love for the poor deriving from a consideration of creation theology, eschatology, Christology, and pneumatology.[25] Both the potential

21. Treucker 1961, 29f.; Ritter 1981, 423.

22. Cf. Savramis 1977, 612.

23. Savramis 1977, 611.

24. The doctrine of the "portion of the soul" maintains that the "soul," that is, God and the poor, is to be satisfied like the firstborn from the estate of the deceased before all other heirs. Ritter 1981, 429, and Hauschild 1979, 22.

25. Beuckmann 1988, 20, shows how Gregory juxtaposes soteriologically the lust for earthly wealth, or greed *(pleonexia)*, with an insatiability *(aplestia)* for beneficence and char-

and the attractiveness of this understanding can be found precisely in this critical theological capacity for throwing the contrasting positions into relief and in the practical possibility of a third path.

We thus find that during a period of increasing social injustice, the Cappadocian Christians manage to create for themselves both a religious and an economic symbolic conceptual framework superior to the competing symbolic worlds of political imperial theology and the ideology of individual and corporate acquisition of wealth. This new symbolic framework of inner-worldly social asceticism, with its revaluation and redistribution of acquired wealth, exercised an emancipatory effect on both the poor and the educated rich.[26]

One can interpret the asceticism of the rich as a counterpart to those who serve God "with their stomachs" and particularly as a sign of solidarity with those whose bodies are plagued by famines caused by injustice.[27] In the same context, one can understand the asceticism of the poor as their liberation from the straitjacket of state and feudal repression. Although the economic straitjacket did admittedly remain in place for most, its symbolic power was broken such that Gregory could even maintain that God laughed at the rich.[28] Even more importantly, however, one must always view the symbolism of this ascetic theology in connection with the enormous injustice threatening the very physical survival of such large portions of the population; only then does its spiritual ethos emerge as the successor to Christ's own self-renunciation and poverty.[29]

In this situation, theologically qualified wealth and worldly wealth inevitably slip into an antithetical relationship or conflict whose significance can hardly be overestimated for a symbolic world based on the elementary unity

---

ity *(euphoria)*. One example of this thinking is Gregory's oration regarding love for the poor, *Or.* 14, which he delivered in 373 at the dedication of a hospital established by Basil near Caesarea. Gregory develops his understanding of love for the poor as a soteriological quality largely from the perspective of Christology and eschatology.

26. In his oration on baptism, *Or.* 40.27, Gregory admonishes the rich to be baptized together with the poor as an expression of the end of previous differences, "and Christ was put upon all in one form."

27. *Or.* 38.6; *Carm.* 1.2.28.86; *Or.* 36.12. Coulie 1985, 205f., shows how the factors leading to the repression of the poor are of significance in Gregory's own work; although Gregory never denied his own membership in the wealthy classes, he did theologically relativize the value of wealth.

28. *Or.* 26.11.

29. The motif of Christ's poverty, physical privations, and renunciation of possessions plays an important role in Gregory's understanding of ascetic ethics. Cf. *Or.* 14.18; 14.4; 40.11; 29.20.

of God, dominion, cosmos, and daily life, as was that of antiquity. A more critical understanding of injustice emerged against the new reference point of mass misery among the poor; this new understanding was then joined by the accompanying influence of a theological understanding of reality that combined trenchant criticism of the unjust acquisition of wealth with an alternative ethics and understanding of practical economics. These considerations — the new understanding of injustice, the emergent criticism of illegitimate wealth, and the accompanying new theological orientation — were of enormous significance for the social transformation of the empire and for Christianity in transition. Cappadocian theology came to understand the reality of those victimized by poverty as a locus of revelation of the triune God. The poverty of Christ is a *present* reality that lends meaning to the reality of his followers in the Spirit.

5. Social Considerations

Unfortunately, of course, this confrontation regarding the understanding and valuation of wealth did not lead to any change in the hierarchical class structure of society. This structure was so firmly entrenched that even Christians did not question the legitimacy of institutionalized slavery. At the same time, however, a profound change was taking place within the inner structure of this hierarchy, a change one might describe as an erosion of solidarity within the vertical structures. The change, however, was actually twofold. While vertical solidarity within the structures of the *state* hierarchy eroded, a new vertical solidarity developed in the *church,* through which it then also manifested itself in society at large.[30] The increasingly differentiated imperial bureaucracy now encountered resistance from the new reference point of mass misery and poverty, of which ever greater numbers among the upper classes were becoming conscious.

Hierarchical administrative structures depend on efficient vertical movement from the various upper levels to the lower ones and on the solidarity of subjects. During late antiquity the increasing use of violence and coercion to keep this structure functioning resulted in a disturbing and increasing

---

30. Concerning the concept of "vertical solidarity," see Assmann 1990, 13f., who distinguishes two ways people can be integrated into a community: either into a vertical/hierarchical structure or into a horizontal/egalitarian one. The concept of vertical solidarity expresses the idea of community without also burdening it from the outset with the notion that subordination necessarily also involves oppression.

reluctance among the various classes to maintain solidarity with those in the hierarchy above them, something attested by the emergence of an ascetic inclination among the upper classes in the empire and by an increasing willingness to redistribute wealth, especially wealth in the form of money, through forms organized by the church. The emergence and reorganization of various movements among women were also a product of this change; by dedicating their bodies and social relationships to God, women in such movements emancipated themselves from entrapment in the vertical hierarchies of familial and sexual subordination.[31]

Countermovements also began to emerge within the empire itself, whose coercive administration was steadily undermining the vertical solidarity on which ultimately it did, after all, depend. These countermovements, however, rather than trying to break out of the hierarchical class structures altogether, were instead trying to introduce *into* that old hierarchy an egalitarian, that is, horizontal, element. This model of new vertical solidarity within a vertical social structure acquired symbolic significance in the organization of the church. This organization, grouping its offices around that of the bishop, attached greater economic value to the distribution and redistribution of goods than to their constant acquisition; socially it taught and indeed tried to actualize the praxis of love for the poor as the highest measure of love for one's neighbor and for God. Cappadocian theology associated ministry to the needy with the question of God. "In the poor, the church is actually encountering Christ."[32]

Cappadocian theology clearly kept a critical distance from the legitimation of the Roman monarchy at the beginning of the century, when the whole landscape "stank" of Monarchianism,[33] not least in the form of monotheistic legitimation based on theological premises. Gregory himself emphasized the monarchy of the Father as guarantor of the unity of the Trinity; he did not, however, understand God as the community of three hypostases with equal power and of equal will,[34] and to that extent his understanding of monarchy was completely wedded to the notion of sociality. As a result, it is impossible for him to relinquish that notion for the sake of theocratic politics.[35]

31. Concerning the emancipation of women from social and physical ties by means of engagement in ascetic movements, see Brown 1986; 1988, 259-84; and Albrecht 1986.

32. Brox 1988, 280.

33. Ehrhardt 1959b, 285.

34. Cf. chap. 3, below.

35. Congar 1981, 197, shows how in *Or.* 31.31 Gregory clearly rejects any assertion that God's monarchy corresponds to earthly realities and thus also rejects any association of the emperor's monarchy with that of God. Cf. also *Or.* 36.11. Pannenberg 1998, 480, maintains

6. Technological Considerations

The development of water mills shows that late antiquity, too, was no stranger to technological innovation. Toward the end of the century the development of this mill technology — technology dependent on water power — emerged in connection with the problems of food provisioning and the absence of a sufficient workforce.[36] This development represented a significant step forward in finally applying the knowledge of nature to technological development. Although such a connection was always a *theoretical* possibility in antiquity, it had never been implemented to any significant *practical* degree. For various reasons, the clearly excellent familiarity with natural processes in antiquity never prompted any of the philosophies of nature to encourage or hasten, as it were, technological development. One likely reason was the ontologically grounded preference for rest over movement. Even though the Greeks based their understanding of nature precisely on the notion of changeability, they were paradoxically less interested in explanations of kinetics than in static relationships.[37]

What we in a technologically highly organized society perceive as a shortcoming appeared to the ancient understanding of the world rather as a synthesis of an extremely high level of knowledge about nature, on the one hand, and a technical way of dealing with nature for the sake of praxis, on the other. Of course, the economic basis of this combination of "high" natural theory and "soft" technology was the institution of slavery. Given the metaphor of the organism on which Stoic philosophy based its understanding of the world and which continued to develop in late antiquity as well, there were still considerable barriers to turning such knowledge into an instrument for the technological subjugation of nonhuman life. In any event, the introduction of water mills to address the need for both a civilian and a military labor force represented a step in precisely that direction.

An even earlier step in the same direction was the exploitation of

---

that the imperial rule is understood as "the earthly image of the rule of the Logos." How can Pannenberg overlook the ideological criticism of trinitarian theology?

36. K. White 1981, 119f., 122, 124. White refers to the implementation of water mills as a new stage in technological development, comparable to the domestication of animals and the introduction of atomic energy (122). The implementation of these mills was closely associated with the lack of a sufficient labor force. Wikander (1980) discusses in depth the significance of water mills in the Roman Empire; in his examination of witnesses up into the sixth century, he also discusses the importance of mills for the Roman army and for the early Christian monasteries.

37. Landels 1980, 226.

Mother Earth through mining, which supplied minerals, in Cappadocia especially silver from the mines in the Taurus Mountains for use in coins.[38] The Stoics vehemently objected to mining practices, their pantheistic understanding of the earth as mother prompting them to view mining as a defilement of her womb.[39] Gregory's use of the "organism" metaphor in his understanding of the world as well as his unequivocal relativization of knowledge of nature and knowledge of God show the extent to which the ancient synthesis of "high" knowledge of nature and "soft" technology played a role in the thinking of the Cappadocians.[40] In any event, no authors in late antiquity offer any justification of human attempts to acquire dominion over the "organism of their mother" through the instrument of technology. What few technological developments we do encounter are invariably prompted by clearly pragmatic considerations lacking sophisticated theoretical justification; indeed, it is precisely this absence of any technological application of the different fields of knowledge that has puzzled historians.[41]

7. Worldview Considerations

In the Cappadocia of late antiquity, elements of cultic and ethnic pluralism joined those associated with the increasing impoverishment of the population and soil and the erosion of vertical solidarity within the hierarchical structures. Whereas the strength of Hellenism arguably lay precisely in its synthesis of religions and cultures, during the fourth century this synthesis begins to fragment and collapse. Mystery cults, astrology, Neoplatonic philosophical schools, Mithraism, Iranian fire cults, magician religions, Hypsistarians, Jewish proselytizers[42] — all these movements presented symbolic

38. Concerning mining and the metaphor of the organism, see Merchant 1987, 20, 34ff., 41-44. Thomson 1985, 242-47, provides a description of ancient mining practices.

39. Documentation in Merchant 1987, 42-44.

40. In *Or.* 28.26 Gregory calls the world the "the common mother of us all," maintaining that even the depths of the sea are also connected with the earth.

41. Cf. K. White 1981, 124-27, and Landels 1980, 225-40.

42. Concerning pagan cults in Cappadocia, see Kirsten 1954, 874-80. Whereas John Chrysostom, one of Gregory's contemporaries, can be viewed as the "spiritual father of anti-Semitism" (Kretzenbacher 1977, 59), Gregory advocated a positive relationship with Judaism. Even though he rejects Arianism as a Judaizing religion, he does acknowledge the integrity of the revelation of the Maccabees in an oration dedication to them (*Or.* 15), and in his biblical interpretation starts with the Origenian premise of a connection between "old" and "new" history.

constructions that, given the ancient assumption of unified being, of necessity also included claims to universality.

The successful exercise of control within the vertical hierarchy of power mentioned above determined the extent to which this bewildering multiplicity of symbolic worlds and their cultic implementation and accompanying truth claims were able to coexist peacefully in such a restricted geographical area. Just as the emergence of Christianity caused the symbolic world of the empire itself with its universal cosmological claims to teeter, it was inevitable that the locally organized symbolic constructions now vying for cultic and philosophical supremacy would also come into increasing competition with one another. It is in this context that the Cappadocians themselves now emphasize and argumentatively advocate *Christian* theology as the true heir of ancient *paideia* over against their critics. And it is in the same context that Gregory becomes so passionately engaged in trying to consolidate Christian festivals for the sake of standardizing life within the church community.[43] Even architecture was influenced by the art of theological construction in late antiquity. One need only consider Gregory's account of the construction of the octagonal church in Nazianzus, an account bringing to eloquent expression the exhilarating joy inspired by the sheer persuasive power of the symbolic Christian world — albeit mixed with not a little patriotism — as manifested in that church construction.[44]

This pluralism of symbolic constructions in philosophical schools, local cults, and universalist religions in the empire was joined by the equally bewildering provocations of ethnic pluralism, all of which now generated the need for new syntheses between the universal symbolic constructions of the empire itself and the heterogeneous gods and differing understandings of nature entertained by the various ethnic groups within the empire. In a word, the formerly self-enclosed culture of ancient Greece was now confronted by the challenge of having to integrate ever more ethnic groups, and it is precisely

43. One of our earliest witnesses for the traditions of the church year is Gregory's own emphatic attempts to articulate the meaning, history, and function of the various festivals. His statements concerning the celebration of martyrdom are of particular interest insofar as they reveal something about how the church's own memory of persecution functioned in the development of communities of faith.

44. *Or.* 18.39. Incidentally, this account also represents the oldest text mentioning octagonal church construction. An — albeit disputed — reconstruction of the church can be found in Hübsch 1863, Plan XIX, 7, 8, p. 44. Gregory mentions that the pillars were decorated with sculptures and colorful ornaments — there was not yet any real cult of images during this period, nor did the Orthodox use of icons develop its own tradition much before the seventh century. Kretzenbacher 1977, 60.

this integration of such "foreigners" with their widely differing constructions of reality that became a cultural problem, something also evident in the Cappadocians' social work, which closely associated love for the poor with love for *aliens* both doctrinally and in the practical organization of welfare institutions.[45] The way the Cappadocians turn their attention to the world itself demonstrates how their understanding of Christianity tries to confront the new challenges posed by their situation within late antiquity; in response to those challenges, they genuinely try to do justice to the ideal of "ecumenical universality and global responsibility" amid new conditions.

8. Summary: The Challenge of Hellenistic Pluralism and Social Injustice

The situation in which Gregory lived and wrote was characterized by the following elements: (a) a plurality (with inevitable conflict) of competing symbolic world constructions from philosophical schools, cultic communities, religious communities, and ever changing imperial political ideologies; (b) increasing social injustice resulting in mass misery and poverty, the ruination of small farmers, and the oppression of aliens, women, and children;[46] (c) a shift of economic institutions from production in autarchic units to the trade of goods and a money economy; (d) the impoverishment and exhaustion of the soil accompanied by an overvaluation (for tax revenues) of real estate resulting in social and ecological injustice from speculation and imprudent land management; (e) initial steps toward the practical application of

---

45. Alongside hospitals, homes for the elderly, funeral welfare, aid for the unemployed, and women's organizations, the institution of homes for aliens represented an independent branch of social organization — for example, in Basil, the settlement for the poor outside Caesarea. See Hauschild 1979, 20ff.; Savramis 1977, 615; and Vischer 1953, 140-44. In *Or.* 44.7, Gregory grounds love for strangers christologically.

46. Songe-Møller shows how the oppression of women as aliens/others in antiquity was closely related to the homoerotic principle of equality. In this respect the emphasis in the Christian doctrine of incarnation that the son was born of a woman certainly represents a significant break in continuity. Although the comprehensive materials in Gregory's writings concerning his understanding of women have not even begun to be satisfactorily examined, one can doubtless concur with Børresen 1989, 158-61, that he was a "patristic feminist." Gregory seems to have had some acquaintance with a specific tradition regarding Christian women in Seleucia going back to Thecla (*De vita sua*, 457ff.). In *Or.* 37.7 he maintains that because Christ became flesh for both men *and* women, the latter, too, were to be redeemed. Similarly, in marriage the husband was to serve his wife and thus also the church and Christ. Cf. E. Schüssler Fiorenza 1995, 276f.

antiquity's knowledge of nature for developing the "hard" technology of water mills; (f) the erosion of vertical solidarity within the imperial hierarchy and its revivification through horizontal countermovements; (g) ethnic pluralism in the military, in the slave trade, and in the introduction of free ethnic groups; (h) the growth of various social countermovements sharing the common vision of a renunciation of property, emancipation from both physical and social oppression, and a willingness to redistribute wealth (otherworldly asceticism, inner-worldly philosophical asceticism, inner-worldly social asceticism).

CHAPTER 3

Gregory's Theological Interpretation
of Creation Set Free

1. Sociality

The idea of a social God, that is, a God of community, plays a key role in Gregory's theology. Indeed, Gregory's originality derives from his incorporation of this notion of sociality into his understanding of both God and the world. For Gregory, sociality is a quality attaching both to the trinitarian God and to the world. Before we examine how the sociality of God and the sociality of the world actually correspond to one another in Gregory's work, it will be helpful to examine the problem to which Gregory's understanding of sociality was responding in the first place. Gregory's thesis regarding God's sociality maintains that God is both one and varied. The presupposition for this unity, however, is precisely the distinction between hypostases in God's immanence and in his economy. Gregory also maintains that the metaphysical God is one with the incarnate God.

That Gregory's God is social is significant for his understanding of the liberation of creation, since such liberation means liberation from evil for the sake of enhanced participation in the sociality of God. As a creation of the triune God, the world is constituted of sociality and relationality. The Cappadocian thus understands the liberation of creation as resulting in the growth and development of precisely that sociality. Just what constitutes an acceptable (i.e., good) form of such sociality Gregory determines theologically from the actual experiences believers have had in their history with the triune God.

The Theological Problem of Sociality

Which theological problem prompted Gregory to develop his understanding of the social God? Gregory himself describes the situation "amid the three infirmities in regard to theology, atheism, Judaism, and polytheism, one of which is patronized by Sabellius the Libyan, another by Arius of Alexander, and the third by some of the ultra-orthodox among us" (*Or.* 2.37). Gregory distances himself from Sabellius's modalist understanding of God because it denies God; from Arius's monotheistic understanding of God because of its Judaism; and from the tritheistic understanding of God because of its polytheism. It is in response to these doctrines of God that Gregory develops his trinitarian understanding of the essential unity of the three hypostases.

Sabellianism

The systematic form Sabellius provided for the modalist Monarchian doctrine of God continued to exert considerable influence even during the fourth century.[1] The Sabellian doctrine of God begins with the unity of God as the mono-personal God. What we call the three "persons" *(prosopa)* of the Godhead are actually nothing more than three different revelatory modes: as the Father in creation and in the law, as the Son in redemption, and as the Spirit in sanctification. Commensurate with the original meaning of the Greek understanding of "person," these persons are like three masks that one and the same actor wears when portraying different roles. The one God appears in three revelations.

Gregory's charge that this position denies God hinges on the idea of the revelatory modes of the actor. He maintains that the unity of the Godhead is grounded in the distinction of the hypostases. By contrast, Sabellius maintains that as revelatory modes the persons can be dissolved, as it were, after their revelation, and are then no longer divine. This extension into "nondivine" persons makes it possible for the Godhead to collapse, as it were, ending the existence of the Father, Son, and Spirit.[2]

The basic presupposition of Sabellianism, then, is the unity of God as a single person. Triunity can develop out of this original unity and then revert

1. Cf. Kelly 1977, 241ff. During Gregory's age, the positions of Sabellius and Marcellus were often hopelessly confused and mistaken for one another; Kelly, 122.

2. The Sabellian notion of "extension" derives from the teachings of the Stoics, who, following Aristotle, developed a doctrine of "relating to something"; Pohlenz 1948, 69ff.

again to unity. The monotheistic unity of person in theology manifests itself modalistically in the economy in the world. Because this position can demonstrate the divinity of the incarnate Word or of the commissioned Spirit neither in theology nor in the economy, Gregory rejects it as a denial of God.

Arianism

The second deviation from orthodox doctrine that Gregory mentions is Arianism, which during his time was revived especially by Eunomius and Aetius.[3] Arius's doctrine of God monistically maintains the unquestionable singularity and transcendence of God. God is the unbegotten beginning *(agennetos arche)*.[4] God's existence *(ousia)* is indivisible; nothing else can participate in it. Arius understands God's unity not as community but as singularity. This monotheistic doctrine of God addresses the question of the divinity of the Son in four points:

1. The Father begets the Son as a creature and creates him as a complete creature fully separate from the rest of creation. Hence Arius understands the procreation and creation of the Son as meaning essentially the same thing. Maintaining the coessentiality of Father and Son would abrogate the singularity and unbegotten nature of the Father. God's transcendence is grounded precisely in being unbegotten, a characteristic attributable to no other being, not even to the Son. Gregory directs one of his key criticisms against the Arian thesis of the unbegotten nature of God, against which he maintains the coequality of unbegottenness, primal originality, and begottenness within the one nature.

2. Because the Son is a creation of God, Arius must also grant him a beginning. The famous assertion of "time before time" is the logical consequence of this doctrine of the one God. By contrast, the Cappadocian assertion of coeternity controverts the Arians' basic monotheistic principle.

3. The Son cannot enter into any sort of ontological community with the Father.[5] Even though the divine logos itself appeared in Christ, as the Word it is still distinct from the Father.

4. Although the Son can indeed be referred to as God, this title is noth-

3. Concerning the significance of Arianism for the development of the Cappadocian doctrine of the Trinity, see Norris 1991, 53-71, and Jenson 1982, 20, 80-89.

4. Kelly 1977, 227.

5. Kelly 1977, 228: "Although He is God's Word and Wisdom, He is distinct from that Word and that Wisdom which belongs to God's very essence; He is a creature pure and simple, and only bears these titles because He participates in the essential Word and Wisdom."

ing more than a name referring not to the Godhead itself, but only to participation in divine grace. When Arius refers to the triad, he is referring to the existence of three persons *(treis hypostaseis)* who are completely distinct from
one another. These three persons cannot share a common essence or nature.
During Gregory's age, and in contrast to Sabellianism, Arianism distinguished the three hypostases from one another by understanding the Son and
Spirit as subordinated to the Father in the sense of an inequality of essence; it
maintained Christ's humanity but not his divinity.

Arianism thus maintained the unity of the essence of the Father and the
inequality of the essences of the hypostases, whereas Sabellianism maintained
the unity of essence as well as the unity of the persons. Gregory counters both
with his doctrine of coessentiality within the divine nature as a community of
the three different divine hypostases.

Tritheism

The third deviation from orthodox doctrine to which Gregory turned his attention was the polytheism of several "hyperorthodox" theologians within
his circle. Here the charge of tritheism is directed not against the multiple
gods worshiped in pagan religion, but against a certain Christian doctrine of
God. The Cappadocians and hence also Gregory had to respond to the objection that they had developed their doctrine of the Trinity as a form of
tritheism. Because they distinguished the three persons as three hypostases,
they were frequently charged with denying the monotheism constituting the
first principle of the Arian and Sabellian doctrine of God. Unfortunately, although the Arian and Sabellian doctrines are known to us from the writings
of other Fathers, no fourth-century texts articulate such a doctrine of
tritheism.

No fourth-century Greek Fathers advocate a Christian doctrine of God
that distinguishes the three hypostases without also maintaining their unity.
It is not until the eighth century that Pseudo-Cyril and John of Damascus
(d. 754) resolve tritheism as a problem inhering in the orthodox doctrine of
God based on the Cappadocian doctrine of the Trinity. Following Gregory of
Nazianzus, these two theologians developed the trinitarian doctrine further
and, in contrast to the tritheism of the Alexandrian bishop John Philoponus,
emphasized the unity of the Godhead even more strongly than did the
Cappadocians themselves. Unlike Gregory of Nazianzus, however, they did
emphasize the unity of the Godhead more strongly than they did the differences between the hypostases, a unity John of Damascus maintains can even

be deduced from creation itself.[6] John weakens Gregory's doctrine by moving from a critique of tritheism to the priority of the unity of the Godhead. Only by recognizing that unity can one also distinguish the hypostases.

Not until four centuries later did Gregory's condemnation of tritheism acquire its real significance. In the meantime, however, the question remained concerning adversaries who advocated polytheism or, as we read elsewhere, the multidominion (*polyarchia; Or.* 29.2) of God.

Even when Gregory makes it easier to defend the charge of tritheism by pointing to others who, quite in contrast to him, advocate a deviant doctrine including multiple gods, we can assume that he is not merely doing so as a rhetorical device but is referring to real adversaries within his own church. This is the only real explanation of the term "hyperorthodox," which may even be referring to the monks who made life miserable for Gregory's father in Nazianzus.[7] On balance, Gregory presumably had little to fear from tritheism in developing the unity of the Godhead in the doctrine of the Trinity.

Plotinus's Doctrine of the Hypostases

Plotinus, whose philosophy derives from the tradition of Platonism that exerted considerable influence in the fourth century, advocates a doctrine of the divinity of the One and the three hypostases within that divinity. Plotinus assumes a polarity between the spiritual — or upper — and the material — or lower — worlds. Within the ontology of the spiritual world we find the three hypostases of the One, the Spirit, and the soul, all of which are connected along a stepped series that Plotinus regards as a natural series of triunity.[8] As the result of a kind of overflowing comparable to a spring, the One tran-

---

6. Franks 1953, 120: "John repeats from Nazianzen the explanation of the One Godhead in three hypostases drawn from the logical distinction of the universal and the particular. . . . But the tendency to individualize the hypostases is corrected by the statement that the hypostases differ only in mode of subsistence *(tropos hyparxeos)*, and still further by the introduction of the idea of perichoresis, i.e. permeation or co-inherence." John picks up Gregory's analogy of Adam, Eve, and Seth as being created in the social likeness of God, deriving from that likeness the unbegotten nature of the Father (like Adam), the begotten nature of the Son (like Seth), and the condition of the Spirit as being neither unbegotten nor begotten (like Eve).

7. See J. Bernardi, in SC 247, 237 n. 9. Cf. the oration on peace that Gregory delivered before these monks and his father, *Or.* 6.13.

8. Plotinus, *Enneads* 2.9.1; cf. Theiler 1971, 108.

scends its own transcendence and begets the Spirit, which also possesses pro-creative power. Insofar as the Spirit emerges from the One, it also actualizes the potency of the One.

Because the concept of emanation removes the discontinuity between God and world in Plotinus's thought, it is probably more accurate to refer to the theological implications of his philosophy as *panentheism*. All being in the spiritual world and all being in the material world move from being an outflow of the One to being part of the One. Everything that is, is from and in the One. Just as the soul does not adopt the world as its body but rather as the world soul actually constitutes the body of the world, so also does the One, rather than entering *into* the world, instead *include* all being within itself.

Plotinus's panentheism constitutes the antithesis to the monistic doctrine of the singular, transcendent God of Arius. No fourth-century Eastern thinker could avoid acquaintance with Plotinus's thought, and it exercised considerable influence on the development of new Christian doctrines of God; at the same time, however, the Cappadocian understanding of the Trinity should not at all be understood merely as a Plotinian variation of Christian theology. In fact, Gregory's theology is quite the opposite of Plotinus's panentheistic understanding of God.

Although Gregory does indeed adopt the Platonic polarity between the spiritual and material world, he subordinates this polarity to the distinction between Creator and creation, that is, between the spiritual *and* the material cosmos, on the one hand, and the essence and being of God, on the other. This fundamental apophatic principle in his understanding of God maintains the complete discontinuity of God and world as opposed to Plotinus's panentheistic thesis of continuity between the two.[9]

Whereas Plotinus interprets both the spiritual and the material cosmos as an outflow of the divine, Gregory views the material world as a "strange" world different from God and the spiritual world as a world that, although also different from God, is nonetheless more "compatible" with God. Both worlds originate in the goodness and will of God, and both participate in God's being, not through their own existence, but only through the will of God. Unlike Plotinus, Gregory maintains that this participation is incomplete and is consummated only historically within the developmental maturation process of those worlds. Gregory counters Plotinus's redeemed spiritual world and eternally mortal world with a spiritual world that is at once both created good and yet fallen, and with a material world related to it. Because

9. Plotinus maintained not only knowledge of God, of the "Good," but also union with God. Cf. *Enneads* 6.9.10f.

Gregory simultaneously draws distinctions within the divine and yet insists on the unity and transcendence of the divine, his theology differs both from Arius's heretically rejected monotheism and from Plotinus's panentheistic doctrine of the hypostases.

The Development of the Idea of Sociality

In which contexts does the Cappadocian theologian develop his understanding of sociality and community? The following discussion of Gregory's understanding of God and world reveals that in his understanding of God he takes the distinction between the hypostases as the basis of their unity as a community, and in his understanding of the world he takes the distinction between parts as the basis of their unity as a totality. What emerges is that Gregory understands the world as a nexus of relationships, and the next task is to examine the quality of the relationships within that nexus and the corresponding locus of human beings within that world. Gregory's understanding of nature's capacity for language will also be of interest in this context, as will an examination of whether and how God's community corresponds to that of the world.

The Perfect Community of the Divine Hypostases

The Cappadocians' major contribution to the history of Christianity, namely, their development of a particular understanding of the Trinity, begins not by positing the unity of the Godhead, but by distinguishing the particular characteristics of each of the hypostases. The characteristic feature of the Eastern understanding of the Trinity was its decision to approach unity along a path beginning with the distinctions within the triunity, a path the Nazianzen explicitly (*Or.* 38.8) describes as a process of unification.[10]

In his understanding of God, Gregory addresses the characteristics of the divine hypostases as a *formal* problem, since ultimately human beings have no access to knowledge of the *real* essence of the deity. Gregory's theology functions not as a speculative exercise attempting to attain to a mystical vision of the underlying divine mystery, but as an instrument making it possible to encounter the Godhead *irrationally;* as such, his trinitarian theology is engaged as a product of human reason fully cognizant of its own insufficiency and limitations.

10. Régnon 1892, 433.

It is the Sabellian understanding of God and its inappropriate "drawing together" *(synairesis)* of the Godhead that prompts the Cappadocian to develop his own doctrine of the Trinity. Gregory accuses the Arians of having "torn" the Godhead "asunder" *(diairesis; Or.* 39.11). He counters these two "evils" — the division of God and modalism — with his doctrine of the unity of essence of the three hypostases, each of which however preserves its own characteristics.

Because Gregory maintains that one can correctly worship the Trinity only if one correctly distinguishes the specific features of each of the hypostases, he also speaks about "one nature but three distinct persons" (20.5; 26.19). Each hypostasis, in and of itself, is God insofar as its particular characteristic is maintained (40.41). Immutability is predicated both of the deity and of the three hypostases: "for neither did the Father cease to be Unbegotten because of His begetting something, nor the Son to be begotten because He is of the Unbegotten (how could that be?), nor is the Spirit changed into Father or Son because He proceeds, or because He is God — though the ungodly do not believe it. For Personality is unchangeable; else how could Personality remain, if it were changeable, and could be removed from one to another?" (39.12). Gregory introduces the schema of trichotomy in explicating the particularities of the three hypostases: "but I open and close my door at the will of that Mind and Word and Spirit, Who is One kindred Deity" (12.1).[11]

One important formal principle of Gregory's understanding of the Trinity is that each individual hypostasis maintains complete unity with the other hypostases and with itself. "Each of these Persons *(hypostases)* possesses unity, not less with that which is united to it than with itself, by reason of the identity of essence and power" (31.16).

Insofar as the Father is himself without beginning and yet is simultaneously the beginning of the Son and of the Spirit, Gregory ascribes special status to him among the three hypostases. Gregory is careful, however, not to understand this priority of the Father temporally; the designation of Father is one of *relation,* whereas time belongs to the essence of the world, not to that of the Godhead (20.6). The Father also enjoys a certain priority among the hypostases in Gregory's understanding because he is the principle and origin of the other two and as such is distinguished from them. "I should like to call the Father the greater, because from him flows both the Equality and the Being of the Equals" (40.43). It would be unwor-

11. Cf. K. Holl 1904, 176; Althaus 1972, 29; Pinault 1925, 48, who discern the trichotomy in Gregory's anthropology.

thy of the precedence and dignity of the Father to bring about creation directly (23.6).[12]

Gregory's assertion of the greater venerability of the Father, however, does not involve the simultaneous depreciation or humiliation of the other two hypostases, since such would cast doubt on the Father's own venerability (40.3). As the principle of origin, the Father also guarantees the unity of the three hypostases: "The oneness of God would, in my view, be maintained if both Son and Spirit are causally related to him alone without being merged or fused into him and if they all share one and the same divine movement and purpose, if I may so phrase it, and are identical in essence" (20.7).[13]

In distinguishing between God and Father, Gregory adduces the distinction between the one nature *(physis)* and unity of the hypostases: "and the three have one Nature — God. And the union is the Father from Whom and to Whom the order of Persons runs its course, not so as to be confounded, but so as to be possessed, without distinction of time, of will, or of power" (42.15). Whereas Augustine's trinitarian principle of unity is the *una substantia*, Gregory's is the priority of the Father, who guarantees the unity of nature, a position also enabling him to concur with New Testament statements about the Father.

If, as Gregory maintains, the hypostases share the same nature, essence, movement, power, and will, then what distinguishes them? He responds that the Father is characterized by being unbegotten, the Son by being begotten, and the Spirit by going forth.[14] The Father is without origin and is unbegotten, the Son is begotten by the Father, and the Spirit has its wealth and substance from God. Gregory thus views the Spirit, which proceeds forth from the Father, and the Son, who is begotten by the Father, as equal (32.5).[15] The Father is both begetter and sender *(proboleus;* 23.11). Gregory maintains that the characteristics of being either unbegotten or begotten distinguishing the Father from the Son are *not* characteristics of being *(ousia)*, nor are they different characteristics of God's actions. Instead the designations "Father" and "Son" refer to the relationships *(schesis)* within the divine being (29.16).

Gregory does, however, also distinguish between the worldly works of

12. In this sense Gregory understands the Son and Spirit as intermediaries between the Father and creatures. K. Holl 1904, 175.

13. Cf. Bulgakov 1946, 39, 89; Schultze 1973, 174.

14. Gregory characterizes this "going forth" as *ekporeusis (Or.* 31.8; 39.12), *ekpempsis (Or.* 25.16), and *proodos (Or.* 23.7); Gregory differs from Basil's understanding of the Spirit. Cf. John 15:26.

15. Understanding Gregory's pneumatology as meaning that the Spirit goes forth from the Father *and* the Son only distorts his position into its opposite. E.g., Schultze 1973, 169f.

God's hypostases. When one acts, the other two naturally are also acting in, through, and from it.[16] At the same time, the distinctions between the various characteristics of the one nature are preserved within the economy of the triune God. In this sense Gregory can speak (34.8) of the hypostases of the Trinity as origin, creator, and perfecter. The Father, who is the origin, initiates the world. The Son, the divine Creator Logos, actualizes the world (32.10; 38.11).[17] "Is it not clear that the Father impressed the ideas of these same actions, and the Word brings them to pass, yet not in slavish or unskillful fashion, but with full knowledge and in a masterly way, or, to speak more properly, like the Father? For in this sense I understand the words that whatsoever is done by the Father, these things does the Son likewise; not, that is, because of the likeness of the things done, but in respect of the authority" (30.11).

Whenever Gregory mentions the Son's creation work, he consistently uses the verbs *demiourgein, pegnynai,* and *teuchein,* which convey a sense of making. By contrast, whenever he mentions the Godhead's creation work, he uses verbs evoking the notion that God bestows being itself, namely, *hyphistanai* and *gignesthai,* suggesting yet again that Gregory maintains his distinction between the hypostases even in their external works (32.10; 38.10; 40.7; 41.2; 7.19; 32.7; 4.20).

As for the Spirit, Gregory understands its particular characteristic to be one that completes or consummates, and as such the Spirit is already at work during creation as the one bringing that particular work to completion (38.9). The Spirit consummates creation; the pneuma is the power of deification, and this power for consummation flows from the source of the Godhead (*Carm.* 1.2.1.1). Everything is through the Spirit (*Or.* 34.15). Everything is from, through, and in God (39.12). The perfection and illumination of the angels is also a work of the Spirit (41.11); indeed, the Spirit reveals its activities in many different forms (31.29). Because the Spirit and the Son are closely related within their economy, Gregory warns against venerating the Son at the expense of the Spirit, "for he [Christ] is not the maker of a fellow servant, but he is glorified with one of coequal honor" (31.12). Gregory also refers to the Father as the true, the Son as truth, and the Holy Spirit as the Spirit of truth (23.11).

Gregory subdivides the revelatory modes of the three hypostases into three temporal periods. Although from the very first day of creation onward

---

16. Kelly 1977, 267, oversimplifies unity of the Godhead in the economy: "[N]one of the Persons possesses a separate operation of His own, but one identical energy passes through all Three." The entirety of the divine self-identity is at work in every act.

17. Gregory understands "Logos" primarily as an economic designation of the Son insofar as he reveals the nature of the Father. *Or.* 30.20. Cf. Lossky 1961, 107f.

the Father, Son, and Spirit are all present in the work of the Godhead, Gregory does detect an element of "progress" within the doctrine of God: "The Old Testament proclaimed the Father openly, and the Son more obscurely. The New manifested the Son, and suggested the deity of the Spirit. Now the Spirit himself dwells among us, and supplies us with a clearer demonstration of himself" (31.26).

On the one hand, Gregory believes that the incarnate Son and the Spirit work together; on the other, the Spirit carries on the incarnate Son's work of liberation.[18] "We are keeping the feast of Pentecost and the Coming of the Spirit, and the appointed time of the Promise, and the fulfillment of our hope. . . . The dispensations of the Body of Christ are ended . . . and that of the Spirit is beginning" (41.5). It is in connection with the work of redemption that the Cappadocian ascribes a key role to the Spirit, and in connection with the work at creation that he ascribes a key role to the Son. As the origin of the Godhead, however, the Father is the source of both creation *and* redemption, according to Gregory.

How does Gregory understand the unity of God? One cannot understand the unity of the divine essence in the Cappadocian view as a logical consequence of the Cappadocian distinction among the hypostases. Gregory finds no element of necessity within the divine essence, nor does the assumption of unity in its own turn constitute a presupposition for distinguishing between the hypostases. Gregory maintains that neither mystical speculation of the sort engaged by Gnosticism nor any logical method of approaching truth of the sort engaged by Aristotelians is sufficient for preserving *and* understanding and articulating for others the mystery of the Trinity. The only way to maintain the unity of God while simultaneously distinguishing between the divine hypostases *without* violating the mystery of the divine existence is to employ the apophatic theology Gregory himself developed — perhaps in critical response to an epistemological theory of skepticism (28.3).[19]

Gregory views the unity and distinction of the hypostases as inextricably connected:

> This I give you to share, and to defend all your life, the One Godhead and
> Power, found in the Three in Unity, and comprising the Three separately,

---

18. Gregory adduces the beginning of the gospel (Luke 9:1), the crucifixion and resurrection, the outpouring of the Spirit upon the disciples (John 20:22), and the tongues of fire after the ascension (Acts 2:3). *Or.* 31.26.

19. I am not aware that anyone has discussed this issue either in historical philosophical studies or in research on Gregory specifically. Is Gregory employing Sextus Empiricus's arguments here regarding "nonknowledge" of God's nature and creation?

not unequal, in substances or natures, neither increased nor diminished by superiorities or inferiorities; in every respect equal, in every respect the same; just as the beauty and the greatness of the heavens is one; the infinite conjunction of Three Infinite Ones, Each God when considered in Himself; as the Father so the Son, as the Son so the Holy Ghost; the Three-One God when contemplated together; Each God because Consubstantial; One God because of the Monarchia. No sooner do I conceive of the One than I am illumined by the Splendour of the Three; no sooner do I distinguish Them than I am carried back to the One. (40.41)

These three distinct and different hypostases constitute the unity of the essence and nature of the deity in their community together. Even though the mystery of the Trinity remains inaccessible to human reason, Gregory is still able to speak about the Trinity as a perfect community — one without correspondence in the created world — which precisely in its threefold character infinitely preserves perfect unity.

Gregory understands the unity of the Godhead as a unity of common will and power. The divine will and the divine power are equally present in all three hypostases. God's will and power are indivisible, and each hypostasis includes within itself the *entirety* of the one will and the one power of the triune God. "[T]he three have one Nature — God. And the union is the Father from Whom and to Whom the order of Persons [*hypostases*] runs its course, not so as to be confounded, but so as to be possessed, without distinction of time, of will, or of power" (42.15).[20] Gregory does not understand the unity of the Godhead as unity of number, even though the number three does indeed most closely approximate the notion of perfection. One can comprehend this community of the three who are one neither as a diversity of three nor as unity in any mathematical sense, since either understanding inappropriately restricts God's essence. "[A] perfect Trinity of three perfect entities; a monad taking its impetus from its superabundance, a dyad transcended (that is, it goes beyond the form and matter of which bodies consist), a triad defined by its perfection since it is the first to transcend the synthesis of duality in order that the Godhead might not be constricted or diffused without limit, for constriction bespeaks an absence of generosity; diffusion, and absence of order. The one is thoroughly Judaic; the other, Greek and polytheistic" (23.8).

Here Gregory parts company with both the monotheism of the neo-Arians and the panentheism of Plotinus, asserting against both a dynamic understanding of unity that comes about in an infinite fashion as an event

20. Cf. Ullmann 1867, 239.

within the Trinity and can be expressed neither in the simple schema of the number one nor in the idea of a One that then pours itself into diversity. Because God and the world are different, the Godhead cannot, like matter, be subdivided into parts.[21]

Gregory maintains that the unity of the Godhead inheres in each hypostasis. Although each of the three reveals the other two, their revelatory *modes* are not the same. Their distinguishing characteristics are preserved in revelation as well. Gregory is thus able to unite two different principles: (1) each of the three hypostases is wholly one with the other two; (2) even if each revelation of one hypostasis does indeed include the other two, the revelatory modes of the hypostases differ depending on their different internal relationships *(schesis)* with one another. "But the difference of manifestation [between the three Persons], if I may so express myself, or rather of their mutual relations one to another, has caused the difference of their names" (31.9).[22] Even when the hypostases mutually reveal one another in various ways, this unity as infinite community remains unchanged: "But each of these Persons [*hypostases*] possesses unity, not less with that which is united to it [*hypostase*] than with itself" (31.16).

The Cappadocian understands the unity of the Godhead as being simple and indivisible. By contrast, things in the material world are divisible because they have been constituted into unities. Because he is different from the world, God is not subject to any such constitution and hence also to no such division (31.14). Moreover, the unity of the divine essence is not subject to time. Accordingly Gregory does not construe the procreation of the Son and the going forth of the Spirit in temporal categories. Instead, the Son and the Spirit, despite the priority of the Father, are of one and the same eternity with the Father.

Gregory understands the beginning of creation as an expansion of the divine community. Instead of remaining restricted to itself, the community of hypostases expands within the creation event out to creatures. Necessity inheres in this expansion of the perfect community out to creatures as little as it does in creation itself; indeed, Gregory emphatically distances himself from the notion of such necessity. Because he construes the unity of the hypostases as a community of different and yet coessential members, yet another expres-

21. Kelly 1977, 268: "In other words, they have transferred their emphasis from mere numerical unity to unity of nature."

22. Cf. Basil, *Adversus Eunomium,* Liber 5.29.756: "You see that sometimes the Father reveals the Son, and then sometimes the Son the Father. Hence the entire Godhead reveals itself to you sometimes in the Father, and sometimes in the Son and in the Holy Spirit." Cited after Staniloae 1984, 276.

sion of this perfect unity is the intention of the Godhead to allow the world to participate in that perfect community. In this sense the mystery of the perfect community already includes within itself the intent or will to have the spiritual and material worlds participate in God's good being.[23]

To what extent does the theologian draw on experiences within the *human* community in moving analogously to an understanding of the *trinitarian* community? Although such experiences can indeed contribute to our understanding of the divine community, Gregory himself admonishes us to remain ever mindful of the limitations of such analogy. "But in this case the common nature [of all humans] has a unity which is only conceivable in thought; and the individuals are parted from one another very far indeed, both by time and by dispositions, and by power. For we are not only compound beings, but also contrasted beings, both with one another and with ourselves" (31.15). Coessentiality among human beings is imperfect and is subject to perpetual change. For Gregory the continuity of human nature is thus both weak and inadequate, while that of the trinitarian community is eternally perfect and unchangeable (31.16).

In any event, although Gregory does not believe that this analogy between divine and human community can lead to knowledge of the perfect trinitarian community, he does indeed adduce one "example from humankind itself" in demonstrating the cogency of the coessentiality as applied to those standing in various relationships, namely, the family community of Adam, Eve, and Seth (31.11). Adam stands for the Father, Eve for the Spirit, and Seth for the Son. Both Eve and Seth come from Adam, albeit in different ways. Seth is begotten (by both), Eve "cut out." Nonetheless, they are both human beings. An inappropriate understanding of Gregory's metaphor here might ask whether he is not saying that the Son is begotten by both the Father *and* the Spirit, or whether he is not trying to say something about the origins of the hypostases. Such was not his intention, however, since he was concerned only with adducing a biblical example demonstrating that a diversity of origins does *not* preclude coessentiality among human beings. Nor is he expressing what might be called the idea of a "social Image of God" in humanity.[24] On the other hand, Gregory does indeed open up an anthropomorphic understanding of God in this familial analogy.

That Eve functions in this analogy as the Spirit and the child Seth as the

---

23. Cf. Jenson 1982, 106f.

24. This notion, rather than representing a new idea for the philosophy of nature in late antiquity, actually represents a mature tradition deriving from Stoic doctrine. Jaeger 1914, 96-137.

Son does not bother Gregory. He rejects the charge that he is saying something about gender-specific characteristics within the Godhead by insisting that he is *not* applying material or physical characteristics to God. His point is that the analogy between the community of the human family and the trinitarian community is to be understood as the coessentiality of those who stand in relationships involving different *origins.* Just as a diversity of genders and generations constitutes the unity of humankind, so also do the procreation of the Son and the going forth of the Spirit from the Father constitute the one Godhead.

The Community of the Created as Mixis and Synthesis

How does Gregory develop the idea of communality in his understanding of the world? In my examination of how the relationality of the created represents a foundational characteristic of creation itself in Gregory's understanding, we encounter the same idea he employs in his understanding of God, namely, that the combination of *different* entities ultimately constitutes the presupposition of *unity.* Gregory understands the world "relationally," that is, as a nexus of relationships. The world is not only a collection of different materials, but also a complex network connecting and juxtaposing different parts. Gregory, too, adopts the older doctrine of *syndesmos,* according to which all being is connected in nature and the spirit. He does so, however, only to describe the structure of creation as a connection of different entities; he has no intention of associating spirit or mind *(nous)* and matter as Plotinus did. For Gregory, God is always the subject that connects and fits together opposing elements within creation without himself being connected by nature with the creature, and without representing any sort of connecting link. "Who mingled [*emixe*] these [heaven, earth, and water], and who distributed them? What is it that each has in common with the other [*koinonia*], and their mutual dependence and agreement? . . . what can this something else be but God?" (*Or.* 28.16).

The Cappadocian maintains that this community *(koinonia)* of elements is characterized by common growth and by what might be understood as a breathing interconnection between various parts.[25] That such antitheti-

---

25. The expressions "community," "common growth," and "common breathing" are to be understood as designations of a concrete understanding of nature deriving from the Stoic philosophy of nature. Cf. also *Or.* 6.15, where Gregory speaks about how creation is guided according to the principles of harmony by a "flowing together or breathing together."

cal elements can be so wonderfully combined and yet still remain separate can only be a sign that God is at work. These connections do not, however, represent God's actual essence; instead, God is revealed as an agent within the community.

Gregory understands the incarnation of the Son as connecting the human and the divine, an activity that is then continued in the indwelling of the Spirit in the corporeal human existence of Christians themselves (31.27). Gregory is quick to point out as well, however, that this connection does not constitute the beginning of an ontological union between the uncreated and creation, but rather a communication of the juxtaposition of God and world. Gregory's goal here is to demonstrate how the creative God is at work in his own creation as the subject that connects and juxtaposes all the various parts of nature in this fashion. That is, it is precisely the *relationality* inhering in creation as a nexus of mutual relationships that reveals the presence of divine activity. This creative God who combines and separates all the differing elements in nature is discernible in the interplay of the four elements, in the mutual relationship between the human soul and body, indeed even in the rhythm of day and night and in the change of seasons and, of course, in the Son who himself became a human being.

Gregory refers to these various connections as mixtures *(mixis, krasis)*, connections *(synthesis)*, and unifications *(synecho, syndeo)*. The four elements, for example, are thus mixed with one another *(mixis;* 32.27).[26] The elements water and earth are "bound together [*epimixiais*] by needs and commerce . . . that things so widely separated by nature should be thus brought together into one for man" (28.27).

In Gregory's world, light pours itself into the air (44.3) and the sun shines on the entire earth (28.29). Heaven gives some of its light to the air and some of its rain to the earth (6.14). Elements providing the constituent parts of bodies are governed by order *(taxis;* 32.8), and the same good organization comes to expression in the sequence of day and night and in the course of the seasons and their changes *(Carm.* 1.1.32; *Or.* 14.23; 6.15). When God created the material world, he created "a system and compound of earth and sky, and all that is in the midst of them" (*Or.* 38.10).

Gregory maintains that God created human beings to unite the spiritual with the material world. Before human beings, the two worlds were nowhere combined *(krama)* and the opposites nowhere mixed *(mixis;* 28.11). Hence, on Gregory's view the spiritual and the material are indeed combined

---

26. Cf. Basil, *Hexaemeron* 4. Homily 5, p. 68. The notion of mixing comes from Chrysippus. Cf. Reinhardt 1926, 8.

in human beings (14.6; 2.75; 2.29; 2.17). Human beings are such a mixture, however, only in the Stoic sense of *mixis,* according to which the combined elements maintain their respective qualities even within the mix.[27] Indeed, even a person's virtues constitute such a "community" (22.14). In the larger sense this mixture is also a source of danger insofar as the various parts can potentially come into conflict with one another, separate, and even dissolve the mix entirely (28.7).

Now, just as human beings represent the combination of the spiritual and the material, so also does Christ represent the mixing and combination of the divine and the human. The two different natures of the uncreated and the created come together in Christ.[28] "God becomes man and suffers with our suffering and through encasement in flesh become poor" (44.4).[29] Gregory's God wants unity, not separation, and the theologian understands such unity as a harmony of interconnections; God's original creation was itself characterized by the law of unity (14.26). For Gregory the world's two dimensions are connected with one another, as are, in a similar fashion, the "letters of nature" *(stoicheia).*[30] Human beings combine elements of the soul with elements of matter. In the Son and then also in the Spirit, God enters into a connection with the element of the human and in so doing thus also enters into a connection with the material world, which is in fact alien to God.

Because Gregory finds the creative and redeeming God at work everywhere in such mutual connections and juxtapositions, he is able to establish parallels between his statements concerning physical, anthropological, and christological *mixis.*[31] In this context, however, he is not adducing an analogy between divine interconnections and worldly ones; instead, God is functioning as the agent of interconnections among created things *as well as* the agent of his own interconnection with human beings. The antithesis of connection is commensurately the disruption and even destruction of relationships. Gregory is quite consistent in portraying the relational nature of the nexus of

27. Concerning the Stoic understanding, cf. Reinhardt 1926, 8. Concerning Gregory's anthropology and understanding of mixing, cf. Ellverson 1981, 37, and Althaus 1972, 57-60.

28. Cf. Barbel 1963, 288ff. In *Or.* 40.29 Gregory maintains that Christ's body is not divided and separated by spaces or gaps.

29. Concerning the parallel between anthropological and christological references to such mixing, see Ellverson 1981, 79f.

30. I do not translate *stoicheia* with the Latin equivalent "elements," but rather as "letters of nature." The original meaning was based on the notion that the elements of the material world were etched or written into material as letters. Cf. Bergmann 1993a, 4.

31. Virtually hypostasized subjects of such interconnecting for Gregory include the divine order, *taxis* (*Or.* 32.8f.); divine providence, *pronoia* (14.33); and the Creator, *Logos* (6.14).

creation as good, and the separation, destruction, and dissolution of those same relations as evidence that evil forces are at work (14.26).[32] Evil enemies try to sunder what God has brought together.

Once again the Cappadocian parallels physical and human life. The same sin causing the disparate relationship between the passions and reason (*nous*) in human beings is responsible for the strife within the cosmos at large (39.7; 6.16).[33] Indeed, the adversary is out to separate and splinter and otherwise disrupt all that has been so wonderfully connected. Gregory now also derives his understanding of our ethical task from this high estimation of relationality within creation, namely, to reconcile and unite what has been separated, and to bring about peace in a general sense. In fact, he believes that such peace — good peace — connects us with God (6.20).

In summary, then, we find that Gregory understands the world as an essentially good human community, as a mixture and series of interconnections. He manages to establish parallels among the interconnections in creation, in human beings, and in Christ by speaking about *mixis* within the relationships in all three. God is the subject of such interconnecting and is the agent of relationality. While the triune God perpetually seeks to connect and bring life together into such relationships, the power of evil chronically tries to destroy and otherwise disrupt precisely these relationships with the help of human sin.

The Qualities of Community: Peace, Beauty, and Nonviolence

If one understands the concept of relation as a situation in which the one is sustained by the other, then interpreting Gregory's writings from this perspective is commensurate with his theology, which does indeed understand the unity of creation as an ontic situation of being sustained by God.[34] But what actually characterizes the community of such connections? Gregory de-

---

32. In *Or.* 6.8 Gregory presents the natural law of the subordination of body parts to the one body as the model for the unity within the church in the context of separation or division.

33. In his oration on the failed harvest resulting from a hailstorm (*Or.* 16.18), Gregory maintains that the cause was actually the wealthy's injustice toward the poor; God intends to teach the wealthy a drastic lesson now. In 6.16 Gregory says that as punishment for sin God could even destroy the very order upon which the cosmos rests.

34. Etymologically the term "relation" in Greek actually derives from the verb *phero* and thus means "to bear, bring, bring by."

scribes the positive qualities of relationality as peace, beauty, commonality, harmony, nonviolence, purity, and newness, and the negative qualities as disorder, divisiveness, dissolution, coercion, and pollution or defilement.

Gregory's theology maintains that a clear correspondence obtains between God and world insofar as the positive qualities of the interconnections within the world emerge from the positive qualities of the trinitarian connections. The relationship between the negative and positive qualities within creation simultaneously reflects for Gregory just how near or far the Creator and creation are to one another. An increase in positive qualities reflects an enhancement of the relation between God and world as this situation of "the one being sustained by the other"; similarly, an increased disruption of that nexus by negative qualities deforms that same relationship.

Gregory's understanding of qualitative *movement* also illustrates this interrelationship between positive and negative qualities. Whenever the nexus of relationships within the world grows qualitatively, God allows the world to approach more closely to him. Conversely, when negative qualities destroy or disrupt relations within the world, the creation moves commensurately further away from its Creator. This relationship between God and world in ancient thought is emphatically *not* to be understood in a primarily *spatial* sense, even though modern thought tends to reduce the notion of relation to such; instead, it is to be understood as a *qualitative* movement that distinguishes between relational proximity and relational distance.[35]

In his second oration on peace (*Or.* 22), Gregory describes peace as a positive quality of interconnection and shows how in God's life this quality corresponds with the life of the angelic and material world.

> These blessings originate with the Holy Trinity, whose unity of nature and internal peace are its most salient characteristic, are received by the angelic and divine powers who are peaceably disposed towards God as well as one another, extend to the whole of creation, whose glory is its absence of conflict, and regulate our own life: in our soul, on the one hand, through the reciprocal and cooperative allegiance of its virtues; in our body, on the other, through the happy marriage of form and function in its constituent members. Of these, the former both is and is called beauty; the latter, health. (22.14)

Just as the anatomy of the body brings the quality of peace to visible expression in the interconnection of its various parts, so also is the "community" of virtues in the human soul such a bearer of peace. Indeed, Gregory maintains

---

35. Cf. Berger 1984, 180f.

that the entirety of creation itself reflects this same quality of peace, as does the community of angels both in their relationships among one another and in their relationship to God. Gregory interprets this peace within creation as participation in the same divine peace obtaining between the hypostases of the Trinity. In this sense the peace of creation lives from the trinitarian peace, which is also why peace is "more Godlike and sublime" than war (22.15). A good peace connects the world with God (6.20), and the peaces that obtain in the state, in the family, and in nature are all intimately connected with one another in the understanding of the Cappadocian (4.120). Nor is it only angels and human beings who qualify as bearers of the quality of peace, since the relationships between the elements in material nature, too, can come together or enter into such alliances (44.11).

Beauty and nonviolence represent additional positive qualities. Gregory maintains that order and good interconnections can always also be discerned as *beauty* (14.23; 16.3; 27.4; 28.6; 43.9). Beauty itself, however, is not only a quality discernible in the visible material world, but also a characteristic of God. "Who is the man who has never beheld, as our duty is to behold it, the fair beauty of the Lord, nor has visited His temple, or rather, become the temple of God, and the habitation of Christ in the Spirit?" (2.97).

It is thus God's beauty that appears in both visible (matter) and spiritual beauty. Unlike modern aesthetic theory, Gregory is quite unable to construe beauty as a "pure" category of aesthetic perception; the appearance of the beautiful is for Gregory always — as in the Platonic tradition as well — associated with the appearance of the true, of the good, and of peace, and thus of the divine itself. Gregory adduces the analogy of the relationship between the artist and the work of art in understanding the world itself as God's work; it is God's perfect beauty that one perceives in the divine work of art (14.31).

Gregory defines *violence* as involuntary privation (40.23) and thus as a restriction of free will and deprivation of potentiality.[36] Violence is a quality of tyrannical power and as such cannot possibly be attributed to God, who admonishes and instructs without resorting to violence (31.25). The quality of being good consists not in violence but in freedom (12.5); Gregory never tires of illustrating this positive quality of nonviolence in imagery drawn from nature. Nature allows not only violence but also its restraint (29.9); only violence — force, power — can change the course of a river flowing in one direction (26.2); a cupped hand cannot measure water, a flat hand cannot weigh

---

36. Cf. in this regard the definition of Galtung (1975, 57), who similarly describes a social structure hindering potential growth as violent or coercive.

heaven, and the human fist cannot grasp the earth and the elements (32.27). And the tree forced to grow in a certain direction inclines toward its original direction once it is freed from its fetters (2.36). The threatened tree resists the iron tool that would fell it (26.10), and the plant forcefully bent down ultimately straightens itself up again (6.8).

Additional *positive* qualities he mentions include commonality, harmony (6.15; 38.10), purity, and newness.[37] He circumscribes negative qualities as, for example, an absence of peace (32.8), as divisiveness (32.2), and as an obscuring of the image of God in human beings (40.7). In a general sense Gregory views as *positive* those relational qualities that enhance communication between interconnected elements and thus initiate qualitative movement *toward God,* and as *negative* those that disrupt or destroy such relations and thus initiate movement *away from God.* Because suffering represents a deformation of relationality caused by evil forces, it also deforms the connection between God and world.

Service, Sanctification, Management: Human Beings within the Community of Creation

How does Gregory now define the place of human beings within the community of creation? In the following discussion I first examine how that particular living being with a body and mind (spirit) and created by the image of God[38] is integrated into that community, and then I examine which position it occupies and what its function is.

---

37. See 32.21; 32.10; 32.23; 33.9 on commonality. "Purity" also serves as the criterion for liberation from sin through Christ (38.14) and is employed in the description of the pollution of the image of God through the fall and sin. In that sense, one approaches God along a path through which this image is purified from its pollution by evil. In 44.6 Gregory speaks about the newness of life. Cf. Eph. 4:22f.

38. Here I expand Aristotle's definition of human beings as *zoon logikon,* i.e., as the living being with the logos. Christian anthropology clearly draws on both the Aristotelian (body and spirit/mind) and the biblical notion (image of God). In this context the criterion of the Christian view is the extent to which the characteristic of being created in the image of God is applied interpretively to the understanding of ancient anthropology. Simply pointing out that Greek-speaking theologians in the early church affirmed the ancient anthropological notion of "duality" is insufficient. The question is rather the extent to which they believed this duality was an expression of being created in the image of God. Gregory associates mind *(nous)* with image of God *(eikon)* and understands the good body, as animated by God, as the enduring presupposition both of the capacity for human reason and for being created in the image of God, which is also why he insists that the "spiritual body" *(soma pneumatikon;* cf. 1 Cor. 15) is also glorified.

Just how are human beings *integrated* into creation? For Gregory the human "being" is creaturely. Its body connects it with the sensuous material world while its soul connects with the angelic world of the spirit or mind. Prior to the creation of human beings, these two worlds were not connected. Through human beings they now become the *one* creation. The two worlds are open to one another and are ultimately connected to one another in this human relationship. For Gregory human beings differ from animals insofar as they have mind *(nous)* and image of God *(eikon)*, and from angels insofar as they have a body *(soma)*. As such a mixture and combination (2.75) of both mind and body, human beings are thus bearers of the divine (38.11) within the created world. Indeed, human beings were fashioned by the very hand of God (45.12; 39.13).

Gregory maintains that the entire corporeal-spiritual human being is completely integrated into creation. On the one hand, the human soul is encompassed in a body of flesh; on the other, the human body has a spirit or mind that shows it what is good. The heart of Gregory's understanding of the "dual nature"[39] of human beings is that this polarity is embedded in a *totality*, and it is the communication between the soul and the body that actually makes a human being into a human being. Human beings are thus integrated into creation from a threefold perspective: physical or corporeal, spiritual or mental, and divine.

Because human beings are accordingly completely integrated into *both* worlds, Gregory prefers to call them "new angels," "at once both mind and flesh," and "a world in miniature," that is, a microcosm (38.11). Human beings are totally connected with their surroundings and constitute part of those surroundings. They actually represent a "second world" or reproduction of the "greater world" (38.11). The salient feature of their nature is this combination of or connection between the spiritual and material world (32.9), and precisely this connection prompts Gregory to speak of human beings as a "world in miniature" or microcosm (38.11; 28.22).

What *position* do human beings occupy in Gregory's understanding of creation? Do they occupy a specific place in the world? Extreme caution is advised in responding to this question insofar as the *modern* understanding of the world tends to reduce "space" to a purely quantitative notion. Hence I will first examine how Gregory himself understands the concept of the *space* of creation; what we discover is that the theologian conceives of the *position* of human beings within creation not as a specifically ontological *place*, but rather as a unified *movement* in relation to (toward or away from) God within

39. Ellverson 1981, 17.

these two worlds. I will also examine why the interpretive category "anthropocentrism" is ill suited for explaining Gregory's anthropology.

What, then, does Gregory say about the "space" of the world? Before asking how an author in late antiquity views or conceives the notion of space in this sense, we must leave behind the perspective modernity normally brings to such thinking. Antiquity was utterly unaware of our notion of space as measured by mathematical and eternally consistent coordinates. In antiquity the term *topos* referred to a region or field within the spherical space "world."[40] The salient feature of such a field is that it is the locus of appearances or phenomena. Antiquity was not familiar with the modern notion of space in the *absolute* sense. One might even say that as far as antiquity was concerned, "space" does not arise except where appearances — phenomena — are involved in the process of arising and then passing away. The celestial course of the stars served to define this region, since they determined the position of the world rather than the idea of an absolute geometrical center.

The underlying notion in Gregory's understanding of the world is that it is divided into two regions: the region of the visible, the material, and the region of the spiritual. Although by distinguishing thus between the material cosmos *(kosmos aisthetos)* and the spiritual cosmos Gregory is essentially following the Platonic view of the world as understood during his age, his understanding of the *origin* of this distinction does differ significantly from that particular view. In *Timaeus* Plato maintains that matter exists from eternity, whereas Plotinus maintains that it is wholly dependent on the spiritual and the One. By contrast, Gregory maintains that both the material and the spiritual were part of the triune God's creation work, and as such each possesses its own intrinsic value. Each also functions differently. Whereas the spiritual was created to serve the Creator, the material reflects his goodness and creative power. For Gregory, then, both parts represent the work of goodness carried out by the triune God, and it is the function of human beings to connect the two worlds. The history of the fall and redemption did not commence until the world had been created as a totality encompassing these two interconnected realms.[41]

Gregory is keen on understanding God as the agent of this distinction. Through the first separation God differentiated the first part of heaven and the angels from God, and through the second he differentiated human beings

40. Picht 1989, 420f.
41. See in this regard Gregory's account of creation in *Or.* 38.9-11, though also the "taxiological," sapiential account of creation in 32.7-10.

(and the material world) from heaven (*Or.* 6.22).[42] By contrast, there is no separation or division at all in God himself (26.19). Gregory's twofold distinction here is not dualistic, since his spiritual and material worlds are indeed open to one another. The cosmic structure is completely self-enclosed, and within this self-enclosed universe two regions emerge: the world of spiritual phenomena above and that of material phenomena below. But again, both fields are part of one and the same creation enclosed or delimited by the uncreated. Antiquity had absolutely no concept of an infinite cosmic All; the firmament of heaven represented the farthest, most extreme boundary of the world. All the same, Gregory does include yet one additional boundary lying as it were "behind" heaven itself whose "veil over the firmament" separates creation itself from the Creator (*Carm.* 1.1.29).

Because the Cappadocians characteristically include the region of spiritual beings in the world of creation, the world of the angels is also part of the world of creation. What delimits the world as a whole is actually its boundary over against the uncreated, a boundary Gregory calls a "great gulf" (*Or.* 41.12; 32.15). And while neither creatures nor even angels can penetrate that boundary, it does remain perpetually open for God, "Who is in all this universe, and again is beyond the universe" (2.76). God remains the Creator and redeemer of spatial order in the material world as well; in describing the work of creation as a work of divine order *(taxis)*, Gregory draws on elements from Old Testament wisdom teachings: "[There is] order in the elements from which bodies are composed. Order has set the heavens in orbital motion; has spread abroad the expanse of the air; has set the earth beneath or even above; has poured forth and harnessed the liquid element; has allowed the winds to blow but not turned them loose; has confined moisture in the clouds but not withheld it, sowing it instead over the face of the whole earth in regular and equitable fashion" (32.8). In his understanding of the interplay of the four elements, Gregory is basically following the tradition that interprets the work of creation within the framework of the Aristotelian doctrine of the combination of the four elements.[43]

As for the category of space in Gregory's understanding of the world, the most obvious references are to an *upper* and *lower* space, or *above* and *below*. By contrast, he seems to have no concept that the earth might have a "middle," and says only that God will in the future redemption stand "in the

---

42. In describing these separations, Gregory employs Philo's metaphor of the two curtains (in the temple) restricting the human view of God (*Or.* 45.23). Concerning Philo's understanding of the cosmos as a temple, see Früchtel 1968, 69ff.

43. Cf. Bergmann 1993a.

middle" of the righteous, who will themselves then be like gods and kings (40.6). Gregory does not, however, assign any *spatially* designated area to God.[44] The Cappadocian does make frequent use of the categories of "above" and "below." Heaven is above, the earth below (6.14). Whereas material nature draws human beings downward (20.1; 2.91), the human spirit or mind tends upward (16.15). After failing in his rebellion against God, Lucifer falls down into the material world (36.5), and whereas worldly rulers rule below, God rules above — from which Gregory also concludes that dominion in the lower world should be accommodated or brought into line with God's dominion above (36.11).

Gregory describes the work of creation as "illumination" in analogy to the visible world in which the sun shines down on the earth from above, illuminating everything in it. Unlike the Gnostic system, which contrasts the darkness in the lower world to the light in the higher world, Gregory's metaphor emphasizes that God's work benefits the *entire* two-part world:

> For God whose will it was to create this world, which is composed of things visible and invisible and is the great and awesome herald of his majesty, to the eternal beings is himself light, and there is no other — for why, when they possess the greatest light, would they require a lesser one? — while lower beings, we among them, are the primary recipients of the power of this light here below. Indeed, it is fitting that the Great Light should have begun his creation with light, by which he disperses the darkness and the chaos and disorder that formerly prevailed. (44.3)

By illuminating the fields of spiritual creation, God's light also illuminates the fields of material creation, connecting the two such that both radiate in the same light. For Gregory, "above" and "below" are oriented *toward* one another rather than *against* one another. Through being set free by the Creator's redemptive work, the darkness below will shine forth with the spiritual world above, and in this sense the shining actually begins with God, flowing from above to below and ultimately reflecting the divine light from below back to the field above.

Significantly, Gregory employs this same directional movement in other contexts as well. Within the redemptive process of human beings, God climbs down while we human beings climb up (41.12; 32.15). Christ's resurrection, culminating ultimately in the ascension from below to above, draws the entire world up with it (45.2). In trinitarian community with the Son, the

---

44. In *Or.* 28.8 Gregory says God has no definite place *(topos)*, and in 32.27 that the Holy Spirit is not spatially bound in any way.

Spirit tries to find a path on earth from below to above; ultimately it goes up with the Son to heaven (14.21), and after Christ has returned home to the Father, the Spirit once again comes "down" to continue his work (41.11).[45] In Christ's own baptism Christ leads the entire world upward (39.16). Elsewhere Gregory makes it clear which direction faith takes: "in order as I conceive by that part of it [the divine being] which we can comprehend to draw us to itself" (38.7).

Hence, instead of understanding the spatial schema of "above" and "below" in Gregory's understanding of the world statically, it is important to note that "above" refers to the phenomenal fields of spiritual natures whose service, however, can just as easily be carried out in the "lower," material world. "Below" refers then to the phenomenal fields of material natures that are bound to the earth itself. Although the two fields are indeed open to one another, human beings alone are able to unite the two.

Although Gregory understands the world in its status as creation as being completely delimited and its boundary over against the uncreated God as being absolutely impenetrable, God himself is both inside and outside the world, and Gregory remarks how utterly remarkable indeed it is to experience this "according to the proportion of their nearness to God" (34.8). Because material and spiritual creatures represent two different parts of the world, their fields of appearance are also different. And because it is only *within* the world of creation that God appears to either group, we must presuppose that God himself *moves* into the world in some fashion. At the same time, however, wherever God does appear to creatures in the phenomenal fields of the world and is actively perceived by them, they are themselves drawn into an upward movement. For Gregory the dynamic process of redemption consists in the Creator drawing the entire world up to himself. Everything now below is ultimately to move upward.

The tectonic structure of Gregory's world is characterized not by organization around a static center, but by this dynamic movement from above to below (God) and from below to above (creatures). Although the two parts constituting the whole of the world are to be understood as the fields of appearance of qualitatively different natures, the two regions and the two natures are always open to one another as parts of the one creation. The existence of humanity binds them inextricably to one another, and the work of divine redemption sets them in motion toward God.

---

45. Cf. *Or.* 41.5, where Gregory says the mysteries of the Spirit only begin when the Son's bodily sojourn on earth — during which the Son still maintains his body in glory with the Father — comes to an end.

Where, however, do human beings fit into this schema? Gregory's world consists of two spatial levels. The created angels are above, the material natures below. The Cappadocians hold that the uniqueness of the human position within the world is that human beings live both above *and* below, and yet are always striving toward God. "A living creature trained here, and then moved elsewhere; and, to complete the mystery, deified by its inclination to God. For to this, I think, tends that Light of Truth which we here possess but in measure, that we should both see and experience the Splendour of God, which is worthy of Him Who made us, and will remake us again after a loftier fashion" (38.11). Gregory is wholly unfamiliar with the notion that human beings occupy a special position within the world in the sense of a place within quantitative space. For him, their position is a qualitative one; they and they only are connected *both* with the world below *and* with that above. Because angels are of a spiritual nature, ontologically they are beings of the upper world; even those who fall down into the lower world do not mix with the material elements of that world. Similarly, while the angels are able to move about freely within the entire space of creation, purely material living beings occupy a special position in the lower world and remain bound to that lower sphere. Human beings alone are able to move about both below — as do animals — and above — as do angels. The uniquely human position in the cosmos is that they are ontologically at home on both levels and are able to move about in both within the limitations of the *diastema* (interspace, boundary). They are also set apart insofar as they were created in the image of God; as such they differ ontologically both from angels and from sensuous living beings, moving about in a similarly unique fashion, namely, either toward or away from God.

In summary, we find that Gregory understands and defines the position of human beings by applying the coordinates of above/below and toward/away from God. This determination of the position human beings occupy is of considerable soteriological significance for Gregory. Because only human beings live below and above, materially and spiritually, and because they are capable of moving toward God, they are entrusted with considerable responsibility in the redemptive process of material creation.[46]

As far as Gregory is concerned, no part of creation goes untouched by the Creator's work of redemption. In one sense the entire redemptive process takes place *in this world*, since if both the earthly *and* the heavenly participate

---

46. The current debate on creation theology in the Orthodox document "Skapelsens förvandling" (11), p. 79 ("Orthodox Perspectives on Creation"), emphasizes this point with reference to Gregory, *Or.* 38.11.

in redemption and transformation because God enters into his creation, a world *outside* the world can never become a reality. It is *this* world and no other that is to be drawn up to God.

Does Gregory's cosmology thus end up being anthropocentric? Meyendorff describes the background common to all patristic theology as a combination of "theocentric anthropology" and "anthropocentric cosmology."[47] The "theocentric" element is allegedly that because human beings are created in the image of God, they are determined not by their autonomy but by their participation in the divine.[48] The "anthropocentric" element is allegedly that because human beings themselves are understood theocentrically, the world as a whole is conceived anthropocentrically. I do not believe that Gregory's cosmology is anthropocentric. Several considerations militate against such a view.

First, the concept of "-centrism" as such — be it theocentrism or anthropocentrism — is alien to patristic thought, nor can one expect to find it there, since the idea of a "center" was utterly alien to antiquity in the larger sense. This has been demonstrated by the Swedish philologist Albert Wifstrand in his neglected essay "Medelpunkten" ("The Center"). Wifstrand documents how our "fellow human beings" in both antiquity and the Middle Ages by no means viewed the earth as the proud center of the universe, but rather more as a "small point compared to the dimensions of the sun's course" (Cleomedes) and as a "point" smaller than the smallest fixed star (Sacrobosco).[49] People of antiquity lived rather in the sludge (Galen) of the earth, *sub luna*, looking upward full of hope at the celestial bodies. This tradition of the minuscule earth continued uninterrupted from antiquity by way of the Arabs through the Middle Ages on down to Copernicus. Wifstrand demonstrates unequivocally that no Greek and Latin writer during this period ever used the word "center" metaphorically.[50] Only after Copernicus understood the *sun* as the center around which the earth revolved could the beautiful woman amid a circle of male admirers be *metaphorically* called the center of society. My criticism of the anthropocentric interpretation here can

---

47. Meyendorff 1983, 34-37. Although Meyendorff speaks about Cappadocian theology in general, he refers — as is unfortunately usually the case — only to Basil and Gregory of Nyssa.

48. Meyendorff 1983, 35: "This element 'akin to God' is, of course, the *imago Dei*, which Gregory [of Nyssa] identifies not simply as a form of participation in divine life but, more specifically, as a sharing in the Creator's 'freedom and self-determination.'" Concerning the concept of "theocentric anthropology," cf. also Meyendorff 1974, 138-43.

49. Wifstrand 1976, 39f.

50. Wifstrand 1976, 41.

also be described — in Wifstrand's words — as a criticism of the "power of language over ideas,"[51] that is, a criticism of the power of the (post-Copernican) metaphor of the "center" over historical interpretation. I understand Meyendorff's thesis of anthropocentric cosmology as assuming that human beings constitute the center of the world space. From the perspective of God, they "stand" at the center. The problem is that Gregory's contemporaries in antiquity knew of no such center.

Secondly, the previous analysis of Gregory's understanding of the position and function of human beings in creation shows that he had no notion that human beings occupied a particular place in cosmic space. The only "place" that might qualify in this sense would be the region of the earth's surface on which human beings stand and that of the lower air into which they raise themselves. Gregory's understanding of the human position is connected with a simple ontological hierarchy in which spiritual beings are above and material beings below. The unique features in his Christian understanding of God are his distinction between creation and the Creator, on the one hand, and between God's various modes of entry into the world through revelation, incarnation, and liberation, on the other.[52]

Thirdly, although ancient philosophy did view circular motion as the most perfect of all motion, the most significant feature of such movement was not the existence of a center around which such movement revolved, but rather the *form* itself of that movement.[53] That is, it is the specifically *circular* movement of the sun and stars that constitutes their perfection rather than their relation to a static center. The Copernican revolution at the dawn of modernity radically altered this basic cosmological understanding. Instead of viewing circular movement from a point of rest, human beings were now *themselves* situated on a moving sphere. The Copernican move to the notion that the earth itself is moving utterly changed the meaning of the category of "-centrism." In response to the question concerning the place occupied by human beings in a world that is itself in motion, one now described the human position as a static center around which other things moved. An examination of the "genesis of the Copernican understanding of the world" (Blumenberg) helps considerably in understanding how the category of anthropocentrism might be applied in addressing the basic anthropological question regarding what is specifically human (in comparison to nature and

51. Wifstrand 1976, 48f.
52. Gregory's understanding of the distance between Creator and creation is to be understood as qualitative rather than spatial.
53. Cf. Blumenberg 1989, 2:509-26.

God). Here I believe Meyendorff introduces a category that might well be applied to this anthropological question *after* the discoveries of Copernicus but is ill suited to understanding writers from antiquity.

Finally, if (as Meyendorff explicitly intends) one wishes to introduce patristic cosmology into current discussion, the thesis that the ancient church entertained an anthropocentric cosmology inevitably leads to misunderstanding. Vehement discussions have been going on for nearly two decades concerning the pros and cons of anthropocentrism and biocentrism. Instead of entering into this debate, Meyendorff is apparently trying to engage the positive connotations of "theocentrism." His concept of anthropocentrism, however, sooner represents a kind of "humanism" that tries to view the intrinsic value of human beings differently than did the Renaissance. In current ecological discussions, the thesis of patristic anthropocentrism suggests that all the church fathers were representatives of what in the twentieth century has been criticized as the kind of anthropocentrism that would dominate nature by autonomous Western rationality. Of course, this is not what Meyendorff intends. If, however, one wishes to introduce patristic thought as a theological contribution into current ecological debate, one must be extremely mindful not to transfer modern interpretive categories on to ancient texts.

This critical discussion raises a fundamental question: How do human beings *function* within creation? What does Gregory view as their purpose or commission? In Gregory's view, human beings connect the material and the spiritual and are connected with God in that they are created in his image, and these two features determine how they function within creation. One might say that for Gregory, God appears in the world as an image in human beings. Gregory believes, however, that human beings not only exhibit ontological and iconic characteristics, but are also to exercise a particular soteriological function he calls "striving": "The words do not mean that you should remain permanently in the same mould, but rather that you should be in constant change, improving, ever a new creature, repenting if you should sin and pressing forward ['striving,' *epiteinonta*] if your life be virtuous" (*Or.* 44.8). Clearly, Gregory does not believe that the commission of human beings is to establish absolute dominion, and he also speaks of the human being as both "King of all upon the earth, but subject to the King above" (38.11). Human dominion on earth is merely one of several functions, and in any case does not represent absolute dominion but merely that of a viceroy and representative.[54] Quite in contrast to any notion of absolute do-

---

54. Concerning the tradition of the viceroy in the ancient church, see Thunberg 1986, 299-304; and 1979. Peterson has shown the extent to which the notion of "king on earth" in

minion, Gregory understands such human dominion as one of service, sanctification, and subordination insofar as the human being is not only king but also worshiper,[55] witness, priest, and subject (38.11). Before the fall, human beings functioned "to till the immortal plants, by which is meant perhaps the Divine Conceptions" (38.12). Each of these functions involves different tasks. In the function of king, human beings administer to the best advantage those gifts of creation entrusted to them. As worshiper, witness, and priest they are to lead creation itself closer to God. And finally, in the function of subject they are to exercise this dominion only in relation to their "subjugation from above."

Gregory describes the human sojourn in the world as that of a king in a palace whose bodyguards are actually all living things (44.4). Although creation was indeed brought about for human enjoyment, at the same time it is incumbent on human beings to acknowledge the honor accorded creation in its own turn and to allow it to lead them to God (16.5). For example, although the elements do indeed give of themselves and their lives to benefit human beings (14.17), and although the earth and the sea might join even more closely in serving human beings (28.27), so also should human beings serve the material world and guide that world toward an encounter with God — that is, they should serve the material world just as the material world serves them. Indeed, Jesus himself honored the body for the sake of its deification (39.16). As the image of precisely this God, human beings should raise up the flesh to God on the wings of the nous (16.15). Unfortunately, however, human beings are certainly not above abusing this dominion, and Gregory addresses two concrete political situations in this context. He held the powerful responsible for an agricultural catastrophe and the resulting famine caused by a storm, maintaining that by unjustly oppressing the poor and withholding from them the gifts of the Creator and by abusing the power of management bestowed on them, the powerful themselves provoked God into visiting on them this natural catastrophe as a sign that they should repent (16.18).

The second example involves the governor of Nazianzus and his unjust exercise of political power. Gregory suggests that in relating to his subjects the regent should consider that as the image of God he is actually ruling over what might be called co-images of the divine, and that certain consequences

---

the Christian church cannot be understood monotheistically in the sense of a political order of creation. The same applies to Gregory of Nazianzus. Peterson 1951, 102f., explicitly understands Gregory's thesis concerning the trinitarian monarchy, to which Gregory opposes anarchy and polyarchy in *Or.* 29.2, as an intensification of Christianity's revolt in the metaphysical and political order.

55. Cf. John 4:23.

follow from this situation. "You are an image of God, but you also control that image. . . . Honor the nature you have in common; respect your archetype; ally yourself with God, not the rule of this world" (17.9). Gregory also points out that "divisiveness" and social differences between the healthy and the rich, on the one hand, and the sick and the poor, on the other, are wholly incommensurate with the image of the Creator: "I ask you to look at that original egalitarian status, not the latter-day discrimination; not the law of the tyrant [the serpent], but that of the Creator" (14.26).

Gregory views the human commission within creation more as service than as dominion in the traditional sense. The human soul should turn the body into a member of God's household (2.17), and should take heed and learn from the order of creation itself (6.14). Even though Gregory acknowledges the differences between human beings and animals (14.23), he is also cognizant of the similarities between them. Indeed, the suffering of creation also brings human beings to know God (16.5). Only Christ exercises full dominion over all flesh (30.6) and consummates and renews all things (30.15). Ultimately everything belongs to God (39.13), and Gregory can say of himself, "I am for the glory of God . . . [I] who exist for God's sake" (42.17).

Gregory also describes the human task christologically. The new creation through Christ reestablishes the original unity, "the law . . . of the Creator" (14.26) in which all things are one (7.23). The uniquely human characteristic is reflected in the witness of the Son, who combines the divine and human nature. As the good shepherd, Christ sacrificed his soul for his sheep and brought the lost sheep home on his back just as he bore the wood of the cross back to higher life (45.26). Christ ultimately shows us that the most appropriate path to exaltation is humiliation (45.26).

Gregory emphatically does not believe that the center of the human task amid fellow creatures means imitating (6.14) this God in the sense of exercising unchecked power over creation; rather it means service and worship in gently and sensitively guiding all fellow living things ever closer to God.[56] The guiding notion is not crude dominion over nature, but the praise of God's glory as sung by human beings, angels, and the material world, something Gregory expresses in the imagery of a cosmic Christmas. The real goal of the human commission within creation is precisely this song of rejoicing within the cosmic Christmas, when all humanity and all spiritual *and* material powers praise God together (38.17).

---

56. Gregory does not conclude from this position the modern notion of "cosmic democracy" and ethical equality; cf. Boff 1985, 34f. Instead, he legitimizes the ontological hierarchy of values obtaining in his own age.

Gregory's eschatological metaphor of "cosmic spring" shows the extent to which he understands this human commission as a function *within* creation at large rather than as dominion *over* creatures. The spring of the resurrection of the new creation is something both visible and invisible for the soul and body, human beings and nature, something Gregory calls "a spring of the world, a spring of the spirit" (44.12).

Gregory thus describes the unique function of human beings within creation from several perspectives: ontological, theological-iconic, political, liturgical, cosmic-doxological, and cosmic-eschatological. Most importantly, he does not understand the commission to "have dominion over the earth" (Gen. 1:28) as unqualified dominion over creatures, but rather as the exercise of a special function within God's overriding cosmic redemptive history. What the Cappadocian sees as the uniquely human quality of this function is the human ability to rule justly and to serve, worship, glorify, witness, manage, and sanctify, and especially to incorporate the image of God — imprinting that image, as it were — in this world. One might even say that for Gregory, being human means to be the image of God *in and for the world*. As such, the life of human beings constantly moves within history toward the goal of having the world itself *be with God*. In trying to describe this eschatological condition of being, Gregory employs the metaphors of the cosmic spring of all life and that of the song of rejoicing that the cosmos itself sings during the eternal Christmas.

The Unity of the Community of Creation as Taxis and Eukosmia

Gregory's Christian theology draws on elements from that particular Stoic doctrine that views uniformity, rationality, and providence as principles that are immanent to the world itself and then develops its understanding of ethics to include the conduct of a person's life in accordance with these same principles. What such a view does *not* include is the idea that human beings might function in some fashion to liberate the world through their very shaping of it.[57] By contrast, the Christian position incorporates the creation doctrine into the heart of its understanding of redemption in which God and human beings together strive to realize the new creation, and it is precisely here that Gregory attributes a decisive role to human beings in mediating the redemption of the material world; in so doing, he positions asceticism against the accumulation of wealth, and love for the poor against self-love.

57. Schupp 1990, 191-99.

Once matter is no longer understood as having existed from eternity, the material, sensory world acquires intrinsic value of its own insofar as, having been created by God, it too is now viewed as good and as willed by God.[58] By understanding evil itself as ultimately deriving from a spiritual origin, Gregory is able to describe evil[59] as a historical process and also assert that the world itself is transformed in a history of redemption from evil.

How does Gregory describe the unity of the community of creation? First, the Cappadocian emphasizes that God created not four worlds, but rather only *one* that he himself orders and maintains (*Or.* 30.11). In Gregory's view it is God who sustains and supports the unity of the world, and he refers to the sustaining subject as order *(taxis),* providence *(pronoia),* law *(nomos),* word and ideas *(logos, logoi),* and spirit *(pneuma).* He refers to the actual unity itself as a mixture or interconnection (*mixis;* 2.75; 38.11), as sustaining (4.47; cf. 7.24; 44.4; 28.16), as preservation or maintenance (6.6), as co-breathing or co-aspiration (6.15), as the beauty of artistic representation (14.31), and finally as the community, symphony, and common breath of all things (*koinonia, symphonia, sympnoia;* 28.16).[60]

For Gregory, God becomes evident in the coherency of the good world order. Because it is God who ensures the enduring existence of things, nature teaches us about his existence (28.6), though Gregory is not intending here to present a proof of God's existence. Indeed, late antiquity had little taste for proving God's existence through rational argument. By contrast, the question of cosmo-dicy, that is, of the relation between the divine order of nature and the disorder of evil, was of central significance. In this context Gregory understands the natural order as *referring* to God rather than *proving* God; that is, it is of referential rather than logically evidential value. Of course, evil can also be discerned in the natural world, and the theologian describes its effects as disorder, as an absence of peace, and as a dissolution of order (6.16). Not surprisingly, he analogously describes the end of the world simply as a perpetual diminution of order leading gradually to complete dissolution, just as the diminution of order and peace in the human body and in society eventually leads to dissolution and death (32.8).

Gregory seems especially inclined to adduce *taxis* (order) as the guaran-

58. Cf. Bergmann 1993c, 465f.

59. Concerning Gregory's understanding of evil in connection with his doctrine of the fall of the angels, see Bergmann 1991.

60. In Stoic teaching, the term *symphonia* refers to the interconnected growing together or fusing together of living beings with the elements and is also used as a term in the theory of sensory perception; cf. Reinhardt 1926, 101-6. In Galen's physiology *sympnoia* refers to the pneuma's living unification of parts; cf. Reinhardt, 55.

tor and principle of unity in the world.[61] One of the basic characteristics of material creatures is that they are sustained by God's *taxis*, whose origin is found in the work of creation itself. In discussing the virtue of moderation in disputes (*Or.* 32), Gregory closely parallels the Old Testament traditions of the divine wisdom *(sophia)* in describing how the divine *taxis* similarly permeates the two-part world of creation.

Here Gregory describes the "order" of the work of creation such that *taxis* is understood in one sense as a characteristic of God and in another as a characteristic attaching to creaturely existence as such. On the one hand he writes that "It was order, then, that assembled the whole," and on the other about "order among the angels; order among the stars . . . order in the elements from which bodies are composed" (32.8). That is, on the one hand, *taxis* is actually the subject of the divine act of creating itself; on the other, it is a constitutive characteristic of what is already created.

Gregory also draws from the creation account in Genesis. In the beginning, when God created the world, his work of seven days also revealed his good order, an order that, as *eutaxia*, human beings should certainly not regard lightly (32.7). At the same time, however, Gregory — apparently aware that a chaotic condition obtained prior to creation according to the account in Genesis — does assume that there was a condition lacking order *before* the definitive "ordering" of the world itself (32.7). Throughout his writings he makes copious references to the "ordered" nature of creation, both as *kosmos* and in its *taxis*. When the angels fell, they brought about a confrontation between evil and that which was created good, and it is that confrontation and the disorder and imbalance it causes that constantly threaten to disrupt and even destroy the good order of creation. In the midst of this very threat, however, Gregory understands creation to be simultaneously characterized by divine *eutaxis* and *diakosmesis*, that is, by *well-ordered governance.*

Gregory understands such order in a twofold fashion in that it represents not only a primal cause in the actual creation work itself, but also the quality of creatures being sustained from the very beginning of time through the present and on to the end of time.[62] Hence, in the unity of the world as creative *eutaxis* and *diakosmesis*, God reveals himself as the unity of time inhering within this temporally changeable life. In describing God's ordering work within the unity of time, Gregory echoes one of Heraclitus's ideas that

---

61. In *Or.* 32.10 Gregory refers to *taxis* as the mother and protectress of all that is. Whereas the *Father* is the principle of unity in the trinitarian being, the *taxis* as the *mother* is the principle of unity in the being of the world.

62. Cf. in this regard the double meaning of *phero* as to bear and to move.

was of fundamental significance for the philosophy of nature in antiquity — the familiar reference to the floating and flowing of nature within the logos — and picks up on the psalmist's reference to the continuity of the law (Ps. 148:6): "[N]ot for a brief period, nor for a single moment or occasion, but from the beginning to the end of time, guided and conducted along the same round, on the one hand fixed in their existence by the Logos, yet in motion thanks to their flux. 'He established them for ever and ever; he fixed their bounds which cannot be passed.' This refers to their fixity, while whatever has or will take place involves their flux" (32.8).

Gregory also adduces the distinctions within the Trinity in describing this sustaining, creative governance of the continuity and interrelatedness of all things. His reference to the ideas of God *(logoi)* that sustain all things (4.47; 7.24) recalls his understanding of how in the beginning the Father "conceived" the world in thought (38.9f.). Gregory proposes that the creation endures as it does because the thoughts of the uncreated inhere *in* the created in some fashion; and the Son, who actualized and shaped the Father's ideas in the beginning, rather than ever abandoning his creation, inheres in all things as the word (30.20).

Picking up on the tradition of the cosmic Christ, the theologian refers to Christ as the redeemer, Lord, creator, and helmsman of all created things (4.78) who also illuminates the entirety of heaven (*Carm.* 1.1.32). And while Christ keeps the cosmos together, the Spirit itself preserves it (*Carm.* 1.1.30). That is, God's Holy Spirit participates in preserving and maintaining creation just as do the Father and Son, and the creative Spirit fills the world with its presence, containing everything, guiding everything — through nature rather than through grace — and ultimately knowing all things (*Or.* 31.29).[63]

It is not just in creation that such order and concord obtain, but also in the interior trinitarian life. In Gregory's view the distinction among the trinitarian hypostases similarly contributes to order in general and to the good order of creation in particular (31.29). It is in this trinitarian unity that Gregory sees the ultimate ground of the unity of creation in the larger sense. The good order characterizing the trinitarian community manifests itself in the good order of creation, and thus as the household of God the world itself is able to enter into ever more intimate community with God. In this sense the creative order of the world is never to be understood as immanent only or exclusively to the world, since it always represents an order maintained by God — which is why references to the "order of creation" in the modern sense would be utterly alien to Gregory, for whom the "order of creation" reveals the Trinity it-

63. Cf. chap. 4, below.

self. Because it is God whom Gregory finds manifestly at work in the ordering of the world, the order of creative acts can never serve to legitimize worldly power.[64]

Gregory's terminology and conceptual forms — taken from antiquity — reflect a concern neither with simple cosmic piety nor with an ethical rationality of the world in the Stoic sense. In a larger sense, Gregory believes that the good unity of the world, generated and grounded in the ever active divine order and providence, also determines the uniquely human task of shaping that very world by confronting the destructive, disruptive powers of evil. In that sense Gregory's doctrine of the world as a "good creation" functions more as part of his soteriology than as part of some evangelized cosmogony. The origin, history, and future of the world are found in God, and the protology, soteriology, and eschatology of the cosmos are all inextricably connected with one another in Gregory's view. Because the origin of the world is found in God's transcendent being, its history and future are also found in the being of the triune God. And because evil originates as a historical process *within* the world itself and includes evil powers, any liberation from evil and any encounter with God must also come about as Christian praxis within the life of this world.

Because Christian cosmology in the early church was concerned with understanding the world as a manifestation of the divine order, the Christians' task was to conduct their lives such that by enhancing the order of the world they also prepared the way for God to be manifest through that order. Gregory's Christian cosmology is quite ill suited as a legitimation of political power of the sort found in Stoic philosophy or in the world-denying ethics of the Gnostics or Plotinus. Gregory's Christian cosmology similarly departs from the kind of "world worship" characterizing cosmic piety in antiquity, since it is not the world in and of itself that Gregory considers sacred, but the world as a transparently divine creation. Understanding the unity of the world as a unity that God perpetually wills also creates theological space in which to engage Christian praxis as the historical shaping of the *new* world through a confrontation with evil forces. By emphasizing the maintenance and preservation of creation in this way, Gregory lays the groundwork for understanding the historical transformation and liberation of life itself as well as for the concrete possibility of a transformation within the ethics of asceticism.

---

64. Cf. Stoic philosophy, which moved from *oikoumene* and *humanitas* to a legitimization of expanded Roman rule over other peoples. Ehrhardt 1959a, 186-94.

The Community of Creation as a
Community of Communication

What we now find is that the theologian associates the idea of community with that of communication and accordingly understands the community of creation itself as a community of communication in which nonhuman creatures communicate not only with each other but also with human beings and with God. "All creation sings the glory of God in wordless strain, for it is through me that God is thanked for all of his works. In this way their hymn becomes our own, since it is from them that I take my song. Now the whole of the animal kingdom is smiling and all our senses are at feast" (*Or.* 44.11). Gregory refers to the language of other living creatures as "praise with wordless voice" and a "silent song of praise" (*Carm.* 1.1.29), distinguishing it thus from language communication among human beings. Here Gregory picks up on the philosophical discussion on whether animals have the capacity for reason,[65] a discussion in which the Stoics maintained that human beings alone possessed reason *(logos)* and animals only had a soul *(psyche)*. The focus was on delineating a boundary between human beings and other creatures based on the capacity for rational language. Although Gregory does not question this boundary, he does develop a concept of "natural communication" in the sense of nonrational language exchange between sensuous creatures.

In developing his concept of natural communication, Gregory points out how moonlight tells wild animals when it is time to hunt, while sunlight tells human beings when it is time to work (*Or.* 28.30). In that sense heaven, sunlight, and sea air all communicate themselves to all things in unrestricted love lacking all envy (4.96). Light pours itself into the air, and air accepts it and takes it up; light thus asperses all things with itself round about human beings, allowing them thus to see (44.3). Forest animals offer themselves to Christians for the hunt (43.7). The ass in the stall in Bethlehem recognized the Lord in the manger (38.17). Angels sing God's praises and guard cities, churches, and other parts of the earth (28.31; 42.9). Hence it is through creation itself that God guides, instructs, and proclaims himself to human beings (38.13; 16.5; 6.14), and in human beings themselves, communication takes place by way of the eyes, the will, the spirit (28.22), the feelings, and the soul (17.1).

What Gregory thus means by the capacity of the physical, material creation for language is this capacity to issue cogent signals, to exchange them, and thus to guide, instruct, and even to proclaim. The question remains con-

65. Cf. Gronau 1914, 106ff.

cerning the relationship between the language bearer and the content sign, between res and *signum*.[66] Gregory responds by pointing out how the entirety of creation is "the great and celebrated sign of God, by which God is heralded in silent proclamation" (6.14). Because creation and the creatures in it reveal God's work, they are of special significance.

From a theological perspective Gregory understands the being of creatures in the cosmos to be a sign and expression of divine action. The world as creation is never merely a world in and of itself; instead, by its very being and history it is an expression of the Creator. Gregory maintains that the entirety of creation seeks to be "proclamations of love and concord, teaching mankind unanimity through their example" (6.15). Unfortunately, what human beings perceive and interpret in the world is not unequivocal. What we actually see, Gregory insists, is not truth but an appearance, a (distorted) image of truth (20.11).[67] Although something does indeed come to expression in the life of creation that genuinely says something about God, it does not express this "something" completely or perfectly. Here Gregory's apophatic epistemological principle comes into play insofar as one is forced to presuppose the rational unfathomability of God's essence while simultaneously trying to say something positive about God's work (28.9).

Applied to the capacity for sensuous language, this means one is forced to presuppose that language is in fact restricted in what it can say about God's essence while simultaneously saying something about God's actions in and with material nature, a situation presupposing that material creatures are indeed capable of communicating something about God's work. Gregory sees nature indeed communicating something about God, and God communicating through nature. In his oration on the hailstorm, Gregory points out how God uses the storm to admonish the powerful to repent; that is, God uses the elements as bearers of language (16.5). In his oration on peace, Gregory understands the elements as language bearers of divine actions announcing peace or violence (6.16). Is Gregory thus advocating a doctrine of natural language?

A "natural language" or "language of nature" in this sense implies that the world as cosmos and creation is construed as a nexus of language. A "nexus of language" does not necessarily assume the use of letters, sentences, and writing, but rather the exchange of information and meaning by signs. The philosophy of nature in antiquity entertained the idea of the cosmos as a nexus of language long before the time of Gregory, conceiving of the four elements as the "basic

---

66. On the relationship between semantics and ontology for the Stoics, see Forschner 1981, 76-84.

67. Cf. Augustine's distinction between res and *signum;* see A. Holl 1963, 35f.

letters of nature" whose constant rearrangement results in ever new messages being "written" into matter. Even the etymology of the term *(stoicheia)* suggests that this is how the concept was understood.[68] In his turn, Gregory now provides a theological grounding for the concept as it was understood in the philosophy of nature, suggesting that the triune God does indeed communicate something about himself to creatures through the language of nature.

Through its very existence before us, corporeal nature posits signs. The master craftsman can be recognized in his work (43.11). On the other hand, God also communicates actively through the language of nature in that the cosmos itself proclaims his greatness (44.3), and it is through signs and changes that nature guides and instructs human beings themselves (38.13; 16.5). In the same context, however, Gregory explicitly rejects any possibility of exclusively *spiritual* or *intellectual* communication between human beings and God. Every path that leads to God of necessity takes us through the material, physical order of things: "[A]s it is impossible for the eye to draw near to visible objects apart from the intervening air and light, or for a fish to glide about outside of the waters, so it is quite impracticable for those who are in the body to be conversant with objects of pure thought apart altogether from bodily objects" (28.12).

Gregory maintains that all creation sings the praises of the Creator: angels, matter, human beings. Conversely, just as all creation sings God's praises, so also does all creation proclaim him (*Carm.* 1.1.29). And though creation may groan and suffer, it still rejoices and exults with the joyous children of God (*Or.* 4.15). Both earthly and heavenly powers participate in this festival of joy (38.17), such that this great cosmic doxology consists of human beings, nonhuman creatures, and spiritual and material elements all communicating with one another and with the Creator (28.31).

The communication taking place *within* human beings themselves between the soul and the body simultaneously acquires a universal dimension for the Cappadocian insofar as it is the *soul* that connects human beings with the spiritual world and the *body* that connects them with the material world (28.12). The human eye establishes a connection with the world of the senses while the human spirit or mind communicates with the spiritual world (28.22). This vision then enables them to move *through* the world of the senses toward spiritual realities (28.13), and ultimately through the visible on to God (28.16).

In Gregory's understanding, the eternal song of praise the angelic chorus sings as it circles around God can be heard not only by God, but also by corporeal living beings, and it is with silent voices — voices *without* normal

68. See further Bergmann 1993a.

language — that the material order then joins in this song of praise (44.12). Similarly, when the four elements communicate with one another through their very interplay (28.27; 28.28; 38.17; 33.9; 32.8; 14.25; 4.96), they not only bring about a communicative exchange between themselves, but also — through the very nature of that exchange — communicate with the human social order as well as with the trinitarian community of God. When society communicates in the kind of exchange that constitutes peaceful relations, the elements of the "letters of nature" are also participating (6.14), and whenever God wishes to communicate a sign to human beings, the elements mediate it by offering something of their own order (6.16).

In one sense Gregory understands the language nexus of creation as emerging on four different levels of "language acts":[69]

1. Within human beings themselves, the body, soul, and spirit or mind communicate.
2. Human beings communicate with the spiritual-corporeal creation as well as with fellow human beings and fellow creatures.
3. Angels and corporeal creatures communicate with one another.
4. God and creation communicate with one another, with God communicating in multifarious ways with angels, bodies, human beings, and the whole of the world.

All four levels are constantly connected with one another, and on all four the triune God becomes manifest as Creator and Redeemer (30.20; 31.29).

In summary, we see that Gregory understands the world as a communicative cosmos, more specifically as a divinely well ordered language nexus through whose sensuous and rational language creatures praise their Creator and in which God also communicates with his world. It is precisely in the communication among creatures of the world that God comes to expression in language.

The Correspondence between the God of Community and the Community of Creation

How does Gregory's understanding of God correspond to his understanding of the world? How does the Cappadocian understand the relationship between the community inhering within the essence and work of the triune God and that inhering within creation itself?

---

69. I here expand on J. L. Austin's notion of the speech-act.

The Conditions of Correspondence

In this section we have seen how Gregory's understanding of sociality comes to bear not only in his understanding of God, but also in his understanding of the world. Gregory's apophatic epistemological premise, however, prevents him from establishing any analogy between the nature of the world and that of God, that is, an *analogia entis*, or analogy of being. This principle prohibits both an *analogia entis* that applies elements of our understanding of the world to God's being and an *analogia Dei*, which applies elements of our understanding of God to the world's being. Our human cognition has only limited access to the nature of the world and of God. The term "analogy" here is actually referring to Gregory's *analogia oeconomiae*, according to which the "economy of the world" allows us to say something about God's work, while experiences and interpretations of the trinitarian economy allow us to say something about the economy of the world.[70]

The concept of "analogy" as such presupposes first a boundary distinguishing two analogues from one another.[71] The analogous relation then implies that despite this distinction, the one is *like* the other. Gregory draws seven such boundaries in his cosmology:

1. between created and uncreated nature, that is, between God and world;
2. between the spiritual and the material;
3. between divine and human nature (in Christ);
4. between the sensory and the rational (in human beings);
5. between human beings and nonrational living beings;
6. between human beings and noncorporeal living beings (angels); and
7. between all creatures and the Creator, though *not* limiting the Creator; this is the most extreme, outermost boundary around the cosmic All that separates all creatures from the Creator.

70. This expression is not found in Gregory's writings. By "economy of the world" is meant what humans can know of the order of nature (the nature of the world), its Being (*on*) in Gregory's terms.

71. The concept of analogy used here lies within a semantic conception of the doctrine of analogy. For Gregory, following Aristotle, such a semantic conception of analogy was a self-evident presupposition. My epistemologically grounded principle of analogy differs freely from his, however. On the history of the concept of analogy, see Track 1978, 630-38, and Jüngel 1964. For the contemporary theological discussion, see Track, 639-48; Pannenberg 1988, 344f.; Tracy 1981, 408-13; and Link 1982, 135-49.

Gregory finds analogous relations thoroughly permeating all these bound-aries. On the one hand, he understands all these different analogues as being ultimately connected by a shared sameness; on the other, he does offer differ-ent interpretations of the actual predicated *content*.[72]

Whereas an *analogous* relationship articulates the relationship of one entity *with* or *alongside* another, a *participatory* relationship articulates how the one is contained *within* the other in a way that does *not* however extin-guish or sublate the one through such containment in another. Gregory pos-its such a relationship:

1. between human beings and the world,
2. between the triune God and all creatures,
3. between Christ and the nature of the cosmos,
4. between the Holy Spirit and human beings and the world, and
5. between God and time and space.

Because human beings are themselves (as discussed above) a world in minia-ture, a microcosm, the world in the larger sense is represented in them. More-over, God's Word and Spirit are in all things. Christ as the logos is in all things (*Or.* 30.20). God's Spirit indwells human beings (31.27) *and* maintains all things without itself being contained (31.29). In the Spirit, God fills the cos-mos without being restricted by it (31.29), encompassing all rational beings at myriad places without being spatially restricted. God's Spirit both initiates *and* consummates all things. God's trinitarian community is neither sepa-rated nor divided by time (31.31). His Spirit "contains" but is not "contained" (31.29).

The Conceptual Figure of Correspondence: Mediation/ Communication — Turning Toward/Away — Social Movement

Recalling that Gregory understands community to be a situation in which the being of the one is *alongside, with, in,* and *around* the other, how then do the community of God and that of creation correspond? What does Gregory say about the liberation of creation in its sociality through the God of commu-nity? We can describe his viewpoint in a conceptual figure with three stages.

---

72. Gregory follows Plato in understanding the principle of analogy as a cosmological structuring principle setting forth all things. On Plato's doctrine of analogy, see Track 1978, 631f.

1. From within the interior of his own communality God posits the beginning of the world. Through human beings the world is connected with itself, and through the specifically human iconic relationship ("in the image"), it is also connected with God. From within the interior perception of his triunity, God communicates himself in community to his work. I call this first stage *creatively social mediation or communication*.

2. As the work of continuity of the God of community, the world itself represents a *community* in Gregory's view. Within Gregory's analogical and participatory thinking, God moves himself and the world by conceptualizing, creatively liberating, and ultimately also by consummating. I call this second stage the *trinitarian movement of the social cosmos*.

Because Gregory's God of community reveals himself in the world, the world itself must be oriented toward or away from him in some way. Angels circle about him or break out of his ring. Human beings similarly move to and fro and are capable — through their senses and reason — of turning toward or away from God. In its own synthetic community corporeal nature praises God and can be raised up or made to fall down by the Spirit and by human beings. Throughout its myriad interconnected parts the community of creation thus either participates in various ways in the trinitarian movement *or* seeks to escape it. I call the trinitarian movement the *turn of the creation community toward or away*.

3. The third stage encompasses the community's growth toward consummation. Whenever humanity itself corresponds to or is commensurate with its trinitarian image or likeness of community, it experiences what it means to exist with or alongside God, a condition Gregory describes as deification — becoming divine. Whenever human senses and reason cooperate peacefully, human beings are serving the social God. Whenever the elements of nature are balanced in a community of cosmic peace and justice, they appropriately reflect God's light and work. Whenever the angels praise God and fulfill their earthly tasks in an eternally uniform movement, they are appropriately around and with God. Whenever human beings correctly carry out their appointed function in the creation community as part of both the angelic and corporeal community as well as in their capacity as the *image* of the divine community, they are contributing appropriately — together with the Son and Spirit — to the history of liberation. I call this third stage the *liberation of the nature of the world as a social movement of God and the world*.

Hence Gregory's cosmology follows a clear temporal sequence. The social God takes initiative in the world. The social world responds by turning either toward or away. If the world turns *toward* God, what follows is the liberation of the creation community by the God of community. Liberation from evil leads to new growth and, ultimately, to completion and consummation.

2. Movement

In his twentieth oration Gregory touches on a problem of particular interest to him, that of movement. Instead of reflecting excessively on the procreation of the Son and the going forth of the Spirit, he examines the connection between soul and body. "How are you dust and an image of God? What is it that makes you move or what that is set in motion? How can the same thing both move and be moved? . . . What is the circuit of the sky? What is the movement of the stars or their order or measurements or conjunction or distance?" (*Or.* 20.11). Gregory's understanding of the phenomenon of movement is of significance not only for the movement of the soul, body, and stars, but also for his trinitarian understanding of God and the world.

It is here, in Gregory's theological reflection on the problem of movement, that his real creative originality emerges. By engaging the notion of movement, Gregory is able to counter Aristotle's famous "unmoved Mover." He does this with a theological system that, by renewing and lending a trinitarian understanding to Plato's idea of the self-movement of the world soul, is able to overcome the presuppositions not only of Aristotle but also of the father of his tradition, Origen.

In this section we examine Gregory's creative contribution with regard to three points:

1. Gregory was the first theologian to understand the idea of movement as a divine attribute; he goes on to develop an understanding of a Creator who is characterized by threefold or triune movement.[73]

2. Instead of juxtaposing the moving changeability of creation negatively over against the Creator, Gregory maintains that precisely that changeability is ontologically positively grounded in God; as a result, Gregory can maintain that knowledge of the changeability of the world can lead to knowledge of the unchangeable God.

3. Because Gregory understands the origin and nature of evil as a spiritual phenomenon within his doctrine of angels and ethically qualifies the idea of movement with regard to *both* humankind *and* the world of the spirit,

---

73. See the further theological discussion of movement in God, in Basil, *Against Eunomius* 2.32, and Dionysius, *Divine Names* 4.14; 9.9.

he is also in a position to articulate his understanding of redemption with the aid of the concept of movement and the associated notions of possibility, change of direction, and the idea of approach. The *source* of redemption is God's Holy Spirit, which perpetually moves forth from within itself and in which both human beings and the world are able to approach closer to God's own being.

Gregory's Development of the Idea of Movement

Gregory held that movement applies to both the spiritual and the corporeal realm, and that both aspects are to be considered in any ontological discussion of movement. He also found the question still unresolved regarding how unity or continuity is maintained despite movement through a variety of different conditions. What is the problem posed by the motion and movements of spiritual and sensuous life? Is movement through a variety of conditions necessarily a sign of evil and sin? Or is it to be perceived as good movement, and as such a gift from the Creator? Indeed, are *all* movements of spiritual creatures to be assessed as either good or bad? The most important question, however, is whether God is to be understood as merely the origin of movement without himself being in motion (as Aristotle assumed), or whether movement can also be ascribed to God's being. What is then the correspondence between movement in God's being and in the being of creation?

One question remained open concerning the way movement within temporal, sensuous, and spiritual life could maintain its continuity and unity despite being subjected to change. In the third and fourth centuries the question concerning the relationship between truth and movement changed to that regarding the relationship between movement and good and evil; this question, too, remained unresolved. As we will see, Gregory in his own turn addresses this question by now understanding movement in connection with the trinitarian idea of God.

I will now examine the seven different *contexts* in which Gregory himself develops an understanding of movement. Starting in each instance with a key passage from Gregory's writings, I will also draw on additional passages as well as on the previous history of the concept in analyzing his understanding of movement.

Inner-Trinitarian Movement

Gregory of Nazianzus was the first theologian to incorporate the quality of movement as a key element into his understanding of God.[74] Just how significant his contribution was can be seen in the adoption of his understanding of movement by Maximus the Confessor, who provides commentary on Gregory's position in two different instances and ultimately incorporates this idea into his own theology and cosmology as a kind of universal law.[75] Gregory's key statement is the following:

> But monarchy is that which we hold in honor. It is, however, a monarchy that is not limited to one person, for it is possible for unity if at variance with itself to come into a condition of plurality; but one that is made of an equality of nature, and a union of mind, and an identity of motion, and a convergence of its elements into unity — a thing which is impossible to the created nature — so that though numerically distinct there is no severance of essence. Therefore unity, having from all eternity arrived by motion at duality, found its rest in trinity. (*Or.* 29.2)

Gregory's concern is to articulate an understanding of God's sole dominion, unity, and monarchy in a fashion that overcomes the antinomies associated with a God whose ultimate essential characteristic is unity.

Gregory's understanding of unity here — a unity that can divide itself against itself and pass into multiplicity — derives from Plotinus, who understood the multiplicity of reality as emerging from the being whose ultimate characteristic was in fact unity, that is, the One. Gregory counters this understanding of unity with his thesis of the quality of movement as the ultimate consummation of the divine essence. The unity of the divine nature is characterized by precisely this perfect concurrence of will and movement among the three hypostases. The consummation of this divine unity manifests itself *not* in the unity of person, however, but rather precisely in the perfect movement constituting unity in the first place.

The problem is to articulate adequately the constitutive nature of this concurrence of the community of the three hypostases without also presupposing that the point of departure involves three discrete points. In addressing this problem Gregory develops the idea of movement as a *characteristic* of the essence of God's unity. The Father's procreation of the Son and the going

---

74. Scholarship has hitherto largely overlooked this point.

75. Maximus Confessor 1860-65, *Ambiguorum liber*, 91:1260B, and his second letter to Thomas. See also Thunberg 1985, 36.

forth of the Spirit from the Father are both expressions of one and the same movement taking place within the divine nature. It is thus movement itself that characterizes the divine unity *as* unity. "Unity" thus refers to the uncreated one nature of God whose perfection comes to expression precisely in the inner-trinitarian movement constituting the one dominion.

One can see how radically the idea of inner-trinitarian movement functions within Gregory's understanding of God by juxtaposing it not only with Plotinus's panentheistic monism of the One, but also with the Aristotelian understanding of God as the eternally unmoved ground of being. Aristotle's thesis of the unmoved mover constituted a kind of logical foundation for his cosmological explanations of changeability and motion, a kind of "metaphysical guarantee."[76] Similarly, Plotinus's thesis of the highest One functioned as the ultimate, ungrounded assumption necessary to explain both evil and multiplicity. What Gregory now does is *reverse* what Aristotle and Plotinus were actually trying to explain. That is, the problem is now no longer the appearance or phenomenon of movement as such. What happens is that the characteristic of movement attaching to uncreated nature — nature remaining perpetually self-identical within the Trinity unaffected by time and space — functions as the ground for explaining created being *amid* change and time. Movement and time are no longer necessarily inextricably connected. Gregory now differentiates God's eternal movement — from which time first emerges — from movement *within* time. God's *uncreated* movement is differentiated from *created* movement insofar as the divine movement moves from the origin through transition and back again to the origin, circumscribing thus the perfect circular movement. In contrast to the movement of creation, that of the Creator is characterized by *synesis,* the capacity for guiding the goal back to the beginning and for perfectly connecting the points of movement with one another.

This position overcomes Aristotelian ontology and its fundamental antithesis between motion and repose. In Gregory's ontology the atemporal, perfect trinitarian movement represents the antithesis to movement within created nature. Compared to creation, God's own being "stand[s] firm and [is] not moved" (*Or.* 7.19) in the sense not of an unmoved Mover, but of a God who is a "movement of self-contemplation" (38.9). In the sense of purely spatial change, God is wholly unchangeable and does not go out of himself to become multiplicity (28.9). One might think of God "being in motion" rather than existence in Aristotelian terms.

Gregory also employs the notion of movement in articulating the

76. Blumenberg 1989, 2:523.

equality of Spirit and Son within the Godhead, deriving both Son and Spirit from a common cause within divine nature. "The oneness of God would, in my view, be maintained if both Son and Spirit are causally related to him alone without being merged or fused into him and if they all share one and the same divine movement and purpose, if I may so phrase it, and are identical in essence" (20.7). Whereas Origen was still more wedded to a monistic understanding of God that tended to associate the Trinity more with the idea of subordination, Gregory articulates his understanding of the equality obtaining between the three divine hypostases by adducing the idea of perfect common movement within the Trinity itself.

In Gregory's understanding, inner-trinitarian movement represents relational movement insofar as the procreation of the Son constitutes a common movement for both Father and Son, just as the going forth of the Spirit represents a common movement for the Father and the Spirit. The Son lets himself be begotten just as the Spirit lets itself be brought forth, and these two — the Son and Spirit — are in their own turn related through the common Father of the perfect community of movement and will. In this sense the inner-trinitarian movement is a movement common to all three separate hypostases,[77] with trinity and unity coming together or coinciding in shared, relational movement within God.

Gregory also posits an unequivocal relationship between the creation of spiritual, corporeal, and human nature and this trinitarian community of movement. Because "this movement of self-contemplation alone could not satisfy Goodness, but Good must be poured out and go forth beyond Itself to multiply the objects of Its beneficence," God thus conceives, creates, and consummates creation in the Father, Son, and Spirit (38.9). By drawing on the idea of movement, Gregory is thus able to develop the analogy between Creator and creation *without* thereby eliminating the boundary between the two.

Movement in the Economy of the Holy Spirit

The doctrine of the Holy Spirit posits the self-movement of the Holy Spirit as a characteristic of uncreated movement in contradistinction to movement within created nature and its creatures.

In his oration at Pentecost regarding the Holy Spirit, Gregory enumer-

---

77. Although aware of its metaphorical inadequacy, Gregory expresses this idea in the metaphor of the glittering ray of sunlight, "flashing upon a wall and trembling with the movement of the moisture which the beam has taken up" (*Or.* 31.32).

ates a whole series of characteristics and capabilities attributable to the Holy Spirit. "The Holy Spirit, then, always existed, and exists, and always will exist . . . invisible, eternal, incomprehensible, unchangeable, without quality, without quantity, without form, impalpable, self-moving *(autokineton)*, eternally moving, with free-will, self-powerful, All-powerful" (41.9).[78]

Gregory's goal here is doubtless to articulate persuasively the full divinity of the Spirit within the trinitarian Godhead. In this context he maintains that the movements of the Spirit and the Son are common since both are related to the Father. What Gregory now emphasizes, however, is that the Spirit is capable of self-movement and of eternal movement or movement independent of time. He thus emphasizes first the equality of the Spirit within the Godhead insofar as it participates in the inner-trinitarian movement, and second the distinction between uncreated and created movement. This means that the Holy Spirit belongs on the side of the Creator and is *not* to be understood as some intermediary being between creation and Creator. Movement within creation is dependent on time, something also applying to spiritual creatures insofar as they do, after all, have a beginning in time even though they are not bound by time. By contrast, the movement of the Holy Spirit is perpetual, eternal, without beginning or end, and independent of time and space. Whereas the movement of all creatures within creation is relational, taking place within mutual relationships, that of the Spirit alone constitutes self-movement or completely free movement. Because the power, being, and movement of the trinitarian Spirit are uncreated, they can be defined only on the basis of the Spirit itself, something applying exclusively to divine being, not to the being of creation.

By defining the movement of the Spirit as timeless, free self-movement and thus as divine, Gregory is now in a position to understand the economy of the Spirit within creation from the perspective of movement. The Holy Spirit, moving from within itself, moves through the boundary between creation and Creator. This boundary between the uncreated and the created is of course always open to the Creator; it applies only to creation, never to the Creator, who is efficaciously present in creation in free movement within the Spirit, in which context Gregory is keen on maintaining the distinction between what the Spirit effects within its own movement and movement within creation itself.

In section 6 of his fifth theological oration, Gregory is concerned with

---

78. With the exception of unchangeable, free-will, self-powerful, and omnipotent (Wisd. of Sol. 7:23 LXX; 2 Cor. 3:17), these characteristics represent Gregory's own predication of the Spirit rather than mere biblical allusions.

maintaining the full divinity of the hypostasis of the Spirit against those who would understand it merely as a force that causes movement. "If he is an activity *(energeia),* he will be effected, but will not effect and will cease to exist as soon as he has been effected, for this is the nature of an activity. How is it, then, that he acts and says such and such things . . . and has all the qualities which belong clearly to one that moves, and not to movement?" (31.6). It is precisely the capacity for self-movement that distinguishes God's Spirit from energy as such insofar as energy is understood as following upon an efficient cause, whereas the Holy Spirit is its own efficient cause even without being in a state of repose. Unlike energy, God's Spirit brings about its own movement, a thesis now raising the question regarding just *how* the Spirit acts efficaciously, if this indeed be the case. Because force or power cannot utter words or choose apostles or be sad or mad, Gregory insists that the being of the Spirit must be understood as endowed with movement. This notion of self-movement also enables Gregory to speak about the Spirit as the agent of human movement or as the agent bestowing upon angels their lethargic movement — disinclination — toward evil (41.11). The Spirit fulfills, guides, sanctifies, deifies, consummates, creates, brings about, bestows life, and indeed is itself light and life (31.29). It is in creation itself that Gregory discerns the economy of the holy, self-moving Spirit as movement, and — again — he does so *without* identifying created movement with the self-moving Uncreated.

The Movement of Creatures and the Creator

Gregory's attribution of movement to God's being raises the question of how God's movement is related to that of creation. The ancient understanding of the world, of course, viewed movement as one of the fundamental characteristics of nature and life, and the Cappadocian not surprisingly adopts this presupposition from the thinking prevalent in his age. One side of the dialectic of movement was that movement constituted the changeability of all living things within time. As part of the understanding of the being of creation in late antiquity, this notion was naturally also part of the early church's understanding of the world. Gregory now develops this idea of movement theologically, and in the process articulates the particular relationship between the self-moved Creator and the motion of creation itself.

In his second theological oration, the Cappadocian begins with the Old Testament idea that God and his Spirit fill and permeate the entire cosmos (Jer. 23:24; Wisd. of Sol. 1:7). He then formulates the problem as follows: "And how shall we preserve the truth that God pervades all things and fills all . . . if God partly contains and partly is contained? For either he will occupy an empty universe . . . or else he will be a body contained in other bodies, which is impossible" (*Or.* 28.8). Gregory's reading of scripture thus prompts him to assume that the Creator permeates creation neither as spatial nor as corporeal movement in the sense of one "body contained in other bodies." His position here, however, does not really solve the problem, since his contemporaries accommodated the notion of noncorporeal movement as the cause of all visible movement in the notion of the "fifth element" (ether or quintessence) that, since Aristotle and the Stoic tradition, had been understood as the spiritual element of the ether endowed with divine features. "But if we are to assert that [God] is immaterial (as, for example, that fifth element which some have imagined), and that he is carried around in circular motion . . ." (28.8). Although Gregory avoids addressing the issue in any substantive fashion here because he is more concerned with maintaining the incorporeality of God, elsewhere he clearly argues against the Aristotelian assumption of a "fifth element."[79]

In the present context, it suffices to demonstrate the contradictory nature of admixing the movement of the Creator with that of creation. One simply cannot attribute to God a place, "or he will be enfolded in them [other bodies], and contrasted with them." Gregory considers it an affront to God, "an insult involved in making the creator subject to the same movement as the creatures, and him that carries all (if they will allow even this) one with those whom he carries." Ascribing corporeal movement to the Creator unavoidably generates insuperable contradictions: "What is the force that moves your fifth element, and what is it that moves all things, and what moves that, and what is the force that moves that? And so on ad infinitum. And how can he [God] help being altogether contained in space if he be subject to motion?" Gregory is absolutely determined to avoid identifying God's being-in-motion with the movement of creation. The idea that God permeates the world is emphatically *not* to be understood as spatial movement, since the Creator of the boundaries of the created is himself limited by no boundaries. As the characteristic of being borne or sustained within time, movement is for Gregory certainly attributable to the created. As Creator, however, God is precisely the one who sustains and supports movement — a condition not identical with being sustained. Although spiritual creatures and their movements are not subject to the limitations of the embodiment the way corporeal movement is, Gregory disallows the conclusion that God himself possesses

79. Cf. Bergmann 1993a.

something resembling the body of an angel (28.8), since the Cappadocian considers angels, too, to be part of creation. Saying that God's movement is like that of spiritual creatures renders meaningless any statements regarding the Lord whom angels serve, since those angels move about in a circle around the Creator.

Gregory's distinction between the movement of the uncreated and that of creatures within creation does not mean, however, that the two are utterly separated. Quite the contrary, his whole point is to speak precisely about God as the one who sustains all movement of the created and as its ground and initiator. It is precisely this God — whose own being is in motion and whose Spirit alone possesses the capacity for free self-movement — who grounds all movements within creation and guarantees their enduring continuity within the changes associated with time. Here the theologian is also clearly delimiting his understanding of movement within creation faith over against any sort of astrological determinism of movement (7.7).

Gregory resists identifying the movements of the celestial bodies with the divine being itself. Because God as the first cause is preceded by nothing, there is also nothing that might set God in motion (31.33). As its initiator, God alone knows the fashion in which the All was initially set into motion, and God alone possesses the power to alter it (16.5).

In Gregory's view human life is characterized by change. Neither poverty nor wealth, possessions nor foreign rule, present nor future is stable, though this situation does indeed attest God's wisdom. Through this very instability, God guides human beings toward acknowledging the limitations of their own being, on the one hand, and God's enduring, stable efficacy, on the other. In this sense, as a guide toward self-knowledge and knowledge of God, the very changeability and instability of creation is to be viewed as something good.[80]

Human Movement

Gregory's anthropology and particularly his psychology address yet another context in which movement acquires significance. In this context he focuses particularly on the union of mortal and immortal elements in human nature, on the changeable nature of human life within time, on the production of tones by the voice (28.22), on the movement of the eyes in connection with their surroundings, on the movement of the will, and on the movement of thoughts in the mind.

80. Contra Althaus 1972, 90f.

One of the fundamental questions of human nature for Gregory is the union of the corporeal and the spiritual within human beings; he uses the idea of movement to express what is specifically human: "how it is that I flow downward and yet am borne upward" (28.22).[81] Whereas the Cappadocian understands the corporeal side of human nature to be subject to the flow of change within time, and as such to be constantly threatened by dissolution, he believes that the spiritual side is maintained and sustained through time from above, that is, by God.

Just as the human will is in motion and ultimately can be understood only as movement (*Carm.* 1.1.34.37), so also the eye, which is moved by the will and through that very movement is connected with the visible objects of its surroundings. Here Gregory finds an analogy between the eye and the spirit insofar as just as the eye connects with the visible, so also does the spirit *(nous)* connect with ideas (*Or.* 28.22; 32.27). Gregory also attributes an important function to movement in his understanding of the human spirit, the human nous, asking, "And how do you conceive of a mind? Is it not that which is inherent in some person not itself, and are not its movements thoughts?" (28.13). As with our thoughts, so he also understands the emotions as being in motion (32.27).

Angelic Movement toward Good and Evil

The idea of movement comes to particularly vivid expression in Gregory's doctrine of angels. The Cappadocian responds to the question about the relationship between angels and God's goodness by referring to the two different movements characterizing angelic service. First, they move around God in a circle of peace; second, they serve in preserving and maintaining certain parts of creation. He responds to the question concerning the origin and nature of evil by referring to the form of movement characterizing the relationship between God and the originally good angel of light. It is the *direction* of movement, prompted by envy and arrogance, that establishes an inappropriate relationship with God and brings about evil, which in and of itself has no being as such.

The angels dwell in intimate proximity to the Godhead, were created by God, and are always round about him.[82] As the first created beings, they are

---

81. Cf. in this regard Plato, *Timaeus* 90A, who describes human beings as plants rooted in heaven rather than in earth.

82. Wyss 1983, 831; cf. Norris 1991, 118.

always around God, directing their movements toward the goodness of the Godhead (38.9) and engaging in a perpetual choral dance around God, the first cause (28.31). Because the angels are so close to God, who is himself harmony and concord, they have no inclination to rebel or quarrel (6.12).

Nothing characterizes God more than the unity of nature and the internal peace obtaining among the hypostases. It is this very peace that now also characterizes the spiritual creatures of the angels, who relate to one another and to God in peace. And because God allows them to participate in that peace, it flows over to the entirety of creation as well (22.14).[83] As a result, the angels are able to live in a community virtually as peaceful as that of the Trinity itself. Gregory does not believe their hasty traversal of the entire universe (28.31) contradicts their intimate proximity to God. Because the existence of the material world — like that of the spiritual world — depends on the triune God, Gregory does not believe it can be conceived as somehow "removed" or "distant" from God. Hence, even within material creation, which is "even more" different from God than the spiritual, those spiritual creatures who are part of God's immediate household maintain their intimate relationship with the triune God.

The Cappadocian believes that the task of the created spiritual creatures is to reveal divine goodness. They themselves have a part in God's beneficent acts by participating in the initial divine work of creation and in the history of the world. As the highest essence and highest being, God is for Gregory the primal ground of peace and order, which in their own turn are intimately related within the work of creation. Indeed, opposition to them can only lead to chaos and separation (32.8). It is Gregory's conviction that by properly shaping and directing their lives, human beings can participate in the good, spiritual being of angels. Just as angels are filled with the peace and unity of God because of their intimate proximity to God, so also can human beings participate in God's peace together with them (22.14).

One burning issue in late antiquity was the question of the origin and nature of *evil*. In examining Gregory's response to this question as a Christian theologian, we can start with an unresolved question the Cappadocian inherited from Origen, namely, why the angel of light is capable of moving toward evil in the first place.

Gregory believes that as beings that God created good, the angels live in enviable community and harmony and without any divisions (*Carm.* 1.1.7.1). As created beings, however, they are also subject to the change inherently

---

83. Gregory does not, however, mention an angel of peace of the sort familiar to Basil (*Commentarius in Jes* 1/16, 260, cited by Michl) and many other traditions. Cf. Michl 1962, 138.

characterizing creaturely existence. Unlike human beings, however, who can quickly change and incline toward evil, angels change in a different way. Although as spiritual beings in intimate proximity to the true, unchangeable being of the Godhead they normally resist change, they are nonetheless subject to the same change characterizing all creaturely existence (1.1.7.45-55; 1.1.7.49b).

On the other hand, in Gregory's understanding the angels are capable not only of change, but also of *movement,* albeit movement inclined toward the good and extremely resistant to any inclination toward evil (*Or.* 38.9). Because of their proximity to God, the angels are also characterized by sinlessness (40.7), albeit not by absolute sinlessness, since such is attributable only to God (16.15).

According to Gregory, in the beginning God created the world of good, imperishable powers without sin. Lucifer, however, the angel of light, rebelled against God and fled, also leading away into darkness the powers subordinated to him (6.13; 38.9; cf. 2 Thess. 2:4; Isa. 14:12ff.). Although Gregory initially insists that spiritual creatures are incapable of moving toward evil (*Or.* 38.9), he revises this to say that they are not absolutely excluded from moving toward evil but that such movement is "difficult" (38.9).

Gregory maintains that it was Satan's arrogance or hubris (38.9) that led him astray and his lust for God's throne above the clouds that made him rebel against God (6.13; cf. Isa. 14:14). The theologian proposes that this angel's rebellion consisted of his lusting after God's unique position, breaking out of the perpetual circular movement around God and moving toward the Uncreated himself, thus attempting to break through the boundary between the created and uncreated and in so doing also violating and sundering the model of peace and goodness characterizing movement within creation. Ultimately, of course, this movement aims at the unattainable, namely, at usurping God's position. God's subsequent judgment is that the angel must leave the angelic circle of light and peace. Movement *toward* God is transformed into flight *from* God, inevitably resulting in evil and establishing a new model of movement within creation. In this schema Gregory thus finds the cause of this new, evil model of movement not in God, but in the fallen angel. That angel of light, instead of being intimately close to God, is now at an enormous distance from God, on earth, where he tries to hide from God's light, "concealing himself, to my way of thinking, in the murk of faction" among the faithful (*Or.* 6.13).

Because he arrogantly lusted after the throne of the Creator himself, the angel of light loses the opportunity to dwell in transfigured proximity to God and flees into the regions of darkness. Because the light of the angels reflects the divine light, and this fallen angel is now cut off from that source of light, he himself becomes darkness. In fleeing the light, he takes his subordinates with him, and yet insofar as he struggles within himself, as Gregory suggests, he has not lost all his angelic qualities. He remains imperishable, spiritual, and invisible as before; only his position and the form of his movement within creation have changed. As such, he and his subordinates introduce evil into creation.

In these explications, however, Gregory does not really answer the question concerning *what* evil is. The substance of evil is not really the essence of the spiritually dark angel, nor is it merely the absence of the divine light. The only thing his doctrine of the fall of the angel of light says is that the root of evil is the arrogant desire to usurp God's position and the resulting movement toward God's throne. Such arrogance ultimately ends in flight from God, and this root of evil now generates movement that in its own turn introduces new evil into God's good creation. Yet the angel of light does ultimately remain a good being of light; it is his removal from God's light and his distorted movement — movement in the wrong direction — that generates evil ever anew. Although the angel's *function* has become destructive, his *nature* remains anchored in God's good creation, and this distinction between the function and nature of the fallen angel will be of considerable significance for Gregory's theological understanding of liberation from sin.

In Gregory's understanding, evil originated at the beginning of creation when the fallen angels fled before God and became powers hostile to everything God had created good. Human beings, connected as they are with both the corporeal *and* the spiritual, are naturally drawn into the actions of these fallen powers and are constantly faced with deciding between them and God. Hence the theologian finds that the struggle against evil and sin is to be directed not against the wounded corporeal world, but against the actions undertaken by these spiritual powers within creation. The Cappadocian emphasizes, however, that in this struggle human beings and the church are not standing alone; they are allied with the Creator's hosts of good angels and with the Trinity itself (6.12; 6.22; 22.14).

Human Moral Movement

One of the fundamental precepts of Cappadocian anthropology is that human beings, composed of both body and spirit and created in the image of God, are always in motion. In his "creation history," Gregory writes that human being is "a living creature trained here, and then moved elsewhere; and, to complete the mystery, deified by its inclination to God" (38.11). From the moment of their creation, human beings are characterized by the possibility of free movement. On earth they move with the guidance of their Creator from one place to another. Being human means being able to incline toward God, turn to God, and direct one's movements toward the Creator.

Ethically Gregory ascribes a moral quality to human movement (40.44). When human movement is in the appropriate relationship with and directed toward the Creator, it is good; if it flees God, it brings about evil just as the movement of the fallen angels does. Because movement in the sense of qualitative change is not only negative but can also mean a change for the better, human movement acquires a moral dimension in that change moves a person either toward or away from the good.

At this point the theologian is careful not to construe this moral quality dualistically to mean that movement swings to and fro *exclusively* between the two poles of good or evil. His alternative is rather that human movement takes a person either toward or away from God's goodness, its ultimate goal being not repose but rather God. Moreover, this entire moral movement in the sense of an orientation toward God and a transformation for the good proceeds as an act of cooperation between human beings and the Holy Spirit. Gregory understands the notion of "re-versal," "con-version," or "turning around" in this sense as a change of movement and direction. Because human beings are indeed capable of moving and orienting their lives toward their Creator, they should *constantly* be striving forward, *constantly* "turning" toward God and examining and correcting their goals and in community with God's Holy Spirit constantly reorienting themselves and their lives toward the Creator.

Movement in Redemptive History

The idea of movement also plays an important role in Gregory's understanding of the redemptive history of the world and humanity. On his view the history of creation is itself a transition in the sense of a qualitative change of direction through history in four stages that are then interpreted as three different modes of revelation of the triune God. The four stages into which Gregory divides the history of creation are idolatry, devotion to the law, the gospel, and the future (31.25). The history of the entire age moves through these four stages by way of three transitions, with the transition from the third (gospel) to the fourth (future) being distinguished from the previous two. Unlike the previous transitions, however, the final one — which is still outstanding — will not be subject to movement.

It is extremely important to the theologian that the *nature* of these transitions within the movement of history be correctly understood. As he points out, "the change was not made on a sudden, nor at the first movement of the endeavor" (31.25). The Creator did not simply force these transitions on his creation because, although he does indeed want change, he wants change effected by conviction rather than by coercion or force. "That no violence might be done to us, but that we might be moved by persuasion. For nothing that is involuntary is durable" (31.25). Only a "tyrannical power" would coerce creatures in Gregory's view. By contrast, God's nature is characterized by nonviolence and especially by an acknowledgment of the human capacity for freely choosing and then practicing the good. God has no interest in forcing good upon human beings "against their will."

Within Gregory's dialectic of creation history, the idea of movement plays a role insofar as history itself "moves" through these transitions that in their turn represent qualitative leaps brought about by God's nonviolent, noncoercive urging, on the one hand, and voluntary, freely engaged human acceptance of the good, on the other. Within time, this movement through history takes places in transitions from an earlier stage to a later one while building on the previous. It might also be noted that Gregory is by no means implying that these transitions necessarily take place in harmony; quite the contrary — here Gregory picks up on Hebrews 12:26 — they can very well represent painful convulsions within history. At the same time, however, they are ultimately characterized by the engagement of God's good will and by an absence of any force or coercion, and also by the emphatically free human acceptance and implementation of his good works.[84]

The Correspondence between God's Movement and the Liberation of Creation

In Gregory's understanding, the being of the triune God is constantly in motion; in his understanding of creation, the life of the whole and that of its parts are also connected through movement. God's uncreated movement and the movement of the created are related and connected, but without losing their respective identities in one another. How is this correspondence to be understood?

---

84. Gregory understands "progress" in theology in analogy to these historical transitions, the transitions through the various stages of the age corresponding to similar transitions toward ever more lucid modes of revelation of the Father, Son, and Spirit (*Or.* 31.26f.).

The Conditions of Correspondence

In what sense is the connection between the idea of movement in Gregory's understanding of God and that in his understanding of the world to be understood as a "relation"?

The Cappadocian uses the concept of "movement" in speaking about both God and creation but does not follow any preceding tradition in doing so. In speaking about "movement" in this context, Gregory uses the two overriding terms "moving" and "sustaining," applying both terms to the Creator as well as to the creation, at the same time. However, he reserves the concepts of spatial movement and movement toward change explicitly and exclusively for references to creation, excluding them from any reference to the Creator. He similarly reserves the compound forms referring to self-movement exclusively for pneumatological references to God while applying the notion of perpetual and good movement to angels and human beings.

The relationship between the idea of movement in Gregory's understanding of God and the world is equivocal insofar as it refers not only to a fundamental dissimilarity between the two, but also to an inherent ontological dependence.

1. God's own movement is uncreated and cannot be identified with anything in motion within creation; and conversely,
2. whatever is in motion within creation is wholly and utterly dependent on the Creator.

That is, the movement of the triune God is atemporal, unchangeable, nonspatial, unrestricted, sustaining, independent, existing within a perfect community of three, and capable of returning to itself. By contrast, all movement in creation is temporally and spatially bound (corporeal creatures), is subject to the *diastema* of creation, needs to be maintained and sustained, is incapable of movement from within itself, and is ontologically moved. Gregory considers it idolatry to identify any movement within creation with the being of the Creator.

With rigorous apophatic awareness of the limitations of thought, Gregory first distinguishes God's being in movement from that within creation, and then argues from the premise of this distinction in asserting that all movements of creatures within creation are dependent on God. This ontological dependence is not however mechanistic or one-sidedly causal; instead, Gregory understands divine movement to be the ground of the possibility, maintenance, and possible goal of all created movement.

Movement within creation, however, is not dependent on the transcendent Creator *only* as its initiator or with regard to its stability or goals. Gregory chooses to describe this dependence as specifically "ontological" precisely because it encompasses *all* dimensions of movement within creation. In that sense, not only the origin and goal of the entire world, but also its perpetual support and maintenance lie within God. Not only do all movements of the human will in freedom acquire the possibility of actualization from the Creator, so also do all possibilities of angels moving either around God or toward evil. Gregory understands the triune God as moving and sustaining not only the orbit of the sun, but also the course of the seasons and even the movement characterizing the human soul. Hence the relationship between the idea of movement in Gregory's understanding of God and world is one between two different entities in which the second depends ontologically on the first.

The Conceptual Figure of Correspondence: Possibility — Orientation — Movement Toward

The correspondence between the idea of movement in Gregory's understanding of God and world can be described as a triple sequence of mutual interplay.

1. God, whose being is in motion, reveals himself in his creation as the ground, possibility, maintainer, and goal of all movement in the world.
2. Creatures endowed with spirit and movement freely direct their own movements either toward or away from God.
3. When creatures do indeed orient their own movements toward the God in motion, those movements partake of the characteristics of divine movement, namely, its goodness and stability; as a result, Creator, creature, and creation all move closer to one another.

The presupposition for the two following stages is the first, namely, what we previously described as the ontological dependence of created movement on God's uncreated movement. The most important consideration in the second stage is open communication between the two movements. As mentioned earlier, God has no interest in forcing creatures to orient the movement of their lives and wills toward the Creator; a genuinely *enduring* orientation toward God results only from sincere acknowledgment and conviction.

In their own turn, angels are easily inclined to movement about God in that perfect circular form that brings about peace and are quite disinclined to flee from God in a movement that brings about evil. By contrast, because human beings — burdened with an imbalance between body and soul — are easily tempted by evil, they are equally capable of moving either toward or away from God.

As a way of dealing with this situation, God thus demands perpetual "re-versal" or "con-version" in the sense discussed above, that is, in the form of constantly examining and, if necessary, correcting one's direction. Because corporeal creatures not endowed with reason are nonetheless still sustained ontologically, they do participate in God's motion; yet they are also affected by the orientation of creatures endowed with reason, and in that sense it is the spirit that is to elevate the flesh.

In the third stage God responds to whether creatures have turned toward or away from him. Turning away means they flee from God, cause evil and sin in the world, and draw other creatures into that flight. Turning back toward God means participating in what is good and enduring in God's movement; the result is that unity, stability, and perfection increase such that creation itself moves a bit closer to God.

This closer approach to God does not, however, overcome the *diastema* or boundary between Creator and creation, since at least from the perspective of creatures that boundary will always obtain. Instead, what is actually enhanced is the *qualitative* proximity between God and creation. The God in motion is closer to his creation when the creatures in it are oriented toward and organize their movements around God instead of around centers within creation itself. Nonetheless, the reciprocal interplay between (2) and (3) as perpetually presupposed by (1) as described above does *not* proceed mechanically. For Gregory the triune God is always the agent who makes this correspondence possible in the first place between created and uncreated movement and enables the reciprocal interplay between nonviolent, noncoercive revelation, free "con-version" and turning, and mutual approach and redemption.

In his dialectical understanding of the transitions of history, Gregory addresses the question of the possibility and future of redemption by focusing on the openness of the present. The future is not determined by the movement of the stars, as many of Gregory's contemporaries maintained, nor by attaining some atemporal condition of repose; it is determined instead by deciding which direction one will take and by approaching ever closer to the moving God precisely at those points at which he reveals his work within creation. It is in this sequence that Gregory finds the possibility that the world itself might be created anew and transformed toward the good. That is, Gregory believes that when the Creator posits this possibility of a liberating future, the creatures will themselves respond by reorienting their movements toward God at precisely those points at which the Creator reveals this possibility within the world; through liberation and growth, the creation and Creator will move ever closer to one another.

3. Suffering

The problem of physical suffering created considerable tension between Christian theology in the ancient church and the understanding of God in ancient philosophy. Because the latter intractably believed that the divine was incapable not only of suffering but also of corporeality in general, it posed an obvious challenge to the Christian doctrine of the incarnation of the Son: either one dilutes or qualifies the ancient notion of divine *apatheia* (not suffering), or the understanding of the suffering of the Crucified is clearly weakened. Both tendencies are attested in the doctrinal developments of the ancient church.[85]

Far from avoiding this question, Gregory discusses it in considerable depth. In his oration on the Son, he summarizes his view in the paradoxical formula "by the sufferings of him [the Son] who could not suffer, we were taken up and saved" (*Or.* 30.5). This question of God's suffering, however, also contains one of the keys to understanding the Christian concept of nature, for suffering presupposes both perception and corporeality.[86]

The choice between pathos and *apatheia* in understanding God involves definite consequences for the soteriology of the corporeal. If God is capable of suffering, then the corporeal suffering of creatures individually and of creation as a whole acquires theological value with regard to redemption. If by contrast God is not capable of suffering (or impassible), corporeal pain loses its function in the history of liberation. For the God that does not suffer, redemption would be liberation from corporeality. By contrast, for the God that does suffer, redemption would mean the possibility of corporeality liberated from suffering. Redemption by the impassible God would be a liberation *from* nature, redemption by the suffering God liberation *to* the possibility of the new being of nature. If faith can see God suffering, it can also see the *entirety* of creation participating in his redemption.

---

85. See Labriolle 1950, 486.

86. Doerrie 1956, 330, points out that the origin of the meaning of *paschein* is actually "undergo, experience, be included in." Extrapolating, I would then understand *apatheia* as "not being included, void of experience," and "lack of suffering."

What, then, is the relationship between God's suffering and that of creatures and creation itself? How does Gregory reconcile the suffering God with the impassible God of his contemporaries? How does his understanding of the suffering God then also affect his understanding of the suffering of creation? In addressing these issues I will:

1. briefly describe the nature of the challenge posed by the notion of corporeal suffering in its fourth-century context;
2. analyze the idea of the suffering of God and his creation in various of Gregory's writings; and
3. examine the role of suffering in Gregory's understanding of God and the world and articulate the theological meaning he ascribes to the notion of the liberation of nature.

The Problem of Suffering

The doctrine of God's impassibility, first articulated by Aristotle, created a serious problem for Christian theologians working in the Hellenistic culture of the fourth century. The first side of the problem is the challenge of reconciling the ancient assertion of God's *apatheia* with the theology of incarnation. The second is the question whether the physical sufferings of creatures and creation have any function in the actions of the liberating God. Gregory's context — in the face of the unjust misery endured by such large portions of the population — raises among the poor the question regarding the suffering of God and Christians. The third side of the problem is the question whether the entirety of creation — including corporeal creatures — participates in redemption. What relationship does the theologian find between the sufferings of groaning creation, the sufferings of the poor, and the suffering of the Son of God?

Three different solutions may be proposed:

1. The *apatheia* of the Godhead is unqualified; this position leads to an ethics of sublime elevation over suffering. Middle Platonism, following the Stoic tradition, embraces this solution.

2. God's corporeal, suffering nature is subordinate to his incorporeal, impassible nature; this position leads to a subordination of the Son and to a reduction of the body to an instrument of liberation. The neo-Arians proposed this solution.

3. The third solution maintains that the divine does indeed suffer in the Son; this position includes all creation in liberation insofar as God does, after

all, love his creation and seeks to suffer in freedom along with his creatures. Gregory embraces this third solution in the tradition of Origen.

In what follows I examine the various contexts in which Gregory develops his understanding of suffering.

Gregory's Understanding of the Capacity for Suffering

The Suffering of Christ

Gregory develops his Christology in a dispute with Apollinarianism, laying the foundation for his later doctrine of the two natures of Christ. In the hypostasis of Christ, human nature enters into union with the divine nature, what Gregory calls "mixing" (*Or.* 38.13), "bringing together" (37.2), "combination" (*Ep.* 101.31 [ET, LCC 3:217]), and "mediator between God and carnality" (*Ep.* 101.49 [ET, LCC 3:220]). Gregory's basic assertion against Apollinarianism is that because only that which God accepts can actually be redeemed (*Or.* 22.13; *Ep.* 101.51f.),[87] Christ adopted the whole of human nature, including body, soul, and spirit or mind. Insofar as Christ genuinely combines the entire divine nature with the entire human nature, Christ as the God-man also takes suffering upon himself. Gregory articulates this unity of the Son's hypostasis in suffering in his interpretation of the crucifixion: "'My God, my God, why hast thou forsaken me?' It was not he who was forsaken either by the Father or by his own Godhead, as some have thought, as if it were afraid of the Passion, and therefore withdrew itself from him in his suffering (for who compelled him either to be born on earth at all or to be lifted up on the cross?) . . . by the sufferings of him who could not suffer, we were taken up and saved" (*Or.* 30.5). Gregory maintains that the Father does *not* abandon the Son of God when the latter suffers the human pain of death on the cross. Nor does he dispossess himself of his divinity. It is precisely the *voluntary, free nature of suffering* that effects redemption, a view also enabling Gregory to overcome the principle of God's *apatheia* by combining the Son's acceptance of suffering with the Godhead's freedom from suffering instead of confronting the two. The Cappadocian maintains that God, who by his very essence is free from suffering, nonetheless is able to combine human suffering with his own essence by entering into this perfect union with the entirety of human nature according to Gregory's principle: "that which he has not assumed he has not healed" (*Ep.* 101.52 [ET, LCC 3:218]). In Gregory's understanding, God

---

87. Cf. Bergmann 1991, 26.

takes human suffering upon himself to free human beings from that very suffering. In this sense God's suffering is a necessary presupposition for redemption.

The theologian now adduces two passages in the letter to the Hebrews in developing this notion of voluntary, free adoption of suffering (Heb. 5:8; 2:18). Through the incarnation the Son comes down to his fellow servants in "the form of a slave" (Phil. 2:7) so that human beings in their turn might partake of his essence by way of this mixture: "Thus he honors obedience by his action, and proves it experimentally by his Passion" (*Or.* 30.6). By taking on suffering himself, the Son shows how "by the art of his love for man he gauges our obedience, and measures all by comparison with his own sufferings, so that he may know our condition by his own." Not even at the restoration of all things will the Son's suffering be submerged in the Father; the Trinity remains self-identical within its threefold community: "the entire Godhead" of all three persons (30.6). The Father does not "consume" the suffering Son; instead, the latter's suffering abides in the entirety of God till the restoration of all things. By asserting that the Son's suffering abides in the Godhead, Gregory is also making unequivocal assertions about the corporeality of the Resurrected, a corporeality that abides after his return to the Father.

In his Easter oration the Cappadocian vividly recounts how the angels fail to recognize the Resurrected at the ascension, and how they even take offense at his crucifixion stigmata.[88] In an allusion to Isaiah 63:2f., Gregory understands the angels as having exclaimed, "how are the garments red of Him that is without blood or body?" (45.25). Gregory counters the angels' astonishment by pointing out how these sufferings in fact *adorned* the body of Christ.

Here the Cappadocian clearly occupies a controversial position within his age, developing his understanding of Christ's two natures by extending this perfect union of human and divine nature into the time *after* the incarnation and ascension. On his view the physical sufferings continued, as did God's experience of the incarnation. "See what even now the Word has to suffer" (38.15; cf. 41.5). "[E]ven now He suffers many dishonors at the hands of the enemies of Christ; and He bears them, for He is longsuffering" (41.5).

God continues to suffer because Christ brings his bleeding body with him into the Trinity. These passages show that this notion was of enormous significance for Gregory precisely because, to extend the redemptive power of the triune God into the present and future, God had to remain involved in

---

88. Christ comes down to earth *without* any such stigmata and ascends to heaven *with* them (*Or.* 45.25).

suffering himself. Indeed, Gregory even goes so far as to adduce the necessity of the incarnation of the Son in asserting that God's Spirit also appears in a bodily fashion.

Although Gregory does discuss at some length his views concerning the Son's willingness to accept suffering, he nonetheless does not abandon the notion of God's *apatheia,* nor can one expect him to, given the significance of this idea during his age. God remains the one who cannot perceive what we know as physical pain (20.8). The divine nature is free from the passions and from suffering (28.11). It seems Gregory might be guilty of a contradiction, namely, that of maintaining God's *apatheia* simultaneous with a theologically passionate insistence on the suffering of the incarnate Son. In Gregory's system, however, this position emerges from two basic considerations rather than from making inherently self-contradictory assertions.

1. On his own free will and out of love, God, standing over against his creation, takes on a body and accepts the attendant suffering.

2. The divine and human natures are combined in Christ such that each maintains its full identity. Gregory finds it inconceivable that *apatheia* and *patheia* might be mixed together. And yet because his two-nature thesis does find that what seems utterly irreconcilable to us is in fact united in Christ, it might be viewed as bringing to expression what in fact was inconceivable to the understanding of God generally held in antiquity, namely, the combination of God's *patheia* and *apatheia.* In his own words: "impassible in His Godhead, passible in that which He assumed" (40.45; cf. 17.12; 30.16).

This theology further undermines the preeminent position of *apatheia* and incorporeality in the ancient understanding of God.[89] That the triune Christian God is now characterized by community, movement, *and* suffering makes it possible to ascribe a function to the suffering of creatures in God's redemptive plans and to incorporate liberation from corporeal suffering into the understanding of redemption. As we can now see, Gregory's understanding of divine suffering has provided the foundation for his soteriology. By incorporating the notion of corporeal or physical suffering into his trinitarian understanding of God, he makes it possible for corporeal nature to participate not merely instrumentally, but actively in the redemptive process. Put briefly, Gregory believes that because the God who is free of suffering nonetheless does love, he chooses to take on the pain of the other, to bear it, to suffer it; and because the Creator himself suffers, his creation can become free.

---

89. Contra Althaus 1972, 137, who interprets Gregory's understanding of Christ's humanity as a "mere schema."

Human Suffering

Insofar as Rosemary Radford Ruether and Anna-Stina Ellverson charge Gregory with entertaining a negative view of the corporeal and physical,[90] they join the interpretive tradition that understands the Cappadocians as Platonist theologians who are accordingly suspected of viewing the body and soul dualistically. Although the dualistic understanding of human beings as espoused by middle Platonism does doubtless constitute one of the presuppositions of Greek-speaking theology in late antiquity, it was nonetheless still quite possible to provide a critical corrective to such dualism even in this context.

The fundamental question here is how Gregory himself understands the corporeal to be functioning within the overall process of redemption. Does the body *impede* the soul? Or is the body, too, to be redeemed? Does the ascetic view diminish the value of the body out of contempt, or does asceticism itself represent an ethical path through which one might free the body from negative ties? In short, does Gregory view the body negatively or positively? In Gregory's writings one can see how on the basis of his understanding of creation and the incarnation he does indeed view the body in an unequivocally positive fashion and how he thoroughly incorporates corporeality into his soteriology. Indeed, he considers the human capacity for physical suffering to be of enormous importance for human redemption. The path to God does not lead past or beyond the body, as the Platonist understanding of redemption would have it; instead, it is through the *entirety* of human nature — as body, soul, and spirit — that human beings move closer to God. One must at the same time allow that Gregory's writings do contain prominent enough passages suggesting a negative understanding of the body.[91] In such passages Gregory does doubtless remain a child of his age.

Gregory's concern is to draw attention to the temptations to which human beings are exposed precisely because of their corporeal constitution and to admonish believers to achieve a state in which the spirit or mind has dominion over the body. The theologian does not, one might add, view the passions as something evil in and of themselves; quite the contrary, they were created good and are just as capable of serving God as are the soul and spirit.[92] Gregory's concern is merely that they *not* gain the upper hand over

90. Ruether 1969; Ellverson 1981.
91. E.g., *Or.* 14.6; 39.6.
92. Documentation in Althaus 1972, 34ff.

the soul.[93] The body and spirit should strive for harmony, subordinating the one to the other. Although Gregory does describe the relationship between the body and soul hierarchically, instead of understanding the hierarchy itself as consisting exclusively in the dominion of the one over the other, he envisions it as a mutual relationship of the one guiding the other for the benefit of both. The body is to serve the human being, life, and God, but to do so it needs the guidance of the spirit, which in its turn is thus to serve the body that the latter might indeed fulfill its purpose.

Gregory's admonitions on the dominion of the body over a person are essentially concerned with the mutual relationship between the body, soul, and spirit, which for Gregory provides the key to biblical anthropology and enables him to view corporeality in and of itself as something good. Insofar as his "negative" statements about the body are always associated with this notion of a mutually beneficial relationship, one cannot really derive from his thinking any contradiction between a negative and positive assessment of the body. It is through *all* parts of the body that a person is connected with God, not just through the spirit. Gregory even engages in a lengthy enumeration of all the body parts and senses that should be purified for service to God: the eye, hearing, tongue, smell, feeling, taste, head, shoulders, hands, feet, stomach, heart, entrails, loins, kidneys, and liver (*Or.* 40.38-40). Gregory's position here hardly constitutes hostility toward the body. Because he believes that consecrating only *one* part of a person to God leads to contempt for the other parts, he maintains that *every* part should thus be engaged in service to God; it is as *whole* persons that human beings should entrust themselves to God.

By grounding his positive understanding of the corporeal in the incarnation of the Son, Gregory is able to overcome Platonic dualism with Christian faith in and knowledge of the resurrection of the flesh (30.21). Precisely because the totality of God is present in Christ, his humanity is also sanctified. In that sense the Messiah, rather than being merely God's emissary, *is* the physically present God. In the Son, God adopted the whole of human nature, uniting in him the body, soul, and spirit, which — as mentioned earlier — remain united even after Jesus' sojourn on earth has ended. Because God's incarnation continues for Gregory, he also views human corporeality and the human capacity for suffering positively.

Gregory's high estimation of corporeality and suffering comes to vivid

---

93. In his poem "On Fear" (which resembles a "theological-psychological instructional piece"; *Carm.* 1.2.25.65-73), Gregory illustrates the emergence of anger using the Platonic metaphor of the rider, in which the horse (emotion) seizes control from the rider (reason).

expression in his oration on love for the poor. At the dedication of Basil's home for lepers in Caesarea, Gregory does not miss the opportunity to castigate the healthy and wealthy for their utter lack of compassion. In this context the Cappadocian also engages his understanding of the "equality of gifts" throughout God's creation with regard to the body, through which God emphasizes the concomitant "equality of creatures" (14.25). In the beginning God created *no* distinctions between the poor and the rich, the healthy and the sick (14.25f.; cf. Matt. 19:8; 14:36).

Elsewhere Gregory asserts that because of their suffering, lepers might even preserve or illustrate the divine likeness better than do the healthy (*Or.* 14.14). In his harsh portrayal of the antitheses inhering in the social injustice between the poor and the wealthy, Gregory underscores not only that love for the poor in fact represents the most sublime form of love for one's neighbor (14.5), but also that beneficent deeds and actions enable a person to partake of God (14.27). Along with leprosy or skin disease, Gregory also mentions the misfortunes of various illnesses and unemployment (14.9). In this oration the Cappadocian presents the rich and powerful with a vivid portrait of physical suffering from the perspective of those who actually suffer. Rather than devaluing physical suffering, he seeks to assess it even more highly in connection with the unredeemed status of creation. That is, because God created all creatures equal, and because Christ was indeed God in the flesh,[94] the suffering of the poor represents the preeminent challenge to the praxis of the Christian faith. In associating the capacity for suffering of the incarnate Son with the concrete physical sufferings of human beings, Gregory also ascribes to the weakest and least among those who suffer the preeminent position with regard to the precept of love for one's neighbor.

Once Gregory establishes this high estimation of the capacity for physical suffering, the next logical step is to incorporate it into soteriology. In a key text in his eulogy for his brother Caesarius (7.21), Gregory writes that after death the soul is "free from the bonds of the body" and immediately attains "a sense and perception of the blessings which await it, inasmuch as that which darkened it has been purged away, or laid aside." Once the soul has "shaken off the fetters which bound it and held down the wings of the mind" and is with God, nonetheless,

> a little later, it receives its kindred flesh, which once shared in its pursuits of things above, from the earth which both gave and had been entrusted with

---

94. Christ was concerned with both the body and the soul of the poor (*Or.* 43.35). Christ took on the body to help suffering creatures (*Carm.* 1.1.2).

it, and in some way known to God, who knit them together and dissolved them, enters with it upon the inheritance of the glory there. And, as it shared, through their close union, in its hardships, so also it bestows upon it a portion of its joys, gathering it up entirely into itself, and becoming with it one in spirit and in mind and in God, the mortal and mutable being swallowed up of life. (7.21)[95]

One sees that Gregory's understanding of human beings clearly distances itself from the idea of an *incorporeal* immortality of the soul and from that of a migration of souls through different bodies. Every individual human being is composed of a totality of body and soul, and just as this is the case during earthly life, so also will it be the case in the new creation when life extinguishes death.

Because Gregory understands the body and spirit to be connected in a mutually beneficial rather than an antithetical relationship, the task of the spirit is to enable the body to participate in the redemptive process (16.15). It is the human spiritual capacity that Gregory associates with the likeness of God; the seat of the image *(eikon)* is the mind *(nous)*. The body is not merely the housing for this likeness, but is connected with it in a way known only to the Creator. Because the spirit strives upward to God in Gregory's understanding, its task is to draw the body up to God as well. As we will discover later, the soul's capacity for enabling its own body to partake of liberation provides Gregory with a foundation for articulating human responsibility for the totality of visible creation.

The goal of this liberation, however, is not freedom *from* the corporeal, but rather the freeing *of* the corporeal itself to a new life free from the power of evil.[96] For Gregory the corporeal is not merely an instrument the human spirit uses for encountering God, but rather is itself an object of liberation by God. Gregory's theology associates the corporeal and spiritual in a necessary and mutually beneficial relationship such that both strive upward to God and both are set free together.

---

95. Gregory is alluding to the Old Testament notion that the earth participates actively in the Creator's salvation history when he says the earth "gave" the brother's body, which is then entrusted to the earth (after death) and which the earth then — through God's gift — will "give back" again. Concerning the tradition of the earth as an active participant in God's work, see Moltmann-Wendel 1993; concerning the reception of the earth as a deity in the ancient church and ecological theology, see Bergmann 1994d.

96. Gregory describes the new life of corporeality as "He will make the flesh immortal" (Christ; *Or.* 38.13) and "the condemnation of the flesh should be abolished" (39.13).

The Suffering of the Cosmos

Just as the thesis of God's corporeal suffering in Christ prompts Gregory to ascribe a positive function to physical suffering in connection with redemption, so also does the understanding of the cosmic Christ and Spirit prompt him to view physical creation as a whole positively.

Because it was as the Father, Son, and Spirit — in community — that God created the cosmos as an expression of his goodness, so also does creation itself participate in the history of liberation. Here Gregory clearly articulates the idea of universal redemption in which corporeal creatures both as individuals and in their totality participate in the Creator's redemptive plan. Gregory does not treat this idea merely as a soteriological addendum, but as an integral part of his theology. Gregory's God is not only the Creator of the divine likeness of the human spirit; he is also the triune Creator of the All, and it is in the history of this All that his economy is revealed. In that sense Gregory finds that creation itself can proclaim God, with God revealing himself in the very being of nature. In Gregory's view corporeal creatures also have intrinsic soteriological value, and since their history is inextricably connected with human history, any suffering in the cosmos also says something about humanity and about its relationship with the Creator.

One of the key texts in which Gregory develops this salvific understanding of the cosmos is his oration to Julian, where following Isaiah (45:8; 49:13) and Paul (Rom. 8:19ff.), he addresses the notion of the groaning of creation:

> Inasmuch as the whole creation and the heavenly powers, such, at least, is my opinion, take an equal interest in these events. For not only does "the whole creation groan with us and is in the pangs of labour, being made subject to corruption" (I mean to things below that are born and perish) "expecting the end of these things and the revelation," in order that itself may then obtain the hoped-for deliverance, as being bound fast to them against its will through the power of Him that created it; but it also joins in glorifying Him, and exults together with the sons of God when they do rejoice.[97]

Gregory believes that creation is connected with misery "against its will," and that creation itself, rather than being the cause or seat of evil, is instead the object and victim of the misery evil imposes. In his interpretation of the fall of the angels as described earlier, Gregory is able to ascribe the activities of

---

97. *Or.* 4.15, ET from C. W. King, *Julian the Emperor* (London: G. Bell, 1888), 9-10, which contains the whole of *Or.* 4 and 5.

evil to spiritual powers. But since the Creator created but *one* world, creation itself also falls victim to evil after the fall, and in this sense, of course, human beings and creation are intimately connected, since both serve "things below," both suffer, and both anticipate the end and the beginning of the freedom they yearn for. Gregory believes that historically the creation was also associated with the suffering of the Crucified.[98]

Here Gregory articulates an idea we might call the *cosmic community of suffering, hope, and joy at liberation.* Humanity and creation are just as intimately connected in this community of suffering as they are in their common joy at God's liberating actions. Because suffering, hope, and liberation all serve as the medium through which various creatures are connected, and because God is the Creator of the *whole,* Gregory maintains that redemption can only be redemption of the *totality.*

Because human beings and nature as a *totality* participate in these events, nature is also in a position to tell us something about the status of the relationship between human beings and God. In his oration on the catastrophe of the hailstorm and the resultant widespread harvest failure, Gregory ascribes an *epistemological* function to the storm itself: "in order that we may be chastised through that for which, when honored with it [creation], we did not give thanks, and recognize in our sufferings that power which we did not recognize in our benefits" (*Or.* 16.5). Greek thought, of course, was no stranger to the notion that gods might reveal themselves in nature, nor does Gregory fail to incorporate allusions to the Old Testament and its prophets. His focus, however, is the connection between the life of society and the life of creation, since nature and society are parts of *one* community: the fellowship of all fellow creatures.

Elsewhere Gregory engages the same conceptual figure in concurrence with the various Greek traditions of cosmic piety.[99] In his first oration on peace, he maintains that

> All these things being so and guided and directed in accordance with the first causes of harmony, or rather of conflux and conspiration, what else could they ever be seen to be but proclamations of love and concord, teaching mankind unanimity through their example? And when matter divides against itself and becomes intractable and intent on destruction through discord, or when God disturbs a measure of the harmony in order to terrify and punish sinners, whether by tidal wave or earthquake, or freak torrential

---

98. Gregory interprets the solar eclipse during the crucifixion in *Or.* 45.29, saying that "it was fitting that the creatures should suffer with their Creator."

99. Cf. Fuchs 1926, 105-7.

storms or solar eclipse, or by prolonging a season or by conflagration, then there is turmoil and fear for the universe and the blessing of peace is shown through the disruption. (6.15f.)

A beautiful cosmos is one that preserves "the blessing of peace." When the All loses that peace, however, it ceases to be a cosmos (6.14). Because Gregory's understanding of the one community of creation inextricably associates the peace of nature with peace among human beings, any disruption in the cosmos itself will also have significance for human beings. In Gregory's view society and nature belong to a shared order, and it is in the condition of *both* parts that the Creator of this community is revealed. Insofar as the sufferings of the cosmos summon human beings to repent and turn around, those sufferings are of ethical significance in Gregory's theology; insofar as they as cosmic groans and sighs also express the entire creation's hope for liberation, they are of soteriological and even eschatological significance.

Gregory discusses the eschatological significance of this cosmic community in the metaphor of the cosmic Christmas, maintaining that "this Festival be common to the powers in heaven and to the powers upon earth" (38.17). The idea that the totality of creation — corporeal and spiritual — will be set free is grounded largely in Gregory's Christology. Christ was "sanctifying the waters by His Purification" at his baptism (38.16). He comes up out of the Jordan waters, and "with Himself He carries up the world" (39.16). Regarding the solar eclipse during the crucifixion, "it was fitting that the creatures should suffer with their Creator" (45.29). Gregory ascribes universal significance to the cross of the Son, whose suffering unto death is of enormous significance for the liberation of all creation (29.20; 45.29; 40.29). God's acceptance of suffering includes not merely human corporeality but the entire world. Liberation will come to the community of all life that still suffers from evil and whose renewed formation God's own suffering inaugurates. Redemption as the new creation of the totality of the community of life comes to expression in Gregory's metaphor of a cosmic spring: "A spring of the spirit, a spring for souls, a spring for the body, a spring visible, a spring invisible, which may we, who have been richly blessed in this life, enjoy in the other as well" (44.12).

Just as Gregory understands the whole person as being related to God, so also the totality of creation. That is, the *whole* world is to be redeemed and drawn up to the resurrection of the Son (45.2).[100] Indeed, the sufferings of the cross shape the entire world anew. In Gregory's view all creatures are united

---

100. See also *Or.* 40.45; 38.14; 40.41.

in a community of suffering, hope, and liberation. Society and nature are parts of the *one* community of creation, and because both suffer under the power of evil, both will also be set free. Gregory's universal soteriology includes all of nature together with human beings.

The Ethics of Compassion

Within the Alexandrian tradition Philo emphasized God's capacity for compassion, while the idea of common or shared feeling and sympathy within the world played an important role in the Stoic system.[101] In drawing on the positive connotations attaching to the concept in both theological and philosophical tradition, Gregory moves the concept of compassion to the center of his ethical thinking by focusing on imitating the God who in Christ freely accepts physical suffering to set corporeal creatures free. It is in compassion that human beings suffer along with their neighbors and in so doing best imitate God; indeed, it is precisely the qualities of sympathy and compassion that best characterize the ethics of *imitatio Christi* that Gregory describes with the expressions "divinization" *(theosis),* "clothe yourself with Christ" (40.25), "man's affinity with God" (14.27), and "imitating God's mercy" (14.26).[102]

In his oration on love for the poor, Gregory writes, "[Love's] most vital part I find is the love of the poor along with compassion and sympathy for our fellow man" (14.5). The value of his path emerges from his Christology. Out of his compassion, "Christ, the gentle and loving . . . experienced pain and was bruised for us that we might become rich in divinity." Gregory views God's Son as a "model of sympathy and compassion" (14.15). Because of this, Christian discipleship should be characterized by active compassion for our neighbors. When Gregory notes that it is through compassion that a person gathers treasures for the future (14.20), he is thinking of the last judgment, when it will be too late for good deeds. Instead, it is only here and now that we can purify ourselves for the better; the time to turn our lives around for the better is now.[103]

Gregory finds that two types of suffering are in fact connected, namely, those of the poor and those of the rich. Whereas the poor suffer from hunger,

---

101. Cf. Reinhardt 1926, 111-21, 178-86; Forschner 1981, 55.

102. Cf. *Or.* 14.24, where Gregory, alluding to an apocryphal writing, summons his listeners to imitate God's righteousness so that no one need be poor.

103. In *Or.* 16.5 Gregory writes that it is better to suffer now than in the beyond, where there can be no purification.

the rich suffer from excess and possessions (36.12; 14.24). The rich suffer in their souls while the poor suffer in body *and* soul (14.18). Ultimately the suffering of the poor and sick should bring the rich and healthy to an understanding of their own situation (14.19). Gregory does not understand compassion as an abstract feeling of pity for others, but rather as a passion prompted by one's experience with others — with fellow human beings as well as with animals (14.28) — which in its turn then prompts us to act, not least by renouncing wealth, which merely causes others to suffer, and ultimately by redistributing wealth, that it might benefit the poor as well. And because Gregory qualifies such renunciation and compassion christologically, a person's ethical path is certainly also of theological significance (45.23).[104]

Gregory's proposition is that genuine *imitatio Christi* acquires concrete form in taking on the suffering of one's neighbor, that is, through solidarity with one's neighbor in the form of an appreciation of that person's suffering and through concrete acts of love. It is absolutely impossible to understand such ethics as the kind of monastic disposition that would flee the world of concrete reality, since it places the responsibility for ethical discipleship squarely in the midst of the physical, corporeal existence of our fellow human beings and in so doing also assigns to the very poorest and neediest among them the highest status, the highest priority for God's love and Christian love.

Here, too, then, Gregory understands the human capacity for suffering positively as the capacity for suffering *with* our fellow human beings. The goal of ascetic ethics is to *free* corporeality redemptively. In the renunciation of wealth and excess, God works together with human beings to liberate and sanctify corporeal nature. Within this process it is those who take up the suffering of others freely and lovingly to whom Gregory ascribes the highest worth (24.11).

God's Suffering and the Suffering of Creation

How does Gregory understand the relationship between human suffering and the suffering of creation, on the one hand, and God's suffering, on the other? Here his universal understanding of salvation provides a point of departure. Because Gregory understands the suffering of Christ's human nature to be of cosmological relevance, he is able to establish a theological connection between christo-dicy and cosmo-dicy. Gregory's understanding of

---

104. Gregory provides an ethical-eucharistic justification in *Or.* 40.31.

the correspondence between God's suffering and the suffering of creation focuses on two issues. First, he is concerned with emphasizing the shared nature of suffering insofar as Christ's suffering is of the same kind as that of other creatures. Second, he is concerned with articulating the meaning of the suffering of this community of creation. Precisely because the Creator himself suffers with and in the same way as his creatures, suffering cannot possibly be void of meaning for believers. Instead, it is understood as the pain of being set free.

The Conditions of Correspondence

Gregory clearly delineates this initial connection between the suffering of the created and the divine natures. In and of itself, God's nature is free from passion and pain, and it is the incarnation that leads the divine freely to take on the sufferings of creaturely existence. Human and divine nature communicate in the one being of the hypostasis of the Son; in so doing, freedom from suffering enters into a connection with suffering, though the two natures do maintain their respective integrity. God's pain — that is, the Son's pain — remains completely human. The result, of course, is that Gregory must continue to maintain that Christ's *divine* nature remains free of suffering. Hence the first systematic presupposition for correspondence is found in Gregory's understanding of the *two natures* that come together in the one hypostasis of the Son. In Gregory's theology God suffers in a human fashion because he has combined the divine and human in Christ.

But can one really say that the triune God suffers in Gregory's view? The premise of a unitarian understanding of the divine community insists that God's being is consistently one.[105] Either God can or cannot suffer, and in that sense Gregory's insistence that the one who is free of suffering nonetheless does suffer contradicts the unitarian understanding of community. In fact, however, Gregory's position is to be understood from the perspective of his trinitarian, social understanding of God. As we saw above, his understanding of God is based on the notion of a perfect community of three different parts. The condition of unity is multiplicity. That is, *community* necessarily involves a threefold distinction rather than uniformity. The second systematic presupposition of such correspondence is Gregory's *trinitarian understanding of community.* Suffering within creation enters into a connec-

---

105. Concerning the distinction between *unitarian* and *trinitarian* community, see Moltmann 2001b, 221-25, 217-21.

tion with the Godhead when the hypostasis of the Son — which is wholly one with the other two hypostases — freely takes on the totality of human nature.

Gregory is thus able to view the sufferings of the Son as the sufferings of the triune God *without* having to allow that the hypostases of the Father and Spirit suffer in the same way as does the Son. As Gregory says, the Father does *not* abandon the Son during the sufferings on the cross. The one who is free of suffering suffers in a different but otherwise unspecified way (*Or.* 30.5). Even though the Spirit is not yet actively engaged in creation in a corporeal way during the period of the Son, the Spirit nonetheless also suffers with the Son (31.26), albeit in the fashion of an accompanying suffering. Only after the ascension will the Spirit continue the work of the incarnate Son through inhabitation; the incarnation of the Son within creation is followed by the indwelling of the Spirit.

A unitarian understanding of the community of the triune God would presuppose that all three hypostases necessarily suffer precisely the same way, whereas Gregory's trinitarian understanding — which we might call "sociality" — maintains that the *specific* sufferings of the Son maintain their separate integrity within the community of the three. One might speak of an inner-trinitarian correspondence of suffering providing the foundation for the activity of the Holy Spirit after the ascension. The Son incorporates human nature into the Trinity, and his suffering provides the basis for the Father's acts of liberation through the Spirit. Insofar as Gregory's theology understands Christ as maintaining his earthly body even in glory with the Father, it is able to envision how creation itself is set free to move closer to God. Just as Christ's own body returns to the triune God, so also is the entirety of the creation community to be guided to life both corporeally and spiritually, that is, "the liberation of the elements, the renovation of the universe" (7.21).

The Conceptual Figure of Correspondence:
Acceptance — Suffering — Liberation

The theological significance of the sufferings of the creation community derives from the incarnation event and especially from its continuation in the economy of the triune God. Assuming that the totality of creation communicates in myriad ways with its Creator, Gregory articulates the meaning of suffering as emerging in three stages:

1. Acceptance: out of love and free will God accepts or takes on human nature and thus the conditions of the possibility of suffering in the Son.
2. Suffering: God endures the same sufferings as do his creatures in the midst of their own community of creation.
3. Liberation: salvation history takes shape as a process through which the entirety of created nature is set free in the Spirit in analogy to the ongoing suffering in the triune God and the resurrection of the Son to corporeal life along with his ascension to the glory of the Father.

These three stages also fit into a trinitarian schema.

1. The Son, begotten of the Father, voluntarily accepts the sufferings of creation; the Spirit accompanies the Son.
2. In the crucifixion the God of community is tested in his love; Father and Spirit both suffer violent death with the Son, who thereby sets human nature free.
3. After the Son has incorporated his earthly body into the glory of the Father, the Spirit enters corporeally into creation to complete the work of liberation whose goal is to set the entirety of creation free to participate in the glory of the Father.

Given this line of thinking, Gregory cannot possibly consider the sufferings of the creation community to be without meaning. Quite the contrary is the case, since for him they reveal the very presence of the Spirit itself, which is now transforming and reshaping creation. Similarly, the sacrifices made by believers themselves, either as practical acts of love on behalf of the poor or in renouncing excess and wealth, rather than merely constituting moral accomplishments, now function as signs that God is genuinely near to us. Gregory seeks to connect God's suffering with that of the creation community at large. His trinitarian cosmology thus manages to transform the *apatheia* of the Greek god into the passionate pathos of the Christian God who is intent on setting the entirety of creation free.

4. The Spirit

The considerable semantic range of the Greek words corresponding to English "spirit" or "mind," namely, *nous* and *pneuma*, includes considerable overlap and variety; the biblical understanding of these concepts is similar in its variety. Christianity during late antiquity did as little to develop a genuine *doctrine* of the Spirit as had the early church itself. Indeed, one of the salient features of the fourth century is that it was really the first generation to examine in any systematic fashion the nature and work of the Spirit. In his own turn, Gregory found the biblical witness regarding the experience of the Holy Spirit to be unequivocal and was not shy about praising Greek antiquity's ability to attain knowledge — however fleeting and conceptually unsystematic — of the (Holy) Spirit (*Or.* 31.5).[106]

The ancient church, then, had certainly experienced and been conscious of God's Spirit even before theologians began examining its activity systematically. God's Spirit had already acted on their behalf even *before* God became a human being in Christ. The issue — still an open one in scholarship today — is rather the late date at which such pneumatological reflection actually commenced.[107] Certainly one of the initiators of this reflection was Gregory of Nazianzus, whose clear thesis concerning the *homoousios* of the Spirit prompted a more thorough development of the doctrine of the Trinity. "What then? Is the Spirit God? Most certainly. Well then, is [the Spirit] Consubstantial? Yes, if [the Spirit] is God" (31.10).

Pressing the question regarding how exactly the world is to be set free inevitably leads us to focus on Gregory's pneumatology. Just as his trinitarian understanding of *God* acquires its final form through the doctrine of the Spirit, so also might we expect that his understanding of the *world* might be shaped by that same doctrine. Anticipating for a moment our findings in this section, we can say that Gregory does indeed advocate a cosmic pneumatology, and it is precisely this pneumatology that we will be examining here.[108] In so doing, we will bear in mind the previous three sections of this chapter and inquire regarding the qualities of sociality, movement, and the capacity for suffering in Gregory's pneumatology: How does the theologian articulate the activity of the Spirit from the perspective of community, the

106. Welker 1994 provides a systematic presentation of the witnesses to the activity of the Spirit in the Old and New Testaments.

107. Concerning the status of scholarship, see Ritter 1988, 194f. and Hauschild 1984, 199-201.

108. Scholarship has egregiously neglected the cosmic dimension of pneumatology, as doubtless attested by numerous biblical and patristic texts. Cf. in this regard Berkhof 1988, 110. This issue was rediscovered in the speech Joseph Sittler delivered concerning cosmic Christology at the conference of the World Council of Churches (WCC) in New Delhi in 1961. Concerning the reception of Sittler's initiative, see Moltmann 1990, 276ff. Thirty years later, in Canberra in 1991, the conference of the WCC also lent expression to the notion of cosmic pneumatology in section I, 1 (p. 67): "The Holy Spirit . . . manifests God's energy for life present in all things and reminds us of the total dependence of all things on God."

movement of all living things (as both moved and moving), and the perfect incarnation of the Son, with whom the Spirit also suffered? The present section also summarizes the preceding ones from the perspective of what one might call pneumatological grammar. We will analyze three different contexts (anthropology, ecclesiology, and cosmology) in which Gregory develops his understanding of how the Spirit is active in the world, in examining his specifically cosmic trinitarian pneumatology.

The Problem of the Spirit

The Crises Prompting Reflection on the Spirit

Why was it even necessary in the first place for theologians in the fourth-century church to reach a theological consensus regarding the activity of the Spirit? What was the critical situation to which Cappadocian pneumatology was a response? The question becomes, which challenge prompted these theologians in late antiquity to address the problem of the Spirit? I cannot see that the ascetic life itself, problems in church politics per se, or specific issues of worship alone (doxological references) fully explain the problem of the development of pneumatological doctrine. Instead, I prefer to follow Hauschild in examining this development in connection with certain crises to which it seems to have been reacting and which it tried to interpret and overcome.[109] Four aspects are worth examining in this context.

1. The *political situation* in the church in the eastern Roman Empire in the fourth century reflected a worsening cultural crisis. The cessation of persecution and the increasing association of Christian institutions with those of the state put the church into a completely unfamiliar position requiring new social models. The freedom that the state accorded Christianity — albeit in no way as a state church — required more sophisticated doctrinal capabilities.

Theological reflection is always related to the contemporaneous social form of the church, a form that changed dramatically during late antiquity. Was the church's own newly acquired social position within the Roman cultural crises related to the theological interpretation of the Holy Spirit?

Whatever else they may involve, crises are always also a matter of survival. The position occupied by the church within the empire might also have been perceived as a threat. The church might have felt that its theological

109. Hauschild 1984, 196.

identity was threatened by the political pressure exerted on it by both the state itself and the spiritual and religious plurality characterizing its own milieu.

Yet another concern might have been to consolidate the ecclesiastical institution itself. During Gregory's age, neo-Arianism and Messalianism posed a threat to the institutional stability of the church, and the Cappadocians became vehemently engaged in unifying Christendom. Indeed, one of Gregory's most pressing concerns was to preserve and solidify ecumenical peace, and to this end pneumatological reflection could also be quite useful. Were the Cappadocians' irenic goals related to their reflection on the activities of the Spirit?

2. I have already mentioned the *ascetic movement*. If this movement did indeed represent a more radical conversion movement within the contemporary economic and cultural crisis, and particularly if its representatives adduced the influence of the Spirit in their support, then ascetic spirituality itself represented a serious challenge requiring a pneumatological response. This spirituality raises the specifically *ethical* question of how the indwelling of the Spirit in a believer influences that person's life, and the *ecclesiological* question regarding the criteria by which to assess genuine charismata. Was the increased interest in pneumatology related to the ascetic movement with its attendant ethical challenges to the church?

This ethical challenge emerged outside Christianity as well. Far from being merely a doctrine, *Platonist* philosophy also involved a certain lifestyle that in part resembled the Christian ascetic life. With its intellectualist, mythical sensibility and its Platonic heritage in the general sense, Platonism represented one of Christianity's most formidable competitors, which is why *mission* considerations certainly demanded a biblically grounded doctrine of the Spirit capable of doing justice to the philosophical criteria of the time and also capable of establishing historical continuity with the ancient philosophers who had already taken a position on the understanding of the spirit. Was the threat represented by the Platonist philosophical position related to the increased interest in Christian pneumatology?

3. Eustathius, whom we know only through Basil, was concerned primarily with clinging in a fearful, *conservative* fashion to the status quo without responding substantively to the questions of the age. The most powerful argument of this position was simply a biblical *argumentum ex silentio* pointing out that, as a matter of fact, the New Testament itself says nothing about the divinity of the Spirit. This argument, which doubtless found adherents in the various camps, did provide a convenient solution to the problem by way of simple circumvention.

One of the presuppositions of Greek-speaking theology since Origen was to assume a relationship between *biblical interpretation* and the activity of the Spirit. By adducing the Bible's own silence on the divinity of the Spirit, the conservatives prompted the need for an interpretation of biblical texts that might make that divinity plausible. Their position also made it necessary to develop a biblical concept capable of *excluding* any subordinate relationship among the hypostases while *maintaining* the equality of the Son and Spirit in relationship to the Father, something Gregory managed by emphasizing the verb "going out of" *(ekporeuesthai)* in the Gospel of John.

The extent to which this struggle toward a proper interpretation of the biblical texts did indeed play a role can be seen in Gregory's thorough enumeration of the "swarm of testimonies" to "the deity of the Holy Spirit . . . to be most clearly recognized from Scripture" (*Or.* 31.29f.); it can also be seen in the difference of opinion between Gregory and Basil, the latter of whom preferred following the texts themselves more closely and as a result hovered between the conservative and homoousian positions. That the conservative rejection of the divinity of the Spirit did represent a serious challenge can be seen not least in the intensity with which the Cappadocians developed their pneumatology; that they addressed a question with this much energy suggests that they viewed it as an urgent problem requiring serious attention. In their opinion the conservatives simply did not recognize the challenge and possibilities of an appropriate pneumatological response.

This conflict between conservatives and spiritual homoousians may also have derived from various views of education in antiquity. We know how clearly the Cappadocians recognized the advantages provided by the thesis of Christianity as the consummation of *paideia.* Persuasively demonstrating that the "spirit of the Greeks" actually represented a genuine if dim recognition of the activity of the Holy Spirit would doubtless have aided in constructing a new ecclesiastical social form within the empire that would *also* better address the needs of the educated. Unfortunately, their opponents were precisely those who had *no* familiarity with the Greek philosophers and did not really perceive the emerging possibilities for the church's existence, those who preferred to rely on the Bible in keeping everything the way it was. Was this conservative clinging to the status quo related to Gregory's constructive development of a doctrine of the Spirit?

4. By characterizing the Son as one of God's creatures, Eunomius thereby also excluded the divinity of the Spirit. While accusing the neo-Arians of professing secular Aristotelianism,[110] Basil himself responded with

---

110. K. Holl 1904, 131-37.

"popularized Aristotelianism" even while sensing that the categories of thing, characteristic, category, and kind were somehow not quite commensurate with the personal element attaching to the divine hypostases.[111] While the original form of Arian theology was not particularly interested in pneumatology, its neo-Arian representatives did not really develop it much beyond Christology.[112]

The charge of Pneumatomachianism (fighting against the Spirit) may have been directed at the neo-Arians, though they were hardly interested in doctrines of the Spirit. What may have happened is that criticism of neo-Arian Christology may have been applied to pneumatology. The thesis regarding the divinity of the Spirit might then have enhanced the thesis of the full divinity of the incarnate Son. The Eunomians, however, were not really up to such pneumatological argumentation. Within the neo-Arian controversy, pneumatology might have been employed as an "auxiliary construction" to overcome the Origenian understanding of the subordination of the hypostases and also to enhance orthodox incarnational theology pneumatologically against Eunomius (and later Apollinarius). Is criticism of the so-called Pneumatomachians related to the conflict between the orthodox and the neo-Arians?

Summary: The Response of Cosmic Pneumatology

I realize that my description of the challenge to which Gregory's doctrine of the Spirit was responding does not directly answer the historical question of why the development of the pneumatological doctrine picked up speed *precisely* between 340 and 381 C.E. Nonetheless, what we have seen regarding this challenge does help us understand Gregory's texts better. To what extent does the Cappadocian's rather comprehensive doctrine of the Spirit represent a response to that challenge?

The connection Gregory's cosmic pneumatology establishes between creation and redemption must be seen in connection with this challenge. Theologically he is insisting that the indwelling of the Spirit includes not only the entire human being, but also the Spirit's community in church and in humankind at large, and that the Spirit vivifies the *entirety* of multifarious creation itself.

This thesis of the *indwelling of the Spirit in corporeal human beings* was

111. Cf. K. Holl 1904, 131-34.
112. Cf. Gregorios 1988, 31.

directed against middle Platonism, which taught a purely spiritual participation of the soul, and against Eunomius, who held a reduced view of the mystery of the incarnation.

The thesis of the *enhancement of community through the Spirit* served ecumenical-irenic goals and facilitated criticism of social injustice. If God's Spirit genuinely was able to bring about peace, then such must be visible in the church itself. And if the Spirit genuinely was the Creator Spirit, then social peace must reflect a similar peace within nature.

The thesis of *vivification through the Spirit* helped overcome Platonist panentheism. The material world was *not* merely the lowest rung in the hierarchy of divine emanations; the Spirit was just as present and efficacious there as in the spiritual realm. Gregory maintained that God was just as indivisible as was the Spirit, which also meant, however, that the Spirit was active in the material world *completely* as God.

This presupposition made it possible to lend theological legitimacy to one's ethical responsibility toward the body as well as toward the poor and sick. Although this responsibility was developed largely as a kind of christological admonition to discipleship in Christ, the thesis of the vivification of all life through the Spirit could have the same goal, namely, to establish the intrinsic value of matter on the basis of its relationship with God.

The thesis of cosmic pneumatology could then also be rigorously developed from the perspective of soteriology, something also quite commensurate with the needs of the present context. The ruler had always been seen as the guarantor of peace in both society and nature, with nature and society reflecting the same cosmic order — one characterized either by peace or by a lack of it. The inclusion of the entirety of life in the redemption of human beings and nature picked up on the cosmo-aesthetic and cosmo-political tradition of antiquity. In this context cosmic pneumatology was responding to the question of why *only* the triune God rather than the emperor was able to redeem the cosmos.

In a word, Gregory's answer is that the Holy Spirit vivifies, liberates, and consummates creation because the Creator Spirit is *also* the redemptive Spirit — in trinitarian terminology: because the entire triune God is at work in the activity of the Spirit within created nature.

The Cosmic Activity of the Spirit

How does Gregory now describe the activity of the Spirit in the world? In examining his theology of the Spirit in connection with the human spirit and body, the church community, and the cosmos, I am certainly not claiming to address *all* the relevant dimensions of his doctrine of the Spirit, which are too extensive and varied for inclusion here.

It is the question of the redemption of nature that prompts me to choose these three contexts. Anthropologically, the question involves the relationship between the human body and spirit. Ecclesiologically, it involves the relationship between the church community and the human community at large. Cosmologically, it involves the relationship between God and nonhuman life.

The Spirit's Indwelling within the Whole Person

Gregory develops his understanding of the historical Trinity in an oration on the Spirit delivered in Constantinople in 381, perhaps as a sermon for participants at the council. He maintains that God's history can be divided into the three trinitarian periods involving the revelation of the Father, the Son, and the Spirit. The Old Testament proclaims the Father clearly and the Son obscurely, while the New Testament proclaims the Son clearly and the Spirit in a hidden fashion (*Or.* 31.26). Gregory believes himself to be living in the third period, the period of the indwelling of the Spirit: "Now the Spirit [itself] dwells among us, and supplies us with a clearer [revelation of God]" (31.26).

Yet a third reason for the Spirit's indwelling is that it will now clarify the doctrines the Son withheld from the disciples: "all things shall be taught us by the Spirit, when he should come to dwell amongst us" (31.27).[113] After the Son has become wholly human and then returns to the Father "above," the Spirit continues the work of the Son. Because the Son took on the human body, so also is it appropriate for the Spirit to act in a corporeal fashion, and in that sense Gregory understands the activity of the Spirit in the world as continued incarnation. Metaphorically the Spirit arrives in the foreign land and home, becomes the citizen of a city, and settles in.

What does this indwelling of the Spirit mean for human beings? Does it affect their spirit or even their bodies? As we saw earlier, Gregory was interested in articulating the christological assertion that God became *wholly* human in the Son. He now maintains the same position in his doctrine of the Spirit in his assertion that the Spirit's indwelling involves the *whole* person,

---

113. The word "dwell" *(endemesantos)* means to be at home. See Gemoll 1965, 274. The New Testament uses the verb to mean "be at home in the body" (2 Cor. 5:6).

both spirit and body, though the human spiritual capacity does ultimately represent the preeminent level at which God's Spirit encounters human beings. In the following discussion I will examine Gregory's understanding of how the Spirit is active in human understanding *(nous)* and in the human body.

Epistemologically Gregory also remains a child of his age. The fundamental principle of ancient epistemological theory was the recognition of like kind by like kind. Greek psychology, which began with Plato's distinction between the three functions of the soul in thinking, willing, and desiring, in its turn distinguished a higher part associated with reason and two lower parts associated with the body; reason *(logos)* and mind *(nous)* referred to the higher, analytical and intuitive parts of the soul, while soul and desire or appetite referred to the irascible and concupiscent lower parts.

The speculative development of the doctrine of the image of God *(eikon)* contributed to the Cappadocian synthesis. The *eikon* is the divine gift bestowed on or breathed into human beings as the breath of life and as the divine likeness. Gregory identifies the human capacity for reason with this divine likeness; because human beings were created in God's image, they have reason, though this capacity does not provide knowledge of God; only the Spirit knows the perfect essence of God.

In Gregory's view human beings communicate with God in a perpetually moving encounter between the human spirit and God's Holy Spirit. The perceivable Spirit *also* draws us toward itself. Knowledge of God leads to participation

> transcending all conception of time and nature, only adumbrated by the mind, and that very dimly and scantily . . . not by [God's] Essentials, but by [God's] Environment; one image being got from one source and another from another, and combined into some sort of presentation of the truth, which escapes us before we have caught it, and takes to flight before we have conceived it, blazing forth upon our Master-part [i.e., reason], even when that is cleansed as the lightning flash which will not stay its course, does upon our sight . . . in order as I conceive by that part of it which we can comprehend to draw us to itself [. . .] and by that part of It which we cannot comprehend to move our wonder, and as an object of wonder to become more an object of desire, and being desired to purify, and by purifying to make us like God; so that when we have thus become like [Godself], God may, to use a bold expression, hold converse with us as Gods, being united to us, and that perhaps to the same extent as [God] already knows those who are known to [God]. (38.7, ellipses in original ET; cf. 2.76)

This linguistically rather turgid citation shows how the Cappadocian describes the activity of the Spirit at the level of human reason as a movement of encounter.

1. Reason discerns God only in a limited fashion from that which is around God; all that can be discerned, however, is the unlimited nature of God's being.
2. Reason is illuminated only "in a flash" so that what is momentarily perceived might awaken longing; it is through this longing that the Spirit draws human beings toward itself.
3. Longing for God leads to purification, similarity to God, and community between a person and God (cf. 21.1f.; 32.24; 42.1).

Gregory describes the activity of God's Spirit with regard to human reason as a dialectical process through which the two approach ever closer to one another. Ontological kinship with the Spirit makes it possible for human beings to incline toward and approach the divine prototype (38.11), a process Gregory describes as illumination, becoming God, consummation or perfection, being created or formed anew, and sanctification. Whereas the Platonic tradition understood this vision as lasting eternally, the Christian tradition understands it as being cosmo-aesthetically and spiritually tied to time, that is, to the historic revelation of Christ and to the historic habitation of the Spirit at a certain time. Whereas the Jews could not endure God's illuminating revelation and thus required that it be veiled or cloaked (39.9), the Christian church begins with the incarnate Christ as God's visible light. Thus for Gregory it is the trinitarian illumination of vision and thought that fulfills both the eternal vision of the philosophers *and* Israel's incomplete vision. The subject of this illumination is always the divine Spirit, which Gregory uses as a guide for his own journey through temporal existence and which maintains that illumination till the very end (31.33; cf. 40.3).

Gregory also associates such spiritual knowledge with the ethical life. One must live according to and in the Spirit to acquire this knowledge (3.7). Gregory's doctrine of the Spirit characteristically associates vision and lifestyle, that is, theory and praxis, which belong together in his theology just as do the doctrine of the Spirit and ethics. Sanctification by the Spirit of gentleness is always accompanied by resistance to sin in the spirit of anger (41.14). Anyone wanting to reflect on God must be tested and strengthened in spiritual contemplation *(theoria)* and purified in body and soul (27.3; 28.2). Ascetic praxis is the presupposition of theological theory. The vision of God and the ethical life are intimately and inextricably related in Gregory's thought.

The *practical* path to God, rather than being inferior to the theoretical, instead constitutes its very presupposition, and it is in this sense that Gregory refers to *theoria* and praxis as the "doorposts of the mind" (16.11). Just as thought provides space for action, so also does action lead to thought (20.12). In a word, theory and praxis are dialectically inextricably connected in Gregory's thought.[114]

In summary, we can say that Gregory follows the Platonist epistemological principle that like kind can only know like kind, and interprets this knowledge dynamically as a movement of communication between God's Spirit and human reason. This perceiving vision of God in its turn awakens further longing for God, to which God then responds in the activity of the Spirit. Rather than being restricted merely to the understanding, such spiritual communication between human beings and God necessarily involves a person's *lifestyle,* since theory and praxis, spiritual knowledge and ethics, are indissolubly connected. Unlike middle Platonism, Gregory's understanding of participation is *communicative* insofar as two different entities (the human being and God's Spirit) make contact. Within this process of becoming like God, however, the human being remains fully human, raising the question of how the body participates in this event.

How does Gregory describe the relationship between the corporeal and the Holy Spirit? He maintains that the Creator Spirit participated in the work of creation itself and indeed is the one "in which all living things receive their life" (*Carm.* 1.1.31). Although the corporeal is characterized by change while God as the Spirit remains unchanged, Gregory does not understand this difference as one between mutually exclusive antitheses. Instead, it constitutes a fertile field of tension in which God acts.[115] In this connection, when the Cappadocian develops his understanding of the indwelling of the Spirit, he thus refers explicitly to the corporeal incarnation of Christ: "For it was fitting that as the Son had lived with us in bodily form — so the Spirit too should appear in bodily form; and that after Christ had returned to His own place, [the Spirit] should have come down to us" (*Or.* 41.11).

Gregory's view is that the Spirit is genuinely active in a *corporeal* fashion. Insofar as it now takes up dwelling in the body and soul of believers themselves after Christ returns home, the Spirit is present not merely in power but also precisely in this indwelling. This physical, corporeal habita-

114. Cf. Spidlík 1971, 153ff.

115. Cf. Jüngel 1978, 511, who believes one must "destroy" the axiom of unchangeability of "older metaphysics" through a theology of the cross. Cf. also Kern's critical response to Jüngel's elimination of this necessary field of tension: Kern 1979, 78-90.

tion of the Spirit now continues the incarnation of the Son, and following Ephesians 2:22 ("dwelling place for God"), Gregory now describes how the Spirit makes believers into the living house of Christ (*Or.* 2.97). Gregory believes the human spirit to be capable, as a creature of God, of also becoming the temple of God's Spirit (34.12; cf. 2.97).

The Cappadocian maintains that the body also participates in the redemptive process (2.17), functioning to prepare a person for the encounter with God that takes place in three sequential stages.

1. The "philosophy of the deed." Here Gregory is referring to the ascetic life whose models include Basil (43.65), the Virgin with the martyr Cyprian (24.10-12),[116] and his own sister Gorgonia (8.14).

2. The opening of the mouth of understanding (2.95; 6.1; 16.1; 28.6; 30.20; 44.6). This metaphor relates the opening of the mouth of understanding (Ps. 119:131) and the breathing in of the spirit of life (Gen. 2:7). The ascetic cleansing of the body is followed by the opening of one's understanding and perception of God so that now both body and spirit can be oriented toward God. For Gregory the initial inspiration of the breath of life (Gen. 2:7) and the filling with the Spirit at Pentecost (Acts 2:2, 4) can take place ever anew as a new creation when believers breathe in the Holy Spirit. Those who draw the Spirit into themselves must no longer drink the cup of death (*Or.* 44.6).

3. Ethical renewal (6.1; 44.6f.). A person's life not only serves to prepare a person to receive the Spirit, it also represents the *effects* of that very reception, thus closing the circle. Gregory believes that a person's longing for God already presupposes practical conversion, which prepares a person for the habitation of the Spirit. In its turn, that habitation further renews the whole person through the Spirit. Gregory describes this conversion as a process of perpetual movement (44.8).

The principle of illumination and withdrawal governs the relationship between the human spirit or mind *(nous)* and the Holy Spirit *(pneuma)*. God, who is both inside and outside the world, both illuminates and withdraws from the spirit the more the latter discerns him, thus leading his friend toward heaven by both drawing that friend toward himself and yet simultaneously slipping away (2.76). Here, too, the theologian envisions that the encounter between the human spirit and God's Spirit is perpetually in motion.

The ancient church was able to establish a special relationship between the Spirit and corporeal life in its doctrine of baptism. Gregory, too, is famil-

---

116. During Gregory's time, traditions of women — here Susanna and Thecla (*Or.* 24.10) — seem to have played an important role. The Marian cult is also attested (24.11).

iar with the analogy between the Spirit and water whose confluence in the sacrament of baptism still represents one of the cornerstones of Christian theology. Because human beings consist of both soul and body, the purification of baptism takes place on two levels (40.8). Whereas *visible and physical* purification takes place in the water sanctified by the baptism of the Son, the *invisible* purification of the inner person takes place in the Spirit. Christian baptism makes it possible to enter into the covenant of a second life and to live purely with God; as *spiritual* purification in the baptismal water, it follows upon the waters of the flood, which similarly cleansed the world itself from sin (40.7). The physical and spiritual purification of baptism guides the *whole* person, with all that person's senses, onto the sanctifying path to God (40.38-40).

In summary, we can note that for Gregory the Spirit's activity also includes the human body; the vessel that accepts the Spirit is certainly not unaffected by its indwelling. God's habitation in the world in the Spirit that has been sent forth involves the whole person — as body, soul, and spirit — purifying that person in preparation for battle with evil along the correct path to God. The body also has an important soteriological function insofar as redemption will involve both the soul and the body; in the two-sided baptismal event the body is cleansed in water, while reason is cleansed in the Spirit. Within the overall process of ethical conversion, however, these two depend on one another and proceed forward only together. Just as theory and praxis presuppose one another in Gregory's theology, so also the soul and body, with the activity of the Holy Spirit encompassing both.

The Spirit's Enhancement of Community

How is the Spirit active in the Christian community? Does the Spirit create an "exclusively Christian" community, or is the community of saints not rather a model of what community ought to be? The relationship between the church community and the human community at large contains yet another key to understanding the problem of the redemption of nature. One would expect that Gregory's unified understanding of creation and redemption would also come to expression in his ecclesiology, in which case the community of Christians would not so much represent the locus of redemption as an *instrument* the triune God engages in redeeming humanity, the world, and nature.

In what follows we will see how Gregory's pneumatological grounding of the community of Christians in fact represents a constituent part of functional ecclesiology. The Cappadocian understands the work of the Spirit in enhancing the community of the *church* as service in enhancing the community of *humankind and the cosmos*.[117]

The church did not reflect on itself as an independent theological theme during the first few centuries. Although Gregory does reflect on various themes associated with the Christian community, including baptism, the Lord's Supper, the Day of the Lord, celebrations, the functions of office, prayer, doxology, creeds, and lifestyle, none of these reflections led to any systematic ecclesiology. The Cappadocian theologians maintained a certain distance between themselves and the various political efforts to standardize the church. Gregory himself envisioned a pluralistic culture quite at odds with the larger political goals of the empire. Whereas Arian ecclesiology sought alliances with the politically powerful,[118] the Cappadocians tried to engage the ideal of love on behalf of the poor while evangelizing the wealthy.

Gregory examined the existence of the church largely from the perspective of pneumatology rather than Christology,[119] his trinitarian pneumatology necessarily expanding ecclesiological reflection beyond the horizon of mere logos-Christology. Gregory divides the Spirit's establishment of the Christian community into three historical stages:

1. the stage before Christ's glorification in suffering
2. the stage after his resurrection
3. the stage after his ascension (*Or.* 41.11)

The power of the Spirit accompanied the Son on earth as one equally honored, then continued its activity in the disciples, in the events at Easter, and within present history. Gregory is obviously concerned with emphasizing the continuity of the Spirit through history from the creation of the world to Israel's patriarchs and prophets, thence to Jesus' earthly sojourn, and finally into the present. "[The Spirit] wrought first in the heavenly and angelic powers. . . . And next, in the Patriarchs and Prophets. . . . And next in the Disciples of Christ (for I omit to mention Christ Himself, in Whom [the Spirit] dwelt, not as energizing, but as accompanying His Equal)" (41.11; cf. 41.13f.).

Rather than constituting the presupposition for the work of the Spirit,

117. By "enhancement of community" I am referring — in analogy to a similar "enhancement of society" — to a progressive, social process of joining together or amalgamation that ultimately reshapes a given social model into an inwardly consistent, intersubjective community.

118. Peterson 1951, 102.

119. Contra Portmann 1954, 128, and Althaus 1972, 152-93, both of whom overlook the textual evidence in which Gregory associates the church and the Spirit.

the community of faith emerges rather only where the acts of the Spirit itself are experienced. That is, the activity of the trinitarian Spirit itself constitutes the presupposition for the emergence of the church. "Will you not reverence even the authority of the Spirit Who breathes upon whom, and when, and as [the Spirit] wills?" (34.14). Gregory's interpretation of the Johannine doctrine of the Spirit plays an important role in his integration of ecclesiology into trinitarian soteriology insofar as the Gospel of John and the tradition of the Paraclete enable him to differentiate between a time of the church with the *Son* and a time with the *Spirit.* In connection with John 14:16, 17:26, 15:26, and 16:7f., Gregory discusses in depth how Christ's ascension constitutes the trinitarian seam for this transition (See *Or.* 41.11-12; 31.27). Here Gregory is intent on incorporating the Spirit's establishment of the church into God's history with the world and with human beings.

This incorporation also illustrates how the work of the Spirit not only provides the community of Christians with a specific identity within God's history with the world, but also endows it with a generalized *social* form enabling it to function in subsequent history as well. In this sense Gregory understands the church of the Spirit as part of God's overall history with his world (12.4), something he also brings to expression metaphorically in showing how the advent of the Spirit in fact fulfills our hope: "We are keeping the feast of Pentecost and of the Coming of the Spirit, and the appointed time of the Promise, and the fulfillment of our hope" (41.5).

One problem confronting the ancient church was the multiplicity of languages. Gregory would like to understand the Christian community as the counterpart to the tower of Babel. That which originally divided and fragmented humanity is now employed for the good by the church of the Spirit; God's Spirit now harmonizes the multiplicity of languages, a multiplicity Gregory views positively (41.16).[120] For Gregory the habitation of the Spirit turns the divided nations of the world into a single people sharing a single capacity for reason *(nous)* (34.6). The old divisions and fragmentation are a thing of the past, the goal of humanity and the world having been fulfilled during the time of the Spirit. For the theologian, being a Christian means entering a new life and undergoing this change for the better (44.6, 8), and in this sense the community of believers is actually the *eschatological* commu-

---

120. Such positive assessment was anything but self-evident. Concerning the ancient church's understanding of how the problem of differentiated languages resulted from the fall or from the creation of humanity, see Thunberg 1974, 46-50, and Borst 1957, 235-38. Gregory of Nyssa viewed this linguistic plurality more negatively than did Gregory of Nazianzus; cf. Thunberg, 48.

nity illustrated by the metaphor of the inbreaking cosmic and spiritual springtime (44.12).[121] The foundation of this community is the doctrine of the unity of the Spirit, which Gregory articulates in the liturgical formula "our worship of the Father in the Son, and the Son in the Holy Spirit" (24.19). A basic principle of Gregory's doctrine of the Spirit in the Trinity is indivisibility, which denies any division of the glory or veneration of the divine hypostases (31.28; cf. 34.11; 34.15).

For the Cappadocian, it is ultimately the activity of the Spirit itself and its veneration that constitute the church. The Holy Spirit enabled the patriarchs and prophets to view God and the future (41.11). By bringing about the "spiritual rebirth" without which no one can view or attain the kingdom, the Spirit that constitutes the church also fulfills a soteriological function (41.14). Gregory emphasizes that it is not merely a power or force *(energeia)* that brings this about (31.6), but rather God's very presence (41.11). Although the ancient church interpreted the Spirit's activity within the community of believers largely from the perspective of baptism, the focus was on baptism not in and of itself, but rather preeminently as the locus of the Spirit's activity.

At the same time, Gregory emphasizes that the Spirit's work is by no means limited only to baptism; in fact, that work actually precedes baptism and remains active after the baptismal event has concluded (31.29; 34.14). The goal of baptism is that one become like God through rebirth and transformation (31.28). Baptism in water and the Spirit establishes the covenant of a second life with God that the believer might walk with God more purely (40.8), and in that sense it is the Spirit acting through the baptismal event that brings about a person's ethical enablement. Through the spiritual illumination of baptism, the believer enters discipleship of the Spirit (40.3), and through this rebirth comes to confess God and is transformed while the earthly element is spiritualized (18.13).

In Gregory's understanding, the scope of the Spirit's baptismal activity extends to four areas. In enhancing the community the Spirit acts with those who are baptized, with the waters, with the fellow human beings of Christians, and finally with the entire world.

What characterizes the community of the Spirit? One of the most important characteristics of the activity of the Spirit in Gregory's understanding is harmony, a concept deriving from music and mathematics denoting balanced proportional relationship and the element of unity within multiplicity.

---

121. This eschatological identity of the community of faith comes to expression especially in Gregory's treatment of Christian festivals.

The harmony characterizing the Spirit's community becomes manifest when the Spirit counters the divisive powers of the multiplicity of languages. Without suspending the plurality of languages, the pouring out of the Spirit nonetheless brings all these languages back into a harmonious state (41.16). Gregory also finds unity in multiplicity with regard to the charismata, the gifts of grace, even though the variety and distinction between the gifts remain in place. He finds that because the various charismata complement one another, all are worthy of equal praise (41.16).[122] Gregory employs the metaphor of the body to illustrate how the Spirit harmoniously shapes the Christian community into an organic unity; here he picks up on biblical imagery in Romans 12:5 (*Or.* 32.11) and Ephesians 4:4 (*Or.* 2.3; 6.8), and refers to the Spirit as the *cause* of this unification (32.11). Here the one Spirit creates *one* people of spiritual Christendom (34.6), caring for that people as its flock and watering it with refreshing drink (6.9). The children of the Spirit also remain one people in battle (6.22); all their relationships are characterized by harmony and peace. Each protects the other, and they all preserve the peace (24.2), burning in passion for instead of against one another (6.4). In the larger sense the Spirit represents the framework of this shared peace (42.13), shaping the community into a single, organic, uniform body (6.4).

The Cappadocian sees the church in the Spirit as a tent set up by the Lord, shimmering in virtuous beauty, a holy temple for Christ consisting of human beings in which the artistic Spirit harmoniously unites all the parts into a whole (19.8). The preeminent characteristic of the community created by the Spirit is harmony and the harmonious unity encompassing a multiplicity of parts within a common whole.

The Vivifying Spirit

Does Gregory understand the Spirit as acting only on behalf of human beings, or is its activity also directed toward nonhuman life? Does the Spirit set all of creation free? The cosmological dimension does not merely represent an addendum to Gregory's doctrine of the Spirit. Quite the contrary, his doctrine of redemption presupposes his pneumatology. Insofar as the Holy Spirit is the agent of the creation, preservation, and consummation of the cosmos, its redemptive activity commensurately also involves the entire cosmos. Understanding God's redemptive activity as being merely partial or in some way

---

122. Gregory is particularly inclined to refer to baptism as a gift of the Spirit (*Or.* 39.14; 40.4). He enumerates various gifts in 32.11.

not universally oriented also necessarily restricts God's activity in creation. To a considerable degree the cosmic dimension of pneumatology constitutes the measure, presupposition, and consequence of the three central elements in Gregory's doctrine of faith, namely, creation, incarnation, and liberation focused on the future.

How does Gregory develop his understanding of cosmic pneumatology? How is God manifested as Spirit within the beauty of the world as a whole? Gregory finds a biblical point of departure in Paul's reference to the Spirit that "searches everything, even the depths of God" (1 Cor. 2:10; cf. Or. 28.6; 14.28; 43.65), in the wisdom text that speaks of how "the Spirit of the Lord has filled the world" (Wisd. of Sol. 1:7; cf. Or. 28.6; 41.9), and finally also in Acts 17:28, which speaks of how "in him [God] we live and move and have our being" (Or. 30.20). On Gregory's view, no living being in the world is ever without God — Godless — since as creatures they are divinely maintained in their very existence and life. Although creation is restricted, temporal, spatial, and corporeal (material-corporeal and spiritual-corporeal), the principle of their origin and preservation is the Spirit, which is atemporal, nonspatial, noncorporeal, and unrestricted (41.7; 31.29; 41.9; 32.27).

Gregory finds God's Spirit in many places. It is active in the angels (41.11), watches over all things (31.29), and brings about things that presuppose a being capable of movement (though it does not cause movement itself; 31.6). As the Holy Spirit it is unrestricted, permeating all things and hastening through all things while yet abiding (32.27). God as Spirit is the one in whom all things exist (39.12), and God is in all things as the Spirit (26.19). For Gregory the Spirit is the source of movement whence emerges the very order in which all things are wisely ordered and distributed (42.1). God's Spirit orders and shapes the parts into a whole and makes them into a unity (32.11). God is a Spirit that displaces mountains (40.10). God fulfills and contains the world in himself within the Spirit (31.29; 41.9). The Holy Spirit provides order and providence for the world (32.10) and renews the world All (7.21). Indeed, the Spirit guides the All in its providence (*Carm.* 1.1.30). The Spirit adds life to everything (1.1.33), and it is the Spirit that bestows life on all that lives so that all life might sing the praises of its Creator (1.1.31).

Gregory understands the very existence of life itself as a manifestation of the Spirit, since in his understanding of the world life presupposes the Spirit. Biology and cosmology always also presuppose pneumatology. Gregory understands the Spirit as the *agent* of all life, as the Spirit that vivifies, not merely as the bestower of life in some mechanical, causal sense.

One particularly striking assertion is that the Spirit guides through nature rather than through grace (Or. 31.29). Here the polarity between the terms "nature" and "grace" does not correspond to that between creation and Creator. God's Spirit acts through *physis;* that is, the Spirit is present and active amid the changing processes of becoming and passing away within nature itself.

Gregory's understanding of the Spirit's cosmic activity is not meant in the sense of immanence, since he clearly emphasizes that the characteristics of the Spirit are different from those of the world in which it is active. On the other hand, however, although Gregory does unequivocally believe that the Spirit's very being fills the world, he nonetheless emphasizes that the unique character of the Spirit's activity in and with the world consists precisely in the confluence, as it were, of that which is in fact different. Gregory's rhetorical figure here simultaneously distinguishes *and* unites the Spirit and the world insofar as although the Spirit is certainly not *like* the world, it is nonetheless *in* the world. The Spirit is unrestricted, the world restricted; yet the Spirit still permeates and abides precisely in that world. Although Gregory insists that nothing fills the Spirit itself, the Spirit does indeed fill the world.

The Cappadocian's understanding of this predication of the Spirit as the bestower of life is comprehensive. Temporally the Spirit not only creates life in the beginning, but also constantly bestows life, functioning as a kind of perpetually flowing source of being whose activity is oriented especially toward the future. The unique characteristic of this activity is consummation. The Spirit guides and renews the world All, its activity encompassing the world's origin, present, and future. Spatially there is no place at which the Spirit is not active, prompting Gregory to assume not that the Spirit is ontologically omnipresent but rather that it is constantly *moving* from one place to another in a fashion more soteriological than ontological. The Spirit searches, hastens, watches, abides, and permeates.

Gregory also maintains that the Spirit inheres *within* the material world. On the one hand, God as Spirit is included in everything; on the other, everything is included in the Spirit. In Gregory's theology the Spirit can inhere within and yet also encompass the limited; that is, the boundaries between within and without that do restrict all that is created do not really constitute boundaries for the Spirit, but rather "passageways."

The elements characterizing the Spirit's enhancement of community now recur in Gregory's description of how the Spirit vivifies the world through establishing unity in multiplicity, whereby the Spirit combines and shapes the parts into a whole. The Spirit is the agent of the cosmos that creates beautiful order. It is not the "cosmetic agent" that might adorn the world, but the very presupposition of the world's beauty.

Gregory describes the Spirit's activity as movement.[123] The Spirit is the source of the world's motion even though it does not actually *constitute* the movement of living things. As the creator of movement, however, the Spirit is in perpetual motion, never resting.

Although Gregory picks up here on the Aristotelian assertion that the principle of movement can be used to explain biological life, he nonetheless counters the Aristotelian "unmoved mover" with his understanding of the Spirit in motion. He also touches on the passage in Plato's *Phaedrus* that asserts that the movement of the soul itself represents the origin of life.[124] Gregory's understanding of the Spirit in motion also enables him to interpret biblical references to the cosmic breadth of the Spirit's activity. Finally, his cosmic pneumatology enables him to qualify the activity of the Spirit from the trinitarian perspective of the incarnation event. The entire cosmos is now to be incorporated into the transformation that began with the incarnation of the Son. The title of this book, *Creation Set Free: The Spirit as Liberator of Nature*, rather than citing or alluding to a specific passage in Gregory's work, summarizes the fundamental thesis of his cosmic trinitarian pneumatology. God's Spirit creates, liberates, and consummates all life that becomes and passes away.

The Correspondence between the Spirit of God and the Liberation of Creation

What is Gregory's understanding of the relationship between the personality of the Spirit and the life of creation? We have seen how his cosmic pneumatology understands the Spirit's activity as manifested in indwelling, in the enhancement of community, and in vivification. What is the relationship between the Spirit and creation? Gregory begins with the assumption that something in the life of creation corresponds to the activity of the Holy Spirit, something he expresses in the metaphor of the harp and harpist, referring to himself as the instrument the Spirit tunes and plays (*Or.* 12.1; 43.67). Because they were created in the image of God, human beings are endowed with spiritual capabilities, while their corporeal nature is the companion of their spirit and the space and instrument of the Holy Spirit. Gregory's theological cosmology also understands spirituality as a characteristic of creation itself, material creation being permeated by the Spirit, receiving its life from the Spirit that it might praise its Creator.

---

123. Cf. above in chap. 3.
124. *Phaedrus* 24.

The Conditions of Correspondence

The *divinity of the Spirit* constitutes the first condition of correspondence between Spirit and nature in Gregory's theology. Cosmological pneumatology
utterly loses its impact and is reduced to an insignificant addendum without
the assertion of the full divinity and personality of the Holy Spirit. Gregory
emphasizes that the Spirit participated in the work of creation in the beginning, was active in an obscure fashion for the Greeks and Jews in pagan philosophy and during the time of the Old Testament, and accompanied the incarnate Son's earthly ministry and suffered along with the Son on the cross.
These considerations suggest to Gregory that the Spirit is indeed of one essence with the Son and the Father, while its specific work can be described as
"consummation." In Gregory's theology the Father, Son, and Spirit bring
about creation and redemption together.

The event of incarnation constitutes the second condition of correspondence between the Spirit and nature. Because the Son became and suffered as a corporeal human being, so also should the Spirit appear corporeally. The Spirit's consummation of creation presupposes that the Son has
already set the redemptive process in motion, the Son's ascension then constituting the historical trinitarian "seam." God's intention is to be present in nature as a result of free will that nature might be redeemed. When the Son returns to the Father "above," the Spirit enters into the world and begins the
new period in God's history with his world that Gregory calls the "indwelling." The Father and the Son have already been revealed; now it is time for
God's Spirit to become visible as well. The *inhabitation* continues the redemptive *incarnation*. The Spirit now corresponds to nature within the redemptive process.

The Conceptual Figure of Correspondence: Permeation — Indwelling — Consummation

In terms of a more modern definition, we can describe the unique characteristic of the Spirit as "the being of the one in or with the other,"[125] a definition
certainly concurring with Gregory's understanding that the Spirit is always
(in essence) the Spirit of God and yet (in its activity) is simultaneously in or
with the created, where it is present according to its *entire* essence. In Gregory's own words, the Spirit permeates, hastens through, abides in, and indeed

125. Lessing 1984, 218.

is in everything while yet retaining its identity as the fully divine Spirit of God. The entire Trinity is present in the activity of the Spirit.

Expressed pneumatologically, this liberation of nature comes about in three stages that can be described with different prepositions indicating the various aspects of this "being with another":

1. The Spirit permeates creation *through and through* and yet is also *with* it.
2. It indwells creation; the Spirit is *in* creation.
3. It consummates creation, leading creation *to* a new being with the Creator.

The first stage represents the *ontic* activity of the Spirit. By actively permeating all created being, the Spirit preserves life and being. The bestower of life moves in and out of the world, moving from the one to the other without being spatially restricted itself. The boundaries separating within from without pose no obstacle to the Spirit. We saw earlier how *dynamically* the Spirit's activity proceeds in bestowing life and permeating nature. Instead of proceeding according to simple mechanistic natural law, this ontic activity represents the perpetually loving, permeating breath of the God who breathes life itself.

The second stage represents the *incarnational* activity of the Spirit. Rather than moving merely in and out of creation, the Spirit now freely chooses a single place to be present within creation, namely, the body and spirit of believers. The Holy Spirit continues the liberating work of Christ by being active not only in believers and in their community, but also outside the church in nature and humankind at large, meaning of course that now believers — filled with the Spirit themselves — no longer enter into a godless world, since the very Spirit dwelling within them now also permeates creation at large. The capacity of the one to be with the other now encompasses the way the Spirit dwells in believers and with creation. God's Spirit is now active both in nature and in humankind and the church. The Spirit's incarnational activity presupposes its ontic activity.

The third stage represents the Spirit's *liberating* activity. The Spirit's indwelling within believers leads to transformation, sanctification, and liberation. Because Gregory believes that the fate of humankind is inextricably bound to the fate of the entire world, however, human redemption necessarily also encompasses not only fellow human beings but also the world in which human beings abide. The agent of this cosmic consummation is the same Spirit that is at once both God's Spirit *and* the Spirit in human beings and with nature, the Spirit that directs through nature, guides all things through providence, and renews the world.

The Spirit's unique characteristic in Gregory's theology is its capacity to be with both the Father and the Son *as well as* with creation. As God's Spirit *in the midst of* creation, it leads God and creation ever closer together. Gregory's cosmic pneumatology articulates his belief in God's liberating activity on behalf of the church, humankind, and nature. Indeed, Gregory's cosmic trinitarian pneumatology and its emphasis on the Spirit's permeation, indwelling, and consummation of creation lends meaning to the idea of a liberation of nature that contextually could have seemed quite plausible not only to Christians of various persuasions, but also to Greeks and Jews.

PART III

Cosmology as Soteriology —
a Constructive Correlation

CHAPTER 4

Correlating the Interpretations
of Late Antiquity and Late Modernity

In this chapter I examine the extent to which one might relate practically the understanding of nature represented by late antiquity and by late modernity to the problems of contemporary ecological discourse as well as to one another. Through historical-hermeneutical correlation I inquire concerning the relationship between the *interpretations* of theological texts from late antiquity and late modernity, all the while bearing in mind the four key concepts discussed in the preceding examination of the patristic position. I identify problems within ecological discourse and then in theological interpretations, and finally enter into critical dialogue with the various proposals for resolving these issues.

1. Sociality

The Problem

The Ecological Question of the Life Community

The question of the nature of community has attracted attention both in biological and in philosophical and ethical discourse. The philosophical question confronting biologists since 1925 is whether life communities are real.[1] That is, does the assumption of a biological community in the smaller and larger sense reflect a reality or rather the observer's prejudice?

The scholarly discipline of ecology differentiates systematically between

---

1. Cf. Trepl 1987, 141.

the various hierarchies of communities, from which it has developed the methodological concept of succession according to which a community is no longer defined as that which is similar but rather as what follows sequentially.[2] That which is connected in a dynamic-genetic fashion as a society represents part of a "successive series."

Since the beginning of the twentieth century, scholars have emphasized the end of such a successive series, and Clements in particular has summarized such an end in the ideal of a concluding society, developing the theory of mono-climax and superorganism according to which a life community in succession necessarily creates its own environmental conditions.[3] In this theory the succession of the life community is totally determined. Just as the progress and demise of human culture — for example, of the West — are universally determined, so also the biological community. Clements's ecological-organismic concept applied the conservative cultural pessimism of his age to nature.

The same climate produced the holistic school with its thesis that the life organism of nature constitutes a totality. Representatives of holism understood themselves as a countermovement to experimental, analytical research. The term "holocoen" summarizes that which relates or connects the various living spaces and areas of plant and animal communities.[4]

This organismic concept encountered vehement resistance. In 1926 Gleason pointed out that changes in vegetation could not possibly be explained deterministically if the ecology of change were examined at the geographical level. In his "individualistic" concept he persuasively demonstrated that succession was characterized by the historical character of a "mere group effect."[5] In 1935 Tansley developed the concept of the ecosystem in his discussion of the spatially conceived holistic concept of totality, thereby initially providing a satisfactory solution to the philosophical problem of the reality of community by proposing that the concept of system constituted the theoretical presupposition of any knowledge of real biological functions. This proposal made the holistic concept of totality operational without also requiring the adoption of its rather questionable organismic conditions.

---

2. Kinzelbach 1989, 15ff. The distinction is between the *organism* and its *surroundings* or *environment,* and between the biozone (life community) and the biotope (and comprehensively the biosphere). Plant ecology focuses on the concept of society, while animal ecologists examine the construction of life communities from below by populations and groups (of populations). Trepl 1987, 162-65. Synecology studies the relationships between species within communities.

3. Trepl 1987, 145.

4. Trepl 1987, 184. Concerning holism, cf. also Meyer-Abich 1988, 89-103.

5. Trepl 1987, 154-58.

In any event, this concept of ecosystem certainly did not end the debate on the problem of the life community. The holistic position acquired new advocates as a result of the increased instrumentalization of the discipline of ecology itself and the increasingly evident devastation of nature.

One can object that the holistic position is not sufficiently cognizant of the presuppositions of its own knowledge. Quite contrary to the intentions of holism, concepts such as "organism," "living whole," and "Gaia" cannot transcend their function as epistemological metaphors. That the biosphere can be *interpreted* as a living being does not yet prove that it really *is* such. One should critically examine the ideological inclinations and methodological monism accompanying the dogmatic concept of the neo-organismic theory.

Ethical problems emerge in connection with the examination of the life community when a sympathetic understanding of the world provides environmental-ethical arguments.[6] One special problem involves the question of the scope of the life community within the moral context. Meyer-Abich, Altner, and Moltmann all argue that the moral community includes *all* life,[7] whereas the utilitarians draw a boundary line beneath animals that are capable of suffering.[8] The urgency of the ethical question regarding the scope of environmental ethics is commensurate with the pervasiveness of the conviction that human technology can manipulate the biosphere in an all-encompassing fashion.[9]

The idea of community plays a central role in communitarian and ecological environmental ethics. Communitarian ethics puts the social criterion before that of the individual. Ecological ethics, picking up on the communitarian initiative, focuses on the idea of a biotic community.[10]

Initiatives deriving from discursive ethical theory postulate a communicative community of interpersonal discourse in which those affected within the biological life community have the right to share in decisions and the

---

6. A "sympathetic" understanding of the world is one that, beginning with a feeling of empathy and oneness, experiences, interprets, and perceives the world as a meaningful nexus to which human beings also belong. Cf. Böhler 1981, 73.

7. Meyer-Abich 1989a; Altner 1991, 108; Moltmann and Giesser 1990, 25. Cf. Bergmann 1992 and 1994b. For a critique of the entire notion of ecologically focused rights of nature, see Irrgang 1992, 82-91.

8. Birnbacher 1986, 121ff.; Singer 1992.

9. Cf. among many others Jonas 1987, 84f., and Ropohl 1987.

10. Examples include the influential "land ethics" initiated by Aldo Leopold in the USA, one of whose basic principles is that "a thing is right when it tends to preserve the integrity, stability and beauty of the biotic community. It is wrong when it tends otherwise." Cited after Weber 1987, 19.

right to representation.[11] This position views the human communicative community as part of a more comprehensive ecological life community, and culture as a specifically human contribution to nature. How do theologians understand the problem of communality? What solutions do they propose?

Theological Interpretations

God as Perfect Ecological Life: John B. Cobb, Jr. Whitehead describes his own thought as the "philosophy of organism," maintaining that the theory of evolution should be encompassed by a fundamental concept of the organism of nature.[12] Together with the biologist Charles Birch, Cobb adopts this position and develops the "ecological model" as an alternative to the mechanistic and vitalistic model: "The ecological model is of entities which are what they are because of the environment in which they are found."[13] This model proposes combining the idea of evolution with that of ecology. "Events" rather than substances are primary.[14] What we usually call "living" and "individual events" Cobb calls "societies of events."[15] What takes place at all levels "is a function of a structure of interacting events"; the ecological model is a "model of internal relations" encompassing both human and other living beings.[16]

Birch and Cobb enlist the popular idiom in referring to a "web of life" whose value consists precisely in multiplicity, and their ethical maxim is accordingly that of "maximising richness of experience" (170-75). For process theology the life community also has an ethical dimension expressed in the thesis of the "intrinsic value" of all beings and of their mutual "instrumental values" (170).[17]

The subtitle of Birch and Cobb's book is *From the Cell to the Commu-*

---

11. Apel 1992b, 248; Bergmann 1994a, 81-84.

12. Whitehead 1926, 157, picks up on the idea of the biological organism: "The doctrine thus cries aloud for a conception of organism as fundamental for nature." When in 1990 Birch and Cobb adopted Whitehead's philosophical reception of Clements's organismic theory from the 1920s, they also inherited the metaphysical and monistic aporia attaching to this theory.

13. Birch and Cobb 1990, 94.

14. Birch and Cobb 1990, 95; Cobb 1972, 113.

15. Cobb 1972, 112.

16. Birch and Cobb 1990, 95. The numbers in parentheses in the following text refer to this work.

17. Cobb 1972, 70.

nity. Anthropologically they explain the body as a "society of living cells." That is, the body should be understood not mechanistically, but rather as a "living community with ourselves." As biological communities, human beings genuinely participate in one another (187f.). The same life the body receives also functions as a "cosmic principle" within the world at large as well as in all its parts. Life is the "ideal power": "Life is creator" (193). Theologically Birch and Cobb identify life and God, maintaining that "life as the central religious symbol is God" (195). Although Cobb's primary goal is to mediate between the Christian understanding of God and that of Whitehead's philosophy, he would also like to provide a theological interpretation of the ecological model of nature: "Indeed, God is the supreme and perfect exemplification of the ecological model of life" (195).

Employing trinitarian theology seems to be important to Cobb, even though it is always Whitehead's understanding of God that provides the perspective from which to interpret the classical trinitarian statements. Cobb interprets the development of trinitarian statements as well as the personality of the Father and Son as a tension between God's creative and responsive love. The Holy Spirit, albeit without personality, becomes the creator of unity.[18]

As the Creator, God remains dependent on his own creation. Without the world there is no God. God embodies the principle of internal relations, contains the world and yet is simultaneously contained within it: "But God includes the world, and the world includes God" (197). The guarantor of development toward the good is for Birch and Cobb life itself, whose goal is the goodness of human communities, of species, and of the overall, total community of all living things. Birch and Cobb speak of "Life as that which transforms and liberates us" (201).

In summary we can say that by reawakening the concept of organism, Cobb unites the evolutionary and ecological aspects of the modern biological understanding of nature in the ecological model. His fundamental concept is the sociomorphic idea of an organic life community, even though he more often speaks about "life" itself as the subject rather than in a more differentiated fashion about the life community. Human society is understood as being wholly integrated into the biological community of internal relations and interacting events while yet allowing for that which constitutes the specifically or uniquely human element. Cobb articulates the life community ethically in the idea of the intrinsic value of all things.

The guiding notion in Cobb's understanding of God is Whitehead's metaphysical idea of God, which hardly distinguishes God from his creatures.

18. Cobb and Griffin 1977, 110.

Because trinitarian theology serves in this tradition more as a common point of contact than as a genuine point of departure for ecological theology, Cobb is unable to access the aspect of a sociality of the divine being itself. The characteristic notion for Cobb is that of a consummation or perfection of creation, a "transformative creation" motivated both biologically and theologically.[19] Within the overriding framework of the one world, Cobb also postulates the comprehensive ecological horizon of divine redemptive activity.[20]

The Bioethical, Evolutionary Totality of Life: Günter Altner Instead of developing a *concept* of the life community, Günter Altner focuses instead on various qualities of life in its totality, emphasizing especially the temporally open nature of life, the common evolutionary origin of all forms of life, and the mutual relatedness of all creaturely existence. Altner confronts the mechanistic interpretation of evolution with a dynamic view of nature as an "open system within time,"[21] and the deterministic natural sciences with ecological science with its consideration of the "formative dynamics" and "self-organization" of nature.[22]

This evolutionary perspective on nature reveals to Altner a totality of "common life history" from which he then derives the equality of human beings, animals, plants, and microorganisms. In that sense, of course, the "argument of a common origin" acquires fundamental ethical significance: "Criteria for our present dealings with one another can be derived from this common life history."[23]

Altner picks up Schweitzer's reverential ethical understanding and applies it to contemporary bioethical problems,[24] taking the conflictive nature of life as his point of departure.[25] For this theologian the preservation and support of life is always good, its destruction and damage always bad. Following Schweitzer's ethical understanding of the world, Altner describes human beings amid the life around them as that particular being that, because it is

---

19. Cf. Welker 1988, 192-96. Welker, 200ff., suggests that Cobb might do well to engage Hegel's concept of the spirit and avoid confusing references to God with references to heaven (which can also be understood philosophically as the sphere of transcendence).

20. Cobb 1982, 112.

21. Altner 1991, 17.

22. Altner 1984, 207.

23. Altner 1991, 205.

24. Altner 1991. Cf. Rockefeller 1997, 59, who makes Schweitzer's principle of "reverence for life" the center of a common environmental ethics for the world religions.

25. Altner 1991, 58-69.

capable of acquiring knowledge of the deeper origins of life and also of ethical conflict, is also capable of accepting responsibility. Human beings must address the question of the unity of the world encompassing all life-forms in the concept of life *(bios)*. Altner derives his basic bioethical criterion from this integrated, evolutionary-historical, antideterministic understanding of the concept of life: "not the guarantee of a life free of suffering, but rather as far as possible the minimalization of pain, destruction, and death on behalf of *all* partners participating in the competition for survival."[26]

Because of the comprehensive nature of this participation of all life-forms in the biological process and the extensive nexus of mutual relationships connecting all of them, Altner considers it imperative that one consider and respect *all* participating life-forms when resolving conflicts of interest. I would call this notion a *bioethically evolutionary life community*.

Altner parts company with Cobb and McFague by emphasizing ethical conflict as the presupposition for the constitution of life itself.[27] Whereas Cobb addresses potential damage to life more as a necessary evil within the overall process of biological exchange,[28] Altner views it as an ethical challenge. Both agree, however, regarding the value of all life-forms and regarding their interconnected communality, and both attribute intrinsic value to such. Altner similarly concurs that there is a "community of the rights of nature" and that this community includes rights of nature as acknowledged by human beings.[29]

Theologically Altner juxtaposes the biblical concept of creation with the Greek and pantheistic concept of *natura naturans*. The "bios as the total-

---

26. Altner 1991, 70.

27. McFague 1993, 174-78, distinguishes between "natural evil" and "sin." McFague maintains that human sin represents the basic ethical problem. On the one hand, she maintains that God cannot suspend the inevitability of death according to natural law; on the other, she understands God to be present among the suffering such that God is with both the living and the dead, since life in the world does, after all, operate within his body (176). I believe McFague slips into a form of quietism here that reduces the universal eschatological claim of the Christian faith to an insignificant remnant.

28. Birch and Cobb 1990, 193: "If we affirm life, it must be a life that includes a continual process of dying and eventuates in death. . . . In this sense evil is an inherent part of good, at least in this world and in this life." I do not believe Birch and Cobb adequately distinguish between *necessary death for the sake of subsequent life*, on the one hand, and *evil, senseless, violent death* on the other. I am disinclined to refer to necessary death as "evil as an inherent part of good" because it makes it impossible to distinguish linguistically between two different kinds of death. Altner (1991) vehemently advocates a Christian *ars moriendi* that will displace the kind of repression of death that in its own turn has brought about the environmental crisis.

29. Altner 1991, 101-7, 111-15.

ity of all creatures" derives its value for Altner solely from the "creation being of all life forms."[30] One of Altner's goals is to free biblical references to a universal history of liberation as well as the relevance of cosmic redemption through Christ from the ancient metaphysics of the biblical worldview and to mediate those references within the contemporary understanding of the world. Altner believes all creatures "participate in the liberation promised to human beings."[31]

The trinitarian understanding of God is of no real consequence in this context. Altner criticizes Moltmann's trinitarian understanding of God as "completely untranslated references . . . with no meaning for secular reason."[32] Altner, like Cobb, finds trinitarian creation theology to be of no use in providing a theological response to an understanding of nature that is open to process. Instead, he finds such a response in a "theology of the cross that dares to interpret the suffering of the world in the light of the cross as the relevant potential of hope for the future."[33]

Altner's intention is to articulate the Christian faith as the "cosmological relevance of the reconciliation of God with the entirety of creation effected by Jesus Christ" in connection and in dialogue with contemporary worldviews.[34] Such a formulation does, it may be noted, bring Altner closer to the classical trinitarian problem, and as such links him to Moltmann and Link in asking the question of *how* the historical Jesus (as the Son) is able to reconcile God (the Father) with the life community of his creation (in the Spirit).

In summary one can say that Altner understands the totality of the world from the perspective of evolutionary history and its common origin as well as from the perspective of the future as a temporally open development, deriving the equality of life-forms and their intrinsic value from the being of creation itself and from their common origin. Unlike process theology, however, Altner follows Schweitzer in emphasizing the bioethical conflict among life-forms as a constitutive factor of the life community and understands human beings to be in a position of having to assume responsibility in that community. Altner concurs with process theology in accepting the importance of a process-oriented understanding of the world and the intrinsic value of life. From the perspective of creation theology, he rejects any "subsequent

30. Altner 1991, 79.
31. Altner 1991, 83f.
32. Altner 1988, 146.
33. Altner 1988, 151.
34. Altner 1984, 206.

dogmatization"[35] of new worldviews and doubts the relevance of references to trinitarian sociality — contra Moltmann — in favor of a universal eschatological interpretation of the cross.

Analogous Sociality in God, Humankind, and Nature: Jürgen Moltmann

The idea of community plays a preeminent role in the theology of Jürgen Moltmann. The social doctrine of the Trinity he worked out in 1980 he then applied to a doctrine of creation in 1985. The "trinitarian concept of life as interpenetration or perichoresis" shapes his "ecological doctrine of creation."[36] Moltmann confronts the understanding of God as absolute subject with that of God as perfect community. God as subject is related to the world as ruler, whereas the social God is related to the world in "an intricate relationship of community." Moltmann understands life as "communication in communion," and at the religious level as "community of creation"[37] whose goal is not destruction, but rather to become a "nonviolent, peaceful, ecological world-wide community in solidarity."[38]

In Moltmann's view this creation community includes a spatial as well as a temporal dimension. Human culture and nature constitute a unity. The generations of humankind through the ages as well as the community of men and women are to be reconciled.[39] Moltmann addresses the evolutionary aspect of the creation community from the perspective of Christology, countering Teilhard de Chardin's *Christus evolutor* with Christ as "a victim among evolution's other victims" and as "the redeemer of evolution."[40] Moltmann has been intensively engaged in the debate concerning the rights of nature, emphasizing the character of the creation community as a community of rights guided by the idea of reconciliation.[41]

It is God's Spirit that connects human beings with their natural environment, an alliance Moltmann calls the "spiritual ecosystem" that relates societies with the system of the earth itself in the larger sense. Human beings and nature together participate in a "eucharistic community of creation" whose cosmic thanksgiving is presented before God.[42] Moltmann seeks to overcome both the monistic and the pantheistic concept of God, tran-

---

35. Altner 1988, 106.
36. Moltmann 1985, 17.
37. Moltmann 1985, 3f.; 1989, 57.
38. Moltmann 1985, 12.
39. Moltmann 1990, 269f.; 1989, 11f.; 2001b, 236-41.
40. Moltmann 1990, 296, 301.
41. Moltmann 1990, 305-12; 1989, 66-71.
42. Moltmann 1985, 69ff.

sitioning then to panentheism. He would also like to overcome the rather one-sided understanding of transcendence and immanence; like Altner, he views creation as "a system that is open," focusing rather on that system's openness to God and to the future.[43]

Moltmann also incorporates the idea of community into his trinitarian anthropology, where he understands the notion of human beings created in the image of God as referring to their "social likeness." God shapes and fashions as the *imago Trinitatis* not only the individual human being but also human society as a whole.[44] In illustrating his understanding of the Trinity, Moltmann historically adduces Gregory of Nazianzus's analogy of the family contra Augustine.[45]

Theologically Moltmann distinguishes between the trinitarian and unitarian concept of community, the former emphasizing multiplicity and an enhancement of community in contrast to unity and uniformity. In Moltmann's theology of "social experience of God," God's community includes self-experience as well as social and natural experience. The source of this community is God's Spirit.[46]

Moltmann discerns the activity of the Spirit in the "drawing of the creatures into a community [*Vergemeinschaftung der Geschöpfe*]," referring to an enhanced variety and organization of information and exchange of energy.[47] "The perception of the divine Spirit in the community of creation corresponds to the new ecological understanding of nature which we seek."[48] The social experience of God brings together love of self and neighbor as well as personality and sociality. This "open friendship" includes the things of the world and everything that holds them together: the "sympathy of the world."[49]

For Moltmann the "trinitarian doxology" represents the consummation of the understanding of the Trinity, that is, of the monarchical (Western), historical, and eucharistic concepts.[50] Instead of being confined to linearly understood self-mediation, the Spirit, Father, and Son are now understood as part of "the self-circling and self-reposing movement of the

43. Moltmann 1985, 103. Moltmann connects to the interdisciplinary theory of the "open systems," which has generated a strong influence on the dialogue between scientists and theologians and philosophers.

44. Moltmann 1985, 234-43; 1991b, 93-97.

45. Moltmann 1981, 199; 1985, 235; 1991b, 94.

46. Moltmann 2001b, 221.

47. Moltmann 2001b, 225.

48. Moltmann 1989, 58.

49. Moltmann 2001b, 255, 259.

50. Moltmann 1981, 151-54; 1991b, 103ff.

perichoresis."[51] Although Moltmann's understanding of *perichoresis* invokes the Eastern Church Fathers, it ignores the fact that the concept was not applied to trinitarian theology until the seventh century. In contradistinction to the Cappadocian Fathers, Moltmann (and Boff)[52] rejects the thesis of the monarchy of the Father as the ground of the trinitarian unity, preferring to understand *perichoresis* more inclusively as an "open Trinity" and as a unity that both invites and unites.[53]

In summary, Moltmann's understanding of community focuses on an analogous sociality obtaining between God, human beings, and nature, a relationship applying to God's communality, to the social constitution of human beings, and to the ecological, process-oriented constitution of nature. The human community resides in the community of nature, and both develop in openness to God's community, which in its turn is open to creation. Here Moltmann presupposes an element of analogous similarity without addressing why and how such an analogy might plausibly be applied to the construction of new forms of social or ecological community. He does not really discuss in any depth the extent to which this differentiation between the three types of community might be significant in this context. Moltmann's anti-unitarian, trinitarian concept of community leaves behind the metaphysical limitations of concepts influenced by antiquity and aims instead to disclose the new theological presuppositions needed for articulating the ontology of an ecological understanding of nature and a pluralistic understanding of society.

Nature as History, Creation as Salvation History: Christian Link   Christian Link maintains that the central problem of creation theology is the contemporary rift between nature and history.[54] Drawing on the modern scientific theories and the contemporary philosophical initiative of Picht, Link tries to establish a positive understanding of the temporality of nature as creation; hence he is more inclined to emphasize the temporal, process-oriented, evolutionary aspect of natural occurrences than spatial ecological relationality.

Link understands human beings as being indissolubly bound to the "solidarity community of creation." From the perspective of human beings, one must speak of the world only to the extent a *temporally* existing subject views it as a *co-world* rather than anthropocentrically as the world *surround-*

51. Moltmann 2001b, 304.
52. Boff 1988, 234f.
53. Moltmann 1991b, 126f.
54. Link 1991, 456. The parenthetical page numbers in the following text are to this work.

ing them. History becomes the determinative category in the ecological model: "Nature has acquired not just a subject, but also a *history*" (466). Link understands the task of theology to be establishing a comprehensive, biblically grounded horizon enabling us to view creation synoptically together with its goal of consummation and to regain the endangered unity of nature and history (462).

Link is aware that one cannot simply identify the ongoing, emergent processes and self-organization of nature with God, which merely places these emanations into God's nature. Instead, Link follows Barth in understanding the relationship between God and world as that of similitude: "If this *capacity* for similitude . . . is the salient feature differentiating creation from mere nature, then there inheres within creatures themselves the potential for being the material of a history of God" (531). Link quite consciously revives the tradition of trinitarian theology in incorporating the history of nature into the history of trinitarian revelation (527).

Link bases his understanding of salvation history on a differentiation of the three articles of the creeds, placing his emphasis on God's "self-representation" in relation to the "transparency" of nature and on an eschatological orientation toward the future.[55] He does not address the classic problem of the inner-trinitarian relationships or of the relevance they might have for creation theology, and only in connection with the third article, on the Spirit, does he mention the aspect of community.[56]

In summary, Link emphasizes the temporal dimension of the life community at the expense of its spatial dimension. Accepting the rupturing of the closed Cartesian concept of nature, he concludes that a concept of God is no longer needed to guarantee the discernible regularity attaching to natural law.[57] In so doing, he creates the theological presupposition for entering into dialogue with the ecological understanding of nature.

The Conflict Partnership of Creation, Moving toward a Community of Peace: Gerhard Liedke and Ulrich Duchrow   Beginning with an ecological concept of nature, Gerhard Liedke tries to mediate between the biblical interpretation of nature as a "fundamental event" and the modern natural sciences.[58] Whereas the natural sciences remain objective and particular, reli-

---

55. Link 1989; 1991, 500f.
56. Link 1982, 221.
57. Link 1982, 332.
58. Liedke 1984, 96-101. Here Liedke picks up Westermann's understanding of the Old Testament creation account as a "fundamental event."

gion is capable of articulating the universality and meaningful totality of temporal events. At the same time, however, nature still represents the "common field of reference" for *both* natural science *and* religion.

Liedke understands human beings as participants in a "community of fate." Liedke associates the biblical thesis of creation in the image of God with the commission to manage nature, understanding both in connection with the comprehensive peace — shalom — commanded by God.[59]

Following the lead of Galtung, Liedke develops his own theory of conflict, taking as his point of departure the biblical idea of reconciliation between human beings and nature before God.[60] Assuming that an element of asymmetry characterizes the initial relationship between society and nature, Liedke focuses on the concept of solidarity. The first step is to acknowledge nature as a conflict partner by according it the status and character of a subject and the position of a partner. He then posits Christ's "comprehensive renunciation of power" as the christological model of conflict resolution "through symmetry below."[61] In a concrete fashion, he proposes understanding the measure of energy exchange as the measure of violence and of a diminution of violence.[62] The "simple meal" qualifies as a "symbolic ecological act" insofar as it expresses an ecologically meaningful act of solidarity.[63]

Because the term "environment" represents only an excerpt, while nature refers merely to the scientific realm of objects, Duchrow and Liedke prefer to use the term "creation" to refer to the totality. Accordingly they understand biblical hope as anticipating "the peaceful restoration of creation"[64] and similarly interpret the concept of righteousness or justice as "conduct conducive to fellowship."[65] God's community with his creation comes to expression in the biblical idea of covenant, albeit a covenant between unequal partners, thus necessarily requiring "behavior commensurate with the community" from all partners.

One might summarize Duchrow and Liedke's understanding of community as a biblical interpretation of the community of conflict between nature and human beings that ultimately is to become a community of reconciliation and of peaceful nonviolence.

59. Liedke 1984, 137.
60. Liedke 1984, 165-78; 1989.
61. Liedke 1984, 177.
62. Duchrow and Liedke 1989, 60ff.
63. Liedke 1984, 200.
64. Duchrow and Liedke 1989, 59.
65. Duchrow and Liedke 1989, 78.

The Concept of Organism as the Norm for Understanding God and Ethics: Sallie McFague   Sallie McFague rigorously engages the organismic concept of nature, paradigmatically juxtaposing it with the obsolete model of the world as a machine. The goal of her ecological theology is to interpret the organismic concept theologically with the metaphor of the "world as God's body." This organic model prompts Christian "postpatriarchal" faith to "rethink humanity's place in the scheme of things."[66]

McFague's point of departure is the common history of creation through which one can explain the interrelated nature of all living things holistically through the ages; this "common creation story"[67] provides the model for cosmological, ecological theology, and the organic model as such can allegedly help "remythologize" the Christian faith.[68] The ethical goal of human beings within this organismic life community is to acquire knowledge of our place within the overall scheme of things. Accordingly, McFague understands sin as a refusal to accept our place (112). On her view, participation in the totality of life ethically obligates human beings.

Although God as the body of the world represents merely a "model" (viii), this metaphor does function as the comprehensive, preeminent guide for our understanding of God in the larger sense. And although McFague does pick up on trinitarian theology, she rejects the designation of the inner-trinitarian relationships as those between Father, Son, and Spirit, citing the gender-specific nature of any Father-Son metaphors. Instead, she prefers to refer in a more abstract fashion to the "mystery," "physicality," and "mediation of the invisible and visible" (193).

McFague's understanding of community essentially elevates the organismic, holistic concept of nature to the unrestricted norm of systematic and ethical theology. By understanding the Christian God "panentheistically" as the body of the world, she lends theological legitimacy and mythological currency to the understanding of the world as an organism. The guiding notion of McFague's theological understanding of nature is the idea of the community of soul and body; just as the soul dwells within the body, so also does God dwell in his world "as the spirit of the body" (135).

---

66. McFague 1993, x.

67. McFague 1993, 27ff.; 1987, 6-14.

68. McFague 1993, 66. The parenthetical page numbers in the following text are to this work.

The Egalitarian and Just Life Community: Rosemary Radford Ruether

Basing her ecofeminist theology on the idea of a "biotic community," Rosemary Radford Ruether focuses on the concept of "ecojustice" in associating dominion over the earth with social dominion. Understanding the concept of nature and world as a living organism — "Gaia" — with which human beings are inextricably connected, she discusses various ways of incorporating the concept of God into such an understanding of nature.[69]

Ruether is quite aware of the significance creation accounts can have for one's understanding of society and nature: "Creation stories not only reflect current science . . . but they are also blueprints for society" (15). Because one's understanding of relationships within the life community of the world depends on a given culture's current, normative accounts of creation, such accounts also possess both a spiritual and an ethical dimension. Ruether would like to see the scientific creation story "remythed" so as to lead to reverential astonishment and valuing of all life and to a vision of humankind living in community with all fellow beings (57f.).[70]

Ruether interprets the Jewish-Christian concept of sin in connection with a comprehensive understanding of justice: "Sin . . . lies in distortion of relationship, the absolutizing of the rights to life and power of one side of a relation against the other parts with which it is, in fact, interdependent" (142). The fundamental notion in this understanding of community is equality. The dissolution of all relationships within the system of dominion leads to the community of "biophilic mutuality" (258). Rather than replacing the patriarchate with a matriarchate, Ruether suggests that "we need new forms of gender parity," new, egalitarian family models in which women are accepted as partners and men commit themselves to sustainable, ongoing life on earth (171f.).

Ruether finds the Christian contribution to the "healing" of the earth in the covenantal tradition whose Jewish origin represents the "intimate unity between justice and right relations" in the relationship between God and Israel (214). She then engages this covenantal tradition in establishing the "rights of nature": "The covenantal relation between humans and all other life forms, as one family united by one source of life, forbids this otherness from being translated into destructive hostility" (227). Ruether, pursuing the same goal as Liedke, Altner, and Moltmann, also views the "living interdepen-

---

69. Ruether 1993, 3f. The parenthetical page numbers in the following text are to this work.

70. Cf. Jeffner 1993 and 1994, who counters the empiricist view of life with a kind of rationality of astonishment.

dence of all things" and the "value of the personal in community" as the basic presuppositions for any ecological spirituality (251).

In summary, Ruether's understanding of community envisions an egalitarian life community; unfortunately, because unresolved and theologically legitimized structures of dominion persist, that community is still characterized by injustice. Instead of developing a communal or trinitarian understanding of God, in a more conventional fashion she views the relationship characterizing the covenant between God and world as a model for the relation between God and Gaia, the understanding of God and the understanding of nature.

The Eucharistic Creation Community in Modern Orthodoxy and the Proto-eschatological Life Community in African Theology Two additional concepts of the comprehensive life community beyond the primary material already mentioned are the eucharistic concept of ecumenically open Orthodoxy and the understanding of life within the African tradition. Beginning with the economic concept of God, the Syrian Orthodox theologian K. M. George focuses on the *philanthropia* of Christ toward humankind, the goal of which is to redeem the entire world. God enters into "total communion" with his creation, his redemptive activity creating, sustaining, and consummating creation through the Spirit. The basic concept characterizing George's understanding of the community of God and creation is "participation." Just as the three persons of the Trinity participate in the essence *(ousia)* of the Godhead, so also do human beings participate in God's work *(energeia)*. As mediators, human beings then expand this participation in God to nature itself.[71] Accordingly, the task of the church is to "transfigure the whole creation so that all that is created is restored from its distortions and made the body of Christ" (53). George then employs the metaphor of the house and body to express God's economic redemptive activity: "An eucharistic theology has the vision of the transfiguration of this cosmic house as the 'house of the Father' and this cosmic body as the body of Christ" (54). This theology is eucharistic insofar as in the Eucharist creation, understood symbolically and anticipating its redemption, is lifted up toward its Creator.

In George's ecological understanding of nature, every part of matter is constituted through a "network of relationships." In contrast to McFague,

---

71. George 1990, 51. George begins here with the distinction Palamite theology makes between God's "essence" and "energy." Gregory of Nazianzus speaks about God's "economy" and about believers cooperating ("synergy") with God's activities. The parenthetical page numbers in the following text are to George's article.

however, he does distinguish the totality of creation as the "ultimate body that has to become the house of the Holy Spirit" (48). Whereas the postulate of creation as God's body constitutes the presupposition for McFague's ecosomatic premise and ethics, George's soteriological premise is that it is only through liberation that the cosmic body *becomes* the dwelling place of the Spirit. George's "oikosomatic or house-body paradigm" serves as a metaphor for the *place* and *object* of God's economy, whereas McFague's metaphor serves to ground organismic ontology.

The African theologian Harvey Sindima incorporates the traditional African understanding of community into his understanding of Christian ecological spirituality, particularly in connection with the Western introduction and expansion of the mechanistic concept in Africa. For Africans "life" is the "primary category" of self-understanding and of any interpretation of the world.[72] In this context Sindima adduces the Malawians and the concepts *moyo* — the divine origin of all that exists — and *umunthu* — the purpose or determination of life. In this view the universe is full of sacred life: "All life — that of peoples, plants and animals, and the earth — originates from and therefore shares an intimate relationship of bondedness with divine life; all life *is* divine life."[73] *Umunthu* refers to the "fullness of life" and is attained through the exchange of life between creatures. It is through the participants of the life community that creation itself acquires new meaning: "In many ways, *moyo* transcends itself as the possibilities for the realization of *umunthu* are created."[74]

In that sense the all-encompassing nature of the African concept of community might even be called proto-eschatological insofar as from the presence of a common source or origin it derives the possibility of genuinely transcending and moving toward the consummation of the universal life community. Sindima's proto-eschatological understanding of community also shapes the concept of justice insofar as "justice is how we live in the web of life in reciprocity with people, other creatures, and the earth, recognizing that they are part of us and we are part of them."[75] Sindima as well as other African theologians are working toward a Christian reception of this understanding of community.[76]

A comparison with Link's understanding of the eschatological histori-

---

72. Sindima 1990, 142. Cf. Bujo 1993, 197-200, and Sundermeier 1988, 22-30.
73. Sindima 1990, 144.
74. Sindima 1990, 145.
75. Sindima 1990, 146.
76. Bujo 1993, 201-4.

calness of nature reveals how the African understanding of community is capable of intimately associating the *that* with both the *how* and the *whence/ whither* of community, whereas Western concepts emphasize either the *that* of creation at the expense of the *how* (Barth), or the *how* of the world at the expense of the *that* (process theology). African thought bases its understanding of humankind and cosmology on the basic universal category of community, which Christian African theologians, in the tradition of trinitarian theology, apply to the understanding of God, to the societal vision of "African socialism," to the *ecumene,* and to ecclesiology,[77] also countering the concept of Western "selfishness" and dualism with the concept of African "community." The salient feature of the African understanding of community is the comprehensive transcending of time, whose unity constitutes the life community in all its multifariousness and transformation.

Summary: Interpretive Common Ground

All these theologians try to interpret theologically the idea of a comprehensive biological life community. None questions the existence of such a life community, and all assume that the human construction of a "sociality of nature" can converge with reality.

The differences in the authors' emphases on particular qualities of the life community function more as complementary perspectives than as antitheses. Cobb and Birch emphasize "life" as the driving force of transformation and evolution, which also constitute the focus of Altner's understanding of nature. Moltmann emphasizes the more physically focused openness of nature's development, a consideration for the victims of development prompting him to distance himself critically from the process of evolution, a position distinguishing him from the more biologically influenced authors (Birch and Cobb; Altner). Link's conservative hermeneutical thinking picks up on the ecological rediscovery of natural history, while Liedke and Duchrow theologically expand the popular ecological understanding of the life community by emphasizing the possibility of eschatological liberation. Whereas McFague wholly subscribes to the popular concept of organism, Ruether emphasizes elements of moral inequality in community.

These various perspectives on a sociality of nature do however exhibit substantive differences regarding details. Differences emerge not least in how these authors perceive the problem of the ethical quality of the biological

77. Frostin 1988, 48-81.

community. Birch and Cobb mitigate the conflict between different interests in favor of an understanding of sociality that necessarily includes both death and transitoriness. Altner bases his premise on this conflict and then derives from the capacity to acknowledge it an important element in his understanding of human beings. Moltmann goes even further in envisioning God himself on the side of the victims of evolution. Liedke and Duchrow also focus on the element of conflict within the life community, and although Ruether does indeed address the phenomenon of inequality and "ecojustice," she (like Liedke and Duchrow) restricts her discussion completely to the notion of the injustice to which nature is subjected because of the inequality inhering in culture — though in doing so she ignores the problem of evil *within* the life community. McFague also ignores this problem, whereas Sindima conceives of justice wholly as the quality of mutuality within the overall life community.

Although all these authors positively embrace the notion of a community of the rights of nature, none considers the extent to which this notion might merely be projecting experiences and concepts of society on to nature. A parallel emerges here with the introduction of the concept of the ecosystem in that because this construction has proven to be practically quite useful and void of theoretical contradiction, the question of the *reality and content* of the construction itself is not addressed.

Additional differences emerge in the form given the theological interpretation of community. Whereas Moltmann employs the analogy between God's sociality and that of nature and society, Birch and Cobb are apparently beginning with the model of identification even if God is occasionally identified as the "symbol" and "exemplification" of life. Like Moltmann, McFague adduces the concept of "panentheism" while nonetheless consistently identifying the world as God's body. Conceiving of the soul and body as a community invokes an identification of cosmology and theology. McFague then no longer needs an understanding of community *within* the deity that might then correspond to the community of nature.

McFague differs substantively from George insofar as she maintains that the world *is* God's body, while for George the world is the body that is to *become* the *dwelling place* of the Spirit. McFague's pantheism represents the antithesis of George's classical doctrine of inhabitation, which expands the activity of the Spirit from the church out to the cosmos itself.

The idea of covenant that is central for Ruether nonetheless necessarily hinders dialogue with nontheologians. Although Altner does emphasize the relevance of faith for the understanding of nature, he does not develop his own understanding of God such that it has any significance for his understanding of nature. Liedke and Duchrow base their vision of creation set free on their understanding of the biblical God of peace. Link also chooses not to apply theological assertions directly to ecological issues, preferring instead to parallel his trinitarian understanding of salvation history only loosely with his understanding of the history of nature; in so doing he surprisingly weakens what from the perspective of theological history is certainly the rather obvious social aspect of the Trinity.

Correlation

The Common Question of the Sociality of Nature

Like modernity, antiquity was familiar with the notion of a community of biological life. Gregory himself picks up on this idea, which during his age was most familiar in the form of Stoic pantheism. For the Cappadocian the world itself is a *koinonia* that breathes and grows and is characterized by mutual interrelatedness, by movement, and by the processes of becoming and passing away. For antiquity, which had no concept of life in the modern sense, physical community was self-evidently constituted in a fundamentally theological way; that is, the divine manifested itself within the natural world.

Although Gregory did not have to address the problem burdening modern theologians, namely, to plausibly demonstrate that the understanding of God can have relevance for the understanding of nature, he, too, was concerned with articulating the Christian theological meaning of the idea of community in connection with his understanding of nature. In this sense creation theology represents the presupposition of the Christian interpretation of life.

The common goal shared by the Cappadocian and modern ecological theologians is to establish a credible theological interpretation of the idea of the sociality of nature. Their common task is to query

1. concerning the relevance of the Christian understanding of God for the social understanding of nature,
2. whether indeed the idea of community attaching contextually to the understanding of nature contradicts or is commensurate with the Christian understanding of creation,
3. concerning models that might mediate between the two positions, and
4. concerning how to apply this theologically considered understanding of community.

For Gregory the issue is largely one of providing a corrective to the alleged metaphysical aspects of nature entertained by other interpretations of life. He enters into dialogue with the Stoic understanding of the divine world body as based on the "metaphysical understanding of the *logos*" (Picht); Plotinus's ontological-ethical, emanatory understanding of nature; and the more popular understanding of the astral gods as the determinants of both human and natural society. In any event, Gregory is concerned more with metaphysical issues (2), modern authors more with questions of relevance (1) and methodology (3), though Gregory can doubtless also contribute important insights to the epistemological issues regarding nature. As for common concerns, the theology of late antiquity and of late modernity do indeed share an interest in ethics (4): Which theological understanding of the sociality of nature best enables us to view and deal appropriately with our environment?

Tradition and Situation: Establishing a Critical Dialogue

The Community of Creation and the Community of the Triune God: Gregory's Understanding of Participation and Redemption   As far as the world of creation is concerned, Gregory is certainly positively disposed toward his contemporaries' ideal of physical community and has no problem liberally invoking Stoic terminology in articulating his understanding of nature. As soon as the theological dimension comes into play, however, he is wholly disinclined to allow any identification of Creator with creation. The body of Mother Earth, rather than actually *being* God, *reveals* God economically. That is, Gaia is a functional *instrument* of God's activity and is not to be identified with God's essence.

Whenever Gregory speaks about creaturely existence, he uses the term "community" *(koinonia)*,[78] and when he speaks about the divine, he uses the term *schesis* as a reference to the interrelatedness reflected in creaturely existence. The uncreated, divine community is related *qualitatively* to the created, worldly community, God's perpetual creation activity manifesting itself as the capacity for peace, justice, life, and love within the relational characteristics permeating the life community. Because Gregory does not really understand the community of God and that of nature to be related in a strictly analogous-ontological fashion, I prefer to call that relationship *analogous and participatory-functional.*

---

78. Basil reverses this position, reserving the term *koinonia* for the divine and speaking of the "community of the Godhead." Zizioulas 1985, 134.

There obtains no *essential* analogy between the essence of God and that of nature to which human cognition might have access; in Gregory's apophatic theology human beings can fathom neither the nature of the world nor that of God. This thesis, which we might call the *mystery of the natures* (of God and the world), prompts Gregory to use the model of the participation and analogy of equal and unequal, of like and unlike.[79] The community of nature participates in the perfect community of God, which in its turn encompasses nature itself. As a God of community, however, God is *also* present in the community of biological life. That which corresponds to God in the otherwise "nondivine" economy of creation Gregory describes from a social perspective as the quality of mutual service; the capacity for peace, harmony, and justice; and the beautiful order of multiplicity and variety, all of which represent those particular characteristics of creation that express or reflect the God of community.

As we have seen, one of the salient features of Gregory's theological understanding of community is its soteriological and proto-eschatological dimension. Although he considers the community of life to be good in and of itself, it was nonetheless created imperfect or incomplete and as a result suffers under evil and thus exists in anticipation of redemption, which in Gregory's universal vision of salvation means the liberation of the entire community throughout all its relationships. Because the life community participates ontologically in the divine community and is capable of communicating — that is, of "speaking" — doxologically, it anticipates and is engaged in its own liberation from evil and its elevation into a qualitatively new condition of openness with God. The salient symbol of this perfect community for Gregory is the complete juxtaposition or coincidence *(mixis)* of divine and human nature in Christ and the inhabitation of the Spirit — through the bodies of believers themselves — in the community of the world.

Several queries for modern interpreters now emerge from this interpretation of Gregory's position.

Is McFague's Body of God the Body of the World?   One question is whether McFague's remythologizing of the organismic concept, which is rooted in Stoic pantheism, can be reconciled with classic creation theology. Can one ontologically identify the world as God's body and still distinguish persuasively between Creator and creation?

Does identifying God's external dimension (as body) ontologically with nature not eliminate the possibility of speaking in any differentiated fashion

79. See chap. 3 above.

about God's activity? Such uncritical blending of cosmological and theological references dilutes statements concerning God's historical incarnation within a specific context, ultimately rendering soteriological assertions — even universal ones — meaningless. If God as body is already present within creation, then the mere acknowledgment of this fact itself should suffice for redemption. I believe McFague runs precisely this risk when she "minimizes" historical Christology for the sake of "maximizing" cosmological Christology.[80]

Gregory's trinitarian soteriology might offer possibilities for resolving this problem. Because Christ already participated in the creation and in the preservation of nature prior to the incarnation, he can also work together with the Spirit in the consummation of community after the resurrection. In the light of trinitarian theology, the basis for our theological knowledge of God's activity remains the revelation of the earthly Jesus and his community of the created and uncreated. By contrast, McFague grounds this knowledge in our experience of an otherwise unspecified cosmic Christ immanent in the world itself. Unfortunately, in this position the Christian interpretation of life no longer provides the criterion of historical revelation and of the writings attesting that revelation.

By simplifying the understanding of conflict ethically in this way, this position now also views the suffering of nature as behavior inappropriate or incommensurate to nature — especially by human beings. By contrast, life commensurate with nature represents the highest maxim. It was in response to precisely this basically Stoic understanding of the rights of nature, however, that the Cappadocians developed their historical christological ethics of sympathy. Oddly, this theologian in late antiquity confronts and indeed overcomes the same metaphysical position among his contemporaries to which the North American theologian of late modernity lends Christian legitimacy.

The fundamental difference between McFague's ecological religion of the body[81] and Gregory's trinitarian understanding of nature derives from the ontological construction. Whereas modern advocates of holism conceive

---

80. McFague 1993, 162.

81. In her last book, although she has revised her position and made it less categoric with regard to ontology, McFague clearly develops her ecological theology after 2001 as a North American liberation theology (2001, 33ff.), even if she still seems to believe that a better life derives from a better theology (see xiv). Even if *Life Abundant* moves McFague's approach closer to Boff's and my project of "an ecological theology of liberation," it still lacks a satisfying trinitarian integration, which is evident by the split of Christology and pneumatology into two separate chapters about salvation and life. I would wish that McFague's next book could start by integrating these two final chapters (2001, chaps. 7 and 8) into one common first chapter about the "trinitarian salvation of life."

being as overriding unity, Gregory understands it communally and rigorously and consistently distinguishes between God's being and that of the world. Here ontological identification is countered by differentiated analogous-participatory relation. In a word, is the life community to be understood as the body of God or as the house or locus of divine activity?

Is Cobb's World Contained in God?   Gregory's position prompts us to ask whether Cobb (and Birch) does not also obscure the distinction between Creator and creation. Gregory maintains that the Spirit — not life — gives and consummates life as the Creator.

Although Gregory's relationship with the philosophy of his age was just as positive as is Cobb's today, unlike Cobb he was quite conscious of the conflict between the biblical and philosophical interpretation of life. Gregory would doubtless reject Cobb's notion that God is somehow dependent on his own creation. Whereas process theology maintains that the world "contains" or "includes" God, the Cappadocian maintains quite to the contrary and quite explicitly that the Spirit contains the world without itself being contained in that world (*Or.* 31.29).

The question is whether by explicitly weakening the sovereignty of God's power as Creator Cobb is not also restricting the forms in which salvation history comes to expression. Is God even capable of setting all life free? Or does he now merely sympathize with the suffering of nature? If God's being depends ontologically on the being of the world, how is one to understand the universal redemptive power of God's "creative-responsive love"? Welker has quite justifiably accused Whitehead (and Cobb) of confusing heaven with God.[82] From the perspective of Gregory's analogy between the various forms of community, one might ask whether Cobb has not confused the notion of God's social being, on the one hand, with the inclusion of the heavenly community of angels within the life community of the world, on the other.

Gregory maintains that although the heavenly powers certainly are contained within the world, God is not. I agree with Cobb that it is meaningless to conceive of the omnipotence of an omnipotent God independent of his creation. The premise of creation faith is, after all, that God reveals himself in his economy as Creator, in which case God's economy is dependent on the creative, responsive love of the world. It seems to me, however, that precisely the assumption that God's essence is inaccessible to cognition and comprehensively transcends the world creates the possibility for speaking in a meaningfully theological fashion about "responsive love" that can also bring about

---

82. Welker 1988, 130-37.

liberation. To speak in Birch and Cobb's terminology: How can life set us free if life is itself created and if God is contained within it? Does God himself become the object of the liberation of life through life? Does not vitalist ontology encounter the limits of expression here?

Cobb's trinitarian premises raise other questions as well. Does his consistent understanding of the Holy Spirit as the guarantor of unity not overshadow the personality of the Spirit's own activity? I also sense that Cobb's interpretation of the Father's creative love as being in tension with the Son's responsive love tends toward a subordinative understanding of the two. Although the Father is contained in the process of the events of the world as the principle of creation, he nonetheless reacts in the Son to the world's weaknesses and suffers together with victims. Does Cobb not get caught here in the same vortex to which Moltmann succumbed in *The Crucified God*? Does this position not take the tension between good and evil out of the life community and put it into the trinitarian community? Does God react to his creation activity "within himself"? Or is creation necessarily faulty? These theologians from late antiquity and process philosophy share parallel ontological intentions insofar as both dismiss the ontology of uniformity and substance and grant preeminence instead to temporal openness. By developing an understanding of how the two parallels of God and world approach ever more closely to one another (doctrine of *epektasis*), the Cappadocians were able to overcome both Origen's cyclical understanding of a return to the point of departure as well as the Platonic notion of matter that remains eternally the same. By picking up on Whitehead's process cosmology, Cobb is able to introduce new modes of expression for universal eschatology.

Does Moltmann Say Too Much about God's Essence? A consideration of Gregory's position enables us to ask whether Moltmann develops the idea of an analogous sociality between God, world, and humankind commensurate with the tenets of apophatic theology. I do not believe this to be the case. Gregory maintains that a theologian can describe in an analogous and participatory fashion only those qualities that God reveals in the world from the perspective of his trinitarian being. By contrast, one must be silent regarding the nature of God's communally interrelated nature. Moltmann has discussed the divine community's openness, its internal movement of circling and resting, and its perichoretic permeation. Unlike Gregory, he does not distinguish between God's communal form and that of the world, giving the impression that the two might indeed be completely congruent.

Theologically constructing a model of society or nature with the help of statements regarding God's own essence, however, inevitably encounters the charge of incommensurability — of the impossibility of translating the one into the other. The theological side of such a model of nature inevitably represents merely a nonessential complement to the otherwise secular description of the model. I believe, however, that this theological figure is now obsolete, not least because the premise of the philosophical grounding of ecological ethics is that any sustainable conception of ethics necessarily depends on religious and philosophical (sapiential) views.[83]

Our interpretation of Gregory suggests that one solution might be to incorporate into our understanding of the various qualities of ecological communal relationships first the classical theological understanding of God's nature and work in scripture and tradition, and second the Christian experience of the living God in society and nature. Establishing these connections enables us to get closer to a rigorous, consistent "theology of nature" in contrast to the conventional dogmatics of creation that Moltmann constantly adduces. Our insights into various ecological relationships could help interpret the classical Christian interpretation of life, and then lead to new insights through specifically *theological* forms of expression, insights that might then be articulated and exchanged in nonconfessional language. Rather than being translated back and forth by various specialists, statements deriving from our understanding of nature and God could mutually interpret one another.

Of course, Gregory is subject to the same charge as Moltmann in that he, too — as we saw above — was inclined to drift toward an immanent-trinitarian theology, something that later earned him the honorific title "theologian" while costing others their lives. In contrast to Moltmann, however, he does not employ the analogy of essence when establishing an ethical or ecclesiological position. Here the contextual differences between the two theologians emerge insofar as while Gregory had access to classical natural theology, Moltmann first had to establish the relevance of faith itself.

Link: The God of Community or Articles of the Trinity? Because the trinitarian understanding of God plays such an important role for Link, his historical conception might very well adduce Gregory, who, as we saw, was the first to incorporate the Trinity into an understanding of salvation history. One notices immediately, however, how little attention Link pays to the idea of communality that was so important to Gregory's understanding of *schesis*.

83. Cf. Næss 1989, 37f., who understands the term "ecosophy" as necessarily referring to the notion of the whole. In his own grounding of ecological ethics, Hösle 1991, 94, operates with the idea of God within the framework of an ideal objectivity. Deane-Drummond 1997, 223, also accuses Moltmann of engaging in excessively speculative trinitarian theology and of paying too little attention to the personality of the Spirit (224).

Has Link been so strongly influenced by Barth's personalism, with its funda-mental premise of the world as a parable of God, and by the labyrinth of Moltmann's development of the idea of analogy that he avoids references to *any* concrete analogy between the Creator and creation?

One principle of Gregory's theology is that those who would conceive God apophatically should also be able to say something positive about him, from which Gregory himself concluded that love, justice, and peace as char-acteristics of the natural *koinonia* do indeed attest God's will and work, which in their own turn are inextricably connected with his communal being. Greg-ory believes that the world itself emerged from within the loving, mutual per-ception of the hypostases within the inner Trinity. Link curiously does not engage the potential of trinitarian theology in connection with the relational model of nature even though he vehemently insists on understanding that model within the trinitarian "horizon." Does his one-sided focus on the tem-poral aspect of the world prompt this reduction? One wonders why Link falls back on the traditional three-article understanding of the Trinity that, similar to Augustine, reduces the third aspect of God, namely, the Spirit, to the activ-ity of establishing unity.

Sin as Damage to the Community: Ruether, Sindima, and Gregory   Both Ruether and Sindima understand sin much the same way as does Gregory. They view sin as damage to the relations within the life community; indeed, Gregory even declared that the sin of social injustice in the distribution of foodstuffs prompted God to visit climatic chaos upon the community.[84]

Although Ruether and Sindima also attach great significance — as did antiquity — on viewing the peace of nature from the perspective of justice, one must keep in mind the difference between the modern understanding of equality and that of antiquity. Ruether and many others follow the tradition of the Enlightenment in their understanding of ideal equality and "horizontal solidarity" (Assmann), a notion alien to antiquity, which tended to tie the idea of equality to that of ontological hierarchy, a position Gregory could hardly escape himself.

Gregory understood peace more as "vertical solidarity" in which the material serves the spiritual, the soul serves the body, and the subject serves the viceroy of creation below and the Creator above. Although Gregory's in-terpretation of baptism did indeed significantly socially radicalize the idea of equality by introducing the idea of classless equality in Christ, he did not ap-ply this ideal to nature.

84. See chap. 3, above.

Like Cobb's understanding of intrinsic value, Ruether's understanding of justice derives from a horizontal understanding of justice in which all living things are of equal value, a notion admittedly difficult to reconcile with biological and evolutionary models. Insofar as Ruether pointedly argues against any apotheosis of the earth as Gaia, she could certainly find common ground with Gregory even though she does leave open the question of how the Christian faith might respond to the new spirituality of the Gaia faith. It seems to me that the Cappadocians' tentatively open posture toward the cosmic piety of their age fulfilled a missiological function that might well be of use in the modern New Age culture. Faith in the divine activity in and with nature made it possible to integrate the faith of older nature religions into the Christian interpretation of life. What the transformation of the doctrine of the four elements and of the Stoic understanding of the organism was able to accomplish during late antiquity could perhaps also happen in the context of new spirituality and its understanding of the world organism.

The Ethical Challenge and the Understanding of God: Altner and Liedke and Duchrow   Unlike Ruether, who begins with the ideal of equality, Altner and Liedke and Duchrow begin with a condition of ethical conflict and asymmetrical relations within the life community. Neither position, however, understands God as standing in any antithetical relationship with the ecological understanding of nature. Because Gregory was so strongly influenced by Origen's theology and its understanding of the fall, he cannot contribute much to this model of a community of conflict. And even though Gregory was apparently familiar with Heraclitus's conflictive ontology, the latter's views did not really influence the understanding of the world of that age. Plotinus had already provided a model for the ethical dimension in Gregory's understanding as the antithesis between matter and spirit, between good repose and evil movement.

Gregory and the Heidelberg theologians do however concur in emphasizing that all of creation is to be set free, and in this sense Gregory offers numerous insights concerning inclusive universal soteriology. The reason is that both groups lived in contexts requiring, each in its own way, new ethical reflection. Gregory developed his trinitarian and incarnational understanding of the life community in countering the devaluation of the corporeal, the feminine, and the material, and to establish a new perspective of social ethical praxis. The premise of the Heidelberg theologians concerning the conflict between human beings and nature ultimately leads to a new openness for the possibility of redemption and the vision of creation set free. All four — Gregory, Altner, Liedke, and Duchrow — adduce numerous biblical witnesses in support of their position. The connection between ethics and eschatology can explain this parallel between the interpretation of tradition and that of the current situation. In answering the question of the ultimate goal of redemption, both Gregory and the Heidelberg theologians address the respective contextual ethical challenges as a problem involving the understanding of God.

Whereas late antiquity was confronted by the increasing impoverishment of the masses, late modernity is confronted by the increasing impoverishment of the Third World and of the environment. All four theologians view the question regarding appropriate ethical praxis as the question regarding God's actions, and do so adhering to their belief in the biblically anticipated idea of universal liberation. Altner proposes a bioethical resolution of conflict with universal participation under the auspices of a theology of the cross. Liedke and Duchrow propose a diminution of violence and a moderation of energy exchange along with a taming and transforming of the global monetary system and its attendant idols.[85] Gregory proposes that creation turn peacefully to God in anticipation of the cosmic Christmas, and that it practice love for the poor and a theologically understood social redistribution of wealth.

Does Gregory's God Redeem the Ontological Hierarchy of the World?

Gregory, too, is open to critical questioning. To what end does he distinguish between the realm of the angels, which is intimately associated with God's own household, and the otherwise alien realm of bodies? Although we cannot really expect him to escape the dualistic understanding of the world regnant during his age, we can ask why he distinguishes so emphatically between an ontological level *distant* from God and another level so *intimate* with God. Here we recall Whitehead in wondering whether Gregory is not associating God and heaven a bit more closely than is really necessary while still not confusing the two.

There are no Old Testament witnesses that Gregory might adduce in support of such a view. From the perspective of Christology, as we saw, he was concerned with articulating the full union of the divine and the human. In this sense the dualistic understanding of the world may have played into the hands of this christological theandric position. That is, one can obviously emphasize the *mystery* of the incarnation more if it is actually alien or unlike elements that are entering into such a union. One interesting aspect of Gregory's understanding of community is his notion that God is both near and

---

85. Concerning the challenge posed to theology by the injustices of the global monetary system, see Duchrow 1992; 1994; 1995.

far. On the one hand, the angels are near to and circle about God. On the other, they are also present for Christians at various places on earth. Does this mean that after the revelation of Christ, God, around whom the angels circle, is now *nearer* to the earth precisely because the angels themselves continue to praise God, but now do so in spatial proximity to the earth itself? Or does Gregory view this presence as a sign that the creation is now moving *toward* its Creator, that is, is being lifted up?

How does Gregory understand the condition Origen described as *apokatastasis?* In combination with the idea of consummation characterizing irenic eschatology, Gregory generally employs imagery and occasionally even the term *apokatastasis* to refer to the rather comprehensively conceived re-establishment of the status prior to the fall, though it is unclear whether he is understanding the liberation of creation as cleansing or purification, as Paul probably does, or as a new creation, as does Irenaeus, or as a gradual redemption within the history of nature itself.

It is also unclear just how Gregory imagined that his universal soteriology might be applied within concrete political contexts. Even though the conditions necessarily attaching to *any* theology conscious of its context probably account for why Gregory — like similar initiatives during our age — could not adequately address the question of how the universal understanding of redemption within the Christian interpretation of life might be translated into ethical precepts for action, there can be little doubt that his trinitarian understanding of God acquired considerable currency in connection with both the irenic process of the churches prior to the council and the social-ethical praxis contributing to a higher valuation of the corporeal; the Roman emperors did, after all, have to reorient their own imperial politics in response to these theologically legitimized applications.

2. Movement

The Problem

The Ecological Question of Movement in the Evolution, Succession, and Self-Organization of Nature

Compared to ancient philosophy, contemporary ecological discussion pays only scant attention to the concept of movement. That this problem also applies to ecology, however, emerges not least from a consideration of the dialectic of the philosophical problem itself, particularly a consideration of the question of the relationship between being and movement and the possibility of identity within time.[86]

No concept of movement as such has been developed, however. Whereas Greek thought understood movement to refer to both *qualitative* change and a change of location, modern thought understands "movement" in a more restricted sense as referring merely to the quantitative change affecting a subject or thing within space. The physiology of the movement of plants does distinguish, for example, four different types of movement, understanding "movement" as functioning on the basis of a supply of energy.[87]

The consideration of *quantitative* change constitutes an important instrument of ecological research that engages the concept of "phylogenesis" in examining the way organisms adapt to a changing environment.[88] Ecology views the environment historically and employs a whole range of criteria (reproduction, number of individuals, differences in distribution, climatic conditions, etc.) in examining changes within the relationships between the environment and organisms.

Three types of biological change are generally distinguished:

1. change of the genotype through mutation or redistribution
2. somatic change under environmental pressure
3. changes in environmental conditio[89]ns

Ecologists initially addressed the phenomenon of *qualitative* change from the perspective of the change in vegetation. In 1896 Warming was the first to recognize the "universality of vegetative change,"[90] giving rise to the concept of "succession" that picked up on the ecological concept of society. "Succession" has been defined as the "development of the ecosystem over the course of phylogenesis together with the coevolution of the accompanying species."[91] Distinctions have also been made between short-term and long-term succession, the former tending toward reestablishing the status of the original point of departure after local disruptions. No one today really subscribes to Clements's envisioned "climax stage" as the absolute goal of succes-

---

86. See chap. 3, above.

87. (a) Free locative movement; (b) turning movement; (c) infracellular; and (d) ballistic movements. Haupt 1977, 1ff.

88. Kinzelbach 1989, 23.

89. Bateson 1990a, 445.

90. Trepl 1987, 143.

91. Kinzelbach 1989, 66.

sion. The individualist understanding of succession counters the organismic understanding in maintaining that vegetation changes in a nondeterministic, historical fashion.[92]

Although interest in problems of evolution receded during the history of ecology, it has reemerged recently under the influence of individualistic and population-focused initiatives.[93] The new interest in the historical dimension of the question probably derives from the need for socially supported prognoses regarding the conditions of various ecosystems. Current discussion is addressing whether coevolution is to be understood merely as the evolution of species with others or as the evolution of a whole that is to be conceived as an ecosystem or superorganism on its own.[94] In this sense the philosophical question regarding the significance of time becomes a problem for scientific ecology, which must ask whether from the ecological perspective on change within time there is anything that nonetheless remains self-identical (as a whole).

Modern physics approaches the problem of movement from a different direction. The theory of "self-organization" rejects the notion of uniform development and instead focuses on the "leaps" a given system makes into a more complex condition.[95] The chemist Ilya Prigogine uses the term "dissipative structures" to describe a formal structure of systems in a condition of imbalance that (contrary to the second law of thermodynamics) export entropy to their surroundings.[96] Paul Davies concludes from these theories that one can speak of "creative progress" in a certain direction and, in this sense, of matter having its own "will,"[97] while Erich Jantsch goes so far as to refer to the dynamic and self-transcendence of evolution and to the self-organization of the universe as "spirit."[98]

Viewed within a philosophical context, what physicists are saying suggests to me that Plato's problem might be reemerging in a new form. Does the self-movement (of the world soul) represent a basic principle of nature?[99] Even though the phenomenon of qualitative change is increasingly addressed within the horizon of the modern natural sciences, one can still legitimately ask whether the notion of an isomorphy of time and space does not still re-

92. Trepl 1987, 147.
93. Trepl 1987, 218.
94. Cf. Kinzelbach 1989, 60, and Trepl 1987, 219.
95. Davies 1989, 98.
96. Davies 1989, 112.
97. Davies 1989, 113, 121.
98. Altner 1988, 110-15.
99. Cf. chap. 3, above.

main determinative.[100] Distinguishing between qualitative and quantitative movement, Georg Picht shows how the founders of the mechanistic view reduce all movements that appear as qualitative changes to the locative movement of atoms,[101] understanding time as a linear parameter and giving space and time a uniform portrayal. The idea of evolution then ruptures this isomorphy of time and space. The past, instead of disappearing, is preserved genetically and eidetically as memory.[102]

Now, it is easy to see how quickly ecological thought can stumble into a thicket of contradictions in that it clearly subscribes to the biological theory of evolution based on the principle of open rather than linear-causal movement through time, and gets caught in the vortex of quantifiable methodologies oriented on the model of mechanistic physics.[103] The epistemological question of the modern natural sciences emerges in all its ramifications precisely in the problem of movement, which ecology addresses in connection with the phenomenon of ecologically qualitative change. One can quite justifiably ask whether a one-sidedly quantitative methodology does not blind ecology's perception of potential significant movement. Picht associates this question with the Greek understanding of movement: "The question is whether the structures of interdependence within an ecosystem can be adequately described in the coordinate system of the time-space continuum according to the prescribed principle of linear causality obtaining there; perhaps those structures are instead obeying principles of movement with a different form and deriving from a different origin — those particular principles of movement which the Greek philosophy of nature described with the general term of *alloiosis,* that is, of qualitative change."[104]

In consideration of Picht's critical query, we might say ecological discourse addresses the problem of movement not as the concept of "movement" itself, but rather in connection with the concepts of evolution, succession, and self-organization. The severity of the problem of ecological movement in the sense of a qualitative change in the pattern of relationships between environment and organisms emerges most fully when one considers the extremely limited explanatory potential of any linear-causal description of the relationships between environment and organisms. Which qualitative

---

100. Concerning the scientific hypothesis that the irreversibility of time constitutes a breach of spatial symmetry, see Prigogine and Stengers 1985, 253f.

101. Picht 1979, 33.

102. Cf. also Sandström's theory concerning the development of pictorial meanings that always precedes logical-discursive thought; chap. 5, below.

103. Cf. chap. 1, above.

104. Picht 1979, 37.

forms of movement can the ecological pattern perceive or discern?[105] How are we to understand and indeed describe the necessary relationship between movement and being, between evolution and life?

Theological Interpretations

Movement as Process: John B. Cobb, Jr.   Although process theology focuses on the changes characterizing reality, it has not really developed a specific understanding of movement. Instead, the concept of process provides the foundation for the concept of system.

Cobb and Griffin maintain that process underlies all reality, an assertion corresponding to the Jewish-Christian understanding of reality insofar as opposing God as the unchangeable one to the changeable nature of the world of necessity also devalues the world, a position that leads to escapism. The Jewish-Christian tradition has however understood God as "active within the historical process."[106]

Following Whitehead, Cobb and Griffin identify two kinds of processes: (1) the temporal process of transition from one real condition to another, and (2) the process of the emergence of real individual events, of concrescence, and of becoming concrete (14f.).

Such processes, rather than being determined by the past, are instead characterized by the realization of possibilities, by "novelty," the conditions for which Cobb and Griffin explain theologically as deriving from the "divine experience." There inheres in God's "primordial envisagement" of the "pure possibilities" an "appetition that they be actualized in the world." The divine reality is understood as "the ground of novelty" (28).

Process theology views the theory of evolution positively. Cobb and Griffin cite Whitehead in explaining why God needed more than four billion

---

105. J. von Uexküll and Kriszat 1983, 43-49, show how some organisms are able to recognize only the movements of other living beings but cannot discern their forms as characteristic features. Bateson 1990b, 90, shows how in a general sense human perception is able to react *only* to events involving change. Should this insight also apply to the knowledge of reason, then our present problem acquires yet additional depth: Is there *any* being that is not in motion? If so, is such being then inaccessible both to human sense perception and to human reason? Can the ensuing question — namely, whether there even exists this sort of unchangeable being attributable to something that remains self-identical over the course of time — be answered rationally at all?

106. Cobb and Griffin 1977, 14. The parenthetical page numbers in the following text are to this work.

years of evolution to create human beings. God's influence "is always persuasive, and can only produce such order as is possible" (64).[107] On this view the
driving force of evolution is the "greater enjoyment." It is not the actual values themselves that are present in God, but rather values only as "possible values" or "in the mode of appetition." "The direction of the evolutionary process is, on the whole, toward more complex actualities, resulting from God's
basic creative purpose, which is the evocation of actualities with greater and
greater enjoyment" (63f.).[108]

Cobb and Griffin emphasize that order and newness are related within
development. Ultimately they assess evolution theologically: "Each stage of
the evolutionary process represents an increase in the divinely-given possibilities for value which are actualized. The present builds upon the past, but ad-
vances beyond it to the degree to which it responds to the divine impulses.
This advance is experienced as intrinsically good, and it also provides the
condition for an even richer enjoyment of existence in the future" (67).

They describe the process christologically such that what the church fathers called the "logos" "is present or incarnate in creatures as the initial aim
in relation to which the creature decides how to constitute itself" (99). Christ
as the incarnate logos is then the "creative transformation."

As perpetual perishing, temporality represents "the ultimate evil," and
religion's ideal vision is thus that of "everlastingness." Cobb and Griffin refer
to the heavenly kingdom as "this everlasting reality" (123).

Welker has critically analyzed Cobb's model of "growth and expansion,"
suggesting that in Cobb's view the community or congregation is able to recognize everywhere that particular force field through which it itself was generated: "Creative transformation would involve recognizing the one force
field everywhere as well as a condition of being maintained in self-
transcendence."[109] Cobb ties this creative transformation as an "inclusion of
newness" to God's own creative love: "Creative transformation is the essence
of growth, and growth is of the essences of life. . . . The creative love of God
produces transformation in creatures."[110]

In summary, we can note that Cobb, following the lead of Whitehead,
develops a relativistic cosmology focused on the idea of qualitative and quan-

107. Quoting Whitehead 1933, 189.
108. Birch and Cobb 1990, 197, do however maintain that there is no plan: "There is no
plan for the future written into Life which it is our task to discern."
109. Welker 1988, 194.
110. Cobb and Griffin 1977, 101f. Cf. Cobb 1972, 133. Cf. Birch and Cobb 1990, 188f.,
where they understand trust in the cosmic power of life as trust in the "emergent possibilities
for creative transformation in each new situation."

titative change, thereby theoretically eliminating the mechanistic isomorphy of time and space. What is past can nonetheless remain present, and something qualitatively new can arise. In this sense Cobb completely appropriates the evolutionary concept of movement.

I do nonetheless get the feeling that Cobb's understanding of the process of reality largely emphasizes the *quantitative* aspect of change under the conditions of a linear understanding of time. God-given possibilities for value are to be "increased," and "growth" is the core of life. One also wonders whether his assumption that the process has a goal does not contradict the basic premise of process theology, which understands movement as being characterized by openness and unpredictability. How persuasively does Cobb actually synthesize classical teleology, on the one hand, and movement as process, on the other? Does he really move away from the isomorphy of time and space, or is there still an evolutionistic remnant?

Cobb mitigates his teleological understanding of evolution with Birch in favor of an "evolutionary ecology," albeit not one that ends in evolutionism.[111]

Because Cobb ascribes ethical significance to temporality, temporal change is bad, whereas "everlastingness" — which I understand here in the sense of enduring self-identity amid change — is good. Even though progressive movement seems good and valuable, temporality represents the greatest evil. Is this position not self-contradictory?

Cobb consistently associates his concept of process with the Christian understanding of God, albeit without describing God himself as process. Instead he assumes that God's immanent presence in things comes to expression in the potentiality or capacity of things for change. God not only brings about change but is himself also fully included in that change. Cobb unequivocally rejects the ancient assertion that God is unchangeable,[112] understanding God instead as the condition of the possibility of movement as process, and as such simultaneously wholly part of precisely that process.

The Movement of Things Themselves within the Temporal Process of Becoming: Günter Altner

Altner's understanding of movement addresses the challenge posed by the theory of evolution. He distinguishes three historical stages of dialogue between the theory of evolution and Christian creation theology and then inquires about the open nature of development and the concept of time itself.

---

111. Birch and Cobb 1990, 65.
112. Cobb and Griffin 1977, 8f.

Altner traces the problematic dialogue between biology and theology concerning Darwin's theory of evolution in part back to Haeckel's mechanistic and universalistic interpretation, showing how the question of evolutionary direction represents a theological problem.[113] Altner leaves the epistemological ground of the isomorphy of time and space — under whose conditions the teleology of nature was able to reveal God — and focuses on the open nature of the process of becoming.

In Altner's view the process of evolution is historical: "Unlike the purely mechanistic course of time in which things move along an ongoing line (cf. a clock), historic time is the movement of things themselves which substantively determines them."[114] Altner criticizes causal-analytical thought because it presupposes reproducibility, an assumption that for all practical purposes — as it were — "reverses" the irreversibility of historic time.[115] Altner suggests instead a "new dynamic understanding of nature" more commensurate with the biblical understanding of creation: "Creation is the process of becoming within time."[116]

Altner suggests interpreting the evolutionary process in a more holistic fashion and discusses several initiatives currently entertained by the natural sciences. Altner himself would like to see this holistic approach developed in connection with the discipline of history,[117] in which case the history of nature and that of society would differ only in their respective objects.

Altner's bioethics derives the ethical principle of equality from the common, shared nature of the evolutionary process itself; he then integrates human beings into this evolving process of becoming as that particular part in which "creation becomes conscious of its own becoming."[118]

In summary we can say that Altner basically understands movement from the perspective of evolution, emphasizing the irreversibility of time and the resulting open nature of development in the biological and physical as well as anthropological and social realms. After discovering how little attention has been paid to the challenge of the evolutionary concept of movement, he finds it imperative that we change our epistemological position and interpret the concept of evolution in a more holistic fashion. From the comprehensive nature of the process of becoming, Altner derives ethical principles for dealing

---

113. Altner (1984), 214, cites Rudolf Otto's judgment of the "Darwinian doctrine" (1929): "Its antiteleological inclination is what really makes it so decidedly antitheological."

114. Altner 1984, 220.

115. Altner 1988, 88.

116. Altner 1991, 105.

117. Altner 1991, 127.

118. Altner 1991, 202.

with life and theologically interprets the biblical concept of creation as the notion of emergence or becoming within time. Unfortunately, he avoids addressing the question of how this position now requires that we revise our understanding of God. After freeing itself from the mechanistic determination of movement, Altner's understanding of movement posits the "movement of things themselves" as the salient feature of the understanding of historic time.

Evolutionary and Messianic Movement: Jürgen Moltmann   Moltmann also draws on recent insights from the natural sciences in emphasizing the openness of nature toward the future. Unlike Jantsch, Moltmann does not identify self-organization with "spirit," preferring rather to understand the world's openness as openness to God.[119] The problem of movement emerges in Moltmann's theological interpretation of evolution. Whereas in 1985 he is positively inclined toward the concept of evolution, in 1989 he subjects it to critical analysis.

His ecological doctrine of creation understands evolution "as a basic concept of the *self-movement* of the divine Spirit of creation" (19). The Spirit is "the principle of evolution" (100). He distinguishes between "evolution" and "creation," understanding the latter as "the miracle of existence in general" and the former as "the continued building up of matter and systems of life" (196). He understands the world theologically as an "open, participatory and anticipatory system" (206) and counters the cyclical and linear understanding of time with a messianic understanding in which the future differs qualitatively from the past (123f.). He charges the exegesis of process theology with having failed to distinguish adequately between God's acts of creation and of separation, between God's work and image. Cobb and Griffin's suspension of the doctrine of the *creatio ex nihilo* ultimately divinizes nature, and the doctrine of creation developed by process theology turns into a doctrine of maintenance and order. God and nature are fused into a uniform world process (78f.).

Moltmann's Christology addresses the problem of evolution under new conditions, clearly distinguishing between *evolution* and *redemption* in critical discussion with Teilhard de Chardin and Karl Rahner: "A *Christus evolutor* without *Christus redemptor* is nothing other than a cruel, unfeeling *Christus selector,* a historical world-judge without compassion for the weak, and a breeder of life uninterested in the victims."[120] Emphasizing the fierce creative

---

119. Moltmann 1985, 103. The parenthetical page numbers in the following text are to this work.

120. Moltmann 1990, 296.

power of nature in the process of selection, Moltmann now addresses the question of theodicy in connection with evolution, also distinguishing between teleology and eschatology in connection with the question of the goal of evolution: "The teleology of creation is not its eschatology."

Moltmann distinguishes between the *redemption* of creation and its *evolution,* insisting that one not mistake or confuse the development or emergence of creation — the process by which it "becomes" — with the advent of Christ. What emerges, however — following Benjamin — is a "dialectical relationship between the purposeful 'dynamic of the profane' and that other direction, 'messianic intensity.'"[121] But Moltmann does not develop his idea of a "self-movement of the Spirit" in his monograph on the Spirit (1991a), nor does he address the problem of evolution in any other pneumatological context.

Although Moltmann's understanding of God focuses theologically on the mutual interpenetration of the divine persons, *perichoresis,* I am yet unclear whether the principle of mutual interpenetration is to be understood dynamically as an expression of movement or ontologically as an expression of interrelatedness.

The Historic Self-Movement of the World and Its Divine Goal: Christian Link   Link suggests that one of the three most important factors prompting a reorientation of creation theology is the discovery of the historicalness of nature; the possibility of no longer having to understand time "in the formula of a law of nature as a linear parameter" poses a real challenge to theology.[122]

Link addresses a whole panoply of theories from the natural sciences, historical materials — especially in connection with the dialogue between theology and biology regarding evolution — and potential solutions offered by theology itself. He accuses process theology of having failed to recognize the problem of the "beginning" and of providing more a doctrine of maintenance and order than of creation (560f.).

Theologically Link classifies the historicity of nature under the history of God. "The trinitarian perspective discloses creation within the horizon of the *history* of the God who comes to the world, which is why the future takes precedence before the present, possibility before reality" (531). Because God not only sustains time but also subjects himself to it, Link no longer finds any

---

121. Moltmann 1990, 303f.

122. Link 1991, 413. The parenthetical page numbers in the following text are to this work.

antithesis between nature and history, evolution and creation. "Although God 'bears' or 'sustains' — to put it metaphorically — the way time brings itself about . . . he is at the same time free to subject himself to the time (world) he himself has created" (450).

Criticizing those (Moltmann, Daecke) who precipitately identify the Spirit and evolution, Link proposes instead that we understand the relationship between these two forms of the Spirit (i.e., as a person of the Trinity and as the principle of evolution) as *temporal* (551). Link's understanding of movement focuses on the historicity of nature. Rather than being created together with time as a "timeless cosmos," the world is rather from the very outset inclined toward *history*, and Link insists that, in any event, the movement of the open world process proceeds "within" movement toward that future (520). Put differently, God's providence provides for the world to move "within" God's own history rather than outside or apart from it. This assertion, however, now raises the important theological question regarding just how the "self-movement of the world" is related to "its direction, as determined by God, toward the eschatological goal." Link's answer is that

> the promise of the new creation represents a proposition that not only cannot be demonstrated, it cannot even be theoretically known. . . . for our only ground of hope has taken the form of a sign, a parable which is already experientially articulating God's future here and now. Theology has no access to any genuinely "historical" perspective. This parable of what is coming, this "ultimate" that has become visible within the spatial realm of creaturely existence, is the resurrection of the Crucified and the outpouring of the Spirit. (598)

One might inquire at this point whether Link is not describing God's historic activity with his world *teleologically*. Although Link does indeed constantly emphasize the open nature of time as the most salient feature of the movement of nature, when he speaks about God coming to the world he seems to intimate that God is actually coming to the world from something *other* than the world. But from where? Or does God come to himself? Otherwise Link assumes that God comes from the future. By contrast, the African sensibility, for example, can certainly also imagine God coming from the past.

I cannot see that Link has really resolved the contradiction between the historic movement of nature and God's goal-oriented eschatological movement. On the one hand, he maintains that the historic movement of nature takes place *within* God's history; on the other, God *comes* to the world from the future. Does Link's thesis of the precedence of possibility over reality not necessarily understand the Creator as the teleological principle behind the movement of nature, even though that movement is now to be understood as temporally open rather than as deterministic?

It seems that Link has lost sight of the question regarding how God's redemptive activity is also able to allow for the integrity of his creation as open historic movement. Might not the "goal" of God's eschatological activity be *precisely* this open movement of his creation, that is, open in the sense that it has neither goal nor direction? How is one to understand the relationship between the "goal" and the totality of the historical process?

Creation as a Basic Event with the Goal of Liberation: Gerhard Liedke and Ulrich Duchrow Liedke incorporates Claus Westermann's interpretation of the biblical creation account into his description of the basic event of nature.[123] On Liedke's view there is in history a "constant," a "primal event." "The basic event is that which endures in an elementary fashion, that which also changes, albeit only over extremely long periods and not really at its core."[124] The theological interpretation of basic event, blessing, and wisdom suggests for Liedke that creation represents "an entity of a unique sort rather than merely a derivative of (salvation) history."[125] On Liedke's view the fact that the basic event underlies all experience provides a common frame of reference for theology and the natural sciences, even though the latter focus only on particular experiences within the basic event.

Theologically Duchrow and Liedke associate this event with God's love: "[B]ut the dynamics of God's love are such that creation continues in time, in the present, past, and future."[126] They also understand creation as an "ongoing creation" moving toward being liberated by God from violence.

The Direction of Creation as Hope in the Expansion of Liberation: Sallie McFague McFague summarizes nature and its development as a "common creation story," emphasizing the significance of acknowledging that because all life shares a common evolutionary origin, all life is also interconnected. In this sense evolution encompasses not only the biological changes associated with humankind, but the accompanying historical and cultural changes as well.[127]

Like Moltmann, McFague discerns a conflict between the principle of

---

123. Liedke 1984, 110-19.
124. Liedke 1984, 96.
125. Liedke 1984, 99f.
126. Duchrow and Liedke 1989, 49.
127. McFague 1993, 41, 45, 171.

natural selection in biological and cultural evolution, on the one hand, and the Christian faith, on the other; the Christian inclination to embrace the oppressed cannot be reconciled with evolution.[128]

McFague understands the metaphor of the cosmic Christ to mean that the cosmos "is moving *toward* salvation," and that "this salvation is taking place *in* creation."[129] On the other hand, she rejects any optimistic teleological understanding of the history of evolution, countering the "prospective" thesis with a "retrospective" one that "takes as its standpoint a concrete place where salvation has been experienced — in the case of Christians, the paradigmatic ministry of Jesus and similar ministries of his disciples in different, particular places — and projects the shape of these ministries onto the whole."[130]

For McFague the experience of liberation thus necessarily precedes the thesis of creation moving toward its liberation. That is, the theological assertion that creation is developing in a certain direction cannot be grounded teleologically in the process of evolution itself, but rather only in various experiences of liberation, where it expresses the hope that such liberation will expand to include *all* of life, a hope guaranteed by the "liberating, healing, inclusive love of God."[131]

What the Interpreters of the Situation Have in Common

First, we find that although all these modern theologians address the idea of movement as a central *problem* of ecological theology, none develops any substantive *concept* of movement. The issue emerges for Cobb in the concept of process, for Altner in the concept of evolution, for Link in the concept of history, and for Moltmann in the concept of the messianic.

Why do none of these authors develop a concept of movement? By deferring to daily language use and avoiding the understanding of movement that has been reduced to quantitative mechanistic movement, are these theologians not losing the opportunity to formulate the problem in a more uniform fashion that is at the same time more open to subtle distinctions? A more broadly conceived concept of movement can doubtless enhance ecological-

128. McFague 1993, 173.
129. McFague 1993, 180.
130. McFague 1993, 181.

131. Because in *Gaia and God* Rosemary Radford Ruether addresses neither the issue of movement nor the problem of evolution, I took up only six positions in the preceding discussion.

theological discourse by making it possible to articulate more clearly a rather comprehensive problem, by facilitating communication between various philosophical and linguistic traditions, and by facilitating the development of process theories applicable to both nature and society. What we said earlier regarding differences in our understanding of community applies here as well. Despite differing philosophical, denominational, and linguistic presuppositions, all these authors are nonetheless addressing the same basic problem. Rather than representing antitheses, their studies complement one another. The common problem is to articulate the challenge posed to theology by the new interpretation of the concept of movement in the natural sciences.

Differences certainly do emerge regarding the preferences of the various dialogue partners. Whereas some authors cede the privilege of formulating the problem to theoreticians in the natural sciences, others approach the problem from perspectives drawn from the tradition of theology itself. Cobb chooses a third path by mediating Whitehead's philosophy with the particular perspectives of modern popular ecology, scientific biology, and the Christian faith.

Three basic positions emerge for addressing the problem of movement: ecological-theological (Altner, Liedke and Duchrow, Link), creation-theological (Moltmann, McFague), and religio-philosophical/theological mediation (Cobb). Rather than being mutually exclusive, these three positions are methodologically related while focusing more specifically on different issues.

Ecological theologians draw on recent results in the natural sciences. Altner focuses on the development of the theory of evolution, Link on the open nature of time and on a suspension of the isomorphy of time and space, and Liedke on popular ecology. From the perspective of creation and biblical theology, Liedke and Duchrow understand the movement of nature as God's *creatio continua*. From the perspective of creation theology, Link incorporates the modern concept of movement into the horizon of universal eschatology, albeit only an eschatology "from the beginning." Altner identifies the open evolutionary process as God's creative action.

Although all these authors try to disclose the ethical credibility of the evidence of the Christian faith, none uses Gregory's idea of ethical movement. None addresses the aesthetic evidence of creation theology.[132]

132. "Aesthetic evidence" of theology refers to the influence exerted by the religious interpretation of life and faith of a socially organized religious community on the social construction of nature. "Evidence" refers here to the plausibility and relevance that participants in a given religious community believe their understanding of God has for the understanding of nature. "Aesthetic" refers to the notion that the understanding of God also influences one's *sense perception* and thus also one's understanding of nature as well as the way one behaves within this social and theological understanding of nature.

The creation theologians try to mediate the modern concept of movement with the doctrine of faith. Moltmann mediates the idea of openness with that of providence, countering an overly interpreted idea of evolution with a Christology focused more on a theology of the cross, thereby juxtaposing evolution with the coming of the Messiah. McFague seeks to reconcile the entire postmodern scientific "common creation story" with the Christian faith. On the one hand, she would like to make the metaphor of organism into the normative model of totality; on the other, she does acknowledge the conflict between evolution in nature and culture and the theology of liberation, proposing as a solution the thesis of deriving our understanding of the *direction* of creation only from our experiences with God. Both McFague and Moltmann counter the teleological figure of movement with an eschatological figure. Whereas Altner draws on the biological concept of movement in the theory of evolution, Cobb focuses on the philosophical concept of process, seeking then to reconcile it with the evolutionary and ecological understanding of movement and to interpret it in light of relevant elements of creation theology.

The theological understanding of movement among these authors manages to free itself from the restrictions of the time-space isomorphy along the following scale. By freeing himself from the old dogma of the natural sciences, Altner is able to discern the "movement of things themselves." Although Link seems to free himself from this philosophical understanding of time attaching to this dogma, his understanding of the divine economy nonetheless still seems bound to it. Although Cobb does indeed suspend the isomorphy of time and space, he nonetheless gives precedence to the quantitative aspect of movement over the qualitative. Although Moltmann fully accepts the findings of modern research, it remains unclear just how these findings also make it necessary to alter our understanding of how God acts within time and space. Neither McFague nor Liedke and Duchrow address the problem.

Correlation

The Common Question: What Can an Ecological-Theological Concept of Movement Accomplish?

Because a comparison between Gregory's understanding of movement and that of modern theologians discloses more differences than similarities, the problem is determining how to relate the various understandings of the movement of nature/creatures with the Christian experience and understanding of God.

Both Gregory and modern theologians wrestle theologically with the idea of movement, taking it seriously in connection with either Platonism, process philosophy, Aristotelianism-Stoicism, or the theory of evolution. Moreover, both feel it challenges them to reinterpret the Christian faith and to articulate their understanding of movement theologically in their respective contexts.

Gregory and these modern authors differ first of all on the term itself. Whereas Gregory was able to draw on a mature tradition of philosophical reflection on movement, contemporary theologians have access only to a reductionist concept of movement. The advantage for Gregory is that his concept is differentiated and sophisticated enough to be engaged in the service of psychology, ethics, the philosophy of nature, cosmology, and theology, whereas modern authors, who do not have access to such a concept, are forced to follow the usage and even modes of thought of the natural sciences.

Hence the first thing our interpretation of Gregory suggests is that ecological theology determine what a comprehensive theological and ecological understanding of movement of this sort might offer today. A sophisticated concept of this sort might first guarantee more comprehensive uniformity as well as the possibility of making more sophisticated distinctions. It might also make the considerable treasures to be found in the philosophical tradition more accessible.

Another difference between the theology of late antiquity and that of late modernity involves the constellation of power of the natural sciences. Although late antiquity did indeed develop qualified theories within the natural sciences, for some unknown reason it did not take the next step and develop any praxis for applying this knowledge within the sociotechnical construction of society and nature. With the exception of water mills, the findings of the natural sciences in late antiquity were put to use in society to a far lesser degree and were certainly less politicized than has been the case in modernity.

Yet another consideration is the extent to which modern findings in the natural sciences have become specialized and particularized. Whereas Gregory was able to begin with a decidedly comprehensive consensus on the understanding of nature, modern theology must first confront the specialization and relativization of the natural sciences.[133] Because modern science has

133. Some authors solve this problem by theologizing "new" comprehensive theories in the natural sciences, e.g., Lovelock's Gaia perspective (cf. Moltmann 1993 and Primavesi 2000), others by way of postmodern relativism and postulated enhancement of sensibilities. A third path is accessible to the ecumenical movement and the local ecclesiastical groups that draw on the syntheses of the environmental movement and relate these to various scientific findings.

lost any consistent concept of movement, and because the natural sciences have also fragmented the original problem in any case, modern theologians must decide under what conditions and with whom they intend to discuss the problem of movement in the first place. Gregory, of course, did not have to make such a decision.

The content of the reflection on movement in late antiquity and in late modernity also differs considerably. Antiquity, of course, had no notion of any theory of evolution. Nor did the ancient church have any notion of evo-lutionist or reductionist interpretation of the biblical creation account. The challenges with which preceding thinkers confronted Gregory involved how to understand the various natural-religious cosmogonies and the determin-istic cosmologies of popular Aristotelian theology. By contrast, the chal-lenges with which preceding thinkers confront ecological theologians in-volve the mistakes made by physico-theology, on the one hand, and modern theological anthropomorphism on the other. Nor did Gregory have any ac-cess to the doctrines of open systems or to a possible suspension of the time-space isomorphy. On the other hand, he was quite familiar with the problem of the relation between the quantitative and qualitative aspects of time and space.

This correlation of the problem of movement is made even more diffi-cult by the ambiguity in the history of the modern natural sciences and by the situation of contemporary upheaval in general. On the one hand, contempo-rary natural sciences surely stand in a certain continuous relationship with an-tiquity epistemologically and to some extent even metaphysically.[134] On the other, they have robbed themselves of many valuable criteria attaching to the ancient understanding of nature.[135] In the present situation in which the natu-ral sciences would free themselves from the strictures of modernity, they un-fortunately can neither return to the past in the form of neo-Aristotelianism nor radically dispense with all historical presuppositions.

In this situation, my interpretation of Gregory's understanding of movement can, I believe, sharpen theology's perception of the depth of the problem and thereby enable it to move more freely within the context of plu-ralism and change. What happens when the interpretation of the understand-ing of movement in late antiquity enters into dialogue with theological inter-pretations of evolution, process, and natural history from late modernity?

---

134. Cf. Groh and Groh 1991, 71; cf. Bergmann 1994d.

135. Picht 1989, 411, e.g., draws attention to the modern natural sciences' destruction of the Aristotelian understanding of the four grounds.

Tradition and Situation Enter into Critical Dialogue

Gregory's Inner-Trinitarian, Inner-Worldly, and God-Worldly Concept of Movement   Gregory develops his understanding of movement by inquiring first about the inner-trinitarian and pneumatological movement of God himself, second about the movement of creation in relation to God, and third about movement within the world. Subjects of such movement in Gregory's thought include the trinitarian God, the Holy Spirit, creatures, the world All, the stars, human beings, angels, and human and salvific history. On balance, Gregory does seem to reside in a thoroughly dynamic world.

As regards the characteristics of movement itself, one notices immediately how much significance he ascribes — probably because of his middle Platonic context and his Origenian roots — to the ethical quality of human and angelic movement. As regards the forms of movement, one notices immediately that, commensurate with the general view in antiquity, circular motion takes precedence over linear form and focus on a center. All the same, Gregory is not really a simple advocate of cyclical motion, since he simultaneously emphasizes that human beings are free to enter into the synergy of God's movement; he accordingly also rejects any salvific determinism. A *universal* understanding of providence is discernible in Gregory's thinking only insofar as the Creator and creation are to move ever closer together in the future. Gregory criticizes Aristotle's restricted understanding of providence and counters it with the biblical notion of universal salvific history whose temporally open nature has been bestowed by God's love and nonviolence.

Gregory develops the idea of movement even further in connection with the doctrine of the Trinity; indeed, in this context Gregory probably represents the beginning of the "historical doctrine of the Trinity" (Moltmann) within the history of theology insofar as he associates the idea of the triune God with a dialectical interpretation of universal salvation history (*Or.* 31.26). One particularly innovative feature of his understanding of movement is the pneumatological connection he establishes. In Gregory's view the Holy Spirit is the only subject capable of moving freely without standing in some psychical or physical relation to other movement within the world. That is, God's Spirit is the only subject capable of moving with complete freedom through time and space. Expressed in modern terminology, Gregory is perhaps saying that the Holy Spirit moves ontologically within different relationships with all entities and all things, and that the Spirit moves simultaneously *within* time and space as well as *through* time and space.

Here Gregory picks up on Plato's late understanding of the self-movement of the soul as the ground of both spiritual/intellectual and physical life (*Phaedrus* 24). By engaging this basic philosophical notion, Gregory is able to counter the idea of the Aristotelian "unmoved mover" with the Christian faith in God's good freedom that sets into motion the liberation of the entirety of creation with all creatures. Gregory's understanding is that the triune God moves freely within the Spirit, liberating in the common movement of synergy everything that is in interrelated motion.[136] This interpretation of Gregory poses several questions to modern theologians.

Is Cobb's God the Transformation, and Is Time Evil?   It seems that both Whitehead's understanding of movement and the modern idea of the evolutionary-ecological model might have excessively influenced Cobb's understanding of God's movement. Gregory differentiates between terms referring to the movement of both the Creator and creation and those referring exclusively to quantitative and qualitative movement involving the created.

By contrast, Cobb operates without such distinctions. For him Christ *is* "creative transformation" and God "*produces* creative transformation."[137] Unlike Gregory, Cobb does not distinguish apophatically between statements about God's actions and nature, a distinction of considerable importance for Gregory and one he rigorously implements in his understanding of movement. The question is then whether Cobb's method does not necessarily lead to immanentism.

Cobb's thesis that temporality represents the greatest evil can also be questioned. Gregory viewed time and space as necessary, value-neutral constituent parts of God's good creative activity. Gregory qualifies such movement *ethically* only with regard to its form and its direction with respect to God. By contrast, within the context of contemporary evolutionary and ecological problems, Cobb comes to focus on the relationship between the biological element and evil. Although in Gregory's view life as such was indeed threatened and sometimes certainly damaged by evil, his doctrine of the fall of the angels and of the spiritual origin of evil provided an explanation that excluded the customary connection made between the corporeal and evil during his age.[138] Quite contrary to his own intentions, Cobb ultimately risks legitimizing temporality as something inherently evil, on the one hand, and atemporality in the form of modernity's illusory concept of immortality, on the other.

---

136. In the terms of Newtonian physics: Gregory understands as the Holy Spirit that which for Newton constituted the existence of absolute time and absolute space and absolute time-space movement.

137. Cobb and Griffin 1977, 101f.

138. Cf. Bergmann 1991.

How are "intransitoriness" and liberation related in Cobb's view?[139] How are we to understand liberation from temporal misfortune to the "everlasting" kingdom of God? How do the experiences of victims in both nature and society figure into his model?

Does Moltmann Eliminate the Apophatic Distinction between God's Essence and Work?   Like Cobb, Moltmann seems to fuse theological statements about God's essence with those about his actions.[140] His ecological doctrine of creation speaks about the Spirit as the "principle of evolution," and even though he does distinguish between creation and evolution, it is unclear how the two relate. Gregory solves the linguistic problem by restricting to creation all references to change of location and characteristics, and in this sense one might say that evolution is a characteristic of creation and as such dependent on God's movement. By contrast, Moltmann delimits "creation" as a "miracle" from "evolution."

Moltmann's trinitarian interpretation of evolution presents yet another problem. On the one hand, God's Spirit is the "principle" of evolution (1985); on the other, Christ is the "redeemer of evolution" (1989). Certainly Moltmann does not mean that Christ redeems the principle of the Spirit, does he? Gregory rigorously incorporates his concept of movement into his trinitarian understanding of salvation history, where statements about inner-trinitarian, inner-worldly, and soteriological movement all correspond. But how are we to understand the correspondence in Moltmann's model between the perichoretic understanding of God and the ecological understanding of nature?

I cannot see that Moltmann does more than establish an undifferentiated analogy between the two. But in doing so, does he not restrict his ability to present a clear theological economy, that is, to speak in a more differentiated fashion about God's actions in, with, and through nature? *How* does Moltmann's Christ redeem evolution? *To what end* does Moltmann's "Spirit of self-movement" effect redemption? Can Moltmann free himself from the presuppositions of the Calvinist understanding of providence and embrace dynamic ecological synergism?

---

139. Cf. Link's careful criticism of the inadequate biblical foundation and lack of clarity of process theology (1991, 437ff.); Altner's criticism of the "unclarified categorial multiplicity" (1988, 109); Welker's criticism of Cobb's inadequate trinitarian distinction between christological and pneumatological statements (1988, 195f.); and Moltmann's criticism of the way process theology amalgamates God and world (1985, 78f.).

140. Moltmann 1985, 78f., directs precisely the same criticism at Cobb.

Does Link Emphasize Movement into the Future at the Expense of Movement from the Past? As did Gregory, so also does Link incorporate the revelatory modes of the triune God into his understanding of creation history, though from the perspective of Gregory's position the question arises whether Link does not understand God's salvific movement within his creation a bit one-sidedly within the temporal modality of the future. In applying his own concept of movement, Gregory is always mindful of the presuppositions attaching to his understanding of the Trinity. For him the divine economy during the time of the Spirit always also implies the Father and Son, and similarly during the time of the Father both the Spirit and the Son are active in salvation history in a preexistent fashion. Gregory's rigorous apophatic trinitarian thinking enables him to juxtapose protology and eschatology insofar as his redeemer is in essence always the Creator, and his Creator is always also active as the redeemer. By contrast, Link is inclined — probably out of consideration for the doctrine of providence in his own Reformed tradition and under the influence of Jüngel[141] — to engage in more one-sidedly futurist eschatology, even though creation theology would sooner suggest examining the proto-eschatological context.

Both Gregory's "transchronological" universal soteriology as well as Picht's philosophy of time and Müller's physics of time (both of which are important for Link) seem to suggest that we understand God's universal economy under the auspices of *all* temporal modalities.[142] It seems to me that one genuinely does justice to the open nature of time only by remaining mindful of how the various modalities of time intersect and overlap, and by simultaneously understanding God's activities as being consciously directed.

Is not the *quality* of the divine movement of liberation central? A whole panoply of questions emerges. How is such liberation to be understood? Where does it take place? When? How? For whom? Liberation from what? To what end? Into what new condition? Link seems to fall back on a conventionally understood model of movement within natural history in which an excessively futurist understanding of the Trinity harmonizes the history of nature with the history of salvation. What does the Barthian "parable of that which is to come" mean? How can something that already "is" analogously represent something different that is to come? Which ontology does such an analogy imply? Does this understanding not ignore the qualitative dimension of movement?

141. Cf. Link 1991, 565-74, 589, and Jüngel 1978, 518.
142. Müller 1978; cf. Link 1991, 447f.

Dynamic Life and Static God: Altner, McFague, Liedke and Duchrow   The positions of Altner, McFague, and Liedke and Duchrow raise the question of how one is to reconcile the concept of movement applicable to nature with that applicable to God. While Gregory dared to incorporate the concept of movement into his understanding of God, neither Altner, McFague, nor Liedke and Duchrow say anything about movement in connection with God's essence, though all emphasize the dynamic character of creation and of life as conceived from an ecological perspective.

Altner and Liedke and Duchrow posit the equivalency "creation = dynamic process of becoming." Could one not just as easily replace "creation" with "world" to throw the concept of God into greater relief? Although doing so is not commensurate with the intentions of the authors, I do believe it unavoidable that we also articulate the concept of movement within the understanding of God if we are to implement ecological theology persuasively. In her own turn, McFague points out how our experiences with God necessarily precede any reflection on or understanding of the particular historic direction of development. Although I wholeheartedly concur with this proposal, I do sense that the next question will be how to communicate and ultimately to universalize such experiences, which are, after all, always contextually shaped. Neither McFague nor Gregory answers this question.

What Does Gregory Mean by "Movement" in God?   What is the relationship between Gregory's inner-trinitarian and his inner-worldly understanding of movement? He speaks of the movement of creation only in connection with changes of location and quality, and of God's "inner" movement as *kinesis*. In Greek, however, movement can also refer to temporal and spatial change. Is not Gregory's distinction between God's movement *(kinesis)* and the world's change *(alloiosis)* semantically questionable? If God's inner-trinitarian movement is *not* referring to change within time and space, to what is it then referring? Is Gregory "merely" trying to address the neo-Arian problem of the relation between the Son and Father by circumscribing their atemporal and yet dialectical relation rather obscurely as "movement from the one to the other"?

One should acknowledge that Gregory perceived the full scope of the problem of the historic plurality of the divine economy better than anyone else during his age and that he made an original attempt to address that problem by engaging his understanding of movement. The work of subsequent theologians with regard to the concept of *perichoresis* as well as Maximus's unequivocal assessment of Gregory's constructive originality show that even if his solution was not entirely satisfactory, it nonetheless pointed out the direction theology would ultimately take regarding the issue.[143] Moltmann's own perichoretic thought as well as modern Orthodox initiatives toward an "ecology of the Spirit"[144] also show how relevant the systematic problem of God's and the world's movement — with which Gregory dealt so intensively — still is and how Gregory's insights can contribute to addressing the problem.

3. Suffering

The Problem

The Ecological Question of the Suffering of Creatures

Ecological discourse encounters the problem of suffering in connection with environmental ethics. By contrast, the empirical natural sciences do not acknowledge the problem. Different representatives of environmental ethics assess the question of the suffering of living beings differently, a question that doubtless represents one of the central problems of ecological ethics. The moral question concerning proper human behavior in and toward the environment is closely associated in Western thought with the notion that suffering is to be understood in connection with human sin and morality.[145]

Historically it was Jeremy Bentham, the founder of utilitarian ethics, who first raised the question regarding the suffering of animals; his famous question "Can they suffer?" still provides the point of departure for many ethicists.[146] In his philosophy of life Arthur Schopenhauer's central idea of a common suffering and a common sympathy between living beings exerted considerable influence on the cultural pessimism of the sociocritical school as well as on Albert Schweitzer's optimistic view of life.[147]

I will examine two positions in the current debate on environmental

143. Cf. Thunberg 1985, 36ff.

144. Archbishop Cyril coined this expression in his important address "On the Ecology of the Spirit" at the First European Ecumenical Assembly "Peace and Justice" in Basel on May 11, 1989.

145. Concerning the history of the concept of suffering in general and this understanding of the connection between suffering, sin, and morality in particular, see Arndt 1980; Scharbert 1990; and Sparn 1990.

146. Bentham 1789, chap. 17, sec. 1, 4.

147. Schopenhauer 1938, 64, also developed the notion of a hierarchy of suffering that ascribes a higher intensity of suffering to human beings, who communicate in concepts, and yet also ascribes "consciousness" to animals.

ethics that ascribe functional significance to the suffering of creatures. The anthropocentric-utilitarian and the ecological-functional positions are to be distinguished from those that either ascribe no or relatively little value to suffering among other living creatures and assume in an unreflected fashion that the only morally defensible norm is the diminution of human suffering. They are also to be distinguished from those who advocate in a biocentrically undifferentiated fashion the equality of suffering among all living beings in all situations and thus strive to avoid suffering altogether.

The Relativization of Suffering as the Norm of Utilitarian Ethics Birnbacher's utilitarian conception argues that a threefold logical connection obtains between human obligation and the creaturely capacity for suffering.

1. Because animals are capable of suffering, human beings have a responsibility toward them.
2. The degree of obligation depends on the animal's capacity for suffering.
3. The degree of obligation toward animals is always less than that toward human beings.[148]

Birnbacher also distinguishes between direct and indirect moral obligation. A direct obligation to mitigate suffering obtains toward animals but not toward landscapes, the key criterion being the capacity of animals for suffering. Like Schopenhauer, Birnbacher and Singer clearly distinguish between the suffering of conscious beings, of human beings, and of animals.[149] Hence the ethical criterion of an avoidance of suffering is central to utilitarian ethics because it establishes and regulates normative behavior and because it subscribes to a quantitative hierarchy of suffering among living beings.

Four objections can be raised against the utilitarian initiative:[150]

1. It is extremely difficult to justify a qualitative hierarchy of suffering from the perspective of the natural sciences. This position does not resolve the problem of how human suffering is related qualitatively to nonhuman suffering, nor can it demonstrate the assertion that only human beings are capable of empathy.

148. Birnbacher 1986, 121.

149. Birnbacher 1986, 121-25; cf. Singer 1990, 133; Hemberg 1976, 109.

150. Concerning the critical discussion of the utilitarian criterion regarding the capacity for suffering, see Strey 1989, 73-76; Altner 1991, 33-41; Bergmann 1994a, 79ff.; and Huber 1990, 229-32.

2. Equating the capacity for suffering with the perception of pain also reduces the assessment of that capacity.

3. By conceiving of the capacity for suffering from an exclusively essentialist perspective, this position does not really consider suffering in its ecological context.

4. This position ignores the problem of intentionally inflicted suffering as well as the question of what leads to suffering.

The Distinction in Ecological Ethics between Ecologically Functional Suffering and Culturally Imposed Ecological Violence   Rolston's environmental ethics formulates an ethical principle that while ascribing lesser value than does the utilitarian conception to the capacity of creatures for suffering, nonetheless understands this capacity as being of *equal* rather than merely *relative* value as it applies to human beings and culture, on the one hand, and to living beings and nature, on the other. Rolston advocates the "homologous principle," according to which the suffering that culture inflicts on nature is to be commensurate with the suffering that already occurs in an ecologically functional fashion: "Culturally imposed suffering must be comparable to ecologically functional suffering — a *homologous principle*."[151]

The central question for Rolston is not Bentham's question whether animals can suffer, but rather deals with the commensurability of culturally imposed suffering in relation to natural suffering. This position makes the thesis of ecologically functional suffering into the norm for environmental ethics. Unlike the utilitarian position, it is not based on the notion of human consciousness, but on the ecological analysis of the various life presuppositions within given ecosystems and for the living beings in those systems. It includes culture in this context.

Altner represents a similar position in advocating that all affected parties participate in resolving conflicts regarding survival and also in helping to avoid suffering (see below). Næss also belongs to this camp, beginning instead with the philosophy of the unity of all life and the principle of nonviolence whose norm advocates the self-realization of all living beings.[152] Objections can however be raised against this position as well. The first question is how in the interest of practical discourse one can establish a sustainable consensus concerning which suffering qualifies as "ecologically functional." Does this enterprise not burden ecological research with having to justify inordinate truth claims? How is one to determine which crite-

---

151. Rolston 1988, 61.
152. Næss 1989, 193-99.

ria regulate the imposition of cultural violence that in any given instance might be exceeding the ecologically functional suffering within the environment?

It is in this context that one might engage the concept of "ecological violence" in the sense of culturally organized actions that inflict both qualitative and quantitative suffering on intrinsically valuable living beings and landscapes in the human environment. Rolston's homologous principle does not sufficiently safeguard against the possibility that one might draw *false* conclusions regarding what at any given time is considered "functionally" defensible suffering and then use precisely those conclusions as the basis for establishing standards for social behavior. I would propose deriving normative standards governing our practical dealings with nature both from the homologous, ecological-functional principle *as well as* from the cultural principle of a maximal avoidance or diminution of violence. Only then can an analysis of ecologically given suffering be commensurate with culturally imposed suffering. Only then will we be able to make an ethically considered distinction between suffering that is justified and suffering that is unjust and thus condemnable and to be avoided.

Theological Interpretations

God's Enjoyment and Empathy: John B. Cobb, Jr.   The thesis of God's sympathetic participation in the suffering of his creatures is an important postulate of Cobb's theology. Cobb and Griffin criticize Anselm's and Thomas's adoption of the ancient axiom of God's immutability that understands God's love to be a love without passion.[153] Process theology understands God having a "consequent" nature that is "receptive" to the world and in connection with which the two characteristics of enjoyment and suffering are emphasized: "God enjoys our enjoyments, and suffers with our sufferings."[154]

Cobb and Birch define the value of life as a maximization of experience.[155] Cobb and Griffin speak of "increasing the enjoyment in the world" as the "degree of order." They respond to the theistic solution to the problem of theodicy by pointing out that although God is indeed responsible for evil, he does not cause it himself. By creating the possibility of deviation, God also

---

153. Cobb and Griffin 1977, 45f. They criticize Nygren's understanding of Christian agape as lacking sympathy (46).

154. Cobb and Griffin 1977, 48.

155. Birch and Cobb 1990, 174.

creates the possibility of evil.[156] Because enjoyment and suffering necessarily belong together for Cobb and Griffin, they ask, "Should we risk suffering, in order to have a shot at intense enjoyment?"[157] They answer in the affirmative.

Birch and Cobb develop this theoretical understanding of enjoyment further in connection with the value of experience. The intrinsic value of creatures derives from their capacity for experience. In animal ethics the criterion of ameliorating suffering is complemented by the positive criterion of enhancing experience.[158] Although Birch and Cobb refer to evil as an integral part of good, they nonetheless insist that one can trust life insofar as death will not have the last word.[159] God's consequent nature is characterized by its capacity for responsive enjoyment and suffering. Although God does complete and perfect the world in Birch and Cobb's view, the world also completes God insofar as life actualizes experiential values.[160]

In summary one can say that Cobb's God is fully capable of suffering and participates responsively in every individual instance of suffering in the world. In addressing what underlies the suffering of creatures, Cobb points out metaphysically that because enjoyment requires suffering, a certain measure of suffering is simply necessary, and because God wants his creatures to be free, evil is always a possibility. Cobb's conventionally formulated response to the problem of theodicy thus remains standing before Auschwitz, his God standing on the side of both those who inflict suffering and those who suffer. Here liberation and a mitigation of suffering refer largely to the quantitative and qualitative enhancement of the whole's capacity for enjoyment. It seems to me that this extremely close association of suffering and enjoyment unintentionally approximates the position of utilitarianism and hedonism, the latter of which ascribes the same function to the enhancement of happiness as Cobb does to the increase of enjoyment. Cobb does not address the issue of just what constitutes the liberating power of the suffering God, and the subject of this liberating seems to be more life than God.

The Theology of the Cross and Learning to Die: Günter Altner   Altner maintains that the suppression or denial of death in modernity has made technological civilization inimical to life,[161] and that the cross of Jesus of Nazareth represents a "symbol of liberation from the 'terrible eternity' bur-

156. Cobb and Griffin 1977, 66, 69.
157. Cobb and Griffin 1977, 74.
158. Birch and Cobb 1990, 152-55.
159. Birch and Cobb 1990, 193, 201.
160. Birch and Cobb 1990, 196f.
161. Altner 1988, 201.

dening modern human beings." Altner believes that the way out of the crisis of survival necessarily involves shattering technological civilization's overriding claim to eternity. The cross of Christ offers the hope that we might learn the praxis of dying and thereby abandon our flight before the power of death.[162]

Following Moltmann, Altner describes the world's future as that of the God who suffers in and with his world,[163] suggesting that a theology of the cross is more commensurate with the open nature of process characterizing the scientific theory of self-organization than is trinitarian theology.

Altner's bioethics (1991) examines the problem of suffering in connection with Albert Schweitzer's ethics of reverence. Anthropologically the human self is constituted by the question of the unity of the world and human oneness with it. "The experience of unity can be gained only at the cost of pain and sympathetic cosuffering."[164] Altner views conscious life as feeling, perception, and suffering. Here he criticizes the utilitarian ethical goal of eliminating human and animal suffering; the center of his bioethics is not the human and animal capacity for suffering but the equality of *all* living beings in their desire for and right to life and their common evolutionary origin within natural history (including microorganisms). His ethical maxim thus demands striving to minimize pain, injury, and death as much as possible, and to include *all* partners involved in the competition for survival.[165] Theologically Altner draws attention to the "liberation effected by Christ," describing it as a "release from anthropocentric restriction," as being "jolted by a universal caring and concern (even unto death on the cross)" that leads to love for neighbor — including both those closest and those most distant — and to a liberation of groaning creation.[166]

God's Essential Capacity for Suffering: Jürgen Moltmann God's capacity for suffering is a central issue in Moltmann's theology. He radically criticizes the notion of God's immutability, maintaining instead that the capacity for suffering in fact represents one of God's most essential characteristics. Surprisingly this idea recedes in his "ecological doctrine of creation" (1985), probably because the book focuses largely on ontological issues in discussion with the natural sciences. It was not until his monograph on Christology

162. Altner 1981, 156.
163. Altner 1988, 151.
164. Altner 1991, 69.
165. Altner 1991, 241.
166. Altner 1991, 98f.

(1989) that Moltmann again addressed the issue from *The Crucified God* (1972), associating God's capacity for suffering with the suffering of the world itself. His pneumatology (1991) addresses the issue only peripherally, in connection with the suffering of martyrs.

Moltmann raises the topic again in connection with his cosmic Christology, focusing on God's ecologically relevant capacity for suffering: "In 'the sufferings of Christ' the end-time sufferings of the whole world are anticipated and vicariously experienced."[167] Moltmann views the destruction of both human beings and their environment within an "apocalyptic horizon." On his view Christ's community includes the starving, the biosphere, and all plants and animals, whose suffering is also Christ's suffering; in that sense the sufferings of the world acquire a universal-apocalyptic dimension: "the cosmic sufferings of this ecological end-time also become 'sufferings of Christ.'"[168] Moltmann also incorporates the idea of Christ's rebirth out of the Spirit into the ecological doctrine of faith, moving away from the "historical-eschatological theology of rebirth" and toward a "historical-ecological theology of rebirth."[169]

Moltmann criticizes the "evolutionary view of the world" of both Rahner and Teilhard de Chardin for ignoring the victims of the process of selection as well as the breaks within the overall world process while viewing Christ as the pinnacle but not as the redeemer of this development. Neither the passion nor the death on the cross plays any significant role in their theology. By contrast, Moltmann identifies Christ as the redeemer of evolution.[170]

The Hermeneutical Function of Suffering: Christian Link   Although Link does attribute a key hermeneutical function to the suffering of creatures within his doctrine of creation, he is also aware of the difficulty presented by modern empiricism's failure to offer any diagnosis addressing suffering. He addresses suffering from the biblical-eschatological (Rom. 8), psychosomatic, soteriological-philosophical, and theodicy-oriented perspectives.[171]

Link closely associates faith with the hermeneutical function of suffering and with the capacity for recognizing and interpreting suffering. "The suffering of the world represents the experiential basis to which Paul directs

167. Moltmann 1990, 155.
168. Moltmann 1990, 159.
169. Moltmann 1990, 247.
170. Moltmann 1990, 292-302.
171. Link 1991, 387-90, 467f., 564, 580ff.

eschatological faith."[172] Suffering functions hermeneutically by drawing attention to a "repressed and discarded truth." It is in suffering that God takes on responsibility for the world, and Link understands the incarnation of the Son as the event in which God takes responsibility for all creatures.[173]

Although Link frequently mentions scientific rationality's inability to discern or recognize suffering, he does not address the problem in any depth. The psychosomatic school of Viktor von Weizsäcker, however, offers him a way out of this dilemma. Weizsäcker maintains that the experience of suffering in the perception of pain is a key hermeneutical guide for knowledge through which the truth of any damage to life interrelationships becomes clearly discernible.[174] Put differently, just as pain helps the body recognize a perceivable threat, so also in Link's view do the sufferings of creation make us aware of a threat to a world whose relationship with its Creator is in danger.

Picking up on Moltmann's lead, Link interprets God's passion as a representative acceptance that includes all of creation. Link, adducing Metz's insistence that the presupposition for the future of liberation is a recollection of suffering, maintains that it is "in suffering that God guarantees the future to which the world closes itself off."[175]

God's Cosuffering under Violence: Gerhard Liedke and Ulrich Duchrow
Duchrow and Liedke focus on the problem of violence from a largely biblical perspective, answering affirmatively the question whether it is even meaningful in the first place to speak about human violence toward nature and adducing biblical evidence in identifying environmental destruction as the suffering of creation. In his Son, God is also affected ("co-affected") by this suffering insofar as he, too, endures ("cosuffers") the suffering of all creation.[176] This cosuffering constitutes God's loving, sympathetic response to the "total corruption" of creation. Duchrow and Liedke's socioethical maxim is the principle of a diminution or reduction of violence, a reduction which from the biblical perspective can be understood as a sign of the new creation.[177]

God's Suffering as the World Body: Sallie McFague   McFague tries to
"remythologize" the relation between God and world by constructing new expressions, metaphors, and models. If we are to remain true to the God of

172. Link 1982, 119.
173. Link 1982, 194f.
174. Link 1991, 467f.
175. Link 1991, 564.
176. Duchrow and Liedke 1989, 52.
177. Duchrow and Liedke 1989, 60ff.

tradition, we must incorporate new images of God's love into our understanding of human beings in the contemporary nuclear and ecological context[178] and articulate God's transcendence in a worldly fashion through the mythology inhering within our context. One of the new metaphors contrasting the world as *king*dom is the world as God's body. [179] Engaging this metaphor means understanding the sufferings of the world as God's sufferings. Because evil enters into and against God's body, God corporeally feels the pain of any part of creation suffering at the hands of evil, "for as this body suffers, so God suffers."[180]

McFague's ecological theology (1993) enumerates two ways in which Christians can enter into solidarity with the oppressed: resistance to evil, and liberation, on the one hand, and sympathy, on the other.[181] As do Christians, so also does God make use of both forms of solidarity. McFague understands this solidarity with the oppressed as the specifically Christian contribution to the history of evolution,[182] and in describing the cosmic Christ maintains that "the shape of God's body also tells us that God suffers with us in our suffering, that divine love is not only with us in our active work against the destruction of our planet but also in our passive suffering when we and the health of our planet are defeated."[183] In summary one can say that as the body of the world, McFague's God also suffers corporeally whenever any of the world's creatures suffer. Is McFague saying that God suffers "within himself"?

The Realism of the Cross: Dorothee Sölle   In her book on creation theology (1984), which focuses on how human beings cooperate in God's creation work, Sölle addresses the problem of suffering only peripherally. Reconciliation with nature, whose cry (Rom. 9:19-23) is to be set free, comes about through human participation in the work of creation in the form of "good, productive, non-alienated work." "Resurrection from sin's power happens in good work." [184] Sölle does address the problem in greater depth in other publications. In *Leiden* (1973) she works out the important distinction between metaphysical and historical suffering, entirely rejecting metaphysical suffering and raising two questions with respect to historical suffering: Why does

178. McFague 1987, xii.
179. McFague 1987, 69-78; 1993.
180. McFague 1987, 75.
181. McFague 1993, 173.
182. McFague 1993, 164, 172.
183. McFague 1993, 190.
184. Sölle 1984, 112.

suffering arise and how can one address its preconditions? What is the meaning of suffering and how can it make us more human?[185] Sölle views the passion of Jesus as the preeminent model of historical, voluntarily accepted suffering in unity with the Father.[186]

In *Gott denken* (1990) Sölle addresses the religious criticism of the cross that accuses Christianity of harboring necrophilia and a death wish. She maintains that the orthodox view within theological history focuses on God's will and plan to redeem the world through the death of the Son. The "liberal paradigm" understands the cross excessively from the perspective of Christ's actions.[187]

Liberation theology was the first to understand the cross as a "realistic event" rather than a symbol. In connection with the Latin American theology of liberation, Sölle proposes developing a "deep realism" and a "new spirituality of the way of the cross": "For the spirituality of liberation, the new ways of the cross are a living form of the appropriation of the tradition, which in Christian understanding is always the depth of historically imposed suffering."[188] The theological presupposition for Sölle's interpretation of the cross is "Christ's unity of *will* with God instead of the speculative *essential* unity of their natures." The basis is God's will to justice, that is, not a reduction of suffering but "God's love, which demands justice," a love encompassing everything. In this sense the cross "expresses love to the endangered, threatened life of God in our world."[189]

The World Suffering of the Cosmic Christ: Matthew Fox   Fox enthusiastically shifts Christology from the historical Jesus to the cosmic Christ, adducing eclectic and overwhelming support from the Old and New Testaments, from the Christian creation mystics, from the New Age movement, and from depth psychology. The new, "living cosmology" he envisions is allegedly the only theology that can save our planet. Fox accuses the Enlightenment of having thwarted the development of such a cosmology (overlooking the fact that the term "cosmology" itself is a product of the Enlightenment).[190] By "cosmology" he understands science, mysticism, and art: the "scientific history of

---

185. Sölle 1975, 5.
186. Sölle 1975, 140.
187. Sölle 1990, 123.
188. Sölle 1990, 132f.
189. Sölle 1990, 134.
190. Fox 1991, 10. The parenthetical page numbers in the following text are to this work.

the origin of the universe," mysticism as the spiritual answer, and art as the imagery of awakening.

The idea of suffering is central to his thinking; he interprets the crisis of survival in which the earth now finds itself as a "history of the crucifixion" of Mother Earth. His understanding of universal suffering is centered on the cosmic Christ (203), who is present wherever pain is present, uniting all in the body of Christ, which is the body of the universe itself: "the cosmic Christ leads the way to cosmic wholeness" (228). Fox describes the advent of the cosmic Christ as a revivification of sexual love mysticism, as respect for the child that overcomes "adultism," as a return of personal art, as a redemption of worship, and as liturgical renewal with the help of nature cults (241ff., 266ff., 292ff., 311ff.). One of the twenty-one criteria Fox mentions for the kind of correct mysticism that through faith in the cosmic Christ will rescue the world is sympathy (80f.), which Fox describes, however, only as an "experience of unity" regarding God's presence in all things.

The Suffering God of Redemption: Choan-Seng Song   Although the Chinese theologian Song's understanding of faith does not address the ecological challenge of Western theology, the presupposition of his understanding of the relation between creation and redemption is in fact God's capacity for suffering.

Song understands God's creation activity as the "salvific response to the pain and suffering of this world" and maintains that theology itself originated in the pain God feels in his heart for the sake of the world. "Creation redemptively carried out is God's theology in action."[191] Although the point of departure of Buddhism, like Christianity, is the suffering of the world, Buddhism separates that suffering from its understanding of salvation; by contrast, the Christian faith understands suffering as an event *in which* redemption comes about in a necessary tension between the historical and the transhistorical dimension. Suffering itself does not bring about redemption; the cross shows us how the new creation necessarily approaches amid pain and suffering. The suffering God is in this sense also the redemptive God.[192]

It is from this perspective that Song criticizes both Kitamori and Moltmann. He criticizes Kitamori's theology of God's pain, which was influenced by the Second World War, for having too closely associated the "passion of the Absolute" with his pain and thus for having internalized the notion of wrath. That is, Song objects that Kitamori internalizes God's salvific

191. Song 1991, 56.
192. Song 1991, 70.

activity by restricting it to the inner-divine conflict between love and wrath.[193] Song similarly criticizes Moltmann (1972) for having interpreted the event of the cross as an event "between God and God," first as separation, then as connection.[194] Song criticizes this "objective" understanding of the cross and resurrection — in which human beings are merely bystanders — because it separates God from any inner participation in human suffering and separates the inner-divine process from human salvation. God's inner conflict becomes irrelevant to salvation history. Song objects that Kitamori ascribes ontological significance to pain: "His God is not only the God who has pain but the God who is pain."[195]

What the Interpreters of the Situation Have in Common

1. The ecological crisis, accepted as a challenge to the interpretation of the Christian faith, has prompted an attempt to integrate the experiences of "ecological suffering" into that interpretation.

2. Theologically God is understood as having taken onto himself the sufferings of creatures in the present ecological crisis. Although all these authors reject the notion that God has no capacity for suffering, they do describe that capacity differently. Cobb, McFague, and Fox understand that participation ontologically; Sölle and Duchrow and Liedke historically-realistically; Moltmann, Link, and Altner eschatologically-dialectically; and Song historically-eschatologically.

3. All these authors understand their initiatives within the historic continuity of Christianity and relate their arguments to the various interpretations of faith within the Christian tradition.

None subscribes to the classic Christology of two natures,[196] and different positions emerge in their understandings of the Trinity: Moltmann and Link constructively incorporate it into their thinking while Cobb, McFague, Sölle, and Fox weaken it even though they do draw from it. Altner rejects the idea of Trinity entirely.

---

193. Song 1991, 76f., though Kitamori does develop his own understanding in a different historical context than that of Song.

194. Song 1991, 77; cf. Moltmann 2001a, 154f.

195. Song 1991, 78.

196. The general view is that the doctrine of the two natures sooner derives from Greek metaphysics than from Christian doctrine. So Moltmann 1990, 53. On the other hand, Moltmann does acknowledge that this doctrine was certainly capable of preserving the origin of "the dual New Testament definitions" of cross and resurrection (49).

4. These authors reject any metaphysical explanation of suffering, searching instead for the theological meaning of suffering commensurate with the conditions of "theology after Auschwitz," that is, commensurate with the experiences of victims. Cobb is an exception.

5. All try to expand the ethical capacity of the Christian faith either in the form of a reduction or mitigation of suffering or in exposing and drawing attention to suffering.

Correlation

The Common Question: How Does God Suffer the Suffering of Creatures?

Contemporary theologians struggle, as did those in the fourth century, with one common, basic problem: What does the suffering of the resurrected God mean for the suffering that evil inflicts on creation and its creatures? How does God suffer the sufferings of creation and its creatures? Gregory had to deal theologically with neo-Arian theism and its "de-divination" of creation, whereas modern theologians find themselves having to reformulate in a postmetaphysical context what it means for God to take suffering upon himself. In his age Gregory was prompted to reflection by the increase in suffering caused by social injustice and by the machinations of ecclesiastical strategy between Julian and Theodosius. The theological thesis regarding the salvific activity of the cosuffering risen One acquired practical missiological as well as socioethical and thus ecclesio-political importance.

Modern theologians are prompted by the general acknowledgment that culturally imposed ecological destruction now poses a threat to our survival, prompting us to reformulate our entire theological understanding of human beings, God, and our environmental ethics. The suffering and impoverishment of two-thirds of the world's population and the impoverished condition of the environment generate the theological challenge of learning how to express anew the notion that God still takes these sufferings upon himself.

Tradition and Situation Enter into Critical Dialogue

Gregory's View of God's Suffering in the Son   Gregory articulates his understanding of God's participation in connection with the incarnational-theological doctrine of the union of the divine and the human nature in the

Son. Christologically the acceptance of suffering is possible because divinity and humanity "come together," "perichoretically" permeating and admixing with one another. God is wholly present in the Incarnate, the incarnation itself encompassing the entirety of human nature in body, soul, and spirit/mind. God wholly takes on the sufferings of creation in the sufferings of the earthly Jesus, experiencing it, as it were, in his own body. Moreover, God takes on human nature and the accompanying corporeal capacity for suffering voluntarily. It remains unclear to what extent Gregory understands God's pain at the disastrous history of his world as having motivated this incarnation; in any event, passages in Gregory's writings that do suggest as much do not really develop the idea further.

On the one hand, Gregory's formula regarding the "suffering of the one who cannot suffer" can mean that it is actually Christ's human nature that suffers while his divine nature remains impassible; on the other, the assertion is that the deity does not fear pain and certainly does not withdraw from the suffering Jesus (*Or.* 40.45; 30.5). That God takes on the entirety of human nature is soteriologically important for Gregory if the whole is to be saved. "For that which he has not assumed he has not healed" (*Ep.* 101.51f.; LCC 3:218). I think this statement can also be applied to God's suffering insofar as only that which is suffered can be set free. In this sense the redemption of creation presupposes the suffering of the incarnate God, something Gregory clearly describes in his references to the glory of the bloody body of the Son with the Father after the ascension. Gregory's reference here is to the *perpetual presence of the experience of the historical suffering of the Son with God,* a perpetual presence that also constitutes the presupposition for the inhabitation of the Spirit in creation and its comprehensive activity of liberation. Gregory's interpretation here raises several questions for modern initiatives.

Do Cobb, McFague, and Fox Displace the Notion of the Pain of the World from the Understanding of the World to the Understanding of God? It seems that Cobb, McFague, and Fox's model of God's specifically ontological capacity for suffering every kind of suffering in the world suspends the uniqueness of Christ's own historical suffering and thereby also diminishes the power of the soteriological thesis of God's cosuffering. If all suffering in the world is simultaneously also God's suffering, how can one maintain the possibility of historical redemption? Does God not effect redemption until God's Son and then the entirety of Mother Earth are hanging on the cross? For Gregory God's historical suffering was an expression of his historical work of liberation and constitutes the presupposition for any further history of liberation. For Cobb, McFague, and Fox the world's suffering seems to constitute the presupposition for speaking about the God who exists in suffering. Fox's "living cosmology" incorporates the history of creation's suffering into the being of the cosmic God. A perception of the world's pain then reveals the *essence* of the suffering God. By contrast, Gregory's trinitarian cosmology understands the suffering of this time from the perspective of the Trinity as the ongoing experience of the historical suffering of God whose goal is the historical liberation of creation. For Gregory the perception of the suffering of creation also prompts the emergence of places where the *work* of the liberating God is revealed.

I believe the objection Song directs against Kitamori can also be directed against Cobb, McFague, and Fox, namely, that by identifying the pain of the world as God's pain, they in fact move it into God's being, thereby unintentionally also weakening the depth of historical suffering inflicted by ecological violence. This ontological conception is not very useful in establishing socioethical and environmental-ethical guides for action. In fact, the only place Fox finds hope for ameliorating suffering is in correct faith in the cosmic Christ and in the praxis of mysticism.

Is Moltmann Able to Establish the Thesis of God's Essential Suffering (Patheia)? Moltmann and Gregory differ in their understanding of God's essence or nature. The Cappadocian speaks only apophatically about God's nature, addressing the issue of suffering as an economic question regarding the meaning of suffering for us. By contrast, Moltmann asks what Christ's sufferings mean for God.[197] Whereas Gregory maintains the axiom of God's immutability *(apatheia)* that he inherited from the theology of antiquity, emphasizing then the notion of the *mixis* of God's immutability and the acceptance of suffering, Moltmann rejects the notion of God's immutability and instead emphasizes the capacity for suffering as central to God's essence. Moltmann actually develops his criticism of the notion of immutability against a position that maintained that the very presupposition for God's redemptive activity was his elevation above the suffering of the world.[198]

Here Gregory's interpretation favors neither position, since for him the presupposition for God's redemptive activity is not divinity qualified as the incapacity for suffering, but rather God's will to consummate his creation

197. Moltmann 1991b, 17. Hough 1997, 73, wonders whether Moltmann does not slip into a kind of "modalist patrology" that so excessively emphasizes the pain of the Father that the Son merely seems to represent the latter, a situation actually no longer applying to Moltmann's Christology (Moltmann 1990). Hough (72) does not discern the differences between Kitamori, Moltmann, and Song.

198. Karl Rahner and many others; cf. Moltmann 1991b, 169ff.

and the incarnation as his voluntary submission to creaturely pain. One question our interpretation of Gregory raises for soteriology is whether the statement about God's immutability does not also constitute a positive statement about God's nature. Those whose basic positive understanding of God's nature includes the negation of God's capacity for suffering can no longer draw support from the apophatic principle of patristic theology. There is also some question whether the assertion of God's immutability as a theological axiom can even be reconciled with one of the most fundamental concerns of Christian theology, namely, the interpretation of the event of incarnation. The danger here is that God's submission to suffering is interpreted too one-sidedly as the suffering of the earthly Jesus, rendering it difficult or even impossible to speak about the pain of the loving God that prompts the incarnation in the first place and about the cosuffering of the Resurrected. Hence Gregory's theology of incarnation offers no support for establishing the notion of God's immutability as an axiom of Christian soteriology.

However, I also believe that Moltmann's criticism of this position can draw only limited support here, in that his inclination to make such *unequivocal* assertions about God's nature seems to abrogate the very mystery of the incarnation. We know that antiquity understood God as being incapable of suffering. We also saw how Gregory's interpretation of the revelation of Christ was concerned with understanding God as a suffering God, as the crucified and resurrected suffering God. The Cappadocian's challenge was to lend meaning to the understanding of God — and to the concrete historical suffering — of his own age from the perspective of a theology of incarnation.

Moltmann pursues the same goal of understanding the historical revelation of Christ as an expression of God's liberating capacity for suffering. Unlike Gregory, however, he construes a logical, two-step argument designed to understand God's nature as being necessarily characterized by suffering.

1. Because God reveals himself as the one who suffers on the cross, his essence includes the capacity for suffering.
2. Because God is essentially capable of suffering, he representatively experiences the suffering of creation.

But does this assertion of God's suffering *(patheia)* not occupy the same position as does the axiom of immutability in the opposing view? Is Moltmann not positing God's *patheia* as a logical presupposition of his redemptive activity? Gregory's apophatic theology disallows deducing statements regarding God's essence or nature from those regarding his work. Saying that God is revealed within the history of endangered creation as one who suffers rather

COSMOLOGY AS SOTERIOLOGY — A CONSTRUCTIVE CORRELATION

than as one who does not suffer actually represents a theological reflection of the experience of God's liberating activity. The portrayal of God's economy also says something positive about God's essence, namely, that God takes on suffering as God. Logically identifying statements about God's nature with those about God's work, however, makes it possible to engage various schematic statements regarding God's nature in order to avoid interpretive difficulties accompanying the interpretation of God's liberating activity.

Moltmann also risks oversimplifying the issue by employing the assertion of God's essential *patheia* in explaining redemptive activity in connection with the ecological crisis. By having the suffering Christ representatively experience the suffering of the *entire* creation community at once, does he not extinguish the onetime, unique quality and individuality of the earthly, historical suffering of ecologically threatened living beings? How can God simultaneously be both Creator and Redeemer of evolution if natural biological selection necessarily results in victims and unjust suffering?

Although Moltmann's thesis of the God whose essence includes the capacity for suffering takes care of the problem of theodicy, he does not address the question regarding the nature and activity of evil, especially in the form of ecological violence. God becomes the God of resistance to threat. In and of itself, however, the essential unity of God's and the world's suffering does not yet tell us anything about why and how liberation is possible and becomes a reality. Although Moltmann's intention of presenting us with a "historic-ecological theology of rebirth" is rhetorically inspiring, it is incomplete if it cannot be related to concrete experiences of ecological liberation by the suffering Son and Spirit.

Song's objection that Moltmann internalizes suffering into the nature of the Father can also be articulated from the patristic perspective. Saying that God *is* the suffering of the creation community says too much about God's nature and too little about his salvific activity. I believe the apophatic self-limitation of theological truth claims prevents soteriology from moving the cross and liberating resurrection *out* of the world.

Although the patristic interpretation is of little use in establishing the axiom of either *apatheia* or *patheia*, Gregory's understanding of the revealed suffering of the triune God from the perspective of incarnation theology does support Moltmann's goal of making the revelation of God's suffering the point of departure for soteriology in the context of ecological challenge.

Does Link's *Analogia Passionis* Lead to Knowledge of the World or of God?
Link concurs with Gregory in emphasizing the proto-eschatological dimension of God's acceptance of suffering in loyalty and anticipation. Link also

emphasizes the hermeneutical function of suffering both as regards the threat to creation and as regards knowledge of God. But on the latter, knowledge of God, a patristic perspective might ask *which* God Link means: God the Father in his glory, the Son that cosuffers in glory, or the Spirit that enters into suffering creation? I am not quite clear what Link's reference to suffering's "capacity for knowledge" means. Does suffering — as *analogia passionis* — lead to knowledge of God in general? If so, then it would be desirable for creatures to suffer. Or does Link's *analogia passionis* mean that knowledge of the inner-worldly threat *then* yields knowledge of how the sympathetic, liberating God acts? This position resembles the paradigm of liberation theology, which attributes an epistemological privilege to those who suffer unjustly as regards knowledge of both the world and God. I am not sure whether Link believes the experience of suffering leads to knowledge of God's nature or of his work.

One question suggested by Gregory and Sölle in this connection involves how one is to understand theologically the liberating presence within concrete historical suffering resulting from ecological violence. Sölle refers here to the presence of the one crucified in history; Gregory refers to the trinitarian perspective on the stigmata of the Son with the Father and the entry of the Spirit from the Son and Father into a creation that is suffering the pangs of birth. How in Link's view does God participate in the suffering of creation *in the midst of* ecological violence? The same question applies to Altner's incomplete theology of the cross.

What does Link's thesis of the hermeneutical function of suffering have to say about violence whose goal is the extermination of, for example, species or even the children of the poor? How is one to understand God as the suffering and liberating God in such contexts? How does the world viewed from the perspective "below" become a "parable" of God? What is the theological meaning of Link's reference to the redemption of a parable?

Must Sölle's God and Church Suffer?   Sölle concurs with Gregory in emphasizing the voluntary nature of the acceptance of historical suffering and the unity of Christ with the whole God. Sölle posits God's "volitional will" in the place of "speculative unity of essence" because in the modern context her Christology wants to avoid the orthodox Lutheran doctrine of the two kingdoms.[199] Viewing this position as a judgment on patristic theology, however, involves an anachronism. As we saw earlier, Gregory tries to articulate persuasively his understanding of the volitional unity of the community of the

---

199. Concerning criticism of the doctrine of the two kingdoms as a far-reaching construction of Lutheran orthodoxy if not of Luther himself, cf. Frostin 1994.

hypostases. By incorporating the notion of the "mixing" of the two natures into his system under the contextual presuppositions of late antiquity, he is developing further the idea of incarnation rather than merely engaging in speculation.

I would suggest that one must begin with an examination of the fourth-century origins of dual-nature Christology to determine whether it can still be of significance in late modernity. Gregory focuses on how God and creation *come together*, later thinkers on the *boundary* between the two natures. One can justifiably ask whether a theology of incarnation allows the assertion — one conservative Lutheran theology is inclined to entertain — that a presupposition of theology is that God and the world are fundamentally different. The acceptance of any fundamental difference of this sort substantially weakens the doctrine of the *communicatio idiomatum* as well as the task of implementing this *communicatio* in a differentiated fashion. The lack of persuasive support from the New Testament or patristic theology requires that we reject as mere speculation any fundamental separation of Creator and creation, a separation that is then often also applied to dual-nature Christology.

A consideration of Gregory's position also raises the question whether by emphasizing the realism of historical suffering Sölle does not beg the question of whether God's love, which demands justice, comes to expression *only* through Christian discipleship in voluntarily accepting historical suffering. If the cross expresses God's love for endangered life, how does that love then come to expression as resurrection from the grave? The understanding of God in Sölle's realism seems to focus one-sidedly on a Christ who *perpetually* suffers death even though the witnesses of the New Testament viewed the resurrection as a historical event. And Gregory himself viewed especially the Son's ascension as an extremely important event in salvation history. Latin American liberation theology, which Sölle herself often cites, emphasizes both the sufferings of believers and the joy accompanying martyrdom and especially the joy at any progress toward liberation. Does Sölle's realism of the Crucified not move on to include the realism of the Resurrected as well? Does God demand justice exclusively through our suffering? Although one certainly cannot insinuate such a position to Sölle, I remain suspicious that she is overemphasizing God's demand for discipleship in suffering at the expense of God's sympathy and solidarity with the unjust historical suffering of his creatures.

Proto-eschatological considerations also raise questions regarding Sölle's pairing of a theology of the cross with a realism of suffering. For the kind of universal soteriology Gregory envisioned, Christ's voluntary acceptance of historical suffering both expressed the loyalty of the Creator to a creation that was originally good but was now threatened by evil and also created the possibility that creation might be set free in the future. God's historical suffering thus emerges protologically from the Creator's suffering at the pain of his creation and eschatologically lays the foundation for the history of liberation toward the new creation. It seems to me that by concentrating on Christ's and Christians' concrete historical suffering, Sölle quite unintentionally risks losing sight of the theological understanding of the prehistory and posthistory of suffering.

How Do the Father, Son, and Spirit Suffer in Gregory's View?   Modern theologians, of course, might question Gregory's insistence on maintaining the axiom of God's immutability. Is Gregory really able to connect persuasively the incarnate Son's acceptance of suffering with God's immutability? Or does he risk slipping into trinitarian speculation that might suggest ascribing *apatheia* to the Father, *patheia* to the Son, and sympathy to the Spirit? Although nothing in Gregory's writings suggests such a classification, his reference to the "suffering of the one who is without suffering" does leave unanswered the question of how *apatheia* and *patheia* are related within the divine.

One can acknowledge, however, that Gregory did persuasively demonstrate the plausibility of a theology of incarnation for the educated Greek critics of Christianity and in so doing skillfully employed the axiom of immutability from Greek theology. But how does Gregory understand God's participation in the painful process of liberation of creation in the Spirit? Does the Spirit, like the Son, also suffer corporeally? If one does not adequately articulate theologically how the Father and Spirit suffer, does an ethics of sympathy — as an ethics of becoming like God — not risk becoming excessively christocentric? Does the Father suffer differently before the incarnation than does the Spirit who takes up habitation in creation after the Son? Because ontologically God contains no evil, Gregory's God cannot suffer from anything. Yet because God simultaneously is active in the world in which evil is regnant, God also takes the sufferings of this world onto himself to liberate the world toward the new creation.

4. Spirit

The Problem

Bateson's Ecological Question
concerning the Spirit or Mind as Form

How does ecological discourse address the problem of the Spirit and of spirituality? First let me point out that I distinguish between the problem of the Spirit and the problem of spirituality. References to "ecological spirituality" recur in various contexts,[200] raising the question of how a given understanding of the world or of life can do justice both to the new ecological stance and to the demands of ecologically structured ethics.[201] Strikingly, the notion of spirituality is rarely associated with that of a *spiritus,* not even — remarkably — by theologians.[202]

In a general sense the question of the Spirit involves how one person or thing can be in or with another ("the being of the one in or with the other").[203] Of course, a definition this broad might qualify a great many issues in ecological discourse as problems of the Spirit. "Problems of the Spirit" might include, for example, the problem of genetic information residing within a physiological form; an (eco)system inhering within a given environ-

200. McDaniel 1990a; Berry 1988 ("spirituality of earth"); McFague 1993, 69 ("creation spirituality"); Boff 1993a; 1993b; 1995; 1997, chap. 10 ("Eco-Spirituality"); Kessler 1990, 72-110 ("creation spirituality"); Mynarek 1986, 42 ("ecospiritual religion and spirituality"). Cf. http://www.religionandnature.com

201. McDaniel 1990a, 30, defines "spirituality" as "the general style or quality of our experience, as that experience is lived from the inside, and as it is oriented around an ultimate frame of reference or center." Ecological spirituality for McDaniel is "the *way* we experience and respond to the data of experience." Unfortunately, this definition sooner obscures than illuminates the concept. How does the ecological experiential mode differ from others? Is the orientation toward (Tillich's) "ultimate being" abstract or concrete; that is, does spirituality find God *in* its experiences, or does this orientation toward the ultimate itself constitute the presupposition for some sort of *special* experience? Does "ecological" refer to *all* sensory human experiences and reactions?

202. Although McDaniel (1990a) does speak about a "spirituality of the gods," despite christological arguments he avoids associating the concept of spirituality with the Holy Spirit. It seems that an excessively indistinct or loosely conceived understanding of the Spirit generally obscures the attendant understanding of God. The concepts of spirituality and Spirit are indeed frequently dissociated. Although Boff 1997, chap. 8, does connect ecospirituality with pneumatology, he does so only in connection with an ontologically all-encompassing "pan-en-spiritualism" (169).

203. Lessing 1984, 218.

ment and in connection with an organism; or the possibility of one epigenetic development inhering within another. Because only a few theoreticians of nature actually employ the concept of Spirit, identifying problems in this way obviously risks overinterpreting the issue; hence I will concentrate on one of the more influential ecological theoreticians who incorporate the concept of the Spirit or Mind (*Geist* in German) into the center of his theory: Gregory Bateson.

Bateson generally follows the lead of Lamarck and Samuel Butler. He admires the way Lamarck "turned the ladder of explanation upside down," such that one no longer understands the Mind or Spirit as deductively explaining life below, but rather derives an explanation of Mind from the study of evolution. Bateson believes that nineteenth-century evolutionary theoreticians avoided the question of the Mind, which then reemerged as a problem during World War II.[204] He admires Butler for showing that Darwin's denial of mind in Nature as an explanatory principle could not really be sustained. He hopes his own definition of Mind/Spirit can overcome not only Lamarck's and Darwin's understanding of the "chain" of being,[205] but also Butler's understanding of the Mind as "supernatural entelechy."[206] Bateson also emphasizes the significance of "random elements" against Butler's model.

Bateson uses the term "mind," which the German translation of his book renders as *Geist*, to cover an extremely wide semantic field. He variously circumscribes "mind" as: "the pattern which connects is a metapattern," "mental process," "system," "aggregate," "ideas," "integrated network," "world of information," "perhaps what some people mean by 'God,'" and "a necessary and unavoidable function of appropriate complexity."[207]

Bateson's basic definition begins: "A mind is an aggregate of interacting parts or components."[208] His point of departure is that there is no opposition between the mind/spirit and nature; instead, the two constitute a necessary unity. He posits six cybernetic criteria of mental/spiritual processes, maintaining that phenomena such as thinking, evolution, ecology, and learning arise only in systems meeting these criteria.[209] The goal of Bateson's theory is

204. Bateson 1990a, 551, who maintains that the war clearly revealed the complexity of spiritual phenomena. The quotation is taken from the English edition (1972, 427).

205. Bateson 1990a, 30f. Here Bateson cites Lovejoy's famous study (*The Great Chain of Being: A Study in the History of an Idea* [Cambridge, 1936]). Bateson 1990b, 17.

206. Bateson 1990a, 229.

207. The first four words or phrases are from Bateson 1990b, 10, 86, 177, and 86 respectively; the final five are from Bateson 1990a, 15, 203, 583, 593, and 619.

208. Bateson 1990b, 85.

209. Bateson 1990b, 86.

COSMOLOGY AS SOTERIOLOGY — A CONSTRUCTIVE CORRELATION

the thesis that the relationship between life and thought constitutes a "stochastic process," that is, a digital *and* analogue relationship combining a component of chance with the selective process.[210] A second goal is the thesis that Mind is the pattern connecting all that lives, which can be discerned from the existence of recurrent forms of mental processes, from the hierarchy of logical types, and from "the transformation of difference."[211]

Because Bateson's ecology of ideas incorporates linguistic forms of expression, trains of thought, and empirical data from a plethora of different areas, I will not burden the reader with additional details of his theory, not least because it does admittedly make rather heavy demands on one's power of imagination. Let me conclude by addressing the theological dimension of his thinking.

Bateson's book *Mind and Nature* is prefaced by a quotation from Augustine's *De civitate Dei* in which the church father positively assesses Plotinus's assertion that blossoms and leaves "could not be endowed with a beauty so immaculate and so exquisitely wrought, did they not issue from the Divinity which endlessly pervades with its invisible and unchanging beauty all things."[212] Here Bateson himself provides the point of correlation between the ecological problem of the mind in the twentieth and fourth centuries. The problem shared by Bateson, Augustine, and Gregory regards the nature of this "place" from which mental form shapes all life.

By emphasizing the "exploratory process — the endless *trial and error* of mental progress," Bateson's theory counters the kind of "dualistic theology" that postulates *within* the biological process of evolution a Creator who is utterly distinct from life.[213] Bateson seeks to address the old problem of the transcendence or immanence of the Spirit in favor of immanence.[214] He is certainly aware that his cybernetic theory contains implications that may well "change or perhaps renew theology," and he emphasizes that mind is immanent not only in the body but also outside the body. "The cybernetic epistemology which I have offered you would suggest a new approach. The individual mind is immanent but not only in the body. It is immanent also in pathways and messages outside the body; and there is a larger Mind of which the individual mind is only a sub-system. This larger Mind is comparable to God, and is perhaps what some people mean by 'God,' but it is still

210. Bateson 1990b, 18.
211. Bateson 1990b, 10f.
212. Bateson 1990b, 2.
213. Bateson 1990b, 172.
214. Bateson 1990a, 407.

immanent in the total interconnected social system and planetary ecology."[215]

Bateson "expands mind outwards" and encourages the posture of humility in recognizing that we are "part of something much bigger. A part — if you will — of God."[216] He also points out the difference between his own theological understanding of the Spirit and the supranaturalistic understanding of God. If human beings conceive God as being *outside* the world and themselves as having been created in the image of this God, they will inevitably also view themselves as being outside of and opposed to the things around them. Once human beings attribute all spirit to themselves, they will view their surroundings as spiritless, discount any moral relevancy in connection with them, and understand and indeed treat them merely as objects to be exploited.

In summary one can say that Bateson creatively develops the concept of mind/spirit by incorporating into it both traditional and more contemporary materials. The being of the One is understood both as being that inheres *within* various constructions and processes as well as being that is *with* or is *intimately connected with* concrete life. That is, Bateson's Mind, rather than "containing" a pig, is the *idea* of the pig. By the same token, without this idea the pig could not *be* a pig.[217] In consciously picking up on Platonic thought, Bateson asserts the reality of ideas, that is, the real existence of the ecology of ideas and of the Spirit, while at the same time avoiding any hypostasization of the Spirit. Bateson in no way understands mind anthropomorphically, since doing so merely diminishes it. The human spirit is instead part of a "greater Mind"; indeed, all life processes, organisms, environments, and events are part of the active mind/spirit.

That Bateson does not explain the relationship between the concept of the Spirit and that of God makes him an important dialogue partner for ecological theology. Although theological judgment cannot determine the extent to which his cybernetic theory serves the development of ecological biology and social theory, the inherent agenda of any Christian, ecological, formative pneumatology must of necessity address his question of whether the "spirit" that as "pattern" connects thought and evolution as a totality is also the Spirit of God.

One wonders whether Bateson's concept of the spirit does not represent a "crutch" similar to the Aristotelian "unmoved mover." For how can we be sure

---

215. Bateson 1990a, 593. English text from the 1972 ed., p. 461.
216. Bateson 1990a, 593; 1972, 461.
217. Cf. Bateson 1990a, 353.

that everything Bateson describes as the spirit genuinely exists in both thinking *and* evolution?[218] One theological criticism is that Bateson does not satisfactorily distinguish between the spirit as pattern and system and the spiritual process. Does his spirit bring something about or *is* it such "bringing about"?

Although Bateson is intent on transforming the ontology of substance into an ontology of form, this certainly does not mean he is able to solve the problems attaching to an ontology of substance, since "form" could just as easily take on the same logical function as did substance in earlier ontology. Although Bateson's emphasis on the form of being of the One in and with the other does doubtless disclose new insights, what about the phenomenon of time? Bateson seems to classify time completely under form and its cybernetic characteristics. Should one not rather maintain the view that time is neither form nor substance? Does Bateson really ascribe to the phenomenon of time a function commensurate with its position as form?

Theological Interpretations

Life as Spirit: John B. Cobb, Jr.   Pneumatology is of little consequence in Cobb's theology. Although the Holy Spirit does not appear in his theology of ecology (1972) until the final pages, the reader does learn that the Spirit "is the God of whom we have been speaking."[219] Cobb views the Spirit as the ground of hope in the face of all destructive forces; he seems to conceive the Spirit as the guarantor of the possibility of future change. Cobb develops his pneumatology more clearly in his introduction to process theology. Griffin and Cobb distinguish between two different concepts of Spirit. On the one hand, the Spirit as "a germ of mentality" is present in all "occasions of experience" as "the capacity for self-determination." This Spirit is associated with the increase of enjoyment and freedom. On the other hand, the Holy Spirit (spirit) is "the effects of God's activity on us."[220]

---

218. That Bateson's understanding of the spirit does indeed acquire a certain function in thinking and is thus real becomes plausible insofar as I am able to present the reader with an analysis of his ideas from having read his books. That is, one can probably assume that Bateson's spirit "has an effect" or is "active" both in me and in the reader of this book. The problem, of course, is proving that the *same* spirit affecting the reader of this book is also at work in the worms in my garden such that what they eat there does indeed taste good to them. Does Bateson not enlist the same "trick" as does Russell, who attempts to solve all problems through a classification of classes?

219. Cobb 1972, 144.

220. Cobb and Griffin 1977, 67, 32.

Although Cobb and Griffin follow the classical doctrine of the Spirit in emphasizing that the "Holy Spirit is fully God," they seem to ascribe God's spirit more to God's "Consequent Nature" and "responsive love" than to God's "Primordial Nature" and "the creative love."[221] In 1980 Cobb and Birch tied the concept of the Spirit closer to the ecological model of nature, picking up on the Hebrew understanding of the Spirit as the "'Breath' of God" and speaking about the "immanence of the divine Life within us that makes us alive." They understand the biblical understanding of the Spirit to be saying that the spirit makes both biological and human experience possible, and from the thesis that the Spirit vivifies in this way they conclude that God is precisely this life: "If it is the Spirit that enlivens us, we may equally say that it is God who makes us alive. If the Spirit is the true Life within us, then God is that Life."[222] Birch and Cobb believe that the biblical authors consciously used the concept of the Spirit in describing biological life and human experience because no image is more central than that of life. They insist "on the identity of the Life that does both of these things."[223]

Their argumentation seems to suggest that one could just as easily do without the concept of the Spirit altogether. If "life" is the ultimate "image" of the divine, why not simply develop a religion of life? Does this position not turn the grammar and conceptual terminology of the Christian tradition into a mere linguistic cloak, and theology into a tool that translates between the language of the natural sciences and that of the church? In 1988 Welker already suggested that Cobb distinguish between the concepts of "aliveness" and "life."[224] I do in any case believe that the tradition of Christian pneumatology is ideally suited for the project Cobb envisions. Why does he constantly give precedence to contemporary philosophical and biological frames of reference over that of theology? Why dissolve the distinction between "life" and "giver of life" in such identification?

The Spirit as the Event of Becoming: Günter Altner   Altner develops his concept of the spirit commensurate with the conditions of evolutionary theoreticians and at a critical distance from theologians who would distinguish between the Spirit of God and that of evolving nature. He objects that Daecke's distinction between the "Spirit of God" and the "spirit of matter" conceives God within Whitehead's understanding "beyond the process

---

221. Cobb and Griffin 1977, 110.
222. Birch and Cobb 1990, 200.
223. Birch and Cobb 1990, 199.
224. Welker 1988, 199.

through which the world becomes" in order then to influence the "dynamic of material self-organization."[225] Altner wonders how in addition to the process of becoming in which God appears, there can be another, second-class transcendence.[226]

Altner also objects that Moltmann's trinitarian initiative inadequately distinguishes between statements regarding the inner Trinity and the dynamic of self-organization.[227] He rejects the trinitarian understanding of God as outdated insofar as it is overly burdened by the metaphysics of the ancient understanding of the world.

> All those involved in the fourth-century trinitarian disputes had enormous difficulty expressing with the conceptual tools of Greek metaphysics the salvific-historical experience of the Christ event in which God becomes a human being. . . . The understanding of the atemporal divine characteristics which emerged from these disputes is a hindrance today, where the goal is quite different, namely, to express the way God becomes world (and thus also time) within the process of evolution. One must acknowledge that these two, fundamentally different paradigms cannot be reconciled, and must simply take the "leap."[228]

Altner takes this "leap" himself, leaving the "conceptual tools" of Greek metaphysics behind. Not surprisingly, he accordingly develops no theological understanding of the Holy Spirit and does not employ trinitarian thought in articulating and grounding his creation theology. The term *ruach* appears neither in his interpretation of the biblical creation account nor in his citation of Psalm 104, and the spirit of the children of God remains similarly absent in his interpretation of Romans 8.[229] Nor does he make any reference to the life-giving Spirit of the creed of Constantinople.

Faced with the alternative between the concept of the Spirit of the Christian tradition and the theory and philosophy of nature, Altner chooses the latter, then argues rigorously against the dualism of spirit and nature and proposes that in accordance with the essay attributed to Goethe[230] we now conceive neither matter without spirit nor spirit without matter.[231] Picking

---

225. Altner 1988, 109.
226. Altner 1988, 149.
227. Altner 1988, 149.
228. Altner 1988, 150f.
229. Altner 1991, 75-79, 83.
230 Goethe 1989b.
231. Altner 1988, 162.

up closely on Jantsch's understanding of the "self-organization of the universe," Altner defines his own concept of the spirit as a circumscription of the reality of the process of becoming. "The reality of the spirit . . . manifests itself in the sense of the theory of self-organization in dynamics and in the self-transcendence of evolution. The reality of the spirit manifests itself in the self-structuring processes of matter, energy, and information."[232]

Following Picht and Müller, Altner also develops his understanding of the spirit in connection with the philosophy of time in order to link that philosophy with the discussion of spirit matter. Here Altner elevates the theory of self-organization into the normative framework for our understanding of both time and the spirit, since on his view neither the spirit not time can be understood as a sort of "special reality" beyond the process of self-organization.[233]

The Trinitarian Spirit as Organizational Form and Mode of Communication: Jürgen Moltmann Pneumatology plays a significant role in Moltmann's understanding of the Trinity, which relates biblical statements and historical theological insights regarding God's Spirit with a plethora of philosophical anthropologies and scientific theories. From the perspective of creation theology, Moltmann's overriding formula is "creation in the Spirit": "Creation in the Spirit is the theological concept which corresponds best to the ecological doctrine of creation which we are looking for and need today."[234] In Moltmann's attempt to establish a "community" of scientific and theological thought, pneumatological considerations represent the theological contribution to the community. Here he draws both on Calvin's doctrine of the immanence of the Spirit in creation as well as on Barth's understanding of the Spirit as "indestructible order."[235]

By emphasizing the immanence of the Spirit's activity, Moltmann skillfully avoids the labyrinth attaching to the problem of energy when he says that "Through the energies and potentialities of the Spirit, the Creator is himself present in his creation."[236] He also articulates his understanding of the Trinity from a christological perspective: "In the unity of created things, Word and Spirit complement one another."[237] Creation in the Spirit is also creation in Christ.

232. Altner 1988, 112.
233. Altner 1988, 112-14.
234. Moltmann 1985, 12.
235. Moltmann 1985, 13, 253; cf. Barth, *Kirchliche Dogmatik* III/2 (1950), p. 391.
236. Moltmann 1985, 9.
237. Moltmann 1990, 289.

In summary, Moltmann speaks about the Spirit as "forms of organization" and "modes of communication in open systems." That is, the Spirit is both the organizational form of ecological systems and "the quintessence of the human being's self-organization and his self-transcendence" and is his consciousness.[238] Moltmann revives the old doctrine of the "cosmic Spirit" and its "cosmic breadth,"[239] emphasizing the Spirit as "principle": the Spirit is a holistic principle, the principle of creativity, of evolution, of individuation, and of intentionality.[240] Moltmann also identifies the cosmic Spirit as God's Spirit: "If the cosmic Spirit is the Spirit of God, the universe cannot be viewed as a closed system. It has to be understood as a system that is open — open for God and for his future."[241] Moltmann also discerns the cosmic Spirit in the anthropological realm. The "creative Spirit" "embraces" corporeality. Moltmann does, however, distinguish the creative spirit from the Holy Spirit, since the latter in fact "transforms" the former.[242] Moltmann finds the Spirit "as" anticipation, communication, and life affirmation in the anthropological just as in the cosmological realm.

Moltmann's monograph on the "Spirit of life" focuses on the context of spiritual experience in the individual, social, and biological realms. An understanding of God's Spirit as the power of creation and the source of life makes it possible to discern God in all things and all things in God.[243] Moltmann's pneumatology culminates in the assertion that the Spirit brings about not only the inner-trinitarian community, but also experience as such at every cosmological and anthropological level. "The trinitarian fellowship of the Holy Spirit is the full community of the Creator, Reconciler and Redeemer with all created being, in the network of all their relationships."[244] In 1985 Moltmann tried to relate recent scientific theories to the biblical and historical Reformed doctrines of the Spirit. In 1991 he drew from a rather broadly conceived understanding of experience that departs from the limitations of subject philosophy in favor of a more broadly ecological perspective; here he related various theories of subjective, relational, social, and natural experience to several largely biblically derived topoi in the doctrine of the Spirit, basing his understanding on a somehow ontologically understood (in

238. Moltmann 1985, 17f.
239. Moltmann 1991a, 10.
240. Moltmann 1985, 100.
241. Moltmann 1985, 103. Contra Jantsch's thesis that God "is not the Creator but he is the Spirit of the universe."
242. Moltmann 1985, 263.
243. Moltmann 2001b, 35.
244. Moltmann 2001b, 221.

the rather unclear concept of "presence") identity between God's Spirit and that of the world. Within this context Moltmann develops his pneumatology from a trinitarian, cosmological, and anthropological perspective, maintaining, following Augustine, that God's Spirit brings about the inner-divine community as well as all communication and organization attaching to created being.

One wonders whether Moltmann has written both too much and too little about the Spirit. Although only an extremely intensive study of his writings could determine just how consistent or contradictory his various statements about the Spirit ultimately are, it seems both statements apply insofar as he wishes to incorporate apparently everything that has been said about the Holy Spirit, the result being that he both says too much and says it too unclearly.

I also have the feeling that Moltmann's understanding of "organization" has been excessively influenced by Barth's understanding of the principle of organization. How does Moltmann propose relating contemporary theories of chaos to statements about the *ruach* hovering above the waters? Even though Moltmann doubtless does not envision a theology of the orders of creation, I do not see that his writings lend sufficient expression to the constantly inculcated ideological suspicion against the organizational inclinations of scientific theories. What critical theological bearing can his ecological and classically actualized doctrine of the Spirit have over against the potentially ideological inclinations of "recent" theories of nature? Moltmann also seems to distinguish insufficiently between the being and activity of the trinitarian Spirit, writing a great deal about *what* the Spirit *is,* less about *how* the Spirit is active, and less still about *what* the Spirit brings about. What is the relationship between the ontological, economic, and soteriological levels of his understanding of the Spirit? We will return to this question in our correlation with Gregory's apophatic thinking.

The Spirit as the Ground of Possibility of God's Manifestation in the World: Christian Link   In contrast to Moltmann's ontological understanding of the Spirit, Link develops his from an eschatological perspective cloaked in a philosophy of time. He, too, draws on Calvin and Barth. Unlike Moltmann, however, he does not interpret Calvin's doctrine of the Creator Spirit as "world immanence" and does not mention Barth's pneumatological "principle of order." He does, however, develop his own understanding of the Spirit commensurate with the conditions attaching to Barth's parable cosmology.

Like Moltmann, Link articulates his understanding of the Spirit within a comprehensive trinitarian understanding of God. Unlike Moltmann, however, whose doctrine of the Spirit begins with God's inner-trinitarian community, Link begins with the more Lutheran tradition of the "grammar of articles" of the confession of faith, and is clearly intent on establishing a foundation for his doctrine of the Spirit in a theology of incarnation and of the cross. Link lends special emphasis to the Spirit's work of unification. It is the Spirit who unites the Father with the Son as well as God with the world. "The Spirit is . . . the unity in the encounter and relationship of God and Son; it unites God with the world. Confessing the Spirit as unity means understanding the Spirit as the ground of possibility of God's manifestation in the world, indeed as the ground of God's 'worldliness.'"[245]

In this sense Link understands the Spirit as the ground of the possibility of God's revelation in the world, a world whose character as "parable" derives precisely from the presence and activity of this Spirit. Moreover, as the ground of possibility, the Spirit is thus also oriented toward the future. For Link the third article establishes the possibility that God may appear "in time, that is, within the boundaries of temporally construed nature."[246] Here Link follows the lead of Barth's reference to the Spirit as the power of light that is cast into the world from the incarnation.[247] Although Link concurs with Moltmann in not identifying the Spirit with structures — as do the process theologians — he objects theologically that the bridge between the second and third articles remains rather obscure. Contra Moltmann, Link begins with Calvin's "sharply" drawn boundary between Creator and creation; that is, it is not creation itself that is sacred, but the transcendent God *in* his creation.[248] It is only as the Spirit of the Son that the Spirit takes up dwelling in believers: "Its world presence is *not* world immanence."[249] It is similarly from the perspective of the theology of the cross that Link answers the question regarding the experience associated with faith in the Spirit: "The Spirit places human beings into Christ's global suffering."[250] Link's thorough exegesis of the Pauline text in Romans 8 emphasizes the "critical power of the Spirit" that disallows any understanding of existence that "objectifies" the world as "accomplishment" and instead remains committed to the "necessarily *pathic* character of our existence."[251]

Link interprets the work of the Spirit completely from the perspective

245. Link 1982, 219; cf. 1991, 547.
246. Link 1982, 221.
247. Link 1982, 229.
248. Link 1991, 445f.
249. Link 1991, 550.
250. Link 1982, 237.
251. Link 1982, 240f.

of the incarnation. The Spirit manifests itself "just as the Logos of John 1:14 manifests itself in the 'flesh.'"[252] In contrast but not in contradiction to the natural sciences, Link speaks of the Spirit that renews reason, maintaining that *all* empirical research necessarily includes "a bit of theology."[253]

The Spirit as the Breath of the World and Mediation: Sallie McFague

McFague's pneumatological considerations within the framework of her ecological theology follow her understanding of the world as God's body. Her organic metaphor emphasizes the Spirit as the breath of the body "world," and in contrast to the traditional trinitarian view she also emphasizes less the Spirit's personality than its role in mediating between the visible and invisible.

Although McFague does emphasize the significance of a new creation spirituality, she does not relate such spirituality to any theological understanding of the Spirit. Instead creation spirituality actually refers negatively to "the critique of a sin-centered, redemption-oriented interpretation of Christianity that focuses on guilt, sacrificial atonement, and otherworldly salvation," and positively to a "celebration of cosmic evolution." Creation spirituality represents a "utopian, eschatological vision" that ultimately is to play a prophetic role.[254]

For McFague the Spirit's significance derives exclusively from its physical basis, that is, from its identity as the breath of life. She maintains that God's body is in fact vivified by God's breath, a metaphor commensurate with her intention of replacing anthropocentrism by cosmocentrism (144) to overcome the understanding of God as the one who orders and directs the universe, and focus instead on the enormous variety of life-forms. "The connection [between God and the world as the Breath] is one of *relationship* at the deepest possible level, the level of life, rather than *control* at the level of ordering and directing nature" (145). McFague understands the activity of the Spirit as "empowerment" in the light of evolutionary development with two different dimensions. The Spirit is not only "empowerment" but also the source of life renewal, "the direction or purpose for all the bodies of the world — a goal characterized by inclusive love" (149). Hence the Spirit as breath not only vivifies God's body with the power of life, it also represents the goal of life, and in that sense McFague's doctrine of the Spirit includes both a vitalist

---

252. Link 1982, 244; cf. 1991, 546.

253. Link 1982, 245.

254. McFague 1993, 70, 72. The parenthetical page numbers in the following text are to this work.

and a teleological dimension. McFague rejects the traditional trinitarian grammar for feminist reasons insofar as its references to the Father and Son necessarily foster a gender-specific understanding of God. As for the Spirit, she suggests quite without reason that one understand it not as the third person, but rather as the "mediation of the invisible and the visible" (193).

What the Interpreters of the Situation Have in Common

Although each of these authors addresses the problem of the Spirit, none develops a full understanding of the relationship between statements regarding the Holy Spirit and spirituality. Three focal points emerge in the discussion of Spirit and creation. The first involves the relation between Spirit and world. Does the Spirit dwell within the world in a fashion one can describe as "immanence," or does God remain completely different from creation even in his worldliness?

The second question asks how what Christians call the "cosmic Spirit" and what theoreticians of nature call "spirit" relate to God's Holy Spirit. *Is* the cosmic Spirit actually the Holy Spirit? Can language even meaningfully distinguish between the two?

The third question asks how the Spirit relates to the triune God. What is the connection between statements about God's being and those about God's activity in the Spirit?

These authors also make different use of theological tradition. Altner, Cobb, and McFague ascribe little value to traditional pneumatological grammar, preferring instead to develop their understanding of the Spirit commensurate with the conditions of ecological spirituality (McFague), ecological theories (Altner), or the understanding of life in process philosophy (Cobb). By contrast, Moltmann and Link are keen on maintaining linguistic continuity with tradition and hence try to mediate between biblical and classical pneumatology, on the one hand, and modern thinking and modes of expression, on the other.

Moltmann and Link differ in their interpretation of Calvin, with Moltmann emphasizing the immanence of the Spirit and Link the transcendence of God's worldliness. Altner and Cobb similarly emphasize this issue, with Altner rejecting any ascription of "special reality" to the Spirit and Cobb identifying the Spirit as life, albeit without making it clear whether the Spirit *is* or *brings about* life. McFague is similarly vague in insisting that as the breath of the world the Spirit is immanent, and yet as the goal and the direction of life is also transcendent.

These authors' understanding of the relation between the cosmic Spirit and the Holy Spirit is even more ambiguous. Altner makes it quite clear that one cannot distinguish between the two; his Spirit is the Spirit of self-organization and evolution. By contrast, although Moltmann's understanding of the Spirit as an organizational form says the same thing as Altner, it also insists that the Holy Spirit somehow transforms the creative Spirit. Cobb and Birch, by identifying Spirit and life, exclude the notion of any subject outside life. By contrast, Link maintains the "sharp" distinction between Creator and creation, anchoring his own understanding of the Spirit in a theology of incarnation and of the cross. Link is the only author who really recognizes the problem of the relationship between christological and pneumatological statements confronting ecological theology whenever the latter draws on the concept of the Spirit articulated by different interpretations of nature.

Differences also emerge regarding the relationship between the ontological and economic understanding of the Spirit. Altner, Cobb, and McFague all understand the Spirit more economically from the perspective of the modern understanding of how nature operates, interpreting the activity of the Spirit as that of nature. Moltmann anchors his understanding of the Spirit ontologically in the being of the triune God and tries to relate the essence of nature to God's essence. By contrast, Link begins with the traditional understanding of salvation history and looks for points of contact between a theological interpretation of natural history and elements of more recent theories of nature. Rather than precipitately identify the activity of nature with that of the Spirit, Link instead tries to interpret the former in the light of the latter.

Despite differences in methodology or use of tradition, all these authors accept the classical understanding (since the fourth century) of the relationship between the Spirit and life. The common question is how to understand the relationship between God as Spirit and the ecology and evolution of nature. What is the significance of the former for the latter, and vice versa?

Correlation

The Common Question: How Does the Spirit Bestow Life?

Whereas modern authors generally develop their understanding of the Spirit in dialogue with the natural sciences, Gregory's understanding emerged within the inner-theological dispute concerning the divinity of the Spirit. It is in the challenge of pluralism that we find the common ground between the situation of late modernity and that of late antiquity.

For Gregory the middle Platonic split between spirit and matter conflicted with the biblically grounded understanding of creation. Today the problem is determining how the notion of "spirit in nature" as understood by the new religiosity and by new science can be related to a Christian doctrine of the Spirit. With this problem in mind, contemporary theology might well learn from Gregory how to articulate the contribution of Christian spirituality to ecological spirituality more rigorously from the perspective of the Holy Spirit.

The association of Spirit and life provides a common point of departure for the various theologies. While Gregory articulates the activity of the Spirit as vivification from the ontic, incarnational, and soteriological perspective, modern authors tend to identify life as evolution, self-organization, and ecological interrelatedness, then associate life and the Spirit either ontologically (in the sense of identification; Altner, Cobb, McFague), pan-en-theistically (Moltmann), or soteriologically (Link).

Another common feature is the ontological and economic understanding of the Spirit. Modern authors increasingly tend to obscure the conceptual distinction that Gregory's apophatic position rigorously maintains between the nature and activity of the Spirit.

Gregory was particularly keen on developing his doctrine of the Spirit from the perspective of both incarnation and salvation history such that cosmic pneumatology constituted the presupposition of Christology, and incarnation the presupposition of soteriological-eschatological pneumatology. A similar undertaking is discernible in Link's initiative. Although unlike Moltmann he does not rigorously develop his trinitarian theology, he does acknowledge the problem that was of such significance for Gregory, namely, the relation between the christological and pneumatological understanding of the divine economy.

Bateson, the theoretician of nature, found that one important point of correlation between the ancient and modern understanding of nature was the question of the *place* from which the spiritual form of all life is actually shaped. This problem was common to both late antiquity and late modernity and can be formulated theologically as the question of *how* the Spirit bestows life and *which* Spirit bestows life.

Tradition and Situation Enter into Critical Dialogue

Gregory's Understanding of How the Spirit Works through and with Creation   By portraying the Spirit as the Spirit of the triune God, Gregory gains a missiological advantage by discerning in the spirit of the Greeks — which preceded Christ — the Spirit of Christ's Father. Gregory is able to constitute both his theology of incarnation and his Christology through his cosmological pneumatology insofar as because *both* the Son *and* the Spirit of the Father participate in co-shaping creation from the very outset, pneumatology and Christology mutually illuminate one another.

By understanding the Spirit's activity as inhabitation, enhancement of community, and vivification, Gregory overcomes the dualistic understanding of the Spirit regnant among the philosophers of his time and at the same time reconciles biblical statements regarding the activity of the Spirit with interpretations of Plato's cosmology. His pneumatology is of particular systematic significance in its understanding of the Spirit as the only subject capable of perfectly free movement.

The salient feature of Gregory's doctrine of the Spirit is its economic perspective. Even when he is unequivocally speaking about the nature of the Spirit as an equally venerated hypostasis within the Trinity, his pneumatology nonetheless maintains a rigorously economic orientation, something clearly evident in his understanding of inhabitation as a continuation of the incarnation and in his understanding of fulfillment and consummation.

Gregory's understanding of the Spirit's activity with respect to creation is twofold. First, the Spirit permeates matter ontically; second, the Spirit acts within creation through its indwelling in believers. Gregory's pneumatological, ontological understanding of nature stands counter to economic, cosmic pneumatology insofar as the Spirit that is active in believers is already present within creation. The various modes of the Spirit's activity correspond within the whole of creation. In that sense Gregory rejects any antithesis between God's transcendent worldliness and the Spirit's immanence in the world. Indeed, the activity of the Holy Spirit is characterized precisely by its ability to transition between its various modes of activity, that is, by its capacity for free movement. This interpretation of Gregory raises several questions for modern theologians.

Does Cobb Understand the Spirit as Life?   Although Cobb and Gregory concur in viewing the Spirit as God in the "fullest sense," Cappadocian theology does not really follow process theology's distinction between God's primordial and consequent natures, since early church theologians closely associated God's creation activity with redemptive activity. Indeed, because one of the fundamental tenets of classical theology is precisely the unity between the work of creation and of redemption, any categorization of two natures for God is antithetical to Cappadocian trinitarian theology. Does Cobb's reference to two "natures" refer to two different modes of God's activity?

A consideration of Gregory's position also raises the question whether Cobb ultimately renders the concept of God superfluous by embracing immanentism. Whereas Gregory maintains that the Spirit does indeed contain the world but is not contained within the world, Cobb and Birch maintain that the world is contained in God.[255] Their total identification of God with "life" begs the question of what the concept of God can now really say about life. Gregory's understanding of the ontic being of the Spirit in and with life makes it possible to relate in a more sophisticated theological fashion statements from theology with statements from the philosophy of nature, something Cobb seems to render impossible. Indeed, is an ecological pneumatology even possible in Cobb's view? Or does his position now sooner represent religio-philosophical vitalism?

Does Altner Prefer the Concept of the Spirit Deriving from the Philosophy of Nature or from Theology? One wonders whether Altner's renunciation of the "conceptual tools of Greek metaphysics" does not exact too high a price. How does he deal with the long tradition of biblical talk about the Spirit and with its linguistic potential for an ecological Christian interpretation of life? Does his proposal that we "take the leap" away from outdated metaphysics not distort the actual state of affairs? One cannot avoid the metaphysical problem simply by abandoning the solution offered by Greek antiquity; it merely resurfaces in a different form. Altner's concept of the Spirit, drawing on insights from the philosophy of nature, is based on recent theories of evolution that certainly also contain certain metaphysical elements. How exactly, to take one example, is one to conceive of the "self" in the self-organization of nature? Pan-psychically? From the perspective of a philosophy of identity? Ecologically?

Altner seems to free himself a bit hastily from the burden of theological concepts of the Spirit from other philosophical contexts. I would propose quite to the contrary that what we need is to examine concepts of the Spirit from various contexts precisely that we may see — through hermeneutical mediation — what the solutions from those other contexts might say about our situation today. Gregory's understanding of the Spirit seems to offer the

255. Cf. section 1 of this chapter, above.

presuppositions for such learning. I would point out that incorporating elements of his conceptual model by no means requires that we also import the contextual metaphysical presuppositions of his age. Quite to the contrary, precisely Gregory's apophatic relativization of the various metaphysical models of his age gives us a tool with which to critique our situation.

Gregory's position suggests that Altner may not have fully recognized that a theological concept of the Spirit standing in continuity with theological history can indeed provide a tool for criticizing the kind of religious overinterpretation characterizing at least some theoreticians of nature as well as some nature spiritualists.

How Does Moltmann Mediate between the Concept and the Experience of the Spirit? Although Moltmann and Gregory concur in maintaining that the *entire* triune God is at work in the activity of the Spirit, Moltmann seems to construe his understanding of the Spirit too one-sidedly from his theological consideration of the divine essence. For Gregory, who frequently emphasizes the experience of the Spirit — which plays him "like a harp" — one experiences the Spirit's activity "from below," from the perspective of the material world. By contrast, Moltmann seems to rely too heavily on an abstract understanding of the nature of the Spirit, from which he then derives his theology of the social experience of God.

Moltmann and Gregory concur in their understanding of the Spirit from the perspective of the Trinity, anthropology, and cosmology. They differ insofar as Gregory rejects any identification of the being of the Spirit with the being of nature, while Moltmann is frequently inclined to entertain precisely this sort of ontological identification, albeit — unlike Cobb — not without qualification. Gregory strictly distinguishes between statements about activity and those about essence, while Moltmann mixes the two and as a result is inclined — something not entirely unfamiliar within the Protestant tradition — to engage in untranslatable kerygmatic theology.

Link: Pneumatological Modalism? In Link's writings the personality of the Spirit seems to recede into the background. Although Link concurs with Gregory in basing his understanding of the Spirit's activity on a theology of incarnation, some question remains on whether his Christology is really constituted *through* his pneumatology. And although he does mention the third article as the basis for the possibility of God's incarnation, he seems to be referring to more than merely the philosophical possibility of thinking and speaking about the incarnation.

Whereas statements about the Spirit's activity *prior* to the incarnation play no role in Link's initiative, they are of enormous significance for Gregory's understanding of salvation history. Because the Holy Spirit is to be understood as the Spirit of the triune God, Gregory does not have to maintain — as does Link — that the Spirit takes up habitation in believers "merely" as the Spirit of the Son. Link's references to the Spirit's work of unifying God and Son sound more Augustinian than Cappadocian, since Gregory viewed the Father precisely as the guarantor of the unity of the Son and Spirit. Link's reference to the unity of God and Son through the Spirit also seems to preserve a remnant of the *Filioque* conflict — a conflict one should in any case probably go ahead and put to rest.

Link also recalls Gregory when in his attempt to preserve what I consider the necessary pneumatological tension between ontology and economy, he maintains that the Spirit is not the *form* within time but rather its *possibility*. What I nonetheless still do not comprehend is how Link understands the Trinity as "the temporal condition" of its own manifestation. In his own turn, Gregory counters the Eunomian thesis by maintaining the supratemporal nature of God, who nonetheless does reveal himself under temporal conditions. Why must the condition of the possibility of appearance within time be temporal? Here I would advise maintaining Picht's distinction between *phenomenality* and *phenomenon*.

A third objection involves Link's suspected modalism. Whereas Gregory constructed his entire pneumatology on the thesis of the full *homoousios* of the Spirit, I believe that Link's reference to the way the Spirit unifies God and world as well as God and Son along with his reference to the Spirit as a "mode" of the divine self-expression excessively weaken the thesis of the full divinity of the Spirit and of its sovereign, free redemptive activity. Here I fear Link succumbs to the burden of his Barthian background.

These differences notwithstanding, more seems to connect than separate Link and Gregory. Both are intent on establishing a close association between the incarnation of the Son and the activity of the Spirit. Like Gregory, Link adheres to the apophatic principle of not translating statements about the nature of the Spirit into cosmological assertions and also emphasizes the eschatological dimension of the Spirit's redemptive activity as well as — in a fashion clearly related to that of Gregory — the critical power of the Spirit inhering within the "pathic character" of existence. Finally, both theologians maintain that the Holy Spirit also influences reason — in Link's case even *empirical* reason.

McFague's World Spirit and God's Holy Spirit   McFague and Gregory do not share much common ground. In fact, for all practical purposes McFague represents a pneumatological position similar to the one Gregory addresses and overcomes in his writings. McFague's spirituality is a "celebration of cosmic evolution." Whereas Gregory theologically qualified the cosmo-aesthetic religiosity of his age from a Christian perspective, McFague tries to lend religious legitimacy to the new understanding of nature. Unlike Gregory, however, she does not employ the traditional biblical, pneumatological frame of reference. Although both draw on the Stoic metaphor of the world as a body, McFague understands the Holy Spirit as the world breath while Gregory demonstrates to his contemporaries that the Spirit permeating the world (inspiration) is the same one that awakens the Son of the Father.

McFague develops her theology commensurate with the conditions attaching to the organic understanding of the world. By contrast, Gregory transforms the philosophy of nature of his age commensurate with the conditions of a biblically oriented understanding of creation and Creator. Whereas McFague understands the developmental activity of the Spirit teleologically, Gregory emphasizes the soteriological dimension of the Spirit's dealings with nature. McFague's criticism of the divine capacity for ordering and directing does reveal an important point at which the contemporary ecological understanding of nature presents a challenge to classical theology, namely, how this understanding of the Spirit's capacity for ordering (Barth, Moltmann) relates to recent insights regarding the processes of nature. Does the Spirit only bring about order? Could one not also understand its work as one of creative *disorder,* that is, as the creation of previously unimagined or unsuspected possibilities for life development? Could one not also — as does the Basque sculptor Eduardo Chillida[256] — understand the Spirit as *space,* that is, as the bestower of space?

How in Gregory's View Do the Spirit and Son Work Together, and How Do Creatures Actually Experience the Spirit of Their Lives?   Notwithstanding Gregory's enormous accomplishment in disclosing to the ancient church the considerable treasures of a pneumatologically shaped theology, we must address two critical questions to him. By beginning with knowledge of the Spirit's divinity to demonstrate precisely that divinity to its doubters and opponents, Gregory inevitably engages in circular argumentation, a procedure Wendebourg understands as a confirmation and authentication of the Spirit's divinity.[257]

By demonstrating that the interpretation of experiences with the Spirit does not contradict the thesis of its divinity, Gregory establishes a credible ar-

256. Cf. Bergmann 1997b, 231.
257. Wendebourg 1980, 234.

gument in connection with his biblical evidence, albeit an argument possible *only* within the confines of the doctrine of the Trinity and Gregory's own context since it presupposes historical knowledge of the incarnation of the Son. Gregory articulates this notion by saying that Jesus "gradually" reveals the Spirit (*Or.* 31.26). That is, knowledge of the divinity of the Son precedes knowledge of the divinity of the Spirit.[258] The goal of Gregory's pneumatology is to articulate the perpetual, ongoing economy of the "whole" God.

What Gregory does not articulate is how the two hypostases work together *after* the ascension of the Son. Is the Son economically passive during the time of the Spirit? Probably not, since Gregory understands the Father, Son, and Spirit as working *together* since the very beginning of creation. Nonetheless, Gregory says nothing about the trinitarian aspect of the economy of the Spirit. The connection between the divinity of the Son and that of the Spirit probably seemed self-evident to Gregory's contemporaries. Today, however, it seems necessary to articulate our understanding of how the hypostases work together economically. How can pneumatological grammar help us articulate how the trinitarian hypostases work together? How are the Son and Father active through and with the Spirit in nature?

A second question to Gregory involves the modern problem of the relation between the cosmic spirit and the Holy Spirit. Although Gregory seems to be acquainted with this problem, he does not really offer any solution. Later the doctrine of the presence of God's logoi in things provided an explanatory model. Does the Spirit permeating all things nonetheless remain alien to those things? What does the notion of the "being of the Spirit in and with things" mean with respect to the matter of creation? Gregory can help us understand and articulate the correspondence between the cosmic, anthropological, and trinitarian activities of the Spirit. The question is how to lend credibility to his model of the correspondence between these realms. How are we to understand the relation between how things are somehow ontologically sustained internally, on the one hand, and yet liberated from evil by the Spirit externally, on the other? How can Gregory's thought help us articulate how the Spirit simultaneously exhibits a clear contour as experienced through its activity while completely lacking such contour as the Spirit of transition between the interior and exterior?

258. Wendebourg overlooks this point. I would object to her reference to God's "external" trinitarian "reference" in the spirit. Does interpreting God's economy as a trinitarian "line" not risk ignoring God's activity in the incarnate Son? This notion of an "external reference" also presupposes that God is outside the world. Does textual evidence support such a view? Must one not assume instead that the Cappadocians' God is both outside and inside the world rather than subject to the discontinuity between world and God?

Although faith in the Spirit's activity presented no problem to Gregory's contemporaries, the question of the *nature* of that Spirit certainly did. That some theoreticians of nature in late modernity make increasing use of a concept of the spirit certainly does not mean they are in fact using a theological concept. Gregory was unfamiliar with the problem of a secular understanding of the spirit, since he simply presupposed that the spirit of the Greeks could without further ado be identified with the Holy Spirit. In today's discourse, however, such an identification involves a considerably more complicated experiment, one that can draw on the patristic model only in a retrospective fashion.

CHAPTER 5

Considerations from the Perspective
of Liberation Theology

In the previous chapter I juxtaposed several interpretations of the liberation of creation whose differences derive from their different background theories. Gregory himself picks up on the contemporary middle Platonic philosophy of nature and on the Origenian tradition of biblical exegesis. Cobb develops his interpretation within the framework of process theology, while Altner draws from recent scientific theories, from Schweitzer's philosophical ethics of life, and from the idea of evolution. Ruether provides ideological criticism of the history of creation theology, while McFague understands theology wholly as part of an organismic worldview. Moltmann and Link remain more independent of background theories while drawing more from theological history itself, with Moltmann viewing system theory and evolution theory positively in 1985, then more critically in 1989, and Link understanding the relation between nature and history from the perspective of Picht's philosophy of time. Only Cobb and Altner really draw on theories from the ecological sciences and human ecology.

In this chapter I intend to establish an ecological theology from the perspective of liberation theology.[1] Does the concept of a "theology of liberation" involve only human beings? Or can liberation theology, which in fact developed in the context of the Third World, also contribute to the First World's theological assessment of the ecological challenge?[2] Rather than providing a complete ecological theology of liberation, I intend to contribute an outline commensu-

---

1. Concerning the history and significance of "liberation theology," see Gutiérrez 1976, 37-42; Frostin 1988, 1-13; Bosch 1991, 438-47.

2. Concerning this question, see Hedström 1986, who answers affirmatively and has already dealt with the problem at the DEI Institute in Costa Rica from the perspective of pastoral and creation theology.

rate with the conditions of the contextual theological paradigm. A discussion of the various conditions needed for such a theology to occur can then provide a measure of guidance for further development. Enlightened by contextual epistemological theory, rather than examining experiences with the Spirit that sets nature free, this chapter instead assesses the *conditions* necessarily accompanying the forms through which such experiences come to expression.

In part 1, I examine the four characteristic features of the paradigm of liberation theology[3] and then qualify each of these ecologically. An ecological expansion of the criteria of liberation theology's interpretation of life enables theological discourse to include nonhuman life-forms. The goal of this section is to mediate ecological theology and liberation theology.

In part 2, I develop an ecological theology commensurate with the methodological conditions of contextual theology and qualified from the perspective of liberation theology, beginning with the four points of correlation in the preceding chapter and examining how the trinitarian understanding of God, the concept of movement, the conceptual form of a theology of the cross, and pneumatology might be enlisted in the service of an ecological theology of liberation.

1. An Ecological Expansion of the Criteria of the Paradigm of Liberation Theology

The Subjects of Nature as Dialogue Partners

The first characterizing feature of the paradigm of liberation theology is its conscious choice of dialogue partners. Beginning with the whole of the human

---

3. Frostin 1988, 6-11, describes these characteristic features. I use the expressions "contextual theology" and "liberation theology" in a twofold manner in the discussion that follows. First, they refer synonymously to the same characteristic features of the new paradigm of theology, viz., (a) the reflexivity of theological subjects and the unified nature of their contexts, (b) the significance of the perception and knowledge of reality from its historic and natural underside, (c) the multilayered conflicts and differences within the global community, (d) the dialectic within time, and (e) the interdisciplinary nature of theology. Second, "liberation theology" refers to the modern phenomenon associated with theological, ecclesiastical, and social history and involving the "re-evangelization" (L. Boff) of Latin America. The expression "contextual theology" occasionally serves simply as a collective designation for the various modes of expression of situational theology, such as feminist theology, black theology, or Minjung theology. Concerning the discussion of contextual theology, see Schreiter 1985, chap. 1; Bevans 1992; and Bergmann 2003a, chap. 1.

social community, the unity of history, the world, and humankind, liberation theology calls into question the alleged autonomy of any one sector of the theological disciplines. This consideration raises the question of the *subjects* of theological dialogue. Which dialogue partners are associated with which presuppositions for our knowledge of God and its various modes of expression? How does one assign the privileges of theological epistemological construction?

Drawing from the sociology of knowledge, liberation theology accepts that sociopolitical factors shape the epistemological constructions of groups, classes, and genders, and that one must critically assess and assign the privileges of such constructions from the perspective of this insight. Prompted by the previously one-sided assignment of such constructions of knowledge, liberation theologians brought about an "epistemological revolution" by ascribing epistemological precedence to the poor and the victims.[4]

This basic principle of liberation theology, however, always involves human beings, its presupposition being the presumed unity of humankind, its social community, and its common history. Under the power of sin, people become either agents of injustice and violence or its victims. Both agents and victims, however, are threatened by the power of evil and are in need of liberation.[5] Liberation theology's analysis of this "devilry" combines different sociological and theological methodologies. Unlike conventional theology, which in interdisciplinary cases always grants precedence to philosophy, liberation theology enters into community with the social and recently also cultural sciences. To expand liberation theology ecologically, we must establish a new interdisciplinary community between theology and ecology.

Can one successfully expand the initial principle of including repressed theological subjects to include an analysis both of human society and of the environment? My hypothetical response of yes assumes that the living world of nature in fact represents a web of relationships common to *both* human and nonhuman life. That is, I would expand liberation theology's understanding of the presumed unity of human history into an *ecological* understanding of the presumed unity of the entire planet as a biosphere shared by both human and nonhuman life-forms.

This expansion places liberation theology's choice of dialogue partners and epistemological subjects into a new light. Can one speak meaningfully about *nonhuman* subjects of knowledge of God? Is it meaningful to speak about "subjects of nature" (Bloch) and "natures" (Novalis)?[6] Does a "libera-

---

4. See Frostin 1992a, 42-45; 1987, 31-33; and Sobrino 1988, 110-14.
5. Goss-Mayr 1981, 64.
6. Novalis coins the term (Germ. *Naturen,* lit. "natures") in "Die Lehrlinge zu Sais,"

tion of creatures" aim at liberation from the deadly dynamics of evolution or from cultural violence?

Ecological thinking, which is currently replacing thinking associated with the philosophy of identity, understands human thought as a process of nature.[7] Why have nonhuman dialogue partners in nature almost entirely receded from recent theological discussion even though plants and animals, the earth and landscapes have played quite varied roles in both biblical and theological history? Have theology and the church marginalized nonhuman organisms much the same way modern culture has marginalized nature? Does this marginalization exhibit the same features as the marginalization of the poor and of women?

Affirming the subjective nature and resulting integrity of creatures and then including these natural subjects in theological discourse raises the question of communication. Can one speak meaningfully about communication between human beings and other biological organisms? How, for example, can animal perceptions be translated into human language? Can we develop a credible theory of communication that includes both nonhuman creatures and human beings? Once we include such organisms in human discourse, how are we to address the problem, for example, of their "legal representation" by human beings?[8]

Advocates of an anthropocentric understanding of nature reject the notion of such subjects in nature, objecting that the gap between human beings and other living beings is too great and that human beings are not capable of really comprehending the truly different nature of nonhuman life-forms. Because human beings are always closest to themselves in this sense, the task is rather to develop a morally upright, humane anthropocentrism ensuring that we impose only a minimum of damage on our environment. Advocates of the biocentric position counter with the thesis of the intrinsic value of nature that human beings should acknowledge and on which they should base their actions.[9]

---

95. In the present study the term "creatures" refers to the various physical life-forms on this planet, including human-corporeal life-forms. By contrast, the term "nature" refers to the totality of being and the forms through which it comes into being and passes away.

7. Picht 1989, 15. In other cultures the notion of the subjective nature of living beings is a constituent part of the understanding of nature. Cf. Sundermeier 1987, 33f.

8. The problem of legal representation of creatures by human beings emerges in connection with the increasing environmental conflicts and is addressed in the discussion of the rights of nature.

9. Cobb 1992, 82-118, arguing that the Christian faith cannot be reconciled with anthropocentrism, discusses thoroughly the forces advocating this faith.

Even if the debate regarding this or that "-centrism" has not yet been decided one way or the other — whether, that is, the "center" of life is to be found *in* or *outside of* human beings — it is obvious enough that since the 1970s the increasing recognition of the ecological damage modern culture has inflicted on nature has increasingly shifted the focus away from human beings and onto their environment, a shift programmatically expressed in ecumenical references to the "integrity of creation." The focal point of the discussion of nature has doubtless shifted from the question regarding human nature to the question regarding what nature can teach us concerning human actions.

The United Nations Conference on Environment and Development in Rio de Janeiro in 1992 provided geopolitical acceptance of this new perspective acknowledging the independence and intrinsic value of all biological life-forms and their ecology. Moreover, new research initiatives have also developed theories concerning the ultimate totality of a differentiated planetary system. In light of these developments, it certainly seems in order that theological discussion of the history of liberation now also include those living beings that share the human environment.

Our discussion of this inclusion can draw on the gospel interpretation of Paul, who maintains that creation hopes along with human beings for liberation (Rom. 8:21). I believe this thesis of the "redemptive need of nature" and of its creatures provides a point of departure for an ecological-theological discussion of the history of liberation.

The Creatures' Perception of the Creator

Liberation theology begins with the assumption that because of their social situation, the poor are especially capable of distinguishing between God and idols. Their theological reflection focuses not on whether God does or does not exist, but rather on how to perceive the liberating Creator in a context of idol worship. Such knowledge or perception does not involve God as some being "existing in and for itself" as discussed in Western intellectual theology, but rather as the one "who is there for others."[10] Theologians ascribe

---

10. Bonhoeffer 1997, 381 (from "Outline for a Book"): "His [Jesus'] 'being there for others' is the experience of transcendence.... Our relation to God is not a 'religious' relationship to the highest, most powerful, and best Being imaginable — that is not authentic transcendence — but our relation to God is a new life in 'existence for others,' through participation in the being of Jesus."

aesthetic-epistemological precedence to the poor because they do indeed experience God's liberating "being there for us," a notion indispensable for our knowledge of God.

In any event, can one ascribe to *nonhuman* living beings and life-forms — in analogy to the poor and women — the same special capacity for perceiving God and even aesthetic and epistemological precedence in this regard? One should not misunderstand the term "precedence" in any ontological fashion here. The perception and knowledge of the poor, of women, and of nonhuman creatures is not a priori "more true" than that of others. Here "precedence" refers instead to precedence within a communicative process, within theoretical and practical discourse in the sense that the poor, women, and nonhuman creatures take precedence in the social perception of a situation and in the choice of the various forms of expression for experiences in that situation, in theoretical discourse, and in practical discourse regarding the development of concepts for action and behavior. In this sense "precedence" is to be understood communicatively. The rich should heed the poor, men should heed women, natives should heed foreigners, human beings should heed other creatures, should learn to see these "others" and let them go first, as it were, in aesthetic, theoretical, and ethical encounters, that we all might learn together how to deal with the path into our common future.

Reference to the "aesthetic-epistemological" priority of nonhuman creatures becomes meaningful if one learns to make certain "epistemological" distinctions in the ecological and social realms. The epistemic capabilities of a worm obviously differ from those of a mathematician. Indeed, the epistemic capabilities of living beings in general are hierarchically organized. Animals with nervous systems possess more complex capabilities than those without them. Plants react to a wider variety of environmental stimuli than do microorganisms.

The adjective "epistemic" in Greek refers to the capacity to understand something. Living beings perceive various phenomena and processes in their surroundings, react to these perceptions, and communicate with their surroundings through various signs. All living beings can come to understand something external to themselves. Theological reference to the aesthetic-epistemological capacity of creatures implies that living beings are capable of perceiving and understanding their existence as that of creatures — as that of created beings. Although this assertion seems utterly meaningless under the conditions of contemporary Western rationality, it is well documented in the theological understanding of nature throughout the history of Christianity.

In the Hebrew Bible psalmists articulate the doxology of nature (Ps. 19:1-7). Mark recounts how the "whole land" reacted physically to Jesus' death on the cross (Mark 15:33). In the writings of Gregory of Nazianzus, "mute beings" also praise their Creator (*Carm.* 1.1.29). Francis sings the praises of the Creator *together with* other creatures. Nature also maintains its theological value in the modern transition from natural theology to the theology of revelation.[11]

Modern ecological sciences employ biological organisms and ecological processes in their function as indicators, meaning that living beings in one place tend to betray the presence of changes to their environment elsewhere. Here, too, one can certainly speak meaningfully about creatures possessing a certain epistemological capacity, albeit one whose manifestations human beings still must interpret. In developing a criterion for defining ecologically "impoverished" living beings in nature — analogous to the sociological criterion for defining the poor within society — one promising path is to do so from the perspective of "cultural-ecological violence."[12] Here the expression "cultural ecology" refers to the influence human culture exerts on the ecology of nature. In this sense the term refers to human and societal interaction with natural resources, a field constituting the subject matter of human ecology. "Cultural-ecological violence" then refers to any cultural interaction with nature that seriously restricts the realization of the latter's ecological possibilities.[13]

In a certain sense, of course, *every* culture must exercise some measure of power over the ecology of its surroundings simply to develop and survive itself, and for this reason our criterion of "cultural-ecological power" must be able to distinguish the boundaries between cultural actions that restrict ecological processes in a commensurate or appropriate fashion (sustainable use for both culture and nature) and those that rob such processes of their very chance of survival (cultural-ecological violence), and must define these boundaries in a reasonable, plausible, and socially operational fashion.

Such criteria can make it possible to speak meaningfully from the perspective of liberation theology about the precedence of the "poor among creatures." One important presupposition of such discussion is the planetary

---

11. Cf. Dembowski 1989, 38, 45.

12. "Violence" in this sense refers to the results of any action by one being that thwarts, hinders, or restricts the development of possibilities of another. Cf. the definition of Galtung (1975, 57), who defines violence as any influencing of the actualization of human possibilities: "[V]iolence is present when human beings are being influenced so that their actual somatic and mental realizations are below their potential realizations."

13. I am using the term "ecology" here — commensurate with common usage — not only in the sense of the first chapter, that is, as a reference to the consideration and discussion of the *oikoi,* their patterns of interrelatedness between organism and environment, but also as a synonym for that very interrelatedness itself.

and ecological unity of creation, expressed theologically: of a creation community that is at once both a community of suffering and one of hope. From the perspective of the natural sciences, this presumed unity of the world can be described in the metaphor of the "organism" as exemplified by the Gaia hypothesis.

Do living beings and life-forms that have fallen victim to the power of evil brought about by cultural-ecological violence deserve precedence in determining the path of liberation? Are the poor among the creatures also those most capable of expressing and communicating to human beings creation's hope for liberation (Rom. 8:21)? Should for this reason we accord to the poor among the creatures precedence in articulating the doxology of the liberating Creator shared by all creatures? Can human beings learn to encounter, acknowledge, understand, and interpret the victims of cultural-ecological violence as well as learn to understand what those victims themselves have come to understand, and can human beings learn how to travel that path with them? What do the poor among creatures teach us about God's liberation?

The Conflict of the Divided Human World as a Conflict Involving the Entirety of Nature

A third salient feature of the paradigm of liberation theology is the understanding of social reality as a reality defined by conflict. The human world is a divided world of conflicting polarities. The foundation of any discussion of this condition is the antithesis between historical reflection "from below" and "from above." Because all participants are influenced by their position within the polarities of a divided world, theological dialogue can take place *only* within the parameters of this condition of social conflict encompassing the world — never outside it. The conferences of the Ecumenical Association of Third World Theologians (EATWOT) describe the polarities of the divided world in terms of the following six dimensions of the conflict of oppression:

1. economic (poor — rich)
2. class membership (capitalist — proletariat)
3. geographical (north — south)
4. sexist (male — female)
5. ethnic (e.g., white — black)
6. cultural (dominating/dominated culture)[14]

14. Frostin 1988, 8.

When liberation theology describes the divided world, it focuses on human societies. Can one expand this perspective to include the entire living world of nature as well?

Such an expansion can add a seventh dimension of conflict to the previous six, namely, an "ecological" (human — nonhuman) dimension, while simultaneously expanding the observation of history "from above — from below" to include an ecological perspective. Ecological liberation theology, in understanding the entire world of life from the perspective of the previously enumerated six dimensions of conflict, also understands the conflict characterizing the divided world as involving the entire ecological world of life on our planet. The collision between human beings and nature can be understood (following Forrester's "world model") from the perspective of economic-scientific, ecosystemic, climatological, and geopolitical models, all of which disclose anew that the conflicts characterizing our technologically and economically highly differentiated global society are intertwined in a completely new way with the changes affecting the ecology of the planet — albeit in a way we admittedly do not yet fully understand.[15]

Any analysis of the ecological conflict between society and nature must assume that an imbalance already obtains between human and nonhuman life in view of the advanced human technological capabilities and developments that took place during the twentieth century.

Such conditions suggest from the very outset that we expand *ecologically* the perspective of our analysis of the social conflicts characterizing our divided human world to include a comprehensive conflict analysis of the entire world of life and its attendant interrelationships. An ecological theology of liberation should begin with a multidimensional analysis of the conflict between human beings and nature, adopting the analysis of the ecologically divided planet as developed by environmental sciences in the stricter sense and then understanding this conflict soteriologically as one of "nature in need of redemption."

Following the lead of liberation theology in ascribing precedence to the poor, our ecological conflict analysis should similarly ensure that the victims in both society and ecological communities become visible.[16] One can then

---

15. Wiman 1991, 237-40, distinguishes two ways of understanding the complexity and changes to ecosystems in relation to the interaction between nature, on the one hand, and society and its environmental policies, on the other: (a) complexity as safeguard and (b) complexity as a generator of surprises. Environmental politics has hitherto paid scant attention to the second of these alternatives, according to which nature follows dynamics that can shift unpredictably from one set of conditions to a completely new one.

16. Concerning the ecological application of conflict research, see Liedke 1989. Paral-

understand "liberation" as a redemption from the same violence and injustice that make victims of members of both human society (the poor) and nature as a whole (the poor of nature).

The Dialectics and Evolution of Society and Nature within Time

Liberation theology's paradigm characteristically also draws on analyses from the social sciences and adopts the dialectical understanding of the relationship between theory and praxis.

Following the analogy of liberation theology, ecological theology draws heavily from nontheological disciplines, integrating into its analyses the findings of the social sciences and environmental sciences.

Liberation theology views itself as the second part of a process in which praxis precedes theoretical reflection. Because the *subjects* of theological reflection add their own theoretical activity to the praxis of liberation, theological reflection maintains constant contact with the practical experience of liberation, understanding this relation as a dialectical one whose two poles are scientific theory and the "culture of silence" (Freire), the latter representing the experiences of the poor who have lost their voice. This dialectical relationship between praxis and theology represents an open process of history in which, in an indissoluble interrelationship, theology *and* praxis constitute the movement of liberation.

Just as liberation theology was the first to accept as a constructive challenge Hegel's and Marx's understanding of social history as a dialectical process, so also does ecological theology constructively accept Darwin's similarly pioneering understanding of the history of nature as evolution. At the same time, of course, one must constantly keep in mind the differences between the premises of biological evolution and those of the social dialectic.

To what extent does the dialectical understanding of human history relate to the ecologically evolutionary understanding of the history of nature? We need to avoid two pitfalls in this context. We should avoid (1) understanding the history of nature excessively from the perspective of social his-

---

lels obtain between victims within humankind and those within nature. While ecofeminism emphasizes the analogy of injustice in the relationship between human beings and nature and in that between the sexes, Spencer's ecological gay theology begins with the experience of "dislocation," which marginalizes homosexuals as something "outside the bounds of natural," and then discusses the parallels between ecological and erotic locations, dislocations, and connections (Spencer 1996, 4).

tory,[17] and (2) understanding society excessively from the constructions of the history of nature.[18]

I propose establishing presuppositions for understanding a *common* social and ecological history of society and nature by first understanding this history as a *movement within common time toward an open future* whose form is subject to various dialectical and evolutionary structures. Although the forms of this movement can be quite different in society and in ecosystems, one can certainly also identify common forms of movement, for example, in a cultural ecosystem in which demographic and ecological patterns appear similar. Such a definition of a common basis of the history of humankind and nature philosophically presupposes the unity of time. It is only against the background of the unity of time that one can discern the phenomena of things coming into being and then passing away within time.[19]

In expanding the fourth salient feature of liberation theology, ecological theology departs from the premise that the dialectic between human thought and praxis differs substantially from the evolutionary processes of all other living beings. Although human thought does indeed constitute the salient feature of human nature, it does not separate or differentiate human beings from nature. An ecological theology of liberation thus presupposes that human thought is not only tied to praxis, but at once also represents a natural process uniquely tying human beings to the history of their environment within time.[20]

17. By forcing the understanding of society as a differentiated system onto his understanding of nature, Luhmann 1990, 74, reduces the environment to a "resonance" object of the social system. Welker's pneumatology (1994, 28-40) uncritically follows Luhmann. Nennen 1991, 255-74, justifiably criticizes Luhmann's application of theory to the ecological sphere for its strategy of legitimation attaching to trust in the system, for the solipsism of its systems, and for the irrationality of the project of rendering ecological responsibility morally neutral. It seems to me that the subtitle of Luhmann's book already betrays the limitations of his perspective: "Can modern society focus on ecological threats?" Apparently this social theoretician is concerned not with the mortal threats to the environment and its organisms and human beings, but rather with society's focus and organization — that is, with preserving the regnant constellation of power.

18. Historically advocates of social Darwinism have operated from within this abyss, and today advocates of the so-called evolutionary epistemological theory (e.g., Wuketis) do the same in trying to explain human reason from a reductionist perspective based on their observations of the evolutionary processes of other species.

19. Concerning the philosophical grounding of the unity of time, see Picht 1989, 449-58; 1990b, 432ff. In the natural sciences Prigogine and Stengers 1985, 300-303, advocate developing a new understanding of time.

20. Picht 1979 has developed an outline for this sort of human ecology. Cf. Scharper 1997, 179f., who charges Latin American liberation theology with being too "harmful and an-

2. The Ecological Theology of Liberation

How can the previous chapter's correlation contribute to the development of an ecological theology whose presuppositions include the epistemological capacity of the poor among creatures, the unity of movement within time as it involves both nature and society, and the fundamental need of nature for redemption?

My constructive intention in this second section adheres to the theoretical and methodological presuppositions of contextual theology. As mentioned earlier, rather than examining the experiences and modes of expression that can be acquired concretely only in the "community of saints," I will instead establish the new presuppositions for these experiences and their expression. The present section draws on our findings in the preceding chapters in experimenting creatively with various theoretical and methodological tools. The extent to which the results of this experiment genuinely can be applied in a concrete fashion to the interpretation of various contexts of life and faith, however, can only be determined outside this book.

This hermeneutical-constructive experiment follows the same procedure followed by any scientific experiment that reconstructs a natural life situation under certain conditions and then reports and tests the results of that construction. After reconstructing the correlation between responses from late antiquity and late modernity under identical conditions — that is, from the perspective of the specific problem points of correlation — I then construct an ecological/liberation-theological response. After this contextual enlightenment, however, it is not I who can then test the results of this experiment within the "laboratory" of this book; only the readers can undertake this task, and *only* at those places where theology genuinely, concretely confronts the ecological challenge. As for the praxis of concrete theological response to the ecological challenge, the "laboratory" can also serve as a "workshop" in which we renew old tools to meet new needs as well as create completely new tools. In the following discussion I focus on the four points of correlation from chapter 4 in inquiring how an ecological theology of liberation can make use of the trinitarian understanding of God and its attendant notion of communality, a new theological understanding of movement, the conceptual form of a theology of the cross, and pneumatology.

---

thropocentric in utopian schemes," albeit without examining further the problem of the relation between the social and biological understanding of time.

Trinity and Ecology

One can legitimately question whether the trinitarian understanding of God genuinely can be applied to an ecological theology of liberation. Is trinitarian theology so bound to the philosophical and metaphysical presuppositions of its original context that its incorporation creates more problems than it solves? Where, exactly — that is, in which discourse — does the idiom of trinitarian thought and reference acquire meaning? Within inner-theological discourse as an expression of what is specifically Christian? In ecological discourse as an expression of the interrelatedness of nature within the larger understanding of God? Can the trinitarian conceptual form contribute to an interpretation of an ecology of nature? Similarly, can the ecological conceptual form contribute to an interpretation of the symbol of God's triunity? What does trinitarian grammar contribute to our understanding of the liberation of nature?

The Convergence of Communality
in the Understanding of God and Nature

Among contemporary ecological theologians, Moltmann especially has drawn from the tradition of trinitarian theology. Although Cobb, Link, and McFague also draw from this tradition, their theologies of nature ultimately focus on other aspects of the understanding of God. Altner entirely rejects the trinitarian expression of faith and asks whether one ought not simply abandon the metaphysical presuppositions amid which the doctrine of the Trinity arose in the first place.

His reservations are certainly justified insofar as the doctrine of the Trinity was indeed brought to its conclusion in critical dialogue with the philosophy of late antiquity. One might even maintain that the historical doctrine of the Trinity actually represents a religio-philosophical expression of the experience and understanding of the incarnation from late antiquity. Altner is quite correct insofar as no doctrine — including the Trinity — can preserve continuity amid the changing contexts of theological history without engaging in critical hermeneutics. Indeed, etymologically the very concept of "tradition" suggests as much in its meaning as both continuation and betrayal.

Be that as it may, these considerations certainly do not demonstrate the irrelevance of the Trinity today. One can interpret this symbol of God's triunity anew without adopting the presuppositions of the classical concept. But one must bear in mind that a modern interpretation of the Trinity need not necessarily concur formally with Gregory's interpretation; otherwise one fails to acknowledge the historicalness of language. What is to be interpreted anew is not *how* Gregory said what he did, but rather *what* he actually brought to expression. Those who would articulate the content of God's earthly, ongoing incarnation and inhabitation within the trinitarian conceptual and linguistic forms, however, must first clarify how this particular theology relates to the philosophical ontology of the contemporary context. Nor is it sufficient merely to refer to the literary structure of creeds or to the significance of this tradition within the history of theology. In this sense, then, Altner's objection discloses the necessity of reinterpreting the concept of triunity and of understanding the convergence between this notion and contemporary social constructions of nature. It is precisely in the auxiliary philosophical constructions of the ecological understanding of nature, however, that the very possibility of this convergence emerges.

Theologically the concept of the Trinity provides the structure for statements concerning the incarnation of the Son and the mission and inhabitation of the Spirit. It also understands the being of God from the perspective of the communality of the hypostases, and the being of nature from the perspective of the communality of life-forms. The theological concept of a "communal being" (of God)[21] converges with the philosophical concept of a "relational being" (of nature) of the sort underlying the ecological view of nature.

The natural science of ecology presupposes the existence of relations between organisms and the environment as well as the existence of ecological communities that can be studied.[22] Ecosophy describes identity as interaction and nature as an interconnected complex of multiplicity within unity.[23] Picht defines ecology as a "'topology' of certain spatial structures, relationships, and conditions" and suspends the notion of any quantitative time-space continuum.[24]

Can the trinitarian understanding of God converge with the ecological understanding of nature? I believe the idea of *community* constitutes the presupposition for such a convergence. A "convergence" in this sense comes about when statements about God's communality "approach" or can be intimately related to those concerning the relationality of nature. This notion helps us understand how the ontologies of Creator and creation can converge *without*

21. I prefer not to use Moltmann's concept of a "social" doctrine of the Trinity here because it does not adequately assess the danger of sociomorphism, that is, of transferring our understanding of society onto the understanding of God.

22. Concerning the problem of the ontological grounding of the existence of relationships and community in biology, cf. chaps. 1 and 3 above.

23. Næss 1989, 164.

24. Picht 1979, 25, 27.

coinciding. Convergence does *not* mean congruence. The characteristics of God's communality and those of nature are not identical; they do not coincide. They converge in the sense that they approach one another. Expressed in the terminology of classical theology: the being of the world is an image of God; creation reflects the Creator without coinciding with the Creator. God's being approaches that of nature and "in-forms" the latter. Nature is God's image, that is, the image through which God "in-forms" himself in creatures.

The trinitarian concept of God converges with the ecological concept of nature without becoming congruent. On the one hand, an understanding of the communality of God's being discloses new possibilities for interpreting the relational being of nature; on the other, ecological ontology discloses new possibilities for interpreting God's triunity. At the same time, new possibilities emerge for interpreting experiences of the activity of the triune God within nature.

A demonstration of the convergence between the trinitarian understanding of God and the ecological understanding of nature lends support to the application of the trinitarian conceptual and linguistic form to an ecological theology of liberation.

The Application of the Trinitarian Conceptual and Linguistic Form

The trinitarian conceptual form provides a structure for articulating various theological genres (liturgy, catechesis, proclamation, doctrine of faith), artistic forms (picture, music, drama, literature), and ecclesiastical actions (diaconate, ecclesiology, social ethics, ecumenics). To that extent it performs a formal function in both practical and theoretical public discourse between theologians in academic settings and in the church. Discourse structured according to trinitarian theology began in the ancient church councils and continues today even though trinitarian theology itself has performed widely varying important functions throughout history.

By contrast, it is still wholly unclear just which function the trinitarian structuring of theological statements is to perform in ecological discourse. Does an understanding of God as a community of three men merely help theologians to avoid confusing the first article (concerning creation) with the second (concerning redemption)? At worst, does the symbol of the Trinity merely help justify patriarchal values? Or can one articulate the notion of God's communality such that it constructively contributes to the expansion and development of ecological discourse?

If so, it seems that ultimately we must develop a new understanding, new images of the communality of the triune God. Our task is that of *re-*

lectura and *re-imaginatio,* that is, of reinterpreting and reshaping, reforming the symbol of the Trinity, and it is the ecological understanding of nature that can articulate the new presuppositions for that task.[25] An ecological reinterpretation of God's communality can perform two important functions. First, it can establish the presuppositions for mediating the *content* of the trinitarian understanding of God within ecological discourse. Second, it simultaneously vitalizes the continuity of trinitarian theology in concurrence with its own tradition. Indeed, I consider this sort of *re-lectura* to be the necessary presupposition both for maintaining the vital continuity of tradition and for communicating that tradition.

Trinitarian Ecology

But how does one actually go about acquiring "new images" of God's communality? Indeed, does it really make sense to speak about an "ecology of God"? Is it perhaps possible to view trinitarian ecology as a *modern* expression of that which *classical* theology understood as the divine economy, that is, of God's work and salvation history? If "ecology" speaks about the relational patterns between organisms and their environment, then "trinitarian ecology" speaks about the *relational patterns between the nature and work of the triune God and the environments of his creation.*

Ecological theory understands the relationship between organism and environment as mutual interaction insofar as the two influence each other within time. An ecological interpretation of God's triunity and of the mystery of the incarnation similarly understands the relationship between Creator and creation synergistically as interaction. Creation, suffering under evil, affects God corporeally in and through the Son; in his own turn, God affects the environments in creation within the Son and the Spirit and allows those environments to influence his actions.

This ecological interpretation of the Trinity focuses on the interaction between God's actions and the environments in his creation. The impossibility of distinguishing between God's essence and work certainly makes it possible to speak about God's essence being affected. Unlike Cobb and Moltmann, who concentrate on the influence the world exerts on God's *es-*

---

25. Contra Boff 1988, 108f., who attributes only little (i.e., merely "formal") value to the "material" symbolism of the Trinity; I would propose rather that it is precisely ecological theology that should draw on the metaphorical wealth of nature and its attendant imagery in reshaping the symbol of the Trinity.

sence, I restrict my "trinitarian ecology" to the interaction between God and world as related to the divine economy in and with the world.

The concept of "trinitarian ecology" acquires additional significance in focusing on the interrelated nature of what is known as the "inner" Trinity, in which case "ecology" then refers to the interconnectedness of different entities in a communal whole. In this sense an "ecology of the Trinity" circumscribes what Moltmann and Boff express in the ancient church terminology of *perichoresis.*

I prefer to reserve the concept of *perichoresis* for the interior relatedness of God's communal essence, while applying the concept of the *ecology* of the triune God to the interaction between creation and the triune Creator within the process of liberation. Four considerations suggest doing so. The expression "inner ecology of the Trinity" seems problematic to me because, first, it begs engagement in speculation regarding essence and, second, it makes it difficult to use the concept of ecology consistently in regard to both a philosophy of nature and theological contexts. Third, the notion of God's "inner" ecology treads precariously close to the abyss of a one-sidedly ecomorphic understanding of God and could too easily be abused to legitimize ecological premises theologically. The Trinity does not *constitute* an ecosystem, even though it certainly is active *in, with,* and *through* ecosystems. A fourth consideration involves terminological history. Gregory of Nazianzus introduced the concept of *perichoresis* into Christology in the fourth century to refer to the mystery of the *mixis* of the uncreated with the created in the incarnate God. Of course, in this sense one could certainly develop the concept of trinitarian ecology christologically from the perspective of *perichoresis;* considering that the concept of *perichoresis* shifted in the fifth century from Christology to the inner doctrine of the Trinity, it seems that any modern attempt to move "behind" this historically significant semantic shift would encounter considerable difficulty.

What, then, is the relation between God's inner-trinitarian *perichoresis,* trinitarian ecology, and the ecology of creation? Boff understands the relation between God's Trinity and society as a "model."[26] Orthodox theologians describe the Trinity as the "model" of their social ethics.[27] Society's sociality

26. Boff 1988, 237. Boff does however employ different imagery: the church as "sacrament" of the triunity (266); "liberation impulses" emerging from the Trinity (236); society as a "mirror" of the triunity (108). Boff views the trinitarian symbol as the "prototype of perichoresis" (110).

27. Since the nineteenth century: Nicolai Fedorov, similarly F. D. Maurice and N. Grundtvig. Cf. Moltmann 1981, 46, who departs from Berdyaev's understanding of the divine love between God and his Other self, the Son, and Ware 1985, 216: "Our social programme, said the Russian thinker Fedorov, is the dogma of the Trinity."

should be the same as or resemble God's sociality. Here the metaphor of a "model" picks up the ancient idea of a prototype *(typos)*, which is then construed as an ethical "model." God's triunity represents the prototype of that which is "informed" or "impressed" upon human beings as an image *(eikon)*. Boff employs this imagery in connection with both social ethics and eschatology. Within the eschatological process of liberation, social ethics should increasingly be oriented and shaped according to God's own sociality.

Critically one might remark here that Boff fails to consider that one's understanding of God's inner perichoretic nature depends on the currently regnant understanding of society. Is Boff interpreting God's *perichoresis* from a perspective possible only after the French Revolution? Is he not placing the allegedly egalitarian quality of the communal being of society *into* the divine essence and elevating it to the status of the primary quality of social being? What about other qualities of social existence? What about, for example, the possibility of being different? What about the fertile hierarchical structures of "vertical solidarity" (J. Assmann)?

The perspective of trinitarian ecology can link the interpretations of *perichoresis* with those of the sociality of culture and nature. It is not the belief that God *is* triune that provides the necessary "model" for an egalitarian social ethics or ecological ethics, but rather the experience and faith that God *acts* in a triune fashion in the history of culture and nature with all beings, and that he acts commensurate with his own being in creating the presuppositions and possibility of discipleship, imitation, and community between human beings and nature in the Spirit.[28] Trinitarian ecology reflects on the experiences of a *perichoresis* of God's actions.

The relationship between ontology and soteriology provides yet another compelling reason for developing this understanding of trinitarian

---

28. Cf. Aulén 1927, 380f., who observes how strongly the idea of community is growing during his own time. Aulén, juxtaposing the Christian motif of community over against the idea of individualism, maintains that "an individualistic Christianity is a *contradictio in adjecto*" (381). He links the motif of community (388f.) with that of eschatology, defining the relationship between the kingdom of God and history such that history's significance derives from being the "battleground" where the victories of the kingdom of God are won. Trigo's reference (1989, 254) to God's kingdom as realized within history *without* coinciding with the kingdom of God itself shows how closely Aulén's perspective resembles that of Latin American liberation theology. Trigo understands history as an open creation (245), and the process of liberation through God's Spirit (with Gutiérrez) as a process of liberation that can be intimated from the backside of history (203).

ecology. By making the Trinity into the "model" for Christian social ethics, Moltmann, Boff, and Orthodox theologians are all pursuing a "theo-naturalistic" analogy for ethics that derives its understanding of the Ought from its understanding of God's being.[29] This model represents an *ontological* analogy: the one should *become* as the other *is;* the world's being should resemble God's being.

Contextual theology should employ a *soteriological* analogy: just as the liberating action of the One is experienced in the other, so also should we act in relationship with others; that is, relational patterns *within* the world should resemble God's own relationships *with* the world.

This figure focuses primarily on the question, "God, why did you create us?" (Buthelezi),[30] as the question asked by all creatures (why have we been created in this environment?) and ecosystems (why have we been created?), and secondarily on what was formerly the primary question, namely, "which God?" (Aulén). Theology itself now focuses not on articulating some universal understanding of God, but rather on understanding the environments in which, through which, and with whose organisms God is acting in the here and now.

A contextual theological understanding of trinitarian ecology adheres to classical apophatic tradition in not speculating about the essence of the Trinity or trying to present a universal trinitarian understanding of God. Instead, it tries to articulate the experiences creatures have with God's liberating actions within their specific sociality and environments, assuming all the while that God is influenced by the environments in his own creation such that he acts in good synergy with the objects of liberation in a way enabling the latter — through, with, and in God — to become subjects of their own liberation. In this sense "trinitarian ecology" becomes synonymous with the

29. The same criticism that addresses the naturalistic perspective in general also addresses this sort of "theo-naturalistic" metaethics. Statements about the being of the good posit metaphysical axioms either as statements about the being of the good in the law of nature or the being of good in God's nature *(physis/ousia)*. Like McFague, Boff, and Moltmann, Gebara's ecofeminist initiative grounds the idea of the Trinity *ontologically*, understanding the "Trinity" as a cosmic structure (1996, 16f.), the earth itself (17), the relationships between peoples and cultures (17f.), between human beings in general, and as the individual personality (18). Like Zizioulas, Gebara also understands being itself as essentially trinitarian, raising the question whether such expansion does not ultimately render the concept of the Trinity itself utterly superfluous and as a result sooner hampers the development of any liberation-theological (ecofeminist) soteriology. For what else does the assertion that the Trinity is "our primary creative reality" (23) mean than the old scholastic thesis that God is the ground of being?

30. Cited in Frostin 1988, 137.

synergy of the triune God with the ecology of his creation. The relationship between God's *perichoresis* and ecology and the ecology of creation might be articulated in the assertion that the perichoretic God acts in a communally liberating fashion with the subjects of his creation in the interrelatedness of nature and culture.

A contextual understanding of trinitarian ecology might focus methodologically on the following three questions within a hermeneutical circle within time:

1. What exactly are these experiences with the God who acts thus ecologically?
2. How can we interpret these experiences in the light of Christian tradition, in this case in historical-trinitarian language?
3. Which practical, normative challenges does this interpretation raise for the discipleship of believers?

This sort of trinitarian ecology is not providing an apologetic for the triune understanding of God; it intends rather to articulate our experiences with the divine economy by using the tools put at our disposal by the tradition of trinitarian theology. Ecological theology is concerned not with defending some confessional understanding of God, but with demonstrating the plausibility of experience with the God who acts socially and ecologically, and in this connection trinitarian theology serves more as a language source and creative grammar[31] whose usefulness emerges in concrete contexts. Contextual theology engages trinitarian language not for the sake of *content,* but as an *instrument* for interpreting the ecological synergy of the triune God with his creation. In its own turn, trinitarian ecology becomes an instrument for interpreting the mystery of the ongoing incarnation of the Son and the inhabitation of God's Spirit and for his liberating work of consummation in the world.

---

31. By "creative grammar" I mean the same thing Chomsky 1973, 15, calls "generative grammar." Unlike Lindbeck's cultural-linguistic theology (1984, 68f.), which understands theological grammar as a regular system — detached from the multiplicity of historically unique situations — of propositional truths, I understand "grammar" to be the language component that develops among subjects *from* and *within* concrete social, historical, and ecological-cultural contexts and whose expressed truths are inextricably bound to those contexts. This initiative associates Chomsky's concept of grammar with the epistemological-sociological analysis of the social presuppositions of both speakers and listeners. Per Frostin alerted me to this epistemological-sociological complement to linguistics shortly before his death in 1992.

The Movement of Liberation — the Liberation of Movement

The Challenge of a Theological Concept of Movement

What can the concept of movement contribute to ecological theology? Gregory freed himself from the metaphysics of his contemporaries by understanding God's being not as eternal repose in the negative sense of a total lack of movement, but as movement that is *not* subject to the time-space continuum. Trinitarian concepts and language enabled him to create the presuppositions for preserving the dynamic dimension of his understanding of God.

Theologically associating movement and being also placed the second theme associated with the concept of movement into a new light, namely, the identity of time and space. Because both were now associated with the earthly experience of the Trinity, the history of nature and of humankind acquired an open form, and the question of the *forms* of movement became Gregory's focal point. Moreover, his dynamic understanding of God enabled him to qualify those forms of movement both ethically and soteriologically. Put succinctly, Gregory's idea is that God acts within the various forms of the movement of liberation in and with creation; God brings about the movement of liberation of the world.

As the modern understanding of nature developed, the concept of evolution threw new light on the problem of movement. The premise of the isomorphy of time and space was abandoned, and the question regarding the forms of movement within time became as urgent as that regarding the space that arises precisely through those forms of movement. As the modern understanding of society developed, the problem of movement appeared under the concept of "dialectics."

The question is whether this problem context now makes it impossible for theology to cling to the ancient metaphysical axiom of God's repose and lack of movement, demanding instead that we develop a new theological understanding of the concept of movement.[32] In the following discussion I will examine what the development of a concept of movement can contribute ontologically and soteriologically to ecological theology.

---

32. Jakob Böhme tried in a completely different context to free himself from the straitjacket of the ancient understanding of movement. Böhme understood the Holy Spirit as the "moveable Spirit in the whole Father," maintaining moreover that "the Godhead, rather than standing still, instead is constantly at work and rising up as a wonderful wrestling, moving, or struggling, like two creatures playing in great love with one another, embracing or strangling one another" (*Aurora* 11, 49, cited in J. Böhme 1983, 55).

Movement within God's Being and the Sacredness of the Earth's Movement and of Movement on Earth

Movement and being are connected. Movement is understood as an ontological quality of God. God's movement "inward" is atemporal, nonspatial, and completely free. God's movement "outward" creates time and space. The understanding of nature associates being and movement such that the qualitative and quantitative movement of living beings and ecosystems appears as being in time and space, though movement itself also creates spatiality. The being of movement and that of space are related through mutual interaction. The possibility of "movement actions" and "movement forms" presupposes the possibility of time and space and is itself constituted by the divine movement that creates time and space.[33] God's movement is the condition of the possibility of an ecology of movement.

In this context faith in a freely moving God generates new respect for the movement of the earth as a presupposition for the entirety of ecological processes. After the "genesis of the Copernican world," for some unknown reason the sacredness of light and of the presumed movement of the sun around the earth was *not* transferred onto the phenomenon of the movement of the earth around the sun. An ecological theology for which God's movement constitutes an important dimension of its understanding of God could prompt new respect for the sacredness of the earth's movement by interpreting the movements of the planets as well as various ecological forms of movement as an expression of the divine economy that preserves the moving vitality of creation.

God's Liberation Movement

God's movement and the movements of creation are connected within God's action. Understood from this perspective, the mystery of the Son's incarnation and the Spirit's inhabitation means that God moves commensurate with the conditions of movement within the time-space continuum. An ecological theology interprets the mystery of the resurrection and of the Spirit's consummation of life as a *transcendence* of the forms of movement of living things and ecosystems.

The question is how an ecological theology of liberation is to under-

33. Paul Klee distinguishes between "movement action," "movement form," and "movement of expression." See Mösser 1976, 19, 34, 82.

stand the transcending of such forms of movement. That is, how is one to describe the forms of movement of God's synergy with the world? This question
can be formulated more concretely on the basis of the Kairos Confession of
Christians of Central America, which speaks of "God, who became incarnate
with humanity through history."[34] How does God move in the Spirit through
the history of a landscape whose organisms and environments are themselves
in movement? The task of ecological theology is to articulate the forms of
movement of the liberating God in and with the world: Where, how, and in
what form can God be discerned in the movement of liberation of nature and
society?

The task of ecology is to articulate the relational patterns between environments and organisms. One dimension of this "pattern of relation" is
movement. Within the ecological context I define "movement" first as a *quality* of this dimension of the pattern. Although ecology generally reflects on
this movement of nature within time with the help of such concepts as "exchange," "succession," and "evolution," movement can also be understood as
the *form* of movement within time as such involves living beings and ecosystems. The being of a given landscape, for example, can be characterized by a
certain kind of movement (relations of exchange, transport channels, etc.)
and simultaneously within the process of movement over time either change
into a different landscape form or remain the same.[35] From an ecological perspective "movement" refers ontologically to a *characteristic* of the pattern of
relationships and then also historically-phenomenologically to the *form of
change* of this same pattern over time.

From the theological perspective I define "movement" as a characteristic of God's trinitarian being and as a form of God's actions in the time-space
continuum. The contents of God's movement and of nature's movement are
distinct. The source of movement is not itself subject to the conditions of
temporal-spatial movement. It is for this reason that God can be understood
as coming *not only* from the "ahead" of the future, as Link emphasizes, but
just as well from the "behind" of the past, as African theology emphasizes,
and from the "cooperation" *(synergeia)* that takes place within the present, as
Orthodox theology emphasizes. The form of the movement of faith is temporally both one of discipleship to him who preceded (Bonhoeffer) as well as
one of recollection of him who suffered and rose (Metz).

The forms of movement of the divine economy are varied and rich. The

34. "Kairos Centralamerika" 1990 (1.5.), p. 12.
35. Concerning the "landscape criterion" in scientific ecological theory, see Allen and
Hoekstra 1992, 54-88, and concerning the fluctuations in and of landscapes, see 74-79.

multifarious appearances of the divine movement as perceived by creatures amid the conditions of the time-space continuum are concealed in the unity of God's inner movement. The phenomena of the divine movements of liberation emerge from the unity of perfect movement in God. The phenomenality of time, space, and movement is concealed in God: God creates everything that is both visible and invisible. The various forms of movement of the divine economy qualify ecological theology soteriologically. In this sense the "movement of liberation" encompasses three stages.[36]

1. First, one must describe the situation of redemptive need such that the *direction* of movement becomes clear. This first stage focuses on the perceptions and interpretations of the condition of ecological violence and on the various forms of movement expressing the power of evil.
2. The second stage focuses on the directions of the forms of movement leading *out* of this situation. The question is: Whither? How do we determine which forms of movement transcend the situation?
3. The third stage focuses on the *quality* of the various forms of movement enabling us to transcend the situation. How in this situation of redemptive need can we discern the form of movement of the Incarnate, for example, in the form of kenosis? What are the specific forms of movement in which God's Son and Spirit act on behalf of liberation?

Concretely one might, for example, apply these three stages to the theological interpretation of a given landscape, moving through each stage in turn.

1. Which forms of movement betray the power of evil over the landscape? Environmental analyses enable us to explain in a more sophisticated fashion how this "power of evil" is threatening survival processes.
2. Which goals and forms of movement can alter this situation of threat to the landscape? This second stage involves practical-ethical discussions that are environmentally informed *and* include all affected parties — including representatives of nonhuman interests.
3. How can one generate models, assessments, and imitations of the various forms of liberating movement that can *change* movements and actions under the power of evil into movements expressing the good? Ecological theology interprets the experiences of how such forms of movement are transcended as experiences of God's movement of liberation.

36. Following the soteriological schema in Thunberg 1977, 12f.

In a landscape in which human beings are able to discern or perceive the rights of nature, of fellow human beings, and of their future, God reveals himself as the *movement of liberation* when the landscape's forms of movement become ecologically "richer" and the landscape itself moves away from a condition in which it is subject to the power of evil. The same landscape movement that ecology describes through a common form of movement as a "transcending" of such movement under the power of evil, theology now understands as movement expressing the liberating God. Ecological theology interprets the movements of liberation in nature and society as liberation toward the community of the triune God with the world.[37]

The Hermeneutics of the Cross of Creatures

The characteristic feature of a theology of the cross is that it articulates that which becomes visible of God in the suffering of this world. Beginning with the historical way of the cross taken by the Incarnate, it interprets the symbol of the cross as the power of evil's most extreme challenge to God. A theology of the cross also provides a methodological criterion for talking about God as formulated by Luther in the Heidelberg Disputation: "That person does not deserve to be called a theologian who looks upon the invisible things of God as though they were clearly perceptible in those things which have actually happened [Rom. 1:20]. He deserves to be called a theologian, however, who comprehends the visible and manifest things of God seen through suffering and the cross."[38] Theology should bring to expression not the God who is turned away from the world, but rather that part of God's nature that is turned toward the world. The object of theological reflection and understanding is not the invisible part of God, but rather that which suffering and the cross make visible to creatures. The experience of suffering includes the experience and knowledge of the liberating God.

Gregory, Luther, and theologians of liberation concur on this criterion. Gregory apophatically rejects any speculation regarding God's invisible nature for the sake of discerning the God who *acts*. Even after the Son is glorified, Gregory's God still experiences the stigmata of corporeal suffering on his

---

37. Contra Comblin 1987, 186, who maintains that the Spirit brings about this movement of the world toward God. Concerning the discussion with Comblin, see below.

38. Luther, *Heidelberg Disputation* (1518), XIX, XX, pp. 361f.: "Non ille digne Theologus dicitur, qui invisibilia Dei per ea, quae facta sunt, intellecta conspicit. . . . Sed qui visibilia et posteriora Dei per passiones et crucem conspecta intelligit."

own body, which the Spirit takes in the world. The Latin American, African, and Asian theologians of liberation interpret the suffering of the poor as the locus of revelation of the redemptive God.[39] In its own turn, the ecological theology of liberation advocated by this book interprets the suffering of the poor among creatures as the locus of revelation of the liberating God.

In the following discussion my first step is to describe from the perspective of the cross of Christ a problem common to theological, ecological, environmental, and practical-bioethical discourse: What path of the cross of survival do both human and nonhuman creatures threatened by ecological injustice take? In describing God's way of the cross with creatures, my second step is to provide a trinitarian understanding of the conceptual figure of the theology of the cross, and the third step is to provide an ecological-semiotic model of the life processes of creatures.

The Way of the Cross of Creatures

The ecological theology of liberation expands the concept of suffering to include organisms in ecosystems. The concept of "ecological violence," understood as unjust endangerment and impairment of the capacity of organisms, ecosystems, and landscapes to survive, enables our theological interpretation of the cross to include *nonhuman* subjects of nature. The power of evil affects human beings and other creatures equally, and the locus of God's visible work of liberation is wherever human beings and other creatures suffer together. Ecological theology today must inquire concerning precisely this community of suffering shared by human beings and nature and must begin by assuming that the Redeemer does indeed also take this ecological cross of creatures upon himself.

An analysis of this cross amid the injustice of ecological violence requires that we implement a combination of social and scientific theories commensurate with the conditions of the victims themselves. The conceptual figure of the theology of the cross assumes that those who suffer violence within cultural ecosystems are best able to perceive or discern not only the situation in need of redemption, but also the presence of the redeeming God *in* this situation.

Empirical science is incapable of analyzing suffering. Even though medicine views pain as one of the preeminent indicators of the presence of a mal-

---

39. Sobrino 1988, 110-14; Song 1991, 175; Koyama 1983, 34; Yong-Bock 1989, 34ff.; Tutu 1985, 97f., 159; Collet 1990, 297f.; Frostin 1987, 17; and Hofmann 1987, 293.

ady, empirical science is guided more by the vision of technical control than by that of healing and developing nature. Environmental sciences, however, tend to shift the normative premises of the natural sciences; increasingly concerned with "rehabilitating" themselves from the consequences of other scientific applications, they are guided more by the vision of a nature that is somehow "other" and "better" and by a vision of an environmentally "friendly" humankind.

The conceptual figure of the theology of the cross enhances environmental science by locating the normative ground of its knowledge neither *naturalistically* in the notion of some natural paradise prior to the fall, nor *anthropocentrically* in the notion of a garden that is eternally, abidingly at the disposal of human beings, nor even *metaphysically* in the notion of the Godhead being somehow reflected into creation. It enhances environmental science by locating that ground of knowledge from the perspective of *incarnational theology* in the experiential vision of the concrete subjects of the community of suffering and hope. By focusing on these subjects, environmental science discloses not only the *place* where creatures struggle for liberation, but also the discernible *features* characterizing the power of ecological evil there. The theology of the cross discloses how God becomes visible in creatures' struggle for liberation and reflects on the function fulfilled by our understanding of God in the struggle for a just survival.

It is the victims themselves who interpret the situations unjustly threatening the lives of both human and nonhuman creatures. It is *their* visible cross that provides the hermeneutics for interpreting the suffering, vision, and mediation of liberation. In this sense the hermeneutics of the cross of creatures themselves is what interprets both the situation of suffering and the vision of liberation. That is, the community of suffering represents both a community of hope and a community of liberation of creatures in the Spirit of God.

God's Pain, Suffering, and Sympathetic Cosuffering

Our analysis of Gregory's writings showed how an understanding of trinitarian distinctions can enhance theology's discourse. The criticism of Moltmann's movement of creaturely suffering into God's essence and of Fox's and McFague's movement of the divine pain into the pain of the world suggested that one develop a new understanding of the uniqueness of the historical suffering of subjects. The narrowness of Sölle's realism as developed from the perspective of the theology of the cross tends to obscure the distinction between liberation and suffering. In the following discussion I propose understanding God's suffering from a trinitarian perspective, such that

1. the discernment of the suffering of the one by another who is *not* affected by that suffering be maintained as a perception of the other;
2. an acknowledgment of the uniqueness of ecological suffering and of the suffering of the earthly Jesus be maintained;
3. the voluntary acceptance of the suffering of the one by another be understood as a necessary step toward liberation.

I refer to the first aspect as "pain": seeing another suffer causes pain; it "hurts." I refer to the second aspect as "suffering": a subject experiences something outside itself that nonetheless makes it suffer inwardly. I refer to the third aspect of suffering as "sympathetic cosuffering" or commiseration: participating in the suffering of another involves subjecting oneself as well to whatever is causing that other to suffer.

Our understanding of God relates these three aspects such that the Father's pain, the Son's suffering, and the Spirit's sympathetic cosuffering *together* constitute the presupposition for the liberation of creatures from their suffering. The Father's pain at the suffering of his world prompts him to take on the suffering nature of humans and of the environment. Suffering thus the senseless power of evil prompts the Spirit to "enter" into the world to participate in and indeed overcome the suffering of creatures. In his own pain the Father participates to the same degree in the suffering of the Son as the Spirit suffers along with the Son. The Son enables the Spirit to suffer in and with creatures whose suffering continues to cause corporeal pain to the Son even with the Father.

The God of the ecological theology of liberation is thus a God who subjects himself to the same suffering endured by his creatures. God becomes visible in the cross and suffering of the creatures who are the victims of ecological violence. The pain caused by God's perception of the suffering of others — of creatures — prompts the Creator to enter into the suffering subjects of nature, into suffering ecosystems, and into suffering landscapes. Filled with the Spirit, those who suffer make this God's work visible. The place where creatures struggle for the right of survival is just as holy as the place where the poor struggle for their human rights.[40] For the life of creatures and of the poor, as bestowed by the Spirit, is holy; and it is there that God acts from within his own pain, suffering, and sympathetic cosuffering.

40. Sobrino 1988, 104f.

The Semiotic Function Cycle of Suffering
and the Wirkwelt *of the Spirit*

Can one speak meaningfully about a community of suffering and hope shared by human and nonhuman creatures? Can human beings and other living beings communicate with one another in the first place? Can one demonstrate the notion that suffering creatures are capable of knowledge of God? Ecological theology obviously needs to develop a theory of communication that makes it meaningful to speak about a community of suffering and hope shared by different subjects of nature. One cannot develop a comprehensive theory of communication of this sort within the utilitarian understanding of reality because the latter views only the more complex animals as physiologically capable of suffering in the first place. Nor is it possible within an anthropocentric construction, since such a perspective views only human beings as subjects. Within a sympathetic ecological understanding of nature, however, it is quite possible to view the relational patterns between organisms and their environment in this comprehensive fashion from the perspective of the experience of suffering.[41]

Here we no longer narrowly understand the concept of "suffering" merely as the physical pain of subjects, but rather more broadly as the "mutual exchange of suffering subjects with respect to ecological violence." Within this broader understanding, "suffering" applies not only to the algae that simply die from lack of acidity, but also to the heath whose botanical makeup is altered by air pollution, to the Indian child injured in the Bhopal accident, and to the small farmers in a Third World country who are robbed of their economic and cultural potential by the global financial policies of the rich.

In the following discussion I examine the three theoretical premises applicable to an understanding of the community of suffering of creatures and their way of the cross: (a) Jakob von Uexküll's theory of the *Merkwelt* (world of perception) and *Wirkwelt* (world of action); (b) Thure von Uexküll's theory of the semiosis of life processes; and (c) the theory of "formative artistic thought" as a presupposition for discursive thought.

Jakob von Uexküll's premise is that a living being's world of perception and world of action are to be distinguished within a "function cycle,"[42] that

---

41. Concerning the tradition of a "sympathetic" view of nature, see Schopenhauer (Stuttgarter Ausgabe), book 4, par. 67, pp. 443-46; concerning its history of reception in Schopenhauer, Nietzsche, and Schweitzer, see Böhler 1981, 78ff.

42. J. von Uexküll and Kriszat 1983, 11. Concerning J. von Uexküll's semiotic environ-

environments *themselves* represent "subjective realities," that the various environments of living beings everywhere "overlap and intersect," that the question of meaning is central for all living beings, and that one subject can understand another by putting itself in the position of the world of that other subject. A living being's *Merkwelt* consists of signs existing within that being's environment that determine that being's behavior with regard to objects in the *Wirkwelt*. Uexküll's understanding of nature led to a revision of the traditional scientific concept of reality by constantly evoking "the concrete spheres of encounter between subjects and objects" in "which nature manifests itself in this or that form."

Thure von Uexküll understands ecology as semiosis, that is, as a sequence of sign processes that represent the "real framework of the 'units of survival.'" He understands the framework of the body as consisting of an exchange of sign processes. This theory understands "action" as a communal undertaking in which role and counterrole "complement" one another in bringing about a communal event.

Jakob von Uexküll has provided a model of such a sign process in the "function cycle" in which "stimuli" are encoded as "signs of meaning" through semantic assignment. This process enables a subject's *Merkwelt* and *Wirkwelt* to be mediated and allows it to enter into an active relationship with the worlds of other subjects. Thure von Uexküll applies depth psychology to his father's model in demonstrating how every insight or acquisition of knowledge simultaneously constitutes a "distortion." His premise is that human knowledge always unites cognitive and affective elements. By shutting out the pain prompted by doubt in our own capacity for knowledge, the striving for knowledge of the "thing in itself" makes it possible to diminish our empathy with others for the sake of exploiting our power. That is, "we would rather deny our own vital nature and the vitality of living creatures and nature than be forced to establish a relationship that might be painful."[43]

The biological-ecological understanding of the semiosis of life processes enables us to analyze biologically other creatures' experience of suffering. How does an organism react within its *Merkwelt* and *Wirkwelt* to destructive processes in its environment? What is the difference between the

---

mental theory, cf. T. von Uexküll 1983; Altner 1991, 140-47; and Hornborg 1994a, 8f., who integrates J. von Uexküll's theory of meaning into an anthropological/humano-ecological epistemological theory. The following presentation is based on J. von Uexküll and Kriszat 1983; J. von Uexküll 1982; Grassi and T. von Uexküll 1950; and T. von Uexküll 1989. The exact documentation is found in the German edition of this book. Concerning the functional circle of contextual, humano-ecological theology, see Bergmann 2003, chaps. 1 and 5.

43. T. von Uexküll 1989, 401-3.

"function cycles of suffering" and the "function cycles of liberation and development"? The psychoanalytical understanding of the connection between cognitive and affective modes of human knowledge makes new modes of knowledge possible that view participative empathy and experience not as antitheses to dissociative knowledge, but as its necessary presupposition.

Art contributes a third theoretical consideration to the development of a comprehensive theory of communication. In his theory of intuition, Sven Sandström persuasively demonstrates how "formative artistic thinking" actually comes about as the formation of meaning within a "semantic space."[44] "Formative artistic thinking" is not the same as linear, discursive thinking, and differs from it structurally and qualitatively as "visual perceptibility" coming about as a spatial "constellation"; by contrast, "discursivity" comes about as digital "confrontation." Sandström also explains how the pictorial, experiential formation of meaning together with the intuitive material of memory constitute the presupposition for any verbal communication, since the latter itself does not really "contain" anything and comes to bear *only* in relation to meanings. Instead of understanding "formative artistic thinking" and intuitive process within understanding as the *alternative* to logical thought, one should rather understand verbal thought (i.e., in language) as the "implementation" of "formative artistic thinking" with the goal of establishing a correlation with earlier conceptual knowledge. Sandström thus believes that a theory of meanings and of meaning formation cannot presuppose language from the outset and must instead be developed independent of the aspects of the specifically linguistic perspective on reality.

Although Sandström's theory of intuition and of "formative artistic thinking" as the formation of meaning refers exclusively to human perception and knowledge, I think it appropriate to apply this question regarding the relation between formative artistic and discursive thinking to nonhuman life forms as well. Might Kant's "imagination" and Sandström's "intuitive formation of meaning" represent a fundamental characteristic and function of *all* living beings of the sort Jakob von Uexküll interprets in his model of the "function cycle" as the semantic assessment and semantic endurance of living beings? Might one combine Sandström's theory of human intuition with Jakob and Thure von Uexküll's theory of life semiosis?

Integrating the pictorial cognitive theory into the ecological-semiotic theory makes it possible to understand in a more sophisticated fashion the similarities, differences, and changes affecting the modes of conceiving and expressing meaning as exercised by human beings and other organisms

---

44. T. von Uexküll 1989, 407.

within their environments. I can summarize in two preliminary hypotheses and accompanying questions my attempt to establish the theoretical presuppositions for understanding the community of suffering of creatures.

1. Experiences of suffering inform the inner human being or imprint themselves pictorially into it; these interior images are then interpreted in a logically discursive fashion within linguistic forms of expression. Can this schema (experience — informing — creation of image meaning — linguistic interpretation/reaction) also be applied to an interpretation of the suffering of *other* living beings?

2. The model of the function cycle in which the worlds of perception and function are connected describes the relation between living beings and their environments. How can we now describe from the *ecological* perspective a function cycle of suffering and a function cycle of liberation?

How can these insights contribute to the development of a new, comprehensive theory of communication, a theory considered from both an artistic-formative and a semiotic perspective and applicable to an ecological theology of the cross?

First, an ecological theology of the cross should remain mindful of the internal processing of the experience of suffering and should try as much as possible to render visible the metaphors and formative artistic expressions of that suffering. Second, an understanding of the semiotic life exchange makes it possible for a theology of the cross to raise the question of God meaningfully within the function cycle of environmental suffering. The biblical belief that creatures and human beings are equally connected with God in both suffering and hope for liberation can now be interpreted ecologically as a reference to how creatures are connected with one another within the function cycles of their intersecting worlds.

Is it possible to interpret the cross of creatures ecologically as a function cycle of suffering? Could it be that precisely this function cycle of suffering shared by different organisms and environments might not also represent the locus of the vivifying, sanctifying, liberating work of the Spirit?

The Spirit as Liberator of Nature

Although many participants in contemporary ecological discourse agree that we need to establish new modes of expression for spirituality as conceived from the ecological perspective, too little attention has been given the question of just *which* spirit's experiences come to expression in the "spiritual." The intention of this book has been to examine precisely the question regarding the work and nature of the Spirit whose experiences contribute to the shaping of ecological spirituality, ecological ethics, and ecological theology. What meaning does pneumatology have for the ecological theology of liberation?

The following discussion begins with the current discussion of the immanence and transcendence of the Creator Spirit — a problem rendered obsolete by the ecological movement — addressing this problem anew as one of location and transparency. The second part challenges us to exploit creatively the freedom offered by the wealth of pneumatological language and concepts within the tradition of trinitarian theology. Here I also propose five criteria of pneumatological grammar that can ensure that we maintain this freedom. The third part provides the outline for an ecological pneumatology of liberation based on the ancient church confession of the Spirit as the movement of the "life of the coming world." After we establish a working relationship between the ecological concept of the Spirit and that of the Christian tradition, we examine in the fourth part several characteristic features of an ecologically enlightened and critical-communicative theology of the Spirit as liberator of nature.

These proposals may well make some rather innovative demands on the reader. This entire section nonetheless carries on an unmistakably classical theological tradition in opening up to the future the same faith in the connection or relationship between *all* life and the activity of the divine Spirit expressed in the Old Testament,[45] mediated anew to the church's creed in late antiquity through the Cappadocian clarification, sustained through both the Eastern and Western Middle Ages, revitalized by the Reformation, emphasized by Enlightenment theologians, and enculturated anew by Third World theology.

The classical understanding of this connection or relationship also generates the central pneumatological question that an ecological theology of liberation must address, namely: In what way does the Spirit actually bestow

---

45. Concerning the connection between the Spirit and life, see in the Old Testament: Gen. 2:7; Job 15:13; 33:4; Jer. 2:24; Ezek. 37:5, 10; Ps. 104:29f.; Schmidt 1958, 170, 172; Stendahl 1990, 15-22; in the New Testament: Rom. 1:4; John 6:63; 2 Cor. 3:6; Nissen 1993, 16-19; Stendahl, 42ff., 48-51; in patristics: Thunberg 1988; 1993b, 206ff.; in mysticism: Andresen 1988, 1:328; in the Reformation: Prenter 1944, 215-32; in the Enlightenment: Hegel 1807, xxxviii; in modernity and late modernity: Rahner 1971; Congar 1983, 213-28; 1986, 122-29; Staniloae 1984, 281; Moltmann 1991a, 83-98; Aagaard 1973, 259ff.; and in Third World theology: Gutiérrez 1986, 72-75; Trigo 1989, 266f.; Boff 1995, 49f.

life — and *which* Spirit are we talking about? The form this question and its answer ultimately take, however, is by no means independent of time and space. Just as the artists of the Vienna Secession insisted "to each age its own art, to each art its own freedom," so also does contextual theology insist "to each age its own experience, reflection on, and understanding of the Spirit, and to each pneumatology its own freedom!"[46]

The Ecology of the Holy Spirit as Transparency of Place

Understanding the all-encompassing Spirit from the perspective of ecology and evolution, Bateson offered an explanation of the Spirit of ecologists and of the theoreticians of evolution. Gregory taught us to distinguish epistemologically between the *nature* and *works* of the Spirit. Drawing from Calvin's biblically grounded thought, Moltmann and Link established the world-immanence of the Spirit, on the one hand, and its transcendence, on the other.

On which of these themes, however, should an ecology of the divine Spirit now focus? In this first part I propose replacing the question of the Spirit's immanence in nature with the question of the *place* where the Spirit is at work and is transparent.[47]

46. Inscription on Johannes Olbrich's Vienna Secession building, 1898, in the Vienna Zeile.

47. In a *general* sense, the concept of place (German, *Ort*) refers to "locality" or "location," that is, to a determination of where one entity is in relation to another within a surrounding space. *Semantically* the English term "place" makes it possible to delimit such a location in space physically as well as socially and mentally. Concerning the problem of integrating "metaphorical space" and "material space," see Gregory 1994, 5. The concepts of *Ort* and "place" presuppose the existence of an open space or spatial surroundings within which the *Ort* place is actually situated.

In the discipline of *geography,* recent epistemological discussion has subjected the concept of place to a considerable degree of differentiation. Recent *ecological* and *geographical sciences* draw on fluctuation theories involving the dimensions of time and movement in examining physical and social processes at *Orten* places as well as in landscapes (see Allen and Hoekstra 1992, 74-79; and Hägerstrand 1988, 16). In *modernity studies,* Giddens emphasizes the tension between space and place in analyzing the separation between the two as a characteristic feature of modernity's constant de- and reterritorialization processes. Giddens 1992, 19, maintains that places are "thoroughly penetrated by and shaped in terms of influences quite distant from them." Although Gregory, 123, concurs with Giddens's criticism of the more abstract models of spatial form, he objects that Giddens ignores the significance of the concrete peculiarities of space, place, and landscape. *Feminist humano-geography* emphasizes the gender-specific experiences of place and their significance for behavior within spaces (see

The question of the relation between the Spirit and nature is meaningful within the larger question of immanence or transcendence only if one can answer it persuasively. Three considerations suggest that this is no longer possible under the conditions of ecological thinking.

1. In the first place, the concepts of inclusion (immanence) and moving past (transcendence) presuppose a *distinction* between Spirit and nature that in its own turn suggests the existence of some sort of "boundary," whereas the ecological definition of the Spirit we developed earlier maintains that the "Spirit" refers precisely to the "being of the one in, with, or alongside another."[48] This definition immediately begs the question of the "porosity," if you will, of precisely that boundary which is so central to the notion of immanence and transcendence in connection with substance. Our focus now turns to the Spirit's ability to shift, suspend, and indeed even redraw both real and ideal boundaries.

2. Viewing the problem of the relation between the Spirit and nature as one of immanence or transcendence under the conditions of the philosophy of substance and identity inevitably results either in unsupportable assertions regarding the nature or essence of the Spirit — that is, in pneumatological *metaphysics* — or in unsupportable assertions regarding the immanent capacity of nature to include or contain something spiritual — that is, in *a philosophical sophiology of nature*.

Viewing the same problem under the conditions of ecological thought, however, enables us to articulate the *transparency* of contexts, situations, and places where creatures themselves experience the Spirit, reflect on those experiences, articulate or represent them, and bring them to practical realization.[49] Taking this path in examining the problem of the relation between Spirit and nature leads us to an *ecology of the Spirit*. The central problem of

---

Gregory, 124f.). Here the concept of "site of settlement" (German, *Ort der Wohnungnahme*) shifts insofar as the conventional temporal-geographical understanding of "places" as "meaningful sites within a symbolic landscape" is expanded and places can now be understood as "sites between and within which identities and subjectivities are negotiated." Gregory, 127. Might this not be the occasion for an encounter between contextual *theology*, which emphasizes the specific geographical and historical meaning of the physical, social, and mental situation for our understanding of God, on the one hand, and critical humano-geography, on the other? Generally speaking, the connections between theology and geography have not been fully developed. To survey scholarship in this area, see Park 1994.

48. Lessing 1984, 218.

49. Cf. Link 1989, who advocates developing a theological "model of representation" of the "transparency of nature" that he understands ontologically (187) as the ability of the world to be a "medium of representation."

this ecology is not the Spirit's *being* in relation to nature, but rather the *how* of that being at places constituted by living beings and environments.

3. A third trinitarian consideration also militates against the particular focus of the problem of immanence. The theological cosmology of the ancient church based its understanding of nature on a double perspective. Epistemologically the boundary between God and world is characterized by both continuity and discontinuity.[50] One cannot simply assume that what appears to human beings as a "boundary" that God "transcends" in the Spirit also seems such from the perspective of the Spirit. I would suggest that we constantly call into question — drawing on the insights of the ancient church itself — the assumption that such a boundary "exists" as presupposed by the debate regarding the problem of immanence or transcendence.

In the fourth century the development of the notion of the historical Trinity addressed this problem by maintaining that our understanding of God as being "more than the world" contradicts neither the idea of incarnation nor that of the universal inhabitation of the Spirit. The existence of neither different religious periods in history nor of different spheres of religious faith called into question the basic Christian trinitarian faith in God as the source of all being *and* as the liberator of specific contexts. Quite the contrary, trinitarian grammar enabled theologians to provide different interpretations of the various modes of action of the one God in different contexts. I believe ecological theologians should accordingly develop creation theology not merely within the "horizon" of the doctrine of the Trinity (Link) or merely "ecologically" (Moltmann), but rather in a fully trinitarian-pneumatological fashion.[51] Any development of an ecology of the Spirit should accordingly draw from a wide variety of historically and geographically differentiated contextual representations of experiences with the triune God who sets nature free.[52]

---

50. Cf. Gregorios 1978, 60-63; 1988, 98f., 128.

51. Panikkar 1993, 99f., pointing out how "trinitarian spirituality" tends to ignore the mystery of the incarnation, thus prefers to develop a "Theandric" spirituality. Although this insight is certainly of value, it should not prompt us to counter the trinitarian tradition with the Theandric. From the perspective of the totality of the trinitarian community, my outline for a trinitarian-pneumatological ecology understands the inhabitation of the Spirit as a salvific-historical expansion of the Theandric mystery. Panikkar's understanding of the cosmo-Theandric mystery (23ff., 103) seems to fall prey to the same inclination we earlier criticized in McFague's position, namely, that of juxtaposing antithetically the historical and cosmic Christ. Cf. Ahlstrand 1993, 178, who shows how Panikkar "does deliberately subordinate Jesus to Christ who is the 'ontic mediator.'" Does the doctrine of the historically concrete inhabitation of the Spirit not create the very presuppositions for overcoming this antithesis?

52. Barnes's initiative toward an "ecology of the Spirit" moves in the same direction,

Inquiring regarding the "how" of the Spirit's activity by implication also inquires regarding the "where," that is, the place where the Spirit actually appears. Precisely this combination of queries regarding the Spirit's mode and locus makes it possible for theology and environmental science to come together quite *apart* from any question of immanence. Put simply: subjects have experiences at specific places constituted by time, space, and movement. Environmental science focuses on the "glassy essence" (Shakespeare) places, the dimensions of which it empirically or hermeneutically examines and explains.

Ecological theology views as the glassy essence of the *Spirit* the same glassy essence whose physical and cultural condition and maintenance constitute the object of environmental science. In this sense environmental science and theology share a common subject even though their respective preliminary understanding of place and the premises governing its examination may differ. Environmental science empirically examines the ecology of a place with the goal of discerning those particular regular features — features remaining constant over time — that allow future prognoses. It hermeneutically examines the ecology of a place as a reflection of the variously manifested meanings whose interpretation may lead to an understanding of its essential nature, of semantic shifts, and of analogies. In concert with environmental science, theology examines the ecology of a place as a *symbol* of the inhabitation of the Spirit, interpreting the various social constructions characterizing this place from the perspective of how the various subjects may perceive its holiness.

With these presuppositions an ecological theology of the Spirit can then establish a new ethical and moral foundation for bioethics whose primary criterion is the situation of victims themselves. Aesthetically such an ecology of the Spirit can also bring to expression the holiness of a place. Insofar as one encounters God precisely where those whose very survival is threatened struggle for their human rights, liberation theologians view such places as holy.[53] Ecological theologians similarly view as holy those places where the struggle for the "rights of nature" is played out, places where nature's peaceful survival is threatened and one encounters God in the Spirit of coming life.

Contrary to anthropocentric theology, the ecology of the Spirit does not understand the glassy essence of place merely as the *place* of activity —

---

albeit largely only formally (as the title of his book) rather than as a fully developed position. Barnes 1994 and Boff 1995, 32ff., 36ff., advocate the same association of physical, social, and inner spiritual ecology.

53. Sobrino 1988, 110f.

neither in the theatrical sense of "scene" nor as a language event in the hermeneutical understanding of nature as an "open book" or "text," nor as a sacrament in the theurgic image of the tectonic "temple," nor certainly from the perspective of natural law in the understanding of life as a "court." For the ecology of the Spirit, such places are simply the locus of the Spirit's inhabitation. The task is then to inquire concerning these places of inhabitation *without* confusing the dogmatic map — which serves as an orientation — with the landscape of appearances of the Spirit.

Pneumatological theological traditions provide maps that can help locate current places where the Spirit has taken up inhabitation. Although these maps — from both Christian and other traditions of faith — do indeed provide the conceptual and systematic tools for such study, they should not be misused for the sake of hasty explanations and assessments of experiences at a given place; instead, they should aid our interpretations of the various local forms in which spirituality comes to expression. In communicating their local, communal experiences of the Spirit, subjects within the community of saints draw on the various forms of spiritual expression offered by the different aesthetic media available to them. It is the task of an ecology of the Spirit to reflect discursively on these various forms of expression of spirituality and its content. An ecology of the Spirit is thus able to provide a *transparent look* through the "eyes" of spirituality at the glassy essence of the places where the Spirit appears without losing sight either of the activity of the Spirit itself or of the change in the ecology of the place. The ecology of the Spirit strives to provide a theological vision of the "transparency of a place within time" as part of a universal vision of the "transparency of world" (Franz Marc) that no single subject alone can provide.[54]

Pneumatological Grammar

The places of the Spirit's inhabitation can become transparent in this sense from different perspectives. Bateson seeks the Spirit as the connecting pattern, while Cobb, Birch, and Altner understand various ecological and evolutionary patterns within time as expressions of the Spirit of life, and

54. The term "world transparency" *(Weltdurchschauung)* comes from Marc, who distinguishes it from "worldview" *(Weltanschauung)* insofar as it seeks to represent the world as "indivisible being." Düchting 1991, 109. Concerning the central theme of the "earthly paradise" in Macke and the search for the unity of human beings and nature in Marc and Macke, see Düchting, 67f.

Moltmann and Link inquire concerning the Spirit's inhabitation while acknowledging the open, temporal nature of the places where the *creatio continua* is discernible. Gregory's understanding of the divinity and salvific activity of the Spirit threw new light on the places where God moves freely through time and space in the Spirit. Today ecological and theological perceptions of the Spirit are joined by a plethora of spiritualities and doctrines of the Spirit currently arising within so-called neoreligious movements.

An Identification of Ecological Spirits versus a Search for Truth at the Places of the Spirit's Inhabitation   Within the context of the ecological challenge and its bewildering profusion of spiritual variety, what considerations militate in favor of drawing from the sources of our own trinitarian-pneumatological tradition?[55] Why not simply nominally identify the Holy Spirit of the Christian tradition with the natural sciences' spirit of evolution, the New Age spirit of new wisdom, the ecologists' invisible spiritual pattern, and the ecosophers' spirit of totality?[56] Or conversely, why not identify the ecosophical spirits as manifestations of the Holy Spirit? Considerations from both epistemology and creation theology militate against this overly facile solution.

Epistemologically I view these different perspectives and their attendant presuppositions as the initial condition for the possibility of a common discursive search for truth.[57] *Not* choosing this point of departure robs us and

55. Contra Boff 1995, 36f., "spirituality" here refers to a form for expressing our experience with the Spirit. Boff uses the terms "mysticism" and "spirituality" synonymously to refer to the "fundamental and all-inclusive experience, by means of which we embrace the totality of things, an organic totality as it were, replete with meaning and value" (42). Boff, 42f., understands spirituality both as an "attitude" (36f.) and as the maintenance of one's "cultivating that inward space" (37). Cf. also his definition of religion: "Religions crystallize as a consequence of religious experience" (149). Cf. also Hill, whose rather sluggish attempt at establishing "connections" between the Catholic doctrine of faith and the environment does not even *mention* the Holy Spirit in his chapter "Christian Spirituality" (1998, 241ff.).

56. Boff avoids this difficult question (1995, 62ff.) by understanding the "return of religious feeling" and the various initiatives toward a "new cosmology" as being prompted by the Spirit's own activity. Although Boff quite correctly points out that the new religious movements risk ignoring the question of social justice (69f.), how does he understand Christian pneumatology contributing anything special to social ethics without restricting one's view of the Spirit to that of pioneering a somehow "immanent" understanding of natural law?

57. Regarding the conditions for the possibility of a common discursive search for truth, I follow — contra objectivist, relativist, and dogmatic postmodern epistemological theories — the discourse ethics of Karl-Otto Apel from the critical Frankfurt philosophical tradition, the Socratic philosophy revivified by Leonard Nelson and Gunnar Heckmann, and the transmodern, intercultural critique of modernity and philosophy of dialogue of Enrique Dussel.

others of any possibility of engaging in philosophical discourse. Abandoning the possibility of dialogue concerning the various theoretical conditions underlying practical concepts of action also robs both us and — especially — any potentially disadvantaged dialogue partners of the possibility of integrating *theory and praxis* in a fashion persuasive to *all* participants and affected parties. Any philosophical dialogue not acknowledging the possibility of metalanguages degenerates into specialized discourse for initiates and the elite. One of the consequences of such a position is that a neoreligious-ecological discourse concerning the Spirit could too easily be engaged on behalf of an obscure justification of new, potentially inscrutable constellations of power. These considerations suggest that the truth claims of theological discourse also be subjected to critical epistemological-theoretical examination by *other* discourses and that they be accessible to and capable of establishing a consensus in connection with those other discourses. Any theological pneumatology not taking these suggestions seriously will risk slipping into the isolation of specialized discourse that in its own turn ultimately will result in the demise of Christian pneumatological reflection.

From the perspective of creation theology, the connection between the Spirit and life discussed earlier in connection with both biblical and classical theology also militates against the facile solution of simply identifying *all* spirits with the Holy Spirit. A Christian doctrine of the Spirit that says something about the Spirit but nothing about life will have little credibility as far as the history of theology is concerned because it is incommensurate with the long tradition of the vivifying, life-giving Spirit. "Where the Spirit is, there is life; and where there is life, there, too, is the Holy Spirit" (Ambrose).[58] As mentioned above, whatever pneumatology says about life must be accessible to and capable of establishing a consensus in connection with other discourses concerning the places of life. If this is not the case, then our confession to the Creator "of heaven and earth" and to the "Spirit who gives life" will degenerate into a mere formula whose meaning is known only to those who speak it.

Criteria for a Pneumatological Grammar of Ecological Theology Anyone not taking the pneumatologically easy way out in the face of ecological and ecosophical challenge faces the rather daunting task of working out a pneumatological grammar capable of serving the spiritualities "from below," their form, and their freedom.

The purpose of the following five criteria for a pneumatological gram-

---

58. Ambrose 1983, book I, XV, 172, p. 113.

mar in the context of ecological theology is to aid in structuring the modes of expression of ecological spirituality. These five criteria involve tradition, experience, the common search for truth, mission, and synthesis.

1. The first criterion, *tradition,* can be understood from the perspective of theological history. It is absolutely necessary that one establish *anew* — in every age and at every location — the classical connection between the Spirit and life described above. Here the trinitarian grammar employed in articulating the doctrine of the Spirit in the fourth century acquires particular significance. The systematic and apologetic reason for continuing to understand the doctrine of the Spirit in trinitarian terms is to maintain the force of the confession that in Christ the creatures of God's world can indeed experience God as both Creator *and* Redeemer. From the perspective of systematic construction, continuing to understand the doctrine of the Spirit in trinitarian terms enables us to develop an inclusive, universal doctrine of the Spirit capable of accommodating the various modes of expression of the historical doctrine of the Trinity. We are then able to understand the Holy Spirit not merely from the larger *cosmic* perspective, but also from *contextually* unique and universal perspectives as the Spirit of the historical and cosmic Christ and as the Spirit of the Father.

2. The second criterion, *experience,* preserves the freedom of subjects whose experiences with the Spirit come to expression in the varied and colorful modes of spirituality. In this sense spiritualities are the *forms of expression* of our experiences with the Spirit. Rather than precipitately classifying spiritual experiences, we should rather respect the *unique* qualities attaching to each such experience. The Spirit moves not only *where* it wants, but also *how* it wants. Pneumatological grammar can accommodate the criterion of experience by acknowledging the unique features of the spiritualities and *pneuma*tologies emerging from other discourses and experiential realms while simultaneously relating these to one another from the perspective of the *one* Spirit of God.

Those who conveniently but precipitately identify *all* spirits with the Holy Spirit cut off the possibility of becoming acquainted with the variety of spiritual manifestations. Spiritual experience can come about in a bewildering variety of both human *and* nonhuman life contexts. While my reference to "spirituality from below" reinforces this insight, the criterion of experience similarly ensures that both rational-discursive *and* intuitive-artistic and other culturally specific, intracultural, and even intercultural-global modes of expressing human spirituality can maintain their uniqueness. It also ensures that we remain mindful that linguistic modes of expression are ultimately "grounded" in ecological life contexts and that we deny neither human beings nor any other creatures the capacity of spiritual experience.[59] The criterion of experience thus aims at integrating the experiences of *all* creatures with the Holy Spirit and at acknowledging the uniqueness and freedom of every creature's spiritual experience.

3. Discussions of "experiences" tend to bog down in the immediate individualism of divided subjects, as if every subject shapes its own spiritual experience. The third criterion is developed Socratically and in the context of discourse ethics with the goal of promoting a *common search for truth* as the principle of discourse concerning the various modes of expression of spiritual experience.

Pneumatology fulfills this criterion by seeking — together with other participants in pastoral-theological, academic-theological, and other ecological discourses — a common understanding of the truth manifested at the various places where the Spirit takes up habitation. Pneumatology within the context of ecological theology must, I believe, restrain itself from fleeing the pain of interpretive conflict that inevitably will emerge within Socratic dialogue and argumentation, and instead draw on the methodology of Socratic maieutic reasoning (midwifery) in interpreting that pain as a sign of the imminent birth of an age to be shared by both life and the Spirit itself (cf. Rom. 8:22f.). In connection with this criterion of a common search for truth and a special consideration of the labor pains accompanying any such birth of truth from within conflicting interpretations, I believe the biblical experience of the Spirit of truth (John 14:17; 15:26; 16:13) and of the Spirit of freedom (2 Cor. 3:17) can flow together.

4. The fourth criterion, *missiology,* refers first to the discursive consideration of the sending of the one to the other.

"Missiology" has a twofold reference. First, it refers to theologians' self-understanding insofar as theological reflection should remain mindful of its own mission to the arena of ecological discourse.

"Missiology" also refers to that particular dimension of pneumatology that emphasizes the connection — one just as "classical" as that between the Spirit and life — between Spirit and mission. Historically the Christian interpretation of life always understood the Spirit as the one sent (and allowing itself to be sent) into the world and into nature — that is, to those places where

---

59. By inquiring concerning the influence exerted by the physical environment on our language world, what I metaphorically call the "grounding" of language in the experiential world of the senses expands Whorf's thesis of language relativity that posits a connection between the language, mode of thought, worldview, and behavior of a culturally identical group.

life comes about within time. Grammatically this complex was accommodated by the use of active and passive verbal constructions expressing the notion of "sending" and "being sent" and by a variety of different prepositions. The pneumatology of ecological theology can remain mindful of this missiological criterion by addressing the question of how the one comes, whence and whither it comes, and to whom. By emphasizing the *dynamic* nature of the Spirit, the missiological criterion works against the tendency to understand the "place" of the Spirit statically and is thus of particular importance for any theological contribution to the discussion concerning the ecological places where the Spirit takes up habitation.

Similar to the theologians confined to the edifice of exclusive, specialized discourse on the Holy Spirit, the convenient identification of the spirits of the various ecological disciplines with the Spirit of theological discourse fails to recognize the spatial and positional character of the Spirit "having been sent," "being sent," and of its "sending" in Christian theological language. The pneumatological grammar of ecological theology can accommodate the missiological criterion by remaining constantly mindful of the question "whence, whither, and to whom?" and of theology's own mission to engage its discussion of the Spirit within the broader community of ecological discourse.

5. The final, fifth criterion of pneumatological grammar for ecological theology is *synthesis*. This criterion involves establishing a *connection* or *relation* between the previous four, a consideration prompted by the threat to the peace of all discourse participants posed by the increasingly challenging phenomenon of pluralism in the global community and by the monistic worship of money.[60]

The criterion of *tradition* prevents pneumatology from falling prey to traditionalism, which restricts the Creator's Spirit to the age of Christianity, and to denominational exclusivism, which restricts the Spirit of life to the community of faith. The criterion of *experience* prevents pneumatology from slipping into ecclesiocentrism, which forces the Holy Spirit of freedom into the social form of the church, and into conservatism, in which the anxieties of the present chase away the Spirit of a recollection of the Son and of liberation.

The criterion of *discursive ethics* prevents pneumatology from slipping into unreasonable isolationism that renders the very Spirit of God invisible

---

60. Concerning pluralism's challenge to theology, see Tracy 1981, ixf.; Welker 1994, 21-27; Frostin 1990; concerning the threat of economic hegemony, see Frostin 1992b and Duchrow 1995.

outside narrow theological life contexts. Finally, the criterion of *missiology* maintains the dynamic nature of the spiritual element within ecological discourse and thus prevents pneumatology from stagnating anthropocentrically within theology itself. By synthesizing these four criteria, the fifth ensures that each can be applied in a balanced, consistent, and coherent fashion.

Applying the criterion of experience to the interpretation of the texts of tradition enables us to view documents from the past as expressions of the experience of the Spirit's inhabitation at a given place that are just as viable as contemporary expressions. Applying the missiological criterion to the same interpretation of tradition enables us to inquire concerning the missiological significance of the text itself as well as concerning the potential missiological dimension of its subject matter. Applying the discursive-ethical criterion to an interpretation of tradition ensures that insights deriving from the history of reception can be integrated into the changing as well as the abiding understanding of the text commensurate with the conditions of theoretical discourse.

Pneumatological grammar can accommodate the synthetic criterion by presenting the four others as the formal criteria for all interdisciplinary-theoretical and intercontextual-practical reflection on the problem of the relation between place and Spirit; in so doing it enhances the possibility that the various — and differing — conceptions of thought and action might reach a practical consensus of the sort that, ideally, views the rich diversity and differences obtaining between the various cultural and ecological perspectives as the *presuppositions* for a peaceful search for truth rather than as potential obstacles.

Again, this brief criteriology of pneumatological grammar for ecological theology represents an outline rather than a fully developed program. Its purpose is to enhance the rational clarity and communicative possibilities of the various expressions of faith and to ensure that we can continue to speak to one another about common interests despite what are sometimes considerable cultural and natural differences. The next step, moving from grammar to pneumatology, examines how reflection on the Spirit functions in a theology of liberation.

The "Life of the Coming World": Ecological Pneumatology of Liberation

What is the function and significance of pneumatology in the context of an ecological theology of liberation? Previous theologies that have focused systematically on the theme of liberation have largely developed their initiatives from the perspective of creation theology and Christology rather than pneumatology.[61] What can pneumatology contribute to cosmology as soteriology?

The Nicene Creed mentions the Spirit who works in a fashion similar to the Lord, and who gives life as well as the eternal life of the world to come. In this section I relate from the perspective of an ecological theology of liberation the "vitalist" and eschatological dimensions of the interpretation of the Spirit's activity as articulated in the third article of the Nicene Creed.

After addressing one particular misunderstanding of trinitarian soteriology and then shifting our focus away from the question of the mediation of God and world through the Spirit to how God as the Father liberates places in the world through the Son in the Spirit, I can establish a counterpart to the understanding of the relation between God and world within time. Finally I will summarize my pneumatological outline in eleven characteristic features of an ecological theology of the Spirit as liberator of nature.

The Misunderstanding of the Spirit as Mediator of God and World   One widespread understanding of the salvific work of the triune God in the world emphasizes the Spirit's function in creation in mediating between God and world, a notion illustrated graphically in the form of two intersecting ellipses:

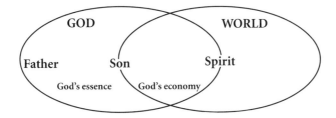

God's essence is on the left, his work and economy in the middle, the world on the right. The Father sends the Son into the world from the "worldless" area of the divine being, of the Father. The Spirit is active in the area common to both God and world, mediating between the two and expanding its own space successively to include the "godless" area of the world.

Examples of this understanding include Wendebourg's summary of her research on the concept of Spirit and energy within the Byzantine tradition.

---

61. Pneumatological initiatives can be found in Sobrino 1988; Gutiérrez 1986, 64-83; Comblin 1987; Boff 1995, 49f.

In coining the concept of God's "external reference," she maintains that in fourth-century theology trinitarian being and trinitarian action corresponded relationally such that "God's external reference" actually "corresponded in a trinitarian fashion to his being."[62] Expressed metaphorically in our graphic schema above: whereas the areas of the divine and worldly being remain separated, the Father, Son, *and* Spirit are all active in the area of the economy.

I am still not quite clear what "external" means in her expression "external reference." Is creation somehow located spatially outside the Creator? Theologically the distinction between God's internal and external reality does not really make much sense. "External" and "internal" are spatial concepts suggesting some sort of "dividing area" that — as we saw above — can be reconciled neither with the double cosmological perspective of ancient church theology nor with the modern understanding of the world in terms of open space.

Liberation theology also includes examples of this problematical understanding of space in connection with trinitarian soteriology. In his book on the Spirit, Comblin evokes the notion of the two intersecting ellipses in speaking about the movement of the giving, living, and loving Spirit: "The Spirit comes at the end of movement in God, but [at] the beginning of God's going-out to creation. It is at the start of creation's road back to the Father."[63] What does it mean to say that "the Spirit comes at the end of movement in God"? Does God somehow go out of himself and into the world that is otherwise essentially alien to him? Are the world and God utterly and completely different in this view? Comblin seems to fall prey to the same notion as Wendebourg, namely, that the Spirit's activity takes place in a kind of interstice between God and world.

Although this spatially rather vague and thus problematical notion and mode of expression is widespread and for that reason may seem self-evident, it combines the Johannine reference to the Spirit going out from the Father (John 15:26) with the Nicene reference to the Spirit giving life such that the Spirit going *out* from the Father is understood as the Spirit going *into* the world, an interpretation obviously presupposing rather unclearly that the Father's place is in fact a different one from that of the world and that the Spirit moves from the one to the other.[64]

62. Wendebourg 1980, 239.

63. Comblin 1987, 186.

64. Moltmann 2001b, 47-51, adduces the Jewish notion of Shekinah in dealing with the spatial problem of the Spirit's indwelling. Moltmann understands the Shekinah as God's presence in the world at a specific place and time. But does his reference (48) to God's "de-

The Gospel of John speaks about the Son who will send the Spirit and who was himself sent (John 16:5-15). Gregory passed along to the future the Johannine reference to the Spirit "going out," speaking of it as that which "went out" from the Father before time just as the Son was "born" of the Father. There is *no* reference in the tradition of the ancient church to God "going out" into creation in the modern sense of the spatial movement of a self out of itself or in the modern sense of "entry" into a mechanistically understood space from some supernatural place.

This whole notion presupposes the modern understanding of the subject that since Descartes has defined its "self" through separation from its surroundings — which it is constantly constituting — and that then projected this division onto its understanding of God. The modern idea that in the Spirit (Hegel) God somehow enters as *part of his Self* into the world he has created can be reconciled neither with classical Eastern theology nor with the premises of ecological thinking, and for that reason I reject it in this context.[65] This supranaturalistic-personalistic understanding of God as an otherworldly Self that reveals that Self to the world in the Spirit is much too indebted to the modern understanding of human beings themselves and as such sooner divides than relates ontology and soteriology, that is, the interpretation of the divine activities of creation and redemption.

Response: In the Spirit through the Son to the Father at the Place of Ecological Liberation   My response to the metaphor of "two spaces" begins with three assumptions in relating the space of creation to the Creator in a different, spatially more differentiated fashion.

1. God consummates his trinitarian liberation of creation — the coming into being of "all in all" through and in God — within a *common*, shared history with creatures.[66] The space of liberation is creation within time. Here is where the "uninterrupted revelation of God" takes place.[67]

2. God appears as the God of sending and movement. Because God's ac-

---

scent" and "habitation" not presuppose that the divine Spirit is actually coming from outside and above the world? Berger 1984, 180, reminds us that the "system" of the New Testament's understanding of reality was quite different from our own and that reality is defined "qualitatively according to nearness or distance from God as the creative center of life."

65. Concerning Hegel's metaphysical concept of the Spirit, see Welker 1994, 289-95.

66. Following the lead of Aagaard 1974, 116: "The trinitarian process — or God's becoming 'all in all' (cf. 1 Cor. 15:22-28) — is consummated not in the depths of his Self, but rather within God's common history with human beings."

67. Aulén 1927, 379. Aulén understands faith in the living God as faith in the Spirit, where "Spirit" refers to the "perpetually present character of divine revelation."

tion and essence are one, he acts as he is. The movement of the triune Spirit appears in the history of the cross and liberation of nature.[68]

3. Creatures' understanding of the world and God reflects the space of action from whose depths God variously appears to creatures. The "area" of God's essence coincides with his area of action in the world. Although the assumption of a boundary *in* God contradicts the traditional Christian understanding of God, this consideration does not necessarily exclude the assumption and experience of a *qualitative* distance between God and creature. Through his essence, however, God also encompasses those spaces that are visible to creatures as spaces of action, and does so insofar as he "hyperwidens" those spaces.[69] The variety of the divine Spirit's modes of appearance and spaces of action in the world points to precisely this "expanded scope and breadth of his essence." Whenever God and creatures approach and encounter one another, a common space of action emerges in which within its liberating history creation becomes a new creation.

Trinitarian soteriology understands the space of creation within time from the perspective of this movement from the old to the new creation. Three circles illustrate this understanding (see diagram on p. 317).

In this salvific-historical schema, the spaces of the divine economy coincide with those of the liberation of creation and yet are transcended by the Creator.

This schema understands the liberation of creation such that nature, instead of moving from itself *toward* God, moves together *with* God in the Spirit toward its consummation in time. In trinitarian terms: the triune God — Spirit, Son, and Father — moves in qualitatively different ways in, through, and with creation. In the beginning it moves as the origin of the world; then within its history it moves as preserver, in the Son in the flesh, in the Spirit through multifarious inhabitations; and at the end it moves as the renewal of all life. An ecological pneumatology of liberation thus focuses on God's movement within creation as expressed in the formula "in the Spirit through the Son to the Father at the place where creatures are set free."

By understanding the being of the world as a being in need of liberation

---

68. Cf. Aagaard 1973, 264.

69. Contra Rahner, whose "axiom" of the identity of the internal and external, immanent and economic Trinity violates the apophatic principle insofar as it allows logical conclusions from the economic to the immanent. The only conclusion we are allowed to draw with regard to God's essence is that God is as he acts, a conclusion that does not however exclude the possibility that God may well be more than our perception of his actions divulges. This is why I speak about the "hyperwidening" of the "area" of the divine essence in relation to the areas of action creatures can experience.

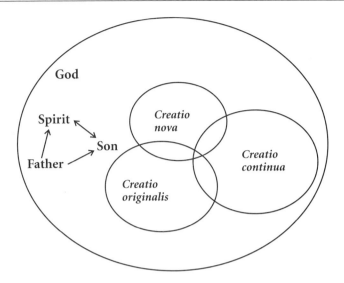

by the Creator, this schema maintains the distinction between ontology and soteriology. It is in its being from and with God that the world contains the possibility of this liberation; it does not contain such a possibility inherently within itself. The source of the church's catholicity ultimately is creation itself and its eschatological new becoming.[70]

Our thesis of God's "hyperwidening" of life and our understanding of time prevent us from identifying life with God as do Birch and Cobb. An ecological pneumatology of liberation must be mindful not to misunderstand the notion of "the emergence of life" within time as being value-free or deterministic or dependent on chance, and must instead interpret this process of liberation from the perspective of the *unity of time,* classically known as God's "eternity." In a proto-eschatological fashion, this soteriology thus presupposes not only the unity of humankind and history, but also that of the history of nature.[71]

70. Here I am following the lead of Yves Congar; Volf 1998, 276. Schreiter 1997, 218-26, advocates a contextually considered, expanded understanding of the catholicity of the church in the current context of globalization. Here he develops further Wiedenhofer's understanding of catholicity as "totality and fullness through exchange and communication," which anticipates that in the future the concept of catholicity will include the ecological relatedness of *all* creatures and will itself be qualified soteriologically.

71. Images of unity often (and easily) take on absolutistic features. I believe metaphorical absolutism is a sign of cosmological reductionism that can be avoided by way of a whole series of images and conceptions. Contra McFague's understanding of the universal image of

Characteristic Features of an Ecological Theology of the Spirit as Liberator of Nature

In conclusion I present eleven characteristic features summarizing the ecological theology of the Spirit as liberator of nature in the form of brief theses addressing theology, ecology, the theology of the cross, pluralism, soteriology, proto-eschatology, epistemology, metaphorology, practical ethics, aesthetics, and the *ecumene.*

1. The Spirit that sets nature free is the triune God; the Spirit is one in essence with the Father and Son, and the three together act in perfect community.

2. With respect to the activity of the Holy Spirit, the glassy essence of places emerges as the place of the Spirit's inhabitation.

3. The Spirit who is and acts as one with the Father and Son appears to the subjects of these places as the Spirit who is "turned toward the world" and is "visible in the cross and in suffering" (Luther). Suffering creatures are thus accorded preeminence in recognizing and articulating the pathic modes of the Spirit's appearance. Because the inhabitation of the Spirit continues the incarnation of the Son — God's earthly act of love for the world — all ecological perception of the transparency of the places where the Spirit has indeed taken up habitation actually consists in perceiving the "fleshly corporeality" of its activity.

4. The multiplicity of the modes of the divine Spirit's appearance in time and space *refers* us both to the unity of time and space of humankind and nature and to the unity of the divine being itself. An understanding of the multiplicity of the Spirit's various modes of appearance constitutes an integral part of any representation of the theology of liberation.

5. "Liberation" means liberation from something, to something, and through something. Under the conditions of pneumatological grammar, cosmology can be understood as soteriology in the following conceptual figure: through their cooperation with the Holy Spirit, the ecology and evolution of nature are led out of bondage to the power of evil and into creaturely freedom.[72] It is not the *being* of the universe that is ethical; it is the spiritual or "mental model" (Bateson) that contributes soteriologically to liberation.

---

the divine body, I prefer a multiplicity of images for expressing the Spirit's activity in, with, and through nature. To avoid the epistemological danger of absolutistic world metaphors, I have in connection with the dialogue between the natural sciences and theology proposed applying the apophatic principle of human reason's self-limitation regarding knowledge of the divine to include our knowledge of nature as well; Bergmann 1993b, 330f., a problem I will address in the last chapter (6) below.

6. The synergy of the Spirit and nature transcends the telos (final goal) of ecology and evolution in a way that would not otherwise be possible. The teleology of nature and the eschatology of the Spirit are nonetheless able to work together because the teleological quality of nature itself actually represents an expression of the creative activity of the triune Spirit within time.

Protology and eschatology are inseparable in an ecological pneumatology of liberation, which must strive to *actualize* the classical symbol of the Spirit that not only gives life but *also* summons the new age; because the Spirit does indeed finish what it begins, the creative Spirit that sets nature free also brings about the consummation of all things within the whole.[73]

7. One cannot simply identify the spirit of evolution and ecology with the Holy Spirit and as such with the triune God. We can just as little discern the essence of the Spirit from our understanding of nature as we can discern the essence of nature from our understanding of the divine Spirit. If we are to discern the activity of the powers of nature *and* of the divine Spirit clearly, we must remain ever mindful of the apophatic principle of the self-limitation of reason as regards our consideration of the essence of *both* nature *and* God.

I would suggest that if we are to emphasize the proto-eschatological dimension of our understanding of the Spirit that gives life and summons the new creation more clearly than has hitherto been the case, we must also develop our overall understanding of the kingdom of God in the light of the ecology of the Spirit envisioned above.

This ecological interpretation of the reign of the Spirit can also resolve Bateson's dilemma. Rather than understanding the Spirit from the perspective of evolution (Butler, Lamarck, Bateson) or evolution from the perspective of the Spirit (Darwin), we must realize that the characteristic features of the reign of the Spirit are precisely that God's Holy Spirit and

72. Daneel 1993 shows how that which is expressed in this rather broadly formulated sentence acquires genuine earthly form. Examining the function of pneumatology in the African Independent Church in Zimbabwe, he shows how the "holistic interpretation of the Holy Spirit's comprehensive involvement in all of life" prevents the prophets of the church from falling prey to the one-sided soteriology of a future, otherworldly redemption of souls (166). He also shows how universal earthly pneumatology leads African liberation theology to refer to the Spirit that heals, liberates, and preserves the earth. In Zimbabwe this "applied" pneumatology fosters the church's sociopolitical and ecological-political positions and actions. Daneel, 162f., adopts Moltmann's (1985) understanding of the immanence of the Spirit and also follows Duchrow and Liedke's (1989, 165) understanding of the suffering and hope of creation.

73. Cf. Moltmann 1996, chap. 4, p. 4, on the eschatology of the space of creation.

the spiritual powers of thought and evolution *together* bring about the renewal of creation.

8. Reference to the "glassy essence of places" shifts the focus of pneumatology to the *places* where the forces of nature work together and where the divine Spirit itself appears and acts.[74]

9. This shift creates room in both ecological theology and the theology of liberation for a perception of and reflection on the Spirit as liberator of nature, thereby making it possible to connect the discourses of ecological theology and liberation theology.

The same shift provides pastoral and contextual methodologies with a new measure of representational freedom in drawing, for example, on models of semiotic-synergistic conceptions of action. It similarly provides theological contributions to the interdisciplinary environmental discussion with a critical tool in their encounter both with the ecosophical grounding of a new, more comprehensive discipline and with the unfortunate pragmatic reductionism of concepts that may utterly lack vision. This shift also provides a new systematic grounding for normative-ethical concepts of action that through correlation with the classical pneumatological tradition can then substantively inform the church's choices regarding its bioethical position and actions.

10. Distinguishing between (a) creaturely experience in the encounter with the Spirit, (b) spiritualities and their various modes of expression, (c) *pneuma*tologies, and (d) pneumatological grammar clarifies the parameters of discursive rationality insofar as the theology outlined here together with its grammar is able to address only that which is theoretically "crystalline" (Simmel), that is, fixed elements of our life experiences and life views.

74. Cf. Hodgson 1994, 291f., who similarly speaks about but in my opinion overly distinguishes between the Spirit's work of liberation and consummation. I would object that by subordinating the Spirit's person to its activity ("the person of the Spirit is formed by the work of the Spirit," 292), he contradicts the classical doctrine of the Spirit and also fails to distinguish between the *person* of the Spirit and its experiential *mode of appearance*. I also object to his defining the liberation of the world as "the whole process of the return of the world from alienated otherness and separateness to its end in divine life" (291f.), because his reference to "return" presupposes a circular understanding of time that classical cosmic soteriology and evolutionary science have surpassed. In the larger sense, his methodological emphasis on the particle "re-" (revisioning theology, reconstruction, restructuring theology, return) presumably suggests that every new interpretation and creative theological initiative remains normatively bound to the author's and church's interpretation of tradition. Does this emphasis on the *re*constructive element not suggest rather that tradition has become more of a "pastiche" than genuinely creative transmission, that is, more imitation than interpretation?

We must necessarily enter the sphere of practical aesthetics if we are to perceive, articulate, and understand the connection between all three spheres. Establishing a practical-theological aesthetics of the Holy Spirit would however considerably expand ecological theology's horizon of question and answer and can only be intimated here as a task yet to be addressed.

11. Because the ecological theology outlined here has been developed from ecological-discursive and pastoral-contextual perspectives as well as in correlation with tradition, it could quite conceivably help address the dilemma of Christ's church, whose global representatives met in Canberra in 1991 with a summons for the coming of the Spirit that renews creation and yet at the same time ran aground in the doxology and in indignation at the inclusive theology of the Spirit.[75] The inclusive soteriological focus of the ecological theology of liberation could also enable the ecumenical movement to exert a practical influence on the changing understanding of nature in modernity.

If the same impulse is driving modernity's changing understanding of nature *and* the ecumenical movement, the conditions for developing a pneumatological ecological theology of liberation seem right, though demonstrating as much must be left up to the reader, since it transcends the capacity of this individual book. The characteristics enumerated above intend merely to provide some presuppositions for recognizing once more the Spirit as liberator of nature and for reasonably articulating our experiences with that Spirit's activity.

75. Concerning an inclusive, ecologically grounded theology of the Spirit, cf. Chung Hyung Kyung 1991. Because no theology becomes real without concrete representatives, and because I could never have written this book without having encountered such concrete representatives, the subjunctive form "could help address" is probably better understood to mean that this theology is indeed already growing "from below" and in that sense has already long served the liberation of nature at the places of the Spirit's inhabitation. The purpose of this present section was to create the theoretical presuppositions for expressing and reflecting upon this spirituality and its theology academically. Accounts of the places where God's Spirit sets the creatures of nature free include: Paul, Rom. 8:22f. (concerning the Spirit who cries for liberation with the Christians in Rome and with the entirety of creation); Kyung (concerning the Korean woman in a Christian basis group in which the Spirit "does much that is good"); Nash 1991, 11-17, 111-16 (concerning the milieu of his childhood in western Pennsylvania, which was destroyed by the steel industry, and concerning the notion of the Spirit's sacramental presence); Santmire 1994, 18ff., 25 (concerning the poorest of the poor in the USA in Asylum Hill and their experiences with "urban justice"); and Hornborg 1994b (concerning the spirituality of place among the Canadian Mikmaq Indians).

CHAPTER 6

Methodological Considerations

Where has our correlation of the interpretations of the liberation of creation brought us? In this concluding chapter I will examine methodologically our findings and the problems still needing attention. The concept of "method/ methodology," deriving from Greek *meta* and *hodos* (way or path to something), refers etymologically to setting out deliberately on a certain path within time.[1]

The contextual paradigm of theology suggests positioning methodological considerations at the *end* rather than at the beginning of our path. Now that we have followed this path of correlation through the landscape of the various theological understandings of nature, what is the methodological yield of our journey? I will first examine the history of the method of correlation in contemporary theology. What can this method accomplish? What can it not accomplish? I will then examine the criterion of tradition. Anyone correlating the past with the present should also provide a precise definition of what is meant by "tradition"; unfortunately contextual theology often neglects precisely this problem. Finally I will discuss why the classical apophatic principle as developed in the Cappadocian tradition of the ancient church can be of methodological use to an ecological theology of liberation as the latter charts its course into "new modernity" and engages in dialogue with the environmental sciences and with other religions.

1. Cf. Gutiérrez 1986, 150, who understands "method" as setting out on the path of discipleship to Christ. One might criticize Gutiérrez insofar as his thesis that reflection on God is (only?) possible for confessing Christians in discipleship risks excluding and isolating theological discourse within a context of pluralistic worldviews. Methodology does not *constitute* spirituality, it only reflects on the problems of the various theological forms of expression.

1. An Assessment of the Method of Correlation

History of the Method

The Concept

The term "correlation" refers to a mutual relationship, a connection in which one is necessarily and mutually related to another. Theologically both Jewish and Christian thinkers make use of such correlation.[2] In developing the concept in the historical sciences, Troeltsch enumerated the three basic categories of the historical-critical method, namely, criticism, analogy, and correlation. He understood the continuity of history as a correlative developmental context.[3]

The methodological application of correlation in theology derives from the nineteenth-century theology of mediation, which tried to mediate between Schleiermacher's emphasis on religious experience and the principle of scriptural exegesis.[4] More recently Paul Tillich and David Tracy have applied the method of correlation within systematic theology.[5]

"Correlation" in Paul Tillich

For Tillich the term "correlation" has three different meanings: statistical, logical, and real, designating "the real interdependence of things or events in structural wholes." He finds correlation between "religious symbols and that which is symbolized by them," "between concepts denoting the human and

---

2. Concerning correlation in Jewish theology, see Piepmeier 1976. It is also used in connection with geometry and statistical mathematics. Cf. *Historisches Wörterbuch der Philosophie* 4 (Basel and Stuttgart, 1976), 1141f.

3. Sauter 1973, 171-75.

4. Concerning the theology of mediation, see Holte 1965.

5. Apart from Tillich and Tracy, in Catholic theology F. Schüssler Fiorenza 1991, 55-59, addresses Schillebeeckx's correlation of the four principles of the tradition of Christian experience with the experience of modern utilitarian individualism, Küng's critical confrontation of the living Jesus with the contemporary situation, and Ruether's correlation involving the prophetic principle in traditions and texts. In Protestant theology one can also mention Moltmann's hermeneutical method of integrating the identity and relevance of faith. In religio-theological anthropology, Panikkar uses the term against the modernist understanding of the subject in emphasizing the inseparable connection between a person's inner life of faith and his or her external reality, discerning a "positive and strict correlation between genuine subjectivity and true objectivity" (1993, 29).

those denoting the divine," and "between man's ultimate concern and that about which he is ultimately concerned."[6] In Tillich's definition of the method of correlation, systematic theology "makes an analysis of the human situation out of which the existential questions arise, and it demonstrates that the symbols used in the Christian message are the answers to these questions."[7]

Tillich intends for this method to preempt three "inadequate" theological methods: (1) the "supranaturalistic," which "takes the Christian message to be a sum of revealed truths which have fallen into the human situation like strange bodies from a strange world"; (2) the "naturalistic" or "humanistic," which "derives the Christian message from man's natural state," "unaware that human existence itself *is* the question"; and (3) the "dualistic," which with the "self-contradictory" notion of "natural revelation" "builds a supranatural structure on a natural substructure."[8]

Tillich thus takes "correlation" to refer to the mutual relationship between the questions of our situation and the answers offered by the Christian faith. In so doing, he prepares the way for the development of contextual theology since the 1960s. By making God's self-revelation dependent (contra Barth) on the mode of the human reception of that revelation, he declares that theology's first step is to *analyze* human existence and the human situation. Moreover, by polarizing question (situation) and answer (tradition), he fails to consider that *every* form of expression of the Christian message is also shaped by the historic situation of its origin.

"Correlation" in David Tracy

Tracy closely follows Tillich's lead in developing a method of "mutually critical" correlation using Ogden's two criteria of "appropriateness to the tradition" and "intelligibility to the situation." Following Max Weber's model of interaction, Tracy develops a theological model of correlation between tradition and situation and also speaks about the correlations between theory and praxis constituting the interpretive process.[9]

The two poles of correlation in this view are tradition and situation. Tracy's hermeneutical method advocates an open presentation of the interpretive process and exhibits three salient features:

6. Tillich 1951, 60.
7. Tillich 1951, 62.
8. Tillich 1951, 64f.
9. Tracy 1981, 25; 1986, 238.

1. The correlation between situation and tradition is to be understood as a logical category that can lead to an identity of the two, to an analogy of similarity in dissimilarity, or to a confrontation of the two.
2. The interpretation of correlation is critically two-sided insofar as both tradition and situation provide questions and answers.
3. The method of correlation consciously tries to be an interpretive process ultimately related to praxis.

Tracy draws on the concept of correlation in his general definition of theology: "theology is the attempt to establish mutually critical correlations between an interpretation of the Christian tradition and an interpretation of the contemporary situation."[10]

Tracy goes beyond Tillich in understanding correlation hermeneutically as a "model of conversation."[11] Rather than being separated, questions and answers arise from within both tradition and the current situation. Unlike Küng and Ruether, who elevate the "living Jesus" or the "prophetic principle" to the criterion of correlation, Tracy emphasizes the Christ attested in the creed and the normative nature of the apostolic scriptural witness.[12]

Three Critical Objections

Francis Schüssler Fiorenza has raised the following three critical and, in my judgment, justified objections to the method of correlation.

1. By distinguishing between reality and the reality expressed in language, the method of correlation diminishes the significance of the historicity of language and culture. The assumption is that although language and culture change, the reality expressed there does not; it can then be correlated.
2. By overemphasizing the continuity and identity of faith, the method of correlation does not adequately consider the elements of change and nonidentity inhering within the development of faith and theology. Schüssler Fiorenza advocates understanding tradition in terms of the categories of change.

10. Tracy 1985, 36; cf. 1986, 234.
11. Tracy 1985, 38-43.
12. Tracy 1981, 300f.

3. The method of correlation ignores the necessary criticism of tradition.[13]

The Method of Correlation in the Present Study

What have our experiences been with the method of correlation in the present study? My application of correlation did not of course begin with Tillich's apologetic method; I did not present the theological tradition of the Cappadocian church father as an *answer* to the theological questions raised by the situation of ecological challenge. Nor is Gregory's theology intended to provide norms for the contemporary development of ecological theology.[14] Nor did I choose Gregory's writings based on previous knowledge of what the Christian tradition is or based on some notion of the normative nature of the theological classics. Instead Gregory's theology represented a theological understanding of the world shaped within a local theology. I did not seek out "the" Christian tradition in Gregory's writings and then correlate that tradition with our contemporary situation. Instead I examined Gregory as the representative of a local theology whose views must be understood both in connection with his situational context as well as with the "social memory" of the Christian tradition during his age, a tradition whose Eastern and Western representatives were already ascribing considerable significance to his theology during his lifetime.

My application of the method of correlation differs from that of Tracy's model. Instead of relating tradition and situation, I relate the local theology deriving from a *single* situation (in late antiquity) to various local theologies deriving from a *different* situation (in late modernity), presupposing that the Christian tradition — as the social memory of interpretations of faith — will come to expression in both poles of the correlation.

The point of this study has been to convince the reader that such correlation can meaningfully disclose new perspectives on contemporary questions and answers; its point was certainly not to demonstrate the normative

---

13. F. Schüssler Fiorenza 1991, 61.

14. In ascribing a normative function to patristics, Zizioulas 1985, 20, focuses on facilitating a rediscovery of the "authentic patristic synthesis" by both Eastern and Western churches and outlines the project of a "neopatristic synthesis capable of leading the West and the East nearer to their common roots in the context of the existential question of modern man" (26). I am concerned here neither with assessing the Eastern authors as fathers of confessional church histories nor with assessing a "patristically" developed initiative in the context of modernity of the sort confessional Orthodox theology is seeking today.

nature of Gregory's theology or even the sustainable unity — however essentially conceived — of the Christian tradition in the larger sense, which is why I also subjected Gregory's position to criticism from the perspective of contemporary thinking.

I drew attention to the background of the Cappadocian's theology in late antiquity to avoid Tracy's dilemma of presupposing the essential continuity of tradition while simultaneously trying to demonstrate that same continuity. Within my overall study, considerations of scope require that this chapter function merely heuristically. Those who would develop the method of correlation further should concentrate on this point in addressing the problem of correlating not only theologies, but especially situations.

One particularly valuable experience involved the problem of identifying questions within the two sets of materials. A correlation that merely relates the theology of one epoch with that of another in a general, overriding sense, or only by adducing various themes and "motifs," risks violating the first two critical objections enumerated above.

One criterion that any method of correlation must fulfill is identifying a *common* problem in the two interpretations, a point Tracy's expresses by insisting that both interpretations share a common object of interpretation, that is, the religious symbol.[15] Such reference to a common object, however, does not suffice insofar as the mere observation that, for example, Gregory and Cobb both interpret the symbol of liberation certainly does not yet establish that both were addressing the same problem — which is why I was concerned with demonstrating that both Cobb and Gregory were addressing the problem of sociality. Hence any meaningful and successful application of the method of correlation necessarily presupposes that both poles are concerned with a substantively common problem.[16]

Yet another presupposition for any successful problem-oriented correlation is that one correlate the *situations* of the two interpretations. It certainly does not suffice merely to assert that because the general situation of an

---

15. Tracy 1985, 35. Concerning the criticism of Tillich's theory of symbols — on which Tracy also depends — see Jeffner 1972, 56-60.

16. This demand for theological answers to focus in a rigorous, substantive fashion on the questions of the past and present also characterizes Christian theology's reception of the philosophy of antiquity. Cf. in this regard Blumenberg 1959, 487: "The point is to acquire an appealable 'reality' . . . Christianity had to establish some *contact* with the world lest it lose the simple capacity for discussion within it . . . it turned everything in the [non-Christian] tradition into a *question* to which it purportedly had a ready *answer*. Because everything new must be able to function as an 'answer,' its content must identify the 'questions' presupposed in that older material and must be able to render them both relevant and urgent."

earlier century so closely resembles that of the present, one can simply deduce constructions normatively applicable to the present from an interpretation of the past.[17]

A correlation of situations must articulate not only the similarity between the two situations, but also — and especially — their differences. Only by remaining mindful of how two contexts *differ* can one objectively assess the potential value the answers articulated by one local theology may have for developing answers with regard to another, different one.

In conclusion, let me mention the significance of the temporal sequence of correlation, which in the present study proceeded through five stages.

1. The first stage consisted in an examination of the situation of ecological theology in late modernity (chap. 1) and of the situation of Cappadocian theology (chap. 2).
2. The second examined Gregory's questions and answers (chap. 3).
3. The third examined the answers of contemporary theologians (chap. 4).
4. The fourth juxtaposed in a mutually critical fashion the various questions and answers of these theologians with regard to the four points of the "problem community" (chap. 4).
5. The fifth stage examined and qualified from the perspective of liberation theology this correlation of theologies from late antiquity and late modernity with regard to the four points.

I implemented the first stage, the correlation of situations, at the beginning of the study so that both author and reader might remain aware of the differences attaching to the various theological positions and of their respective contextual ties. Any correlation that truncates or dispenses with this stage risks degenerating into idealistic analogy.

At the fourth stage, it seemed prudent to identify the various problems in a separate section to render as plausible as possible why and how this concern with a common problem comes to expression in the two interpretations. One must first demonstrate exactly what establishes the community — the shared nature — of questioning, something that admittedly only the method itself constitutes and reconstructs, before the mutual interplay of responses can really bear fruit commensurate with the conditions of the question at issue. That is, one must persuasively demonstrate the shared concern before

---

17. So Wingren 1983, 9f.; because he recognizes in the contemporary century the gnostic adversary of Christianity in the third century, he believes he can ascribe normative status to his own interpretation of Irenaeus's theology for contemporary theology.

any subsequent establishment and examination of the correlation of answers can be meaningful. The continuity of this concern for a common question ultimately proved to be a stimulating presupposition both for a more substantive development of the correlation and for liberation theology in general.

In this sense the method of correlation represents a kind of "hermeneutical labor," albeit one in which *only* under the previously enumerated conditions can one successfully disclose new, broader perspectives with regard to the questions and answers posed by the current situation. By subjecting situations, questions, and answers to precisely this sort of mutually critical interaction that relates the past and the present and thereby establishes new presuppositions for the future, I do believe the method of correlation can participate in the transmission of the Christian faith. By thereby demonstrating that substantive issues from the past can be rendered of service to both the present and the future, the method of correlation also shows how temporal modalities are intertwined: through precisely such correlation, both past and future become present.

Insofar as its form is objectively oriented toward specific problems, the method of correlation also accommodates the rational demands made on any hermeneutical undertaking. I do not believe, however, that this method can really fulfill Tillich's demand that the symbols of the Christian tradition be presented as answers to the existential questions of the current situation. Those responding *theologically* to the current situation must move beyond correlation itself, since ideally it merely discloses new perspectives on the various questions and answers. Although we must thus draw from *other* methodologies in developing the answers, correlation can certainly supply valuable presuppositions. Living communities of believers must create these answers at the actual places of faith's experience, answers that must be examined in open discourse. Theology's function is to provide the *instruments of query* for the community of believers.

To encourage reflection on these experiences as well as a mindful approach to the rationality of their various modes of expression, and to help lay the groundwork for subsequent, reasonable theological reconstruction, I expanded this correlation (chap. 4) by qualifying ecological theology itself from the perspective of the theology of liberation (chap. 5). Although the method of correlation can contribute to the ongoing transmission of the Christian message — that is, to its contemporary continuity — I do not believe, as Tracy apparently does, that it can demonstrate the unity of this tradition's continuity.

2. The Criterion of Tradition in Contextual Theology

The method of correlation creates presuppositions for transmitting our experiences, modes of expressions, and reflections on God's actions. Using this method bestows on past documents a measure of authority that must constantly be subjected to critical examination. Otherwise the correlation merely represents an extension of the present into the past and ultimately derives from its own interpretation of the past normative claims for the future.

Theologians have understood tradition criticism in different ways over the course of history. The Reformation corrected the understanding of tradition during its own age by means of the principle of *sola scriptura*. Current Catholic discussion subjects tradition to criticism as something static, as something in demise, or as something in ongoing development. Liberation theology uses the tradition of the oppressed as a critical corrective to the interpretation of the Christian tradition.[18]

My question here is how one can understand the concept of tradition such that it serves as a *positive criterion* of contextual theology.[19] A successful application of the method of correlation in constructing local theologies requires that one first determine the content of tradition and its formal function within the methodology of contextual theology.

In the following discussion I will demonstrate both the necessity and the significance of accommodating the criterion of tradition when engaging in any contextual theology. My earlier correlation of Gregory's trinitarian cosmology with the ecological theology of liberation provides an example of how the interpretation of the tradition of one *specific* local theology can enhance the construction of a *different* one. Which concept of tradition best serves not only the specific kind of ecological theology envisioned here, but also contextual theology in general?

Beginning with Robert J. Schreiter's understanding of tradition as a "series of local theologies," I will then draw on Walter Benjamin's materialist understanding of history in distinguishing between the history of victors and

18. Gutiérrez 1991, xvi, mentions the dialogue "between history and history" in which the situation of the oppressed shapes biblical exegesis and biblical exegesis itself is then able to throw new light on the situation. Concerning the biblical interpretation of Latin American liberation theology, cf. Johnson 1984. McAfee Brown 1978, 87, offers a differentiated and academically and pastorally useful schema for clarifying the relationship between the interpreter, the others, the context, text, and historical context. Cf. Frostin 1992b, 129f.

19. Concerning the content and history of the concept of tradition, see Wiedenhofer 1990. Concerning the concept itself and for a thorough introduction to the theory and praxis of contextual theology, see Bergmann 2003.

that of victims, showing how a recollection of the suffering and "tradition of the oppressed" characterizes Christian tradition. Identifying the "birth pangs of nature" provides a hermeneutical key for articulating the tradition of the oppressed past of nature. This procedure can contextually shape one's understanding of ecological theology and address the challenge of linking tradition and modernity anew.[20]

Tradition as the Social Memory of a Series of Local Theologies

In understanding the church tradition as a "series of local theologies" corresponding to variously obtaining cultural conditions, Schreiter distinguishes four theological forms of expression: variations of a sacred text, wisdom, pure knowledge, and praxis.[21] All these forms emerge commensurate with the conditions of the attendant cultural context. For example, the discipline of theology emerged during a period of social upheaval that was urbanizing the agrarian economy and in so doing also creating the conditions in which more specialized functions necessary for a complex society could be developed at the institution of the university.

Schreiter describes the relation between tradition and culture as a dialectical interplay in which a local theology can emerge,[22] with theology drawing its themes from an analysis of the cultural situation and from various documents of culture. The analysis of tradition gives rise to a series of local theologies commensurate with the needs of the specific contexts. Any local Christian theology must somehow be connected with the larger Christian tradition. Although the tradition naturally influences the development of any local theology, each local theology also influences tradition by both forgetting and recalling anew and by providing its own contribution toward the future. A local theology also enduringly influences its attendant cultural situation. Culture and tradition thus mutually shape and influence one another, though they can certainly mutually change one another as well.

Schreiter assumes that tradition contributes to human society in a general sense by providing sources of identity, a system of communication fostering coherence and continuity, and the possibility of accommodating innova-

---

20. Gabriel 1991, 71, shows how what is currently understood as a "break in tradition" represents the dissolution of a certain, historical form of the intertwining of tradition and modernity. A revised version of the following discussion of tradition can be found in chapter 3 of my book *God in Context* (1997a = 2003).

21. Schreiter 1985, 80-93.

22. Schreiter 1985, 25.

tion.[23] He develops his theory linguistically by applying to the Christian tradition Noam Chomsky's distinction between "competence" and "performance" as well as Chomsky's "generative grammar."[24] In this view "tradition" refers to "the entire language system," with "faith" then corresponding to "language competence," theology and the various expressions of tradition to "language performance," and the "loci of orthodoxy" to the grammar that mediates between competence and performance.[25] Schreiter thus understands tradition as a language system containing more than merely unarticulated faith, the loci of orthodoxy, and the history of theology. The competence of faith, the performance of theologies, and the grammar of orthodoxy mutually shape one another. On the other hand, one should not misunderstand Schreiter's "loci of orthodoxy" statically or as rules fixed in scripture. The grammar of tradition is also subject to change.

One possible criticism of Schreiter's theory is that one can probably not draw a parallel between the language competence of a culture and the competence of faith without some qualification. Not only does the competence of faith include both linguistic *and* artistic modes of expression whose transmission follows different patterns, but in a situation of "secularization" the relation between the language competence of a cultural context and the competence of faith is simply too laden with conflict. It would probably be more meaningful to speak of a parallel between the competence of religious language and the competence of "other" languages.

Schreiter's theory also fails to clarify just how theological performances and the development of grammar mutually influence one another. Although we have a fairly good idea of how, for example, Gregory's pneumatology influenced the council, how did the "grammar of the council" then influence the development of additional "local *pneuma*tologies"? Schreiter's theory also contributes little to the problem of determining the significance of tradition in supporting claims of ecclesiastical authority.

Despite these objections, three considerations militate in favor of adopting Schreiter's concept of tradition.

1. First, it excludes the kind of static understanding of tradition that constantly threatens to emerge in the terminology distinguishing between *traditio* and *traditiones*. There *is* no tradition "in and of itself."[26] Tradition is

---

23. Schreiter 1985, 105.

24. Cf. Chomsky 1973, 14f.

25. Schreiter 1985, 115.

26. Contra Beinert 1987, 515, who defines "tradition" as the "process of God's self-mediation in the Christ event through the Holy Spirit in the medium of church proclamation" and as the criterion of knowledge. Beinert does not really differentiate between "tradi-

to be understood as a consequence of transmission. On the other hand, it is not simply the sum of transmitted content; as the language system of the Christian faith, it represents instead a kind of "social memory" of the community of believers.

2. If following Schreiter one maintains that *every* theology emerges within the context of a culturally shaped situation and that tradition represents the result of local theologies, then "tradition itself" — expressed in the singular — *cannot* represent the criterion of Christian truth.[27] The danger, of course, is that of elevating a contextually shaped social construction of tradition to normative status over other local theologies; that is, a given local theology's necessarily local understanding of that which constitutes "tradition" in the larger sense is universalized into a norm for others. The *understanding of tradition* entertained by the powerful is confused with Christian *tradition.*

Because every Christian community and by extension every local theology should also be characterized by catholicity in the sense of concurrence with the whole, the connection between every local theology and the Christian tradition should also be evident. If we are to maintain a vibrant consciousness of the contextual and cultural conditions shaping theologies and their tradition, then our common search for the truth of tradition — commensurate with the conditions of discourse ethics — should focus not on establishing the *normative status* of this or that tradition, but on establishing a *consensus* in the conflict so often arising between the interpretations of tradition among any given series of local theologies. It is not the various forms of social church organization (liturgy, office, creed) that constitute the primary objects of such consensus, but the content of the different theologies *and* the forms of the church's being.

3. A third factor favoring the adoption of the dynamic and contextual concept of tradition is the significance the future acquires for our understanding of tradition. Without developing the insight further, Schreiter

---

tion" and "understanding of tradition," and ultimately restricts tradition to the medium of church proclamation. Church proclamation, however, can only sketch out a certain understanding of tradition; it cannot itself represent the normative authority for examining that same understanding of tradition.

27. Contra Kasper 1985, 399, who understands traditions as the evocation or representational articulation of the *one* tradition and offers a typological-sacramental understanding of tradition. Traditions viewed as a series of local theologies, on the other hand, representationally articulate not "a tradition" but rather God in the Spirit. Kasper seems to be confusing the social function of tradition with its object. Elevating tradition into the criterion of knowledge necessarily also elevates particular interpretations — that is, a certain contextual understanding of history and tradition — to normative status.

points out how every local theology influences not only the whole of tradition, but certainly its local cultural context as well. I consider it imperative that we remain mindful of the significance of the future if we are to maintain a dynamic understanding of tradition as a language system of faith generated by local theologies.

A culture will die if its monuments cause it to become so rigid that the flow of living water is cut off. That same flow of tradition will dry up if one understands tradition primarily as a remembrance of past monuments. If human beings really are "creatures of tradition" (Max Seckler), being so is probably also a necessary part of physical survival. The functions of memory also enable human beings to react appropriately in a physical sense in different situations.

The function of remembering the past and oneself in that past is always to enable a person to deal successfully with the future. Remembrance rarely takes place merely for its own sake and is generally engaged in instead in connection with the conditions of the present and future. In this sense, although functionally the social memory of tradition is certainly subordinated to the experiences of the present situation, it is absolutely necessary and extraordinarily valuable in dealing with both the present and the future.

In other words, the past tradition that the community of believers recalls always functions for the sake of the present and future.

Precisely because the present situation shapes our recollection and understanding of tradition, any development of our understanding of tradition is well advised to consider the various attendant power interests. Because our recollection of the past inevitably also shapes life possibilities for the future, there inheres within every understanding of tradition various possibilities for maintaining and even enhancing power. To avoid confusing the understanding of tradition entertained by the powerful — that is, the history of the victors within church history — with the Christian tradition itself — that is, with the *content* of salvation history — every interpretation of collective memory must also analyze the relationships of power necessarily inhering within every understanding of tradition.

Tradition is not, as Schreiter believes, the series of local theologies, but rather *the social memory in which the communities of saints remember the series of local theologies.*[28] New Testament tradition referred to the Holy Spirit as the

---

28. Concerning the concept of "social memory," see Cavalli 1991. Cf. also Halbwachs's concept of "collective memory," which maintains that images of the past become the object of dispute between various social groups. The interpretation of tradition in connection with the concept of memory (that is, as that which is worthy of remembrance) is already discernible in the sixteenth century. See Wiedenhofer 1990, 626f.

subject of this social memory, while early church creeds associated the Spirit with the life of the church. In this sense, of course, tradition "itself" does not really have any independent existence, representing instead a social function. Theologically tradition refers to the activity of the Holy Spirit that at various times and in various places causes the community of saints to recall its experience with God's history of salvation. The *agens* of Christian tradition and its social memory, the *agens* that is "identical in all,"[29] is the Holy Spirit that brought about, brings about, and consummates the history of liberation.

The Tradition of the Repressed Past of Nature in the Christian Tradition

In his text *On the Concept of History,* Walter Benjamin turns against those historians who try to determine "the way it really was."[30] Benjamin counters this history of those in power — whom he calls the heirs of all who have ever been victorious — with the real picture of the past, the picture that flits past us, the picture of the past "which unexpectedly appears to man singled out by history at a moment of danger."[31] Because Benjamin believes that not even the dead are safe from the victorious enemy, the historical materialist must read history "against the grain." Benjamin proposes that we take the "tradition of the oppressed" as our presupposition for a new understanding of history that runs counter to the notion of progress within history. History should portray not the "the eternal image of the past," but rather "a unique experience with the past."[32] By countering history as a "monad" and discerning within it "the sign of a Messianic cessation of happening," Benjamin intends to fight for "remembrance" of the past.[33]

One should not overestimate the theological import of Benjamin's statements. Although it is not quite clear what he means by the tradition of the oppressed, he does not seem to refer to "God having come in history."[34] In any event, theologically Benjamin's text does unremittingly challenge the Christian understanding of tradition.[35] His thesis of how the oppressed understand tradi-

---

29. Schleiermacher 1884, 518.

30. ET as "Theses on the Philosophy of History," in W. Benjamin, *Illuminations* (New York, 1969), quotation from Thesis VI.

31. Benjamin 1991, 695; ET, Thesis VI.

32. Benjamin 1991; ET, Thesis XVI.

33. Benjamin 1991, 702f.; ET, Theses XVII, XVIII, A and B.

34. John 1991, 77.

35. In his discussion of the theological significance of Benjamin's philosophy of his-

tion differently than do the victors articulates a key element in Christian social memory, namely, its recollection of the suffering and failure of the Messiah.

Benjamin can teach us how to discern the conditions affecting our understanding of the tradition of the oppressed past: "It is not given to every person at every place and at every time, but rather only at the moment of danger."[36] From the perspective of this difference between the victors' and victims' interpretations of history, we must develop "the tradition of the oppressed as the guiding theme of our theological hermeneutics."[37]

The christological foundation of this hermeneutics is our remembrance of Christ's sufferings. The pneumatological subject is the Holy Spirit that makes this remembrance possible in the first place. The necessary condition for understanding salvation history in this hermeneutics is that we recall not only God's history of suffering, but also that of the martyrs of the ancient church and of victims in both history and the present.[38] Understanding the concept of tradition from the perspective of the Trinity and a theology of the cross enables us to ascribe epistemological precedence to the oppressed in the representational articulation of the Christian tradition. Yet precisely because the tradition of the oppressed is not simply accessible everywhere and to every person, we must address the question of just who are the *subjects* of this discernment of tradition. The tradition of the oppressed is found "only among those who are poor and despairing right now and only at the places where they suffer — only near to them."[39] It is precisely their situation that provides them with a powerful impetus to believe and to hope and to experience and reflect on God's liberation.

---

tory, Wiedenhofer 1994, 70, ascribes to it an "important critical and diagnostic function." Although Wiedenhofer reads church and religious history as "a catastrophic history which nonetheless does bear the saving tradition within itself to the extent the promise of forgiveness sustains it" (71), the question is then how one can plausibly speak of history bearing this saving tradition *within itself.* Is Benjamin's whole point not that one *must* distinguish between the losers' view of the *events* of history and the victors' *writing* of history? How is theology to meet the important challenge raised by the question of the *subjects* of historical writing? I believe that understanding God rather than tradition as the bearer of forgiveness and liberation suggests developing a functional rather than an ontological understanding of tradition.

36. John 1991, 76.

37. With John 1988.

38. Metz has been especially concerned with positioning this insight at the center of Christian theology. Cf. also my discussion of the contextual-theological paradigm in connection with anamnestic reason in Metz and its recollection of the suffering of God and creatures, in Bergmann 2001.

39. John 1988, 524.

Just as the remembrance of God's historical suffering prompts liberation theology to accord to the poor a central function within the social memory of Christian tradition, so also would I like to accord not only suffering humanity, but also suffering creatures a central function within the memory of tradition. The tradition of the oppressed should include the ecological victims of cultural violence.

To take but one example, one might certainly associate the remembrance of species that human colonialism has rendered extinct with the remembrance of nature's participation in the events at Golgotha as portrayed by the Gospels (Mark 15:33; cf. Amos 8:9; Matt. 27:45, 51; Luke 23:44f.). Just as the martyrs suffered for their faith, so also did these species suffer for their Creator. A remembrance of their suffering fulfills an important function in the ecological theology of liberation insofar as it keeps hope alive in a resurrection of the dead for them as well.

Paul mentions nature's "birth cry" and its anticipation of liberation (Rom. 8:22).[40] Modern biology suspects that all organisms possess the function of memory within the parameters of what is known as "morphic resonance," which can certainly be understood as "recollection" or "remembrance."[41] Because the considerable extent to which painful experiences contribute to shaping the memory functions and behavior of organisms is already well known, there is really nothing preventing us from assuming that nonhuman life-forms also possess what we might call social memory.

Of course, my assertion that there is also a *tradition of the oppressed past of nature* does not mean that the subjects of nature themselves are the conscious bearers of that tradition. Those interested in examining the extent to which such is even possible will have to draw on biological and ecological theories for both information and inspiration. Theologically the tradition of the oppressed past of nature means that the social memory of the Christian tradition includes not only a remembrance of the suffering of Christ and of our fellow human beings, but a similar remembrance of the suffering of God in his creation and of the suffering of other creatures.

As is the case in the history of humankind, the defining features of this tradition are different from those of the traditions of the victors, that is, of those living beings who have been victorious in the evolutionary process. The tradition of the victims of natural selection and of cultural-ecological violence is a necessary part of the Christian tradition that the community of saints can discern through its perception of the suffering of its ecological siblings and through its

40. Cf. Schottroff 1989, 140ff.
41. Cf. Sheldrake 1988, i, 159ff.

remembrance — as enabled by the Spirit — of nature's birth cry throughout its history.[42] Indeed, nature's birth cry provides ecological theology with a hermeneutical key for remembering the past tradition of oppressed nature.

3. The Principle of Apophatic Knowledge: God and Nature in Ecological Theology

One salient feature of Gregory's theological method was his distinction between the nature and activity of God, between theology and economy. Gregory maintained that human knowledge has as little access to the essence of God as it does to the essence of creation (*Or.* 28.31). He did, however, link this negative principle of knowledge of God with the positive insistence that one be able to say something positive about that which one has already qualified negatively (28.9). The apophatic principle is one of theology's creative instruments.

Through their reception of the Cappadocian's theological method, both Dionysius and Maximus developed apophatic theology further.[43] The apophatic principle of knowledge of God enables Christian theology to free itself from the strictures of Greek ontology that understood the being of God and that of the world according to the same conditions. Now God's being could be distinguished from that of the world, and the cleft between the ontological otherness of God and world could be bridged not by "nature" or "essence," but by God's active love, a situation Zizioulas articulates by understanding the goal of apophatic theology as having been to move questions concerning truth and knowledge out of the sphere of Greek ontology and into that of love and community.[44]

42. In the history of theology, Saint Francis's perception of the suffering of nature remains exemplary.

43. Gregory does not actually use the term *apophatikoi;* it is Dionysius and Maximus who first use it epistemologically to refer to a negation of God's attributes. Cf. Lampe 1976, 219. For a thorough discussion of the "language of negation" in Gregory of Nazianzus, Gregory of Nyssa, Basil, and Macrina, cf. Pelikan 1993, 40-56. Concerning apophatic theology and its influence on scholasticism, see LaCugna 1993, 324-35, who, like Tracy recently, unfortunately completely fails to discern the difference between Eastern apophatic and Western negative theology because she does not perceive the positive element of apophatic thinking that was ultimately lost in the Western *theologia negativa.* In the West the doctrine of analogy also adopted the apophatic principle.

44. Zizioulas 1985, 91f. Like Gregory, Zizioulas emphasizes the monarchy of the Father, who on this view does not however seem to be relationally constituted. Zizioulas then bases his own anthropology of Christians and of the church on the ontology of person and love. An initial objection to Zizioulas's analogy — following Volf's detailed analysis of his

In this concluding section I will examine how the apophatic principle is methodologically useful to ecological theology.[45] Why, one might ask, should one speak apophatically about both God *and* nature? Here I will draw from Gregory's analogy; in his second theological oration he tried to demonstrate that human reason is subject to analogous limitations with regard to its knowledge both of God and of creation. Ecological theology might similarly consider distinguishing not only theologically between the essence and activity of God, but also ecologically between the essence and activity of nature.

Six considerations militate in favor of ecological theology integrating the apophatic epistemological principle into its own methodology as well. Here "apophatic" means that in all statements about the essence and activity of God and nature, we should express those regarding *essence* negatively, since a complete or perfect vision of essence is impossible in any case, and those regarding *activity* positively, that we may simultaneously say something in a limited fashion about essence as well insofar as essence and activity are necessarily related. An acknowledgment and discernment of the limitations of theological knowledge create the necessary presupposition for positively expressing the unknowable; in this sense the *via negativa* represents the condition of the possibility for a *via creativa* that remains mindful of its own limitations. Why should ecological theology speak apophatically about creation and the Creator?

Theology as Soteriology

By prompting our understanding of God to remain mindful of its presuppositions within our experience of God, the apophatic principle prevents theology from being limited to a philosophy of religion. Instead of turning into

ecclesiology — is that it represents an overrealized eschatology (see Volf 1998, 101) insofar as despite everything he still does understand salvation from the perspective of ontology rather than from that of creational soteriology. A second objection is that his emphasis on the monarchy of the Father results in the hierarchical preeminence of the bishop (= Christ) over the community and believers within the analogy of trinity and church (cf. Volf, 109-16). A third objection is that he does not at all clarify how the being of the human person relates to that of God. And finally a fourth objection, following chap. 3 above, is that Zizioulas's neopatristic exegesis of the Cappadocians completely ignores their understanding of the equality of will and power among the divine hypostases; instead, he merely develops normatively the notion of the monarchy of the Father (1995, 52ff.) for his own purposes — something utterly at odds with the intention of Gregory of Nazianzus.

45. See the discussion of my main points from this section in Degen-Ballmer 2001, 273-80, who works against a reductionistic conception of nature/creation, in dialogue with process and Orthodox theologies.

theosophy, that is, wisdom concerning God's essence, apophatic theology becomes soteriology, that is, a reflection on our experience with God's liberating activity. Within the parameters of Gregory's method, human reason ultimately encounters God through his *work* in and with creation. Because the Cappadocian rejected any path to God that did *not* adhere to the natural conditions of existence, his theology became economy, that is, a consideration and portrayal of the salvation history of creation.

Because positive statements regarding God's essence derive *exclusively* from our limited knowledge of his actions, the apophatic principle avoids any speculation regarding the content of the concept of God.

Of course, precisely such knowledge of God's actions presupposes that, commensurate with the condition for the possibility of theological understanding, we do indeed experience the divine activity. The object of theological reflection is thus our experience of God's liberating action. What we are able to say *positively* about God is precisely that which one can perceive in the encounter between God and creature. In that sense the object of theological statements is not the concept of God — who can never be such an object — but rather the reflection on our experiences with the one who liberates. Apophatically theology thus becomes soteriology, the doctrine of God's universal liberating action. Adherence to this apophatic principle means that the object of the reflection of ecological theology is the experiences human beings, living beings, and landscapes have with the God who sets free. This feature separates the ecological theology of liberation from the wisdom of new theological spirituality insofar as the latter derives its statements about nature from speculative theological statements about essence.[46]

---

46. Maxwell develops a completely different concept of wisdom than the inclusive-esoteric version I am alluding to here. This philosopher of science advocates developing a "new, more rigorous kind of inquiry" focused on problems and solutions that are of significance for all life. Distinguishing between a "problem-solving" and an "aim-pursuing rationality," Maxwell proposes basic guidelines for both, and in so doing links the methodologies of the social and natural sciences. The "new inquiry" Maxwell envisions consists in a "philosophy of knowledge" in the forms of these two rationalities and in a "philosophy of wisdom." Whereas the philosophy of knowledge contributes to creating a better world, the task of the philosophy of wisdom is to "apply" the rules of the philosophy of knowledge. Maxwell understands wisdom as "the capacity to realize what is of value in life" (1992, 205; cf. 218). One of the basic problems of his philosophy of knowledge and wisdom is the question, "how can we best *learn* how to realize what is of value?" (225). Although Maxwell is apparently not acquainted with Næss's ecosophical initiative, he nonetheless clearly shares its conviction that any practical-normative philosophy in an ecological context necessarily includes an eco*sophical* dimension. Cf. chap. 1 above. One critical objection is that Maxwell seems to make things a bit easy on himself regarding just *who* it is that can, may, and

Ecological theology also separates itself apophatically from those theologies that derive their statements about salvation history from postulates of a universal concept of God. Because one can know about God's essence only on the basis of the actual appearances of the acting God, apophatic theology declines to draw any conclusions concerning God's work from statements about God's essence. The question "which God?" can be answered meaningfully only as the question "which God for me and us here and now?" This position links the classical principle of apophatic knowledge of God with contextual theology's epistemological criticism of the truth claims of modernity's understanding of God.

Apophatism and the Pluralism of Knowledge

The apophatic principle not only prevents us from making God and nature into objects in this sense, it also prevents us from mystifying them. The apophatic criticism of the modern scientific understanding of nature is that it reduces the essence of the life of nature to knowledge of its mechanisms, whereas the essence of nature in fact includes considerably more than what can constitute the object of scientific investigation. The apophatic criticism of the concept of God that limits God's essence to his attributes is that attributes such as "omnipotence," "infinity," or *apatheia* characterize the divine essence only negatively, whereas God's essence includes considerably more than what can be understood in terms of theological attributes. The apophatic principle prevents us from making either nature or God into an object by maintaining that neither the whole of nature nor the whole of God can be rationally comprehended.

Because statements about the being of nature and God are ontologically only negatively possible, the apophatic principle prevents us from slipping into mystifying speculation. Nature "is" not a dance, as Capra maintains, nor "is" God life, as Cobb and Birch maintain. The apophatic distinction between essence and activity ensures that we remain mindful that our understandings of God and nature ultimately represent cultural

---

should "realize what is of value" and why. Maxwell's initiative will not withstand ideological scrutiny if it does not offer an epistemological-sociological analysis of the presuppositions and inevitable conflict attaching to any discussion of the unjust distribution of possibilities for implementing or actualizing subjectively and collectively understood values. Maxwell might also want to include the analytical methodologies of religious studies in his initiative if he is to avoid having to engage an esoteric concept of wisdom after all in the final analysis.

constructions made up of anthropomorphic, sociomorphic, and biomorphic notions. The apophatic principle disallows any equivalency between words or images, on the one hand, and the essence to which they presumably point, on the other.

The apophatic principle applies to our understanding of human beings in the same way it applies to our understanding of nature and God. Because we can never come to a complete or perfect understanding of human "being," we can only negatively circumscribe what human beings "are." Although human beings "are" not animals, they do obviously share an enormous number of behavioral patterns with animals. Rather than "being" good or evil, human beings are instead characterized by a moral capacity. Applying the apophatic principle anthropologically could well help preserve the integrity of what it means to be human insofar as it would deny specific, individual theories from making universal claims concerning some comprehensive truth about human existence. The apophatic principle thus fosters a pluralism of theories and a pluralism of epistemological methods without which one constantly risks falling victim to totalitarian worldviews.[47]

Apophatism and Critical Rationality

By ultimately bringing down the scholastic schema of natural theology, the apophatic principle enables rational theology to connect with the classical apophatic method. Scholasticism understood God as the ultimate or highest being, as the being in which the sustaining features of every other being come to fulfillment. As such, God became the quintessence of the being of the objects of nature.

Kant brought this schema of natural theology down. He was wholly unable to understand God as the quintessence of objects and as thus being subject to the categories of the understanding. "The content of the negative part of rational theology is to demonstrate the dialectical illusion that forces rea-

47. Cf. Tillich 1951, 59f., who insists that method and object correspond and warns against methodological imperialism, which "is as dangerous as political imperialism" (60), and Jaspers 1974, 59, who maintains that only a systematic understanding of disciplines rather than a single understanding of the world can make truth claims. Jaspers understands each such understanding of the world as a "particular world of knowledge" that is not to be understood absolutely as representing *the* being of the world (59). Quite commensurate with the apophatic tradition, Rasmussen 1998, 129, speaks about faith as "the great unknowing" whose "experience of finitude" "crushes any homocentrism and exposes all our efforts to know *the* truth as self-deceptive."

son to imagine God as an object of thought even though he can never be such an object."[48] In this sense Kant repeats the movement of classical apophatic theology whose goal was to free theology from the strictures of ontology. Kant similarly maintains that the task of rational theology is not merely the negative one of revealing the "dialectical illusion," but also the positive one of articulating the "ideal of pure reason" as the object of transcendental theology.[49] At the same time, however, Kant remains fully cognizant that this ideal is by no means identical with the reality of God.

Although the "ideal" of God — our understanding of God — is indeed necessary for attaining any reason-based knowledge of the being of objects and appearances of nature, that ideal does not coincide with God's reality. Indeed, God demonstrates his reality precisely in "being incapable of being exhausted by that which we call reality; instead he is only real as the infinite task of reason."[50] This Kantian interpretation of apophatic theology demonstrates how the apophatic principle serves the rationality of theology by self-critically preserving reason against its own claims. Although reason-based knowledge of the objects and appearances of nature does indeed lead to knowledge of God, it does *not* lead to any *positive* knowledge of the reality of God's essence. As Kant suggests, however, it is precisely by discerning and acknowledging this limitation of knowledge that the knowledge of reason itself demonstrates its own capacity for truth. That is, only a rationality that constantly remains critically aware of its own limitations can meet the demands of a rational theology.

Applied to ecological theology, the apophatic principle disallows drawing conclusions about God's being from the being of nature.[51] What this exclusion does, however, is put ecological theology into a position to interpret the objects and appearances of nature with the aid of the ideal of reason — the understanding of God — and at the same time creatively to articulate positive statements concerning the appearance of God's reality *within* the limitations of its knowledge of nature.

---

48. Picht 1990a, 572.

49. Kant, *Kritik der reinen Vernunft*, B 608, 3.390 (*Critique of Pure Reason*, B 608).

50. Picht 1990a, 601.

51. This disallowance was not shared by the theology of late antiquity, which quite unaffectedly also used the figure of natural theology. Although thinkers did indeed apophatically free the understanding of God's essence from the understanding of being, they nonetheless continued to support the ontological proof of God's existence that was a self-evident part of their ancient context. Kant's critique of ontology itself as *metaphysica generalis* first excluded the possibility of this combination.

Apophatism and the Postmodern Conflict
between Ontological Atomism and Holism

Apophatic knowledge of God and nature leads neither to poststructuralist relativism nor to particularist universalism. What is known as postmodern/poststructuralist philosophy has justifiably criticized the interweaving of the structures of language and power. Postmodern philosophers criticize the modern constructions of the presumed unity of reality and experience and question the real connection between sign and signified in the representation of language.[52] Given the rejection of the possibility of conceiving the unity of reality, postmodernism has also struck the question of the possibility of a unity of reality from its agenda. The epistemologically justified criticism of modernity's particularist understanding of unity and its universal truth claims has thus merged into epistemological relativism that in its own turn ultimately has also called into question the conditions of the possibility of theoretical and normative-practical discourse as such. Poststructuralist criticism thus often leads to cynicism, and rather than engaging in new construction, its exclusive deconstruction of the existing merely presents a combinatorial selection of remnants among the ruins. Nor has anyone really carried through on the promises to articulate an alternative to modernity.[53]

But the essential question above remains unanswered, namely, whether the deconstruction of the various understandings of the unity of reality and experience necessarily also negates the conditions of the possibility of such unity. Because it is the conditions of our *understanding* of unity rather than the conditions of unity *itself* that are called into question, one cannot logically draw this conclusion. If, then, one can at least potentially not exclude the possibility of the unity of reality, the question becomes *whether* and, if so, *how* knowledge of this unity of reality might indeed be possible.

It is at this point that an application of the apophatic principle can perhaps take us further insofar as it maintains the simultaneity of the revelation of the unity of reality *and* of the limitations necessarily attaching to any knowledge of that unity. That is, precisely because reason can never come to a full recognition of the unity of reality, that very unity emerges as a possibility. Of course, one can object that in this "boundary knowledge" of reason it is precisely *not* the "unity" of reality that appears, but rather the complete "differentiation" and fragmentization of its various parts, which cannot be medi-

52. Cf. Foucault 1993, 78ff.; Derrida 1994, 422-42; Barnes and Duncan 1992, 8f.
53. Beck (1986; 1988) does persuasively show that the alternative is to enter into a second modernity.

ated in any event. What we then have is an antithetical confrontation between ontological atomism and ontological holism. As long as ontological holism is advocated in a modern, that is, universalist, fashion, it is subject to postmodern criticism. That criticism does *not* apply, however, if ontological holism is engaged within the construction of transcendental theology together with the apophatic principle, since in that case it is not making any positive statements about the being and essence of reality itself. The disclosure of the "dialectical illusion" (Kant) is then in an excellent position to adopt the methods of deconstruction and the hermeneutics of suspicion. Although these considerations admittedly still do not resolve the question of the existence of the unity of reality, apophatic rational theology can nonetheless still maintain the possibility of such unity.

On the other hand, of course, ontological atomism in postmodernity must submit to the criticism of apophatic theology. In the larger sense, can ontological atomism be rationally supported at all? Can one not more accurately classify it as an ontological confession of faith? Is it not by assuming the atomism of being that one first creates the rational conditions under which the understanding of the postmodern reality of differences (alterity) becomes plausible? If theoretical discourse as such becomes impossible because our rejection of any unity of reality also renders the intersubjective search for truth meaningless, then why even discuss ontological and epistemological atomism further? Although this criticism does not demonstrate the thesis of apophatic theology that God's reality comes to appearance in the "boundary knowledge" of our understanding of nature, it does clearly show that ontological atomism's criticism of universalist holism is justified only if one metaphysically construes the unity of being by also viewing God as an object, that is, by identifying the concept of God with God's reality. It is precisely this construction that apophatic theology avoids by distinguishing between the unity of reality (God's being) and our experience and discernment of this unity within nature (God's salvation history).

Yet another criticism of ontological atomism as perceived in postmodernism in the phenomenon of language involves a pragmatic issue of language philosophy. The question is whether the analysis of representation in the various forms of linguistic expression and the criticism of the lack of ontological correspondence between sign and signified really demonstrate that *no* connection at all obtains between the object of nature, its human perception *(Vorstellung)*, and its representation in a sign. But then how is communication through language able to serve human social needs at all? Or is this merely illusory? I believe theoreticians of representation ascribe too little significance to the referential capacity of language. From a purely pragmatic perspective, the social application of language suggests that consensus regarding the reference of a given sign to something signified is more the norm than the exception.

Empirically this referential capacity of language constitutes the possibility of language communication. It is of less importance whether one understands the connection between the sign and the signified ontologically as in the period Foucault calls "classic" or sociologically as in the theory of the sociology of knowledge. Even if the linguistic sign itself does not ontologically represent the signified, this still does not allow the conclusion that *no* connection at all obtains between the object, perception, and sign. Given the referential capacity of the sign, it seems more appropriate to assume that perceptions, rather than arising in the interior of an atomistically isolated subject, instead represent perceptions of something *in* nature, and that thus what is actually outside human beings does indeed appear through language in the interpersonal human sphere. A critique of the perceptions of such representation justifiably reminds us that what actually does appear may not be appearing *as* it actually is. This consideration does not, however, mean that the *same* thing is not being both perceived and referenced through a sign. This understanding acquires cogency if one views thinking itself as a natural process and the subject as a constitution of relationships.[54]

The Transparency of Nature as the Presupposition for Knowledge of God's Appearance

The apophatic principle enables the transparency of nature to move into our purview. Applied to our investigation of nature, the apophatic principle enables us to discern the capacity of nature for transcending itself. Unlike modernist physico-theology, which associates the being of nature nominalistically with the being of God, apophatic ecological theology frees itself from having to view the being of nature in terms of the divine being.[55] Ecological theology

---

54. Picht 1989, 46-54; Bateson 1990b, 18.

55. Russell follows the modernist–physico-theological figure in combining the findings of the history of science, the modern natural and ecological sciences, and the Gaia understanding of nature and in adducing these theologically in his concluding chapter to justify technological optimism (1994, 143) and a continuation of human instrumental dominion over nature (146ff.). Russell, wanting "to make the Gospel more accessible to our contemporaries" (151), teleologically defines the goal of the earth *as* "part of God's purpose" (148), then defines ecological ethics in a practical sense *as* the ethics of faith (147), and finally defines the value of the earth itself metaethically *as* God-given (143). Without subjecting his theological statements to any translation at all, he nominalistically and selectively combines them with

draws on those ecological theories that contribute to our understanding of the interplay between organisms and their environments. Whereas scientific ecology focuses on the "glassy essence" of this interplay, however, theology inquires concerning the *transparency* of that interplay.

By "transparency" I am referring first of all to the natural phenomenon of transcending, to nature's own capacity to move "beyond itself." Evolution, for example, is capable of bringing forth something new. The living forms of a given ecosystem might change into different ones. The development of higher levels of complexity becomes discernible over the course of evolutionary history. The apophatic principle enables us to understand nature's capacity for "self-transcendence" (Bosshard) positively in relation to the appearances and objects of the interrelatedness of various life-forms. Concerning this capacity for self-transcendence, the apophatic principle only allows us to speak negatively about nature's "being." That is, nature "is" not evolution or selection; instead, nature itself evolves and selects. The being of nature "is" not complexity; instead, the complexity and variety of its life-forms constitute a reference to it.

One can express this transparency of nature scientifically, aesthetically, and theologically. Scientifically we speak about the "self-organization" or "self-transcendence" of nature. Aesthetically we speak about "natural beauty" (Adorno) or about nature's "depth" (Cézanne). And theologically we speak about the "representational power" of God's future (Link).[56] From a critical perspective, of course, one may well ask whether such talk about "transparency" does not simply represent a projection of our understanding of God into our understanding of nature. Can one really simply assume that what the ecologist calls "self-organization" simultaneously functions as a medium of God's representation? Or does there not lurk here yet another physico-theological version of the ontological proof of God's existence? Apophatic theology does indeed require that we concur with the critic on this point. The fact that the theologian views the phenomenal form of the ecological pattern from the perspective of its transparency with regard to the divine certainly does not yet mean that God actually reveals himself *as* such a pattern. Natural theology tried to demonstrate the integrity of this ontological capacity.

---

theories of nature. By simply appending reflections on the creation dogma to his discussion of nature, Russell manages to avoid all the problems of an ecological theology. His creation dogmatics utterly ignores the pluralism of worldviews and religions; the late-modern fragmentization of discourse concerning nature, human beings, and God; the chasm between scientific and humanistic culture; reflections on our experience with God and on modern subjectivity; and the moral-philosophical basis of traditional natural law. What Russell has done is simply dress the figure of historical physico-theology in a new garb.

56. Link 1989, 187.

By contrast, ecological theology is concerned with demonstrating the *capacity* of the transparency of nature, that is, the *possibility* of being transparent with regard to its own essence and God's activity. While assuming that nature is capable of such transparency does indeed constitute the *condition of the possibility* of an appearance of the acting God in nature, it is by *no* means maintaining that the being of nature is somehow ontologically connected with the being of God. This construction presupposes that ecological discourse continues to distinguish the partial discipline of scientific-ecological discourse from that of ecological-theological discourse. The common object linking the two is the transparency of the pattern of ecological interplay. What separates them is their different questions.

The apophatic principle prohibits identifying nature's self-transcendence with God's activity. God is not evolution, nor does God evolve. From the perspective of transparency, any statements about God's appearance *within* transparent nature are to be apophatically distinguished from statements about nature's transparency. The apophatic principle also prohibits mixing statements about the transparency of nature with statements about God's being. That is, we must maintain the tension between statements about the ontological transparency of nature and those about the nature *in* and *with* which God acts. Instead of offering an ontological proof of God's existence, ecological theology articulates its experiences with God's actions in nature in connection with the latter's transparency toward the divine. Whereas natural theology followed the premise that "the being of nature reveals God's being," ecological theology follows the premise that "God can be perceived in transparent nature." Once more, we must remain apophatically mindful that the "transparency of world" (Marc)[57] reveals not the essence of God, but God's liberating actions with the world.

By adhering to the classic apophatic principle, ecological theology is following the soteriological lead of the theologians of the Eastern church tradition who understand universal salvation history as a "transfiguration" of all creation.[58] In this sense the history of creation becomes transparent toward its transfiguration and liberation by its Creator.

---

57. Cf. Bergmann 1994f, 43f.

58. "Skapelsens förvandling" 1987, 15: "God's gracious activity for the reintegration and transfiguration of all reality." ("Orthodox Perspectives on Creation," p. 6.) In his understanding of transparency, Link speaks about God's "temporal relation with the world" and understands God's being as coming freely to the world rather than being analogous to it (1989, 190). Here we encounter the difficult question whether the being of transparent nature also contains allusions to its own eschatological liberation. Can one somehow assume the presence of "eschatological logoi" in ecology? Concerning the significance of the Eastern church understanding and terminology of logoi for creation theology, see Thunberg 1985, 132-43.

The Apophatic Understanding of Nature in the Dialogue of Religions

In conclusion I would like to point out how the apophatic principle can create new presuppositions for the understanding of nature within the theology of religion.[59] In the transformation of natural theology in late antiquity, the apophatic principle made it possible for Christian theology to regulate theological statements about God and nature linguistically,[60] and the same principle can now also help clarify not only the language of theological discourse among religions about creation, but also the language of practical-ethical discourse about the ecological world ethos.

It is especially in the dialogue with Buddhism and with the so-called animist nature religions that a negative theology of nature can help shape the Christian understanding of nature such that the idea of nature's transparency can function as a common feature of interreligious respect for nature. McDaniel has pointed out how the notion of the nonself *(anatta)* in Zen Buddhism presents a challenge to Christian personalism.[61] Buddhist anthropology understands the self as being constituted by relationality rather than by substance. In this context Cobb has suggested moving on into "postpersonal Christianity."[62] Buddhism's transpersonal experience also challenges the Christian understanding of God insofar as it calls into serious question whether God really is better understood as a "self," as a

59. I realize that the expression "theology of religion" is not without problems. Here it refers to our theological reflection on the problems of dialogue between different religions. Concerning the establishment of a dialogue between religions from the perspective of creation theology, see Sundermeier 1988, 275-81. Cf. Bergmann 1994e. Gerlitz documents contributions of the world religions to the ecological challenge. The project "Religion and Ecology" at Harvard University is coordinating a comprehensive interpretation of the world religions in the light of the ecological challenge: http://environment.harvard.edu/religion/. While the many publications from the Harvard series one-sidedly focus on the constructive potentials of religions for the solution of the global environmental crisis, the forthcoming *Encyclopedia of Religion and Nature* (New York and London: Continuum, 2005) offers more detailed and balanced insights on the different practices and ideologies of "ecospirituality" in many different regions, contexts, and traditions.

60. Pelikan 1993, 115.

61. McDaniel 1990b, 237-42. Cf. also Kazuo 1994, 340, who draws attention to the significance of the Japanese, Zen Buddhist understanding of the simultaneous negativity and positivity of nothingness, "as, one might say, emptiness and at the same time thus-ness (reality as it is; *ku soku nyoyitsu*)."

62. Cobb 1975, 220.

subject with essence, rather than as "the ultimate reality of each and every self."[63]

By applying the apophatic principle ecologically, we are not quite as constrained to defend the personalism of our understanding of God as the *only* way of understanding the divine essence. Apophatic theology is concerned instead only with circumscribing God's essence negatively. Although it is obvious enough, of course, that God is more than a human person, I doubt whether a "postpersonal" Christian theology can really do justice to the mystery of the incarnation. In connection with our investigation and knowledge of nature, an application of the apophatic principle thus strongly suggests that in its transparency, nature appears as a holy creation precisely because it does point us toward spiritual and divine reality.

The religion of Australian Aboriginals views landscapes as the topography of mythology.[64] Nature is read as a "text" containing concrete traces of the activity of spiritual ancestors. Those who move about in this landscape and have been initiated into the language of this text are able to participate in the history of their landscape, their people, and their spiritual fathers. It is the land that constitutes a person. In a sense, myth "reads" a person through the landscape as a dream. In the Aboriginal understanding of the world, nature contains references to the spiritual reality constituting the physical, psychological, and social world.

Christian missionaries found the Aboriginals' nature religion to be primitive, pantheistic, and animistic — hardly a surprise given the enormous differences between the nature religion of Aboriginals and the physicotheological thinking of eighteenth-century European missionaries. By freeing us from having to conceive the essence of God, human beings, and nature essentialistically, however, the apophatic principle opens the door to dialogue between the Christian understanding of creation and the understanding of nature of a religion that ascribes greater reality to the spiritual transparency of a landscape than to its physical features.

Perhaps the creation theology of a new modernity can learn anew from the wisdom of Aboriginal religion in focusing on the transparency of a land-

63. McDaniel 1990b, 246. Concerning the Buddhist understanding of nature, see Panikkar and Stolz 1985.

64. Concerning the Aboriginals' mythological understanding of landscape, see *Aratjara*, especially Ryan 1994, and Caruana 1993. Concerning the history of Christian mission among the Australian Aboriginals, see Kolig 1988 and Hume 1988. Concerning the basic religious experience of the country and life of the Pacific tribes and the Australian Aboriginals, and the challenges this faith presents to Christian theology and the church, see May 1990, 33-39.

scape with regard to the appearances of the Spirit. Might the traditions of the Hebrew and Christian Bible perhaps also contribute to an interpretation of the so-called animist perspective on nature as a medium for God? Might we perhaps recognize in the spiritually transparent landscapes of the Aboriginals the traces of the Spirit whose breath gives life to creatures (Ps. 104)?

This nomadic digression into the expansive land of religio-theological dialogue concerning the appearances and objects of nature draws attention to an area in which a rigorous application of the apophatic principle of knowledge of God and nature might well relieve Christian theology of some of the burdens with which it has saddled itself through enculturation over the course of its Western history. Just as the apophatic principle itself arose in a situation in which Christianity became increasingly concerned with mission and with its dialogue with different theological understandings of God, so also can it create new presuppositions here at the beginning of the new millennium for interreligious discourse concerning the ecological transparency of nature.

Summary

Much favors incorporating into an ecological theology of liberation the classical methodological form of the apophatic principle of knowledge of God and nature as developed within the Cappadocian context of late antiquity. Ideally the apophatic principle prevents us from engaging in speculation concerning essence and prompts us to focus instead on our experiences with God's activity within salvation history. It prevents us both from making God into an object of knowledge and from incorporating elements of mystification into our understanding of nature and God and also helps preserve epistemological and methodological pluralism. By keeping reason mindful of its transcendental epistemological boundary, the apophatic principle fosters theological rationality and the capacity for substantive critique. Rather than leading to postmodern relativism or to particularist universalism, an apophatic ecological theology takes us beyond the conflict between ontological atomism and holism. Finally the apophatic principle directs our vision to the transparency of nature; enhances the dialogue between natural and ecological science, on the one hand, and theology, on the other; and creates new presuppositions for those engaging in religio-theological discourse who are trying to come to a mutual understanding of the spirit amid differing understandings of nature.

Summary Theses

Part I

1. Modernity's understanding of nature is changing. Our cultural crisis has generated an "ecological crisis" in which modern human interaction with nature in many instances threatens or destroys nature's chances for survival. Ecological discourse reflects on this crisis theoretically and practically-normatively from the fundamental perspective of the relationships between living beings and their environments.

2. The various ecological disciplines address this basic problem from the perspectives of cultural history, the natural sciences, philosophy, aesthetics, sociopolitics, and ethics. The queries of ecological discourse and its subdisciplines also include a metaphysical dimension.

3. From the perspective of cultural history, the establishment and reception of the concept of "ecology" has since 1866 been associated with the disparate elements of modernity's understanding of nature that, since 1800, has largely understood nature dynamically, historically, and instrumentally and has been characterized by an optimistic metaphysics. Ecological science has adopted the dialectics of the modern understanding of nature as part of its discipline.

4. Within the natural sciences, ecology has developed in a context shaped by social dynamics and characterized by the tension between two poles: system-functional utilitarianism and holistic research into nature. The first pole focuses on quantifiable, exact, nomothetic knowledge oriented toward application but runs the risk of ideological reductionism. The second focuses on qualitative observation with the goal of understanding but runs the risk of ideological holism.

5. The classical philosophical questions of ontology, the philosophy of nature and metaphysics, ethics, anthropology, and epistemology all recur within the framework of the ecological crisis. An incipient ecological aesthetics of nature offers valuable guides for developing new practical and theoretical forms of knowledge.

6. Since the 1970s an increasing awareness of the connection between social growth and the biological environment of society has prompted the demand for new sociopolitical concepts of action and for new models of production and consumption. This demand involves a plethora of different participants in a common, dynamic, open process of social development. Ethical focus has shifted to the task of developing a practical planetary bioethics and of grounding that ethics morally in a way accommodating a pluralism of participants.

7. The theological response to ecological challenge takes three basic forms: (a) the conjunctive model connects fundamentally different interpretations of faith and life; (b) the syncretistic model uncritically identifies nature and God; and (c) the critical-integrative model interprets and transforms in a theologically differentiated fashion the overall interpretation of life within a common ecological-theological community.

8. This critical-integrative model follows two methodological paths: the path of ecological creation dogmatics moves from the question of God to the question of creation, and the path of theological ecology moves from the question of nature to the question of God. The two methods can mutually inform and complement one another.

9. Despite differing denominational, historical, gender-specific, and geographical presuppositions, theologians in the First World have since 1972 been developing in a systematic, critically integrative fashion the Christian interpretation of life in response to the ecological challenge. This interpretation includes initiatives developed from the perspective of process theology (Cobb), the theology of the cross and of life (Altner), biblical and social ethics (Liedke and Duchrow), the history of nature and creation theology (Link), an ecological dogmatics of creation (Moltmann), ecological feminist theology (McFague), and ecofeminist theo-cosmology (Ruether).

10. In connection with the ecological challenge facing late modernity, my decision to examine the writings of the Cappadocian theologian Gregory of Nazianzus from late antiquity was prompted by historical (including the history of reception), philosophical, ecumenical, and systematic-theological considerations.

Part II

11. Important problems confronting Gregory's theology within his specific situation included pluralism, increasing social injustice, the replacement of the household economy with that of trade and money, the agricultural impoverishment of the earth, an increasing technical exploitation of nature, a general dissolution of social ties and obligations within the empire at large, and the emergence of social countermovements.

12. The notion of God's sociality occupies a key position in Gregory's theology and ultimately shapes his understanding of both God and world as well as the correspondence between the two in his dispute with modalist, monotheistic, and tritheistic Christian initiatives and in his critical-integrative dialogue with the middle Platonist understanding of reality and its doctrine of hypostases.

13. Ascribing central significance to the distinction between the three divine hypostases in his overall understanding of God leads Gregory to develop his soteriology in a fashion that includes a more differentiated understanding of the trinitarian economy. For Gregory the unity of the divine essence necessarily derives from the infinite interconnection between the three different parts of the Trinity in the one perfect community of will and power.

14. In Gregory's understanding of the world, communality comes to expression as good inner-worldly and human relationality understood as a mix, composition, interconnection, and union of all creaturely existence; it comes to expression positively as peace, beauty, and nonviolence, and negatively as any disruption or damage to these relations.

In construing the integration of human beings into creation from both a corporeal and a spiritual perspective, Gregory is actually defining his position topologically-dynamically rather than anthropocentrically. On his view human beings function as God's image in and for the world; the unity of creation is conceived as continuity, totality, and good order within the world, and the creation community itself is understood as a community of communication.

15. Gregory understands the correspondence between God and the world from the perspective of sociality in three stages: (a) God's own creative social communication or mediation; (b) the trinitarian movement of the cosmos whose creatures move either toward or away from God; and (c) the liberation of creation from evil as a movement of the triune God and the world.

16. The double dialectical thematic issues associated with the idea of movement among thinkers prior to Gregory — from Parmenides to Origen — remained open. That is, the question of the enduring unity of movement

through a multiplicity of conditions continued to pose an unresolved problem. Once the dispute concerning God's relationship with corporeality reemerged in the neo-Arian controversy, Plotinus's dualistic understanding of movement became questionable insofar as it antithetically juxtaposed spiritual repose and corporeal movement. In late antiquity the earlier question concerning the relation between truth and movement was transformed into the open question concerning the ethical relation characterizing movement toward evil or good. The central question Gregory addresses is whether God is only the source of movement without himself being in motion (as Aristotle assumed), or whether movement is also part of God's being.

17. Gregory was the first theologian to understand movement as a divine predicate and then develop the idea of the triune God in motion who moves creation itself. The Cappadocian develops this understanding of movement from the perspective of the inner Trinity, pneumatology, creation theology, psychology, angelology and hamartiology, ethics, and soteriology.

Gregory explains the origin and nature of evil in connection with his doctrine of angels as a spiritual phenomenon, ethically qualifies the idea of movement in connection with humankind and spirits, and shapes his understanding of redemption in a threefold manner in connection with the idea of movement as (a) the creation of the possibility of the various movements of creation, (b) creatures moving toward or away from God, and (c) creatures moving ever closer to God. The source of redemption is God's Holy Spirit, which perpetually moves out of itself and in and with which humankind and the world move closer to God's own being.

18. The problem of physical suffering created considerable tension between the theology of the ancient church and ancient philosophy's understanding of God. The challenge facing Christian philosophy was first to reconcile the ancient understanding of God's *apatheia* with the theology of the incarnation, second to show how the physical sufferings of creation acquire a function in connection with God's liberating actions, and third to articulate the significance of the suffering of God and of other Christians together with the poor in the context of mass misery. Yet another question was whether the entire creation would participate in redemption.

During Gregory's age three solutions were being offered: (a) the middle Platonist insistence on God's *apatheia* and on the ethics of sublimity; (b) the neo-Arian subordination of God's pathic to God's apathic nature together with the soteriological instrumentalization of the physical; and (c) God's acceptance of suffering in the Son and the inclusion of all creatures in liberation. Gregory represents the third solution.

19. Gregory develops the idea of suffering from the perspective of Chris-

tology, the Trinity, anthropology, cosmology, soteriology, ethics, and eschatology, emphasizing the voluntary nature of Christ's acceptance of suffering
as a presupposition for the liberation of creation and the inclusion of corporeality in the liberation of human beings, who are liberated not *from* the corporeal, but rather from evil and *to* new corporeal life. Beginning with the notion of the suffering of the cosmos, Gregory develops a universal soteriology
that includes the entire cosmos; the human capacity for suffering comes to
positive expression in an ascetic ethics of sympathy and cosuffering. Gregory
understands the correspondence between God and the world from the perspective of suffering as a linking of christo-dicy and cosmo-dicy and in the
three-part conceptual figure of the acceptance of suffering, the endurance of
suffering, and the liberation of all that is created.

20. Between 340 and 381 the theology of the ancient church was forced
to reflect on experiences with the Holy Spirit. Gregory responded to this challenge by developing a cosmic pneumatology.

He directed his thesis of the Spirit's indwelling within corporeal human
beings against middle Platonism, which taught a purely soul-oriented participation of the Spirit, and against Eunomius, who unnecessarily reduced the
mystery of the incarnation. Gregory's thesis of the Spirit's enhancement of
community served ecumenical and irenic interests and criticized social injustice. His thesis of vivification through the Spirit helped him overcome
Platonist panentheism.

Gregory's understanding of the liberation of nature includes three
pneumatological stages: the Spirit (a) permeates creation and is *with* it;
(b) dwells within creation, is *in* creation itself; and (c) consummates or perfects creation, leading creation *to* new being with the Creator.

Part III

21. The sociality of nature and the ideas of movement, suffering, and the
Spirit all represent significant concerns in Gregory's theology, in ecological
discourse, and in current ecological theology.

22. The solutions offered by ecology and by theology in both late antiquity and late modernity can be related through critical "dialogue." A correlation between the interpretations of the four problems as offered by theology
from late antiquity and by late modernity (a) expands our understanding of
those problems, (b) provides a critical corrective to the various proposals,
(c) opens new possibilities for addressing various issues, and (d) helps qualify
and mediate theological contributions to ecological discourse.

23. From the perspective of sociality, one particular problem is the relation between ontology and soteriology. From the perspective of movement, a problem is the relation between movement, time, and evil. From the perspective of suffering, it is the differentiation between the uniqueness of suffering with regard to the triune God, creatures, and creation. And from the perspective of the Spirit, it is the various ontological and soteriological ways of expressing the relation between the Holy Spirit and life.

24. The ecological perspective expands liberation theology to include the subjects of nature themselves as partners in theological dialogue and as subjects capable of perceiving the Creator. The conflict of the divided world is now viewed as a conflict involving all of nature. The ecological sciences join the social sciences as partners to theology. And finally, the dialectic within social history is now linked to evolution within natural history.

25. Within the contextual theological paradigm, an ecological theology of liberation with regard to the four problem areas of correlation emerges in which the trinitarian God, a new theological concept of movement, the conceptual form of the theology of the cross, and a topologically shaped pneumatology all play a central role. Trinitarian ecology focuses on the convergence between God's perichoretic communality and relational nature.

The idea of movement within God's being leads to the notion of the holiness of the earth's movement and indeed of all movement on earth, and to the concept of God's liberating movement.

A hermeneutics of the cross of creatures is able to draw not only on J. von Uexküll's semiotic model, but also on the expressive forms of modern art.

An ecology of the Holy Spirit can be developed in the sense of the "vision of the transparency of place," making it possible to develop criteria for a pneumatological grammar that then enhances both our experiences with the Spirit and the various modes of expression of spirituality.

The ecological pneumatology of liberation reconstructs the Nicene Creed — specifically the confession to the Spirit of triunity as the creator of life and of the coming world — such that the Spirit, rather than functioning as the mediator between the Father/Son and the world, appears instead as the triune God who acts at places within a world in need of redemption.

26. Although the method of correlation can help maintain the vitality of the ongoing transmission and continuity of theology, it cannot demonstrate the unity of that tradition's continuity. It does, however, demonstrate the intertwined nature of temporal modalities by making the content of past forms of theological expression accessible to the present and future.

Our experience with the method of correlation showed us that those using the method must (a) carefully identify the problem common to the two interpretations, (b) correlate not only the problems themselves but also the situations of the different interpretations of those problems, and (c) remain mindful of the temporal sequence of the various stages of correlation.

27. The concept of tradition functions as a positive criterion in the service of contextual theology when understood as the social memory of a series of local theologies. The Christian concept of tradition can include the history of losers among nonhuman creatures as the tradition of nature's oppressed past.

28. The constructive incorporation of the classic apophatic principle as used in Gregory's theology can help develop theology as soteriology, overcome the problem of epistemological pluralism and the ontological dilemma of late modernity, enhance the critical rationality of theology, articulate the theological understanding of nature from the perspective of transparency, and enhance dialogue between the religions.

Works Cited

Aagaard, Anna Marie. 1973. *Helligånden sendt til Verden.* Aarhus.

————. 1974. "Der Heilige Geist in der Welt." In *Wiederentdeckung des Heiligen Geistes: Der Heilige Geist in der charismatischen Erfahrung und theologischen Reflexion*, 97-119. Ökumenische Perspektiven 6. Frankfurt am Main.

Adams, Carol J., ed. 1993. *Ecofeminism and the Sacred.* New York.

Ahlstrand, Kajsa. 1993. *Fundamental Openness: An Enquiry into Raimundo Panikkar's Theological Vision and Its Presuppositions.* Studia Missionalia Upsaliensia LVII. Uppsala.

Albrecht, Ruth. 1986. *Das Leben der heiligen Makrina auf dem Hintergrund der Thekla-Traditionen.* Forschungen zur Kirchen- und Dogmengeschichte 38. Göttingen.

Allen, Timothy F. H., and Thomas W. Hoekstra. 1992. *Toward a Unified Ecology.* Complexity in Ecological Systems Series. New York.

Althaus, Heinz. 1972. *Die Heilslehre des heiligen Gregor von Nazianz.* Münster.

Altner, Günter. 1974. *Schöpfung am Abgrund: Die Theologie vor der Umweltfrage.* Neukirchen.

————. 1981. *Tod, Ewigkeit und Überleben.* Heidelberg.

————. 1984. *Fortschritt wohin? Der Streit um die Alternative.* Neukirchen-Vluyn.

————. 1987. *Die große Kollision: Mensch und Natur.* Graz.

————. 1988. *Die Überlebenskrise in der Gegenwart: Ansätze zum Dialog mit der Natur in Naturwissenschaft und Theologie.* Darmstadt.

————. 1991. *Naturvergessenheit: Grundlagen einer umfassenden Bioethik.* Darmstadt.

————, ed. 1989. *Ökologische Theologie: Perspektiven zur Orientierung.* Stuttgart.

Ambrose. 1983. "On the Holy Spirit." In *Some of the Principal Works of St. Ambrose*, translated by H. de Romestin, 93-158. Select Library of Nicene and Post-Nicene Fathers of the Christian Church, vol. 10. Grand Rapids.

Andresen, Carl. 1975. *Geschichte des Christentums: I. Von den Anfängen bis zur Hochscholastik.* Stuttgart.

————, ed. 1988. *Handbuch der Dogmen- und Theologiegeschichte.* Ungekürzte Studienausgabe, vols. 1-3. Göttingen.

Apel, Karl-Otto. 1986. "Verantwortung heute — nur noch Prinzip der Bewahrung und Selbstbeschränkung oder immer noch der Befreiung und Verwirklichung von Humanität?" In *Zukunftsethik und Industriegesellschaft*, edited by Thomas Meyer and Susanne Miller, 15-40. Munich.

———. 1992a. "Diskursethik vor der Problematik von Recht und Politik: Können die Rationalitätsdifferenzen zwischen Moralität, Recht und Politik selbst noch durch die Diskursethik normativ-rational gerechtfertigt werden?" In *Zur Anwendung der Diskursethik in Politik, Recht und Wissenschaft*, edited by Karl-Otto Apel and Matthias Kettner, 29-61. Frankfurt am Main.

———. 1992b. "The Ecological Crisis as a Problem for Discourse Ethics." In *Ecology and Ethics*, edited by Audun Øfsti, 219-60. Trondheim.

Aristotle. 1950 (1932). *Politics*. 3rd ed. London.

———. 1953. *De caelo*. Edited by W. K. C. Guthrie. 3rd ed. London.

———. 1969. *Metaphysics: Books X-XI*. In *Aristotle in Twenty-three Volumes*, vol. 18. London and Cambridge, Mass.

———. 1983. *Physique (I-IV)*. Edited and translated by Henri Carteron. Paris.

———. 1986. *Physique (V-VIII)*. Edited and translated by Henri Carteron. Paris.

Arndt, M. 1980. "Leiden." In *Historisches Wörterbuch der Philosophie*, 5:206-12. Basel and Stuttgart.

Assmann, Jan. 1990. *Ma'at: Gerechtigkeit und Unsterblichkeit im Alten Ägypten*. Munich.

Augustine. 1911, 1914, 1916. *Gottesstaat*. In *Des Heiligen Kirchenvaters Aurelius Augustinus Ausgewählte Schriften*. Bibliothek der Kirchenväter 1, 16, 28. Translated by Alfred Schröder. Kempten and Munich. *(The City of God.)*

Aulén, Gustaf. 1927. *Den kristna gudsbilden genom seklerna och i nutiden: En konturteckning*. Stockholm.

———. 1983 (1931). *Christus Victor: A Historical Study of the Three Main Types of the Idea of the Atonement*. London.

Bakken, Peter W. 1995. *Ecology, Justice, and Christian Faith: A Critical Guide to the Literature*. Westport, Conn.

Barbel, Joseph, ed. 1963. *Die fünf theologischen Reden: Text und Übersetzung mit Einleitung und Kommentar*. Düsseldorf.

Barnes, Michael, ed. 1994. *An Ecology of the Spirit: Religious Reflection and Environmental Consciousness*. Annual Publication of the College Theology Society, vol. 37. Lanham, Md.

Barnes, Trevor J., and James S. Duncan, eds. 1992. *Writing Worlds: Discourse, Text, and Metaphor in the Representation of Landscape*. London and New York.

Bateson, Gregory. 1990a. *Ökologie des Geistes: Anthropologische, psychologische, biologische und epistemologische Perspektiven*. Frankfurt am Main. In English, *Steps to an Ecology of Mind*, 1972.

———. 1990b. *Geist und Natur: Eine notwendige Einheit*. Frankfurt am Main. In English, *Mind and Nature*, 1979.

Bätschmann, Oskar. 1989. *Entfernung der Natur: Landschaftsmalerei 1750-1920*. Cologne.

Baudelaire, Charles. 1976. *Le peintre de la vie moderne*. In *Oeuvres compl. 2*, edited by Cl. Pichois. Paris.

Baumgarten, Alexander Gottlieb. 1973. "Aesthetica." In *Ästhetik als Philosophie der sinnlichen Erkenntnis*, edited by Hans Rudolf Schweizer. Basel.

Bayer, Oswald. 1990. *Schöpfung als Anrede: Zu einer Hermeneutik der Schöpfung*. 2nd enlarged ed. Tübingen.

Beck, Ulrich. 1986. *Risikogesellschaft: Auf dem Weg in eine andere Moderne*. Frankfurt am Main.

————. 1988. *Gegengifte: Die organisierte Unverantwortlichkeit*. Frankfurt am Main.

Beinert, Wolfgang. 1987. "Art. Tradition." In *Lexikon der katholischen Dogmatik*, edited by Wolfgang Beinert, 513-16. Freiburg, Basel, and Vienna.

Benjamin, Walter. 1991. "Über den Begriff der Geschichte." In *Gesammelte Schriften: Abhandlungen, Band I. 2*, 691-704. Frankfurt am Main. In English, "Thesis on the Philosophy of History," in *Illuminations*, 1969.

Bentham, Jeremy. 1789. *An Introduction to the Principles of Morals and Legislation*. Oxford.

Bergant, Dianne. 1998. *The Earth Is the Lord's: The Bible, Ecology, and Worship*. Collegeville, Minn.

Berger, Klaus. 1984. "Geist/Heiliger, Geist/Geistesgaben, III. Neues Testament." In *Theologische Realenzyklopädie*, 12:178-96. Berlin and New York.

Berger, Peter L., and Thomas Luckmann. 1977. *Die gesellschaftliche Konstruktion der Wirklichkeit: Eine Theorie der Wissenssoziologie*. 5th ed. Frankfurt am Main. In English, *The Social Construction of Reality*, 1966.

Bergmann, Sigurd. 1991. "Andliga är ondskans rot och rörelse — en detalj i änglaläran hos Gregorios av Nazianz i ljuset av det moderna förnuftets kris." In *Florilegium Patristicum: Festskrift till Per Beskow*, 19-39. Delsbo, Sweden.

————. 1992. "Naturens rättigheter — teologiska perspektiv på naturens egenvärde i en rättsgemenskap av allt levande." *Vår Lösen* 6, no. 7: 379-96.

————. 1993a. "Gregory of Nazianzen's Theological Interpretation of the Philosophy of Nature in the Doctrine of the Four Elements." In *Studia Patristica Vol. XXVII*, edited by Elizabeth A. Livingstone, 3-8. Louvain.

————. 1993b. "Varför bildkonsten och trostolkningen vet något om världen." *Vår Lösen* 5, no. 6: 325-32.

————. 1993c. "Die Welt als Ware oder Haushalt? Die Wegwahl der trinitarischen Kosmologie bei Gregor von Nazianz." *Evangelische Theologie* 53, no. 5: 460-70.

————. 1994a. "Diskursiv bioetik — för offrens skull." In *Miljöetik — för ett samhälle på människans och naturens villkor*, edited by Uno Svedin and Anne-Marie Thunberg, 68-89. Forskningsrådsnämnden Rapport 94, 2. Stockholm.

————. 1994b. "Naturens värde och människans vördnad: Varför man bör tillerkänna naturen dess rättigheter." *Retfærd* 65: 76-86.

————. 1994c. "History of Mission — History of Liberation?" In *Mission in a Pluralist Society*, edited by Werner Ustorf, 81-104. Studies in the Intercultural History of Christianity 97. Frankfurt am Main.

————. 1994d. "Jord, kultur och Ande — komposten i humanekologisk och teologisk belysning." In *Kontextuell livstolkning: teologi i ett pluralistiskt Norden*, edited by Sigurd Bergmann and Carl Reinhold Bråkenhielm, 224-50. Religio 43. Lund. In

German, "Erde, Kultur und Heiliger Geist — Praktische Theologie des Kompostierens," in Bergmann 1997b, 296-328.

————. 1994e. "Att genom bilder finna kors." *Vår Lösen* 6: 447-55.

————. 1994f. "'Landskapet har gått under i dammet' — Den moderna bildkonstens naturbild utmanar kulturteologin." In *Kontextuell livstolkning: teologi i ett pluralistiskt Norden,* edited by Sigurd Bergmann and Carl Reinhold Bråkenhielm, 57-90. Religio 43. Lund. In German, "'Die Landschaft ist am Staub zugrunde gegangen' — Die Herausforderung der Theologie durch die bildende Kunst der Moderne," in Bergmann, *Geist, der lebendig macht: Lavierungen zur ökologischen Befreiungstheologie,* 34-70, Frankfurt am Main, 1997.

————. 1997a. *Gud i funktion: en orientering i den kontextuella teologin.* Stockholm.

————. 1997b. *Geist, der lebendig macht: Lavierungen zur ökologischen Befreiungstheologie.* Frankfurt am Main.

————. 1998. "Das Fremde wahrnehmen: Die öko- und ethnologische Herausforderung der Bildkunst und Theologie." In *Kunst-Positionen: Kunst als gegenwärtiges Thema evangelischer und katholischer Theologie,* edited by Wolfgang Erich Müller and Jürgen Heumann, 96-120. Stuttgart.

————. 2001. "'Ich kenne ihre Leiden. Darum bin ich herniedergestiegen . . .' Das neve Paradigma der kontextuellen Theologie." *Studia Theologie* 55, no. 1:4-22.

————. 2003. *God in Context: A Survey on Contextual Theology.* Aldershot.

Berkhof, Hendrikus. 1988 (1968). *Theologie des Heiligen Geistes.* 2nd ed. Neukirchen-Vluyn. In English, *Doctrine of the Holy Spirit,* 1964.

Bernardi, J. 1968. *La prédication des Pères Cappadociens: Le prédicateur et son auditoire. Saint Grégoire de Nazianze.* Marseille.

Bernstein, Ellen, ed. 1998. *Ecology and the Jewish Spirit: Where Nature and the Sacred Meet.* Woodstock, Vt.

Berry, Thomas. 1988. *The Dream of the Earth.* San Francisco.

Beuckmann, Ulrich. 1988. *Gregor von Nazianz: Gegen die Habsucht (Carmen 1. 2. 28). Einleitung und Kommentar.* Studien zur Geschichte und Kultur des Altertums 2, 6. Paderborn.

Bevens, Stephen B. 1992. *Models of Contextual Theology.* Maryknoll, N.Y.

Binswanger, Hans Christoph. 1991. *Geld & Natur: Das wirtschaftliche Wachstum im Spannungsfeld zwischen Ökonomie und Ökologie.* Stuttgart and Vienna.

Birch, Charles, and John B. Cobb, Jr. 1990 (1981). *The Liberation of Life: From the Cell to the Community.* Denton, Tex.

Birnbacher, Dieter. 1979. "Was kann Verantwortung für die Natur heißen?" In *Frieden mit der Natur,* edited by Klaus Michael Meyer-Abich, 91-111. Freiburg im Breisgau.

————, ed. 1986. *Ökologie und Ethik.* Stuttgart.

Bloch, Ernst. 1977 (1959). *Das Prinzip Hoffnung.* Vols. 1-3. 4th ed. Frankfurt am Main.

Blumenberg, Hans. 1959. "Kritik und Rezeption antiker Philosophie in der Patristik." *Studium generale* 12: 485-97.

————. 1989 (1975). *Die Genesis der kopernikanischen Welt.* Vol. 1, *Die Zweideutigkeit des Himmels/Eröffnung der Möglichkeit eines Kopernikus.* Vol. 2, *Typologie der frühen Wirkungen/Der Stillstand des Himmels und der Fortgang der Zeit.* Vol. 3, *Der kopernikanische Komparativ/Die kopernikanische Optik.* 2nd ed. Frankfurt am Main.

———. 1993 (1981). *Die Lesbarkeit der Welt.* 3rd ed. Frankfurt am Main.

Boehm, Gottfried. 1986. "Das neue Bild der Natur: Nach dem Ende der Landschafts-malerei." In *Landschaft,* edited by Manfred Smuda, 87-110. Frankfurt am Main.

Boff, Leonardo. 1985. *Saint Francis: A Model for Human Liberation.* London. In Portuguese, *São Francisco de Assis: Temura e Vigor,* Petrópolis, 1981.

———. 1988. *Trinity and Society.* Tunbridge Wells. In Portuguese, *A trindade, a sociedade e a libertação,* Petrópolis, 1986.

———. 1993a. "Ökologie und Spiritualität: Kosmische Mystik." *Evangelische Theologie* 53, no. 5: 438-51.

———. 1993b. "Religious Experience and Ecology." *COELI Quarterly,* no. 64: 16-23.

———. 1995. *Ecology and Liberation: A New Paradigm.* Maryknoll, N.Y. In Portuguese, *Ecologia Mundialização-Espiritualidade: A emergência de um novo paradigma,* São Paulo, 1993.

———. 1997. *Cry of the Earth, Cry of the Poor.* Maryknoll, N.Y. In Portuguese, *Ecologia: Grito da Terra, Grito dos Pobres,* São Paulo, 1995.

Böhler, Dietrich. 1981. "Naturverstehen und Sinnverstehen: Traditionskritische Thesen zur Entwicklung und zur konstruktivistisch-szientifischen Umdeutung des Topos vom Buch der Natur." In *Naturverständnis und Naturbeherrschung: Philosophiegeschichtliche Entwicklung und gegenwärtiger Kontext,* edited by Friedrich Rapp, 70-95. Munich.

Böhme, Gernot. 1989. *Für eine ökologische Naturästhetik.* Frankfurt am Main.

Böhme, Hartmut. 1988. *Natur und Subjekt.* Frankfurt am Main.

Böhme, Jakob. 1983. *Die Morgenröte bricht an: Zeugnisse der Naturfrömmigkeit und der Christuserkenntnis.* Edited by Gerhard Wehr. Herderbücherei "Texte zum Nachdenken" 1077. Freiburg im Breisgau.

Bonhoeffer, Dietrich. 1997. *Letters and Papers from Prison.* New, greatly enlarged ed. New York.

Børresen, Kari Elisabeth. 1989. "Patristic Inculturation: Medieval Foremothers and Feminist Theology." In *Feministteologi idag,* 157-72. Religio 30. Lund.

Borst, Arno. 1957. *Der Turmbau von Babel: Geschichte der Meinungen über Ursprung und Vielfalt der Sprachen und Völker.* Vol. 1, *Fundamente und Aufbau.* Stuttgart.

Bosch, David J. 1991. *Transforming Mission: Paradigm Shifts in Theology of Mission.* American Society of Missiology Series, no. 16. Maryknoll, N.Y.

Bouma-Prediger, Steven. 1995. *The Greening of Theology: The Ecological Models of Rosemary Radford Ruether, Joseph Sittler, and Jürgen Moltmann.* American Academy of Religion Dissertation Series 91. Atlanta.

Brown, Peter. 1971. *The World of Late Antiquity: From Marcus Aurelius to Muhammad.* London.

———. 1986. "The Notion of Virginity in the Early Church." In *Christian Spirituality,* vol. 1, *Origins to the Twelfth Century,* edited by Bernard McGinn and John Meyendorff, 427-43. London.

———. 1988. *The Body and Society: Men, Women, and Sexual Renunciation in Early Christianity.* New York.

Brox, Norbert. 1982. "Zur christlichen Mission in der Spätantike." In *Mission im Neuen Testament,* edited by Karl Kertelge, 190-237. Quaestiones Disputatae 93. Freiburg im Breisgau.

———. 1988. "Diakonie in der frühen Kirche: Die Erde zum Himmel machen." *Concilium* 24, no. 4: 277-81.

Bujo, Bénézet. 1993. *Die ethische Dimension der Gemeinschaft: Das afrikanische Modell im Nord-Süd-Dialog.* Studien zur theologischen Ethik 49. Fribourg, Switzerland, and Freiburg im Breisgau.

Bulgakov, Sergij [Serge Boulgakof]. 1946. *Le paraclet.* Translated from Russian. *Paris. Utesitel', O Bogoce-lovecestre,* 1936.

Bultmann, Rudolf. 1977 (1948-53). *Theologie des Neuen Testaments.* 7th enlarged ed. Tübingen. In English, *Theology of the New Testament,* 1956.

Burns, J. Patout. 1994. "The Unicorn and the Rhinoceros: A Response to Matthew Fox." In *An Ecology of the Spirit: Religious Reflection and Environmental Consciousness,* edited by Michael Barnes, 75-82. Annual Publication of the College Theology Society, vol. 36. Lanham, Md.

Buthelezi, Manas. 1968. *Creation and the Church: A Study in Ecclesiology with Special Reference to a Younger Church Milieu.* Madison, Wis.

Campenhausen, Hans Freiherr von. 1973. "Einheit und Einigkeit in der Alten Kirche." *Evangelische Theologie* 33: 280-93.

Carson, Rachel. 1962. *Silent Spring.* Boston.

Caruana, Wally. 1993. *Aboriginal Art.* London and New York.

Cavalli, Alessandro. 1991. "Soziale Gedächtnisbildung in der Moderne." In *Kultur als Lebenswelt und Monument,* edited by Aleida Assmann and Dietrich Harth, 200-210. Frankfurt am Main.

Chomsky, Noam. 1973. *Aspekte der Syntax-Theorie.* Frankfurt am Main. In English, *Aspects of the Theory of Syntax,* 1965.

Cobb, John B., Jr. 1972. *Is It Too Late? A Theology of Ecology.* Beverly Hills, Calif.

———. 1975. *Christ in a Pluralistic Age.* Philadelphia.

———. 1982. *Process Theology as Political Theology.* Manchester and Philadelphia.

———. 1990. "The Role of Theology of Nature in the Church." In *Liberating Life: Contemporary Approaches to Ecological Theology,* edited by Charles Birch, William Eakin, and Jay B. McDaniel, 261-72. New York.

———. 1992. *Sustainability: Economics, Ecology, and Justice.* Maryknoll, N.Y.

Cobb, John B., Jr., and David R. Griffin. 1977. *Process Theology: An Introductory Exposition.* Belfast.

Collet, Giancarlo, ed. 1990. *Theologien der Dritten Welt: EATWOT als Herausforderung westlicher Theologie und Kirche.* Neue Zeitschrift für Missionswissenschaft, Supplementa XXXVII. Immensee, Switzerland.

Comblin, José. 1987. *The Holy Spirit and Liberation.* Tunbridge Wells and Maryknoll, N.Y. In Portuguese, *O Espírito Santo e a Libertação,* São Paulo.

Congar, Yves. 1981. "Der politische Monotheismus der Antike und der trinitarische Gott." *Concilium* 17, no. 3: 195-99.

———. 1983. *I Believe in the Holy Spirit.* Vol. 2. London.

———. 1986. *The Word and the Spirit.* London.

Cooper, David E., and Joy A. Palmer, eds. 1998. *Spirit of the Environment: Religion, Value, and Environmental Concern.* London and New York.

Coseriu, Eugenio. 1982. "Naturbild und Sprache." In *Das Naturbild des Menschen,* edited by Jörg Zimmermann, 260-84. Munich.

Coulie, Bernard. 1985. *Les Richesses dans l'Œvre de Saint Grégoire de Nazianze: Étude littéraire et historique.* Louvain-La-Neuve.

Daecke, Sigurd Martin. 1979. "Auf dem Weg zu einer Praktischen Theologie der Natur." In *Frieden mit der Natur,* edited by Klaus Michael Meyer-Abich, 262-85. Freiburg im Breisgau.

Daneel, M. L. 1993. "African Independent Church Pneumatology and the Salvation of All Creation." *International Review of Mission* 82, no. 326: 143-66.

Darwin, Francis, ed. 1887. *Leben und Briefe von Charles Darwin.* Vol. 3. Stuttgart.

Davies, Paul. 1989. *Den kosmiska planen.* Stockholm. In English, *The Cosmic Blueprint,* 1987.

Deane-Drummond, Celia E. 1997. *Ecology in Jürgen Moltmann's Theology.* Lewiston, N.Y.

Degen-Ballmer, Stephan. 2001. *Gott–Mensch–Welt: Eine Untersuchung über mögliche holistische Denkmodelle in der Prozesstheologie und der ostkirchlich-orthodoxen Theologie als Beitrag für ein ethikrelevantes Natur- und Schöpfungsverständis.* Frankfurt am Main.

Dembowski, Hermann. 1989. "Natürliche Theologie und Theologie der Natur." In *Ökologische Theologie: Perspektiven zur Orientierung,* edited by Günter Altner, 30-58. Stuttgart.

Derrida, Jacques. 1993. *Vom Geist: Heidegger und die Frage.* 2nd ed. Frankfurt am Main. In French, *De l'esprit. Heidegger et la question,* Paris, 1987.

————. 1994. *Die Schrift und die Differenz.* 6th ed. Frankfurt am Main. In French, *L'écriture et la différence,* Paris, 1967.

Descola, Philippe. 1994. *In the Society of Nature: A Native Ecology in Amazonia.* Cambridge Studies in Social and Cultural Anthropology 93. Cambridge.

Des Jardins, Joseph R. 1997. *Environmental Ethics: An Introduction to Environmental Philosophy.* 2nd ed. Belmont, Calif.

Doerrie, Heinrich. 1956. *Leid und Erfahrung: Die Wort- und Sinn-Verbindung von παθειν-μαθειν im griechischen Denken.* Akademie der Wissenschaften und der Literatur in Mainz. Abhandlungen der Geistes- und Sozialwissenschaftlichen Klasse, no. 5. Jahrgang 1956. Mainz.

Dörries, Hermann. 1966. *Wort und Stunde: Gesammelte Studien zur Kirchengeschichte des vierten Jahrhunderts.* Göttingen.

Duchrow, Ulrich. 1989. "Gerechtigkeit, Frieden und Befreiung der Schöpfung." In *Ökologische Theologie: Perspektiven zur Orientierung,* edited by Günter Altner, 349 62. Stuttgart.

————. 1992. *Europe in the World System, 1492-1992: Is Justice Possible?* Geneva. In German, *Europa im Weltsystem 1492-1992: Gibt es einen Weg der Gerechtigkeit nach 500 Jahren Raub, Unterdrückung und Geldver(m)ehrung?* Bremen, 1991.

————. 1994. "Kyrkor mellan världsmarknad. världsriken och Guds rike — biblisk hågkomst och världsekonomiska perspektiv." In *Upptäckter i kontexten: teologiska föreläsningar till Per Frostins minne*, edited by Sigurd Bergmann and Göran Eidevall, 20-51. Skrifter från Institutet för kontextuell teologi 3. Lund.

———. 1995. *Alternatives to Global Capitalism: Drawn from Biblical History, Designed for Political Action*. Utrecht. In German, *Alternativen zur kapitalistischen Weltwirtschaft: Biblische Erinnerung und politische Ansätze zur Überwindung einer lebensbedrohenden Ökonomie*, Gütersloh, 1994.

Duchrow, Ulrich, and Gerhard Liedke. 1989. *Shalom: Biblical Perspectives on Creation, Justice, and Peace*. Geneva.

Düchting, Hajo. 1991. *Franz Marc*. Cologne.

Dussel, Enrique. 1995. *The Invention of the Americas: Eclipse of "the Other" and the Myth of Modernity*. New York. In German, *Von der Erfindung Amerikas zur Entdeckung des Anderen: Ein Projekt der Transmoderne*, Theologie Interkulturell 6, Düsseldorf, 1993.

Ehrhardt, Arnold A. T. 1959a. *Politische Metaphysik von Solon bis Augustin*. Vol. 1, *Die Gottesstadt der Griechen und Römer*. Tübingen.

———. 1959b. *Politische Metaphysik von Solon bis Augustin*. Vol. 2, *Die christliche Revolution*. Tübingen.

———. 1969. *Politische Metaphysik von Solon bis Augustin*. Vol. 3, *Civitas Dei*. Tübingen.

Ellenius, Allan. 1992. *Landskapsbilden: Ur den europeiska naturkänslans historia*. Stockholm.

Ellverson, Anna-Stina. 1981. *The Dual Nature of Man: A Study in the Theological Anthropology of Gregory of Nazianzus*. Uppsala.

Finger, Thomas N. 1997. *Self, Earth, and Society: Alienation and Trinitarian Transformation*. Downers Grove, Ill.

Finley, Moses I. 1977. "Die Schuldknechtschaft." In *Seminar: Die Entstehung der antiken Klassengesellschaft*, edited by Hans G. Kippenberg, 173-204. Frankfurt am Main.

Forschner, Maximilian. 1981. *Die stoische Ethik: Über den Zusammenhang von Natur- Sprach- und Moralphilosophie im altstoischen System*. Stuttgart.

Foucault, Michel. 1993. *Die Ordnung der Dinge: Eine Archäologie der Humanwissenschaften*. 12th ed. Frankfurt am Main. In French, *Les mots et les choses*, 1966.

Fowler, Robert Booth. 1995. *The Greening of Protestant Thought*. Chapel Hill, N.C., and London.

Fox, Matthew. 1991. *Vision vom kosmischen Christus: Aufbruch ins dritte Jahrtausend*. Stuttgart. In English, *The Coming of the Cosmic Christ*, 1988.

———. 1994. "Creation Mysticism and the Return of a Trinitarian Christianity." In *An Ecology of the Spirit: Religious Reflection and Environmental Consciousness*, edited by Michael Barnes, 61-73. Annual Publication of the College Theology Society, vol. 36. Lanham, Md.

Fragomeni, Richard N., and John T. Pawlikowski, eds. 1994. *The Ecological Challenge: Ethical, Liturgical, and Spiritual Responses*. Collegeville, Minn.

Franks, R. S. 1953. *The Doctrine of the Trinity*. London.

"Fred genom rättvisa: De europeiska kristna kyrkornas bidrag till världskonferensen i Seoul 1990. Antaget på den ekumeniska europeiska konferensen i Basel." 1989. In

Tiden är inne — ekumenisk teologi i uppbrott, edited by Sigurd Bergmann and Gunborg Blomstrand, 122-69. KISA rapport 5. Uppsala.

Frey, Christofer. 1988. "Theologie und Ethik der Schöpfung: Ein Überblick, H. E. Tödt zum 70. Geburtstag." *Zeitschrift für Evangelische Ethik* 1: 47-62.

Frohnhofen, Herbert. 1987. *Apatheia tou theou: Über die Affektlosigkeit Gottes in der griechischen Antike und bei den griechischsprachigen Kirchenvätern bis zu Gregorios Thaumaturgos.* Frankfurt am Main.

Frostin, Per. 1987. *De fattigas evangelium — befrielse för svenskar?* Stockholm.

————. 1988. *Liberation Theology in Tanzania and South Africa: A First World Interpretation.* Studia Theologica Lundensia 42. Lund.

————. 1990. "Systematisk teologi i ett pluralistiskt samhälle." *Svensk teologisk kvartalskrift* 66, no. 4: 154-62. In English, "Systematic Theology in a Pluralist Society," *Studia Theologica* 46 (1992): 15-27.

————. 1992a. "Kristendomens kairos — vågar kyrkorna säga nej till mammon och ja till de fattigas Gud?" In *De nedtystades Gud — diakoni för livets skull,* edited by Sigurd Bergmann, 13-53. Stockholm.

————. 1992b. "'Tredje världen-teologierna' som ekumenisk forskningsuppgift." In *Ekumeniken och forskningen: Föreläsningar vid den nordiska forskarkursen "Teorier och metoder inom forskning om ekumenik" i Lund 1991,* edited by Sigurd Bergmann et al., 125-35. Uppsala.

————. 1994. *The Two Kingdoms Doctrine: A Critical Study.* Studia Theologica Lundensia 48. Lund.

Früchtel, Ursula. 1968. *Die kosmologischen Vorstellungen bei Philo von Alexandrien: Ein Beitrag zur Geschichte der Genesisexegese.* Arbeiten zur Literatur und Geschichte des hellenistischen Judentums 2. Leiden.

Fuchs, H. 1926. *Augustin und der antike Friedensgedanke.* Berlin.

Gabriel, Karl. 1991. "Tradition im Kontext enttraditionalisierter Gesellschaft." In *Wie geschieht Tradition? Überlieferung im Lebensprozess der Kirche,* edited by Dietrich Wiederkehr, 69-88. Quaestiones Disputatae 133. Freiburg, Basel, and Vienna.

Gallay, Paul. 1943. *La Vie de Saint Grégoire de Nazianze.* Paris.

Galtung, Johan. 1975. *Är fred möjlig? Studier i fred och imperialism.* Stockholm.

Gebara, Ivonne. 1996. "The Trinity and Human Experience: An Ecofeminist Approach." In *Women Healing Earth: Third World Women on Ecology, Feminism, and Religion,* edited by Rosemary Radford Ruether, 13-23. Maryknoll, N.Y.

Gemoll, Wilhelm. 1965 (1908). *Griechisch-Deutsches Schul- und Hand-Wörterbuch.* 9th ed. Munich and Vienna.

George, K. M. 1990. "Towards an Eucharistic Ecology." In *Justice, Peace, and the Integrity of Creation: Insights from Orthodoxy,* edited by Gennadios Limouris, 45-55. Geneva.

Gerlitz, Peter. 1998. *Mensch und Natur in den Weltreligionen.* Darmstadt.

Giddens, Anthony. 1992 (1990). *The Consequences of Modernity.* Cambridge.

Goethe, Johann Wolfgang. 1972. *Faust: Der Tragödie erster und zweiter Teil. Urfaust.* Edited and commented on by Erich Trunz. Munich.

————. 1989a. "Recht und Pflicht. Zur Naturwissenschaft II. 2." In *Zur Naturwissen-*

schaft überhaupt, besonders zur Morphologie: Erfahrung, Betrachtung. Folgerung durch Lebensereignisse verbunden. Münchner Ausgabe Band 12. Munich.

———. 1989b. *Die Natur.* In Picht, *Der Begriff der Natur und seine Geschichte,* 38-42. Stuttgart.

Goss-Mayr, Hildegard. 1981 (1976). *Der Mensch vor dem Unrecht: Spiritualität und Praxis gewaltloser Befreiung.* 4th enlarged ed. Vienna.

Grassi, Ernesto, and Thure von Uexküll. 1950. *Von Ursprung und Grenzen der Geisteswissenschaften und Naturwissenschaften.* Munich.

Green, Elizabeth E. 1994. "The Transmutation of Theology: Ecofeminist Alchemy and the Christian Tradition." In *Ecofeminism and Theology* (Yearbook of the European Society of Women in Theological Research), edited by Mary Grey and Elizabeth E. Green, 48-58. Mainz and Kampen.

Gregorios, Paulos. 1978. *The Human Presence: An Orthodox View of Nature.* Geneva.

———. 1988. *Cosmic Man: The Divine Presence.* New York.

Gregory, Derek. 1994. *Geographical Imaginations.* Cambridge, Mass., and Oxford.

Gregory of Nazianzus. Greek sources: Patrologiæ cursus completus. Series graecae [PG] 35-38, edited by J.-P. Migne, Paris, 1886; Sources Chrétiennes (Paris): *Discours 1-3,* edited by Jean Bernardi (1978) (SC 247); *Discours 4-5,* edited by Jean Bernardi (1983) (SC 309); *Discours 20-23,* edited by Justin Mossay and Guy Lafontaine (1980) (SC 270); *Discours 24-26,* edited by Justin Mossay and Guy Lafontaine (1981) (SC 284); *Discours 27-31,* edited by Paul Gallay and Maurice Jourjon (1978) (SC 250); *Discours 32-37,* edited by Claudio Moreschini and Paul Gallay (1985) (SC 318); *Discours 38-41,* edited by Claudio Moreschini and Paul Gallay (1990) (SC 358); *Discours 42-43,* edited by Jean Bernardi (1992) (SC 384); *Lettres théologiques,* edited by Paul Gallay and Maurice Jourjon (1974) (SC 208); *La Passion du Christ: Tragédie,* edited by André Tuilier (1969) (SC 149); *Gregor von Nazianz. De Vita Sua: Einleitung. Text. Übersetzung. Kommentar,* edited by Christoph Jungck, Heidelberg, 1974; *Gregor von Nazianz. Briefe,* edited by Paul Gallay, Berlin, 1969; *Gregor von Nazianz. Über die Bischöfe (Carmen 2. 1. 12). Einleitung. Text. Übersetzung. Kommentar,* Beno Meier, StGKA 2. 7, Paderborn, 1989; *Gregor von Nazianz. Gegen die Putzsucht der Frauen,* Griechischer Text mit Übersetzung, motivgeschichtlichem Überblick und Kommentar von Andreas Knecht, Heidelberg, 1972.

———. English translations: *S. Gregory Nazianzen,* in NPNF, 2nd ser., vol. 7, Grand Rapids; reprint, 1983; *Saint Gregory Nazianzen: Selected Poems,* translated by John McGuckin, Fairacres and Oxford, 1986; *Selected Orations,* translated by Martha Vinson, FC 107, Washington, D.C., 2003; "Theological Orations," in *Christology of the Later Fathers,* translated by E. R. Hardy, LCC 3, Philadelphia, 1956; *Three Poems,* translated by Denis Molaise Meehan, FC 75, Washington, D.C., 1986.

Griffin, David Ray. 1994. "Whitehead's Deeply Ecological Worldview." In *Worldviews and Ecology: Religion, Philosophy, and the Environment,* edited by Mary Evelyn Tucker and John A. Grim, 190-206. Maryknoll, N.Y.

Griffin, Susan. 1987. *Frau und Natur: Das Brüllen in ihr.* Frankfurt am Main. In English, *Woman and Nature,* 1978.

Groh, Ruth, and Dieter Groh. 1991. *Weltbild und Naturaneignung: Zur Kulturgeschichte der Natur.* Frankfurt am Main.

Gronau, Karl. 1914. *Poseidonios und die jüdisch-christliche Genesisexegese.* Leipzig and Berlin.

Gutiérrez, Gustavo. 1976. *Theologie der Befreiung.* 2nd ed. Munich and Mainz.

————. 1986. *Aus der eigenen Quelle trinken: Spiritualität der Befreiung.* Fundamental-theologische Studien 12. Munich and Mainz. In Spanish, *Beber en su propio pozo.* In English, *We Drink from Our Own Wells: The Spiritual Journey of a People,* London, 1984.

————. 1991. *The God of Life.* London. In Spanish, *El Dios de la Vida,* 1989.

Haeckel, Ernst. 1866. *Generelle Morphologie der Organismen.* Berlin.

Hägerstrand, Torsten. 1988. "Landet som trädgård." In *Naturresurser och landskapsomvandling: Rapport från ett seminarium om framtiden,* edited by Bostadsdepartementet och Forskningsrådsnämnden. Stockholm.

Hallman, David G. 1994. *Ecotheology: Voices from South and North.* Geneva and Maryknoll, N.Y.

Hanson, R. P. C. 1988. *The Search for the Christian Doctrine of God: The Arian Controversy, 318-381.* Edinburgh.

Haupt, Wolfgang. 1977. *Bewegungsphysiologie der Pflanzen.* Stuttgart.

Hauschild, Wolf-Dieter. 1979. "Armenfürsorge II, Alte Kirche." In *Theologische Realenzyklopädie* 4 (1979), 14-23. Berlin and New York.

————. 1984. "Geist IV, Dogmengeschichtlich." In *Theologische Realenzyklopädie* 12 (1984), 196-218. Berlin and New York.

Heckmann, Gustav. 1980. *Das sokratische Gespräch: Erfahrungen in philosophischen Hochschulseminaren.* Hannover.

Hedström, Ingemar. 1986. *Somos parte de un gran equilibrio: La crisis ecologica en Centroamerica.* Otras publicaciones de la editorial DEI. San José.

Hegel, Georg Wilhelm Friedrich. 1807. *Phänomenologie des Geistes.* New ed. Frankfurt am Main, Berlin, and Vienna, 1983.

Hemberg, Jarl. 1976. *Djuretik.* Stockholm.

Hill, Brennan R. 1998. *Christian Faith and the Environment: Making Vital Connections.* Maryknoll, N.Y.

Hodgson, Peter C. 1994. *Winds of the Spirit: A Constructive Christian Theology.* London.

Hoffmeyer, Jesper. 1988. *Naturen i huvudet: Om biologisk vetenskap.* Stockholm.

Hofmann, Manfred. 1987. *Bolivien und Nicaragua: Modelle einer Kirche im Aufbruch.* Münster.

Holl, A. 1963. *Die Welt der Zeichen bei Augustin.* Vienna.

Holl, Karl. 1904. *Amphilochius von Ikonium in seinem Verhältnis zu den grossen Kappadoziern.* Tübingen.

Holm, Jean. 1994. *Attitudes to Nature.* Edited by John Bowker. London.

Holte, Ragnar. 1965. *Die Vermittlungstheologie: Ihre theologischen Grundbegriffe kritisch untersucht.* Acta Universitatis Upsaliensis, Studia Doctrinae Christianae Upsaliensia 3. Uppsala.

Hornborg, Alf. 1994a. *Ecology as Semiotics: The New Monism and Its Implications for Anthropological Knowledge Construction.* Lund.

————. 1994b. "Environmentalism, Ethnicity and Sacred Places: Reflections on Modernity, Discourse and Power." *Canadian Review of Sociology and Anthropology* 31, no. 3: 245-67.

Hösle, Vittorio. 1991. *Philosophie der ökologischen Krise: Moskauer Vorträge.* Munich.

————. 1992. *Praktische Philosophie in der modernen Welt.* Munich.

Hough, Adrian Michael. 1997. *God Is Not "Green": A Re-examination of Eco-Theology.* Herefordshire.

Huber, Wolfgang. 1990. "Über die Würde der Natur." In *Konflikt und Konsensus: Studien zur Ethik der Verantwortung,* 227-35. Munich.

Hübsch, W. 1863. *Die altchristlichen Kirchen nach den Baudenkmalen und älteren Beschreibungen.* Karlsruhe.

Hume, Lynne. 1988. "Christianity Full Circle: Aboriginal Christianity on Yarrabah Reserve." In *Aboriginal Australians and Christian Missions: Ethnographic and Historical Studies,* edited by Tony Swain and Deborah Bird Rose, 250-62. Australian Association for the Study of Religions 6. Bedford Park, South Australia.

Irimoto, Takashi, and Takako Yamada, eds. 1994. *Circumpolar Religion and Ecology: An Anthropology of the North.* Tokyo.

Irrgang, Bernhard. 1992. *Christliche Umweltethik.* Munich.

Jaeger, Werner. 1914. *Nemesios von Emesa: Quellenforschungen zum Neuplatonismus und seinen Anfängen bei Poseidonios.* Berlin.

Jaspers, Karl. 1974. *Einführung in die Philosophie.* 16th ed. Munich.

Jeanrond, Werner G. 1994. *Theological Hermeneutics: Development and Significance.* London.

Jeffner, Anders. 1972. *The Study of Religious Language.* London.

————. 1993. "Förundrans livshållning." *Vår Lösen* 5/6: 318-20.

————. 1994. "Vetenskapens anda." In *Upptäckter i kontexten: teologiska föreläsningar till Per Frostins minne,* edited by Sigurd Bergmann and Göran Eidevall, 176-87. Skrifter från Institutet för kontextuell teologi 3. Lund.

Jenson, Robert W. 1982. *The Triune Identity.* Philadelphia.

John, Ottmar. 1988. "Die Tradition der Unterdrückten als Leitthema einer theologischen Hermeneutik." *Concilium* 24, no. 6: 519-26.

————. 1991. "Fortschrittskritik und Erinnerung: Walter Benjamin, ein Zeuge der Gefahr." In *Erinnerung, Befreiung, Solidarität: Benjamin, Marcuse, Habermas und die politische Theologie,* edited by Edmund Arens, Ottmar John, and Peter Rottländer, 13-80. Düsseldorf.

Johnson, Bo. 1984. "Något om bibelanvändningen i latinamerikansk befrielseteologi." *Svensk teologisk kvartalskrift* 60, no. 1: 64-70.

Jonas, Hans. 1979. *Das Prinzip Verantwortung: Versuch einer Ethik für die technologische Zivilisation.* Frankfurt am Main.

————. 1987. "Warum die Technik ein Gegenstand für die Ethik ist: Fünf Gründe." In *Technik und Ethik,* edited by Hans Lenk and Günter Ropohl, 81-91. Stuttgart.

Jones, A. H. M. 1981. "Überbesteuerung und der Niedergang des Römischen Reiches." In *Sozial- und Wirtschaftsgeschichte der römischen Kaiserzeit,* edited by Helmuth Schneider, 100-108. Darmstadt.

Jüngel, Eberhard. 1964. *Zum Ursprung der Analogie bei Parmenides und Heraklit.* Berlin.

———. 1978 (1977). *Gott als Geheimnis der Welt: Zur Begründung der Theologie des Gekreuzigten im Streit zwischen Theismus und Atheismus.* 3rd ed. Tübingen. In English, *God as the Mystery of the World*, 1987.

"Kairos Centralamerika." 1990. *Missionsorientering* 144, no. 1: 2-25. Swedish translation of *Kairos Central America*, Nicaragua, 1988.

Kandinsky, Vasily. 1927. "und." In Kandinsky, *Essays über Kunst und Künstler.* Zürich, 1955.

Kant, Immanuel. 1974. *Kritik der reinen Vernunft.* In *Werkausgabe*, edited by Wilhelm Weischedel, vols. 3 and 4. Frankfurt am Main. *(Critique of Pure Reason.)*

Kasper, Walter. 1985. "Tradition als theologisches Erkenntnisprinzip." In *Dogmengeschichte und katholische Theologie*, edited by Klaus Löser, Karl Lehmann, and Matthias Lutz-Bachmann, 376-403. Würzburg.

Kazuo, Muto. 1994. "Das Christentum und der Gedanke des Nichts." *Evangelische Theologie* 54, no. 4: 316-46.

Kelly, John Norman Davidson. 1977. *Early Christian Doctrines.* London.

Kern, Walter. 1979. "Philosophische Pneumatologie: Zur theologischen Aktualität Hegels." In *Gegenwart des Geistes: Aspekte der Pneumatologie*, edited by Walter Kasper, 54-90. Quaestiones Disputatae 85. Freiburg.

Kertsch, Manfred. 1976. "Ein bildhafter Vergleich bei Seneca, Themistios, Gregor von Nazianz und sein kynisch-stoischer Hintergrund." *Vigiliae Christianae* 30: 241-57.

———. 1977. "Ergänzende Bemerkungen." *Vigiliae Christianae* 31: 298-307.

———. 1980. *Bildersprache bei Gregor von Nazianz: Ein Beitrag zur spätantiken Rhetorik und Popularphilosophie.* Grazer Theologische Studien. Graz.

Kessler, Hans. 1990. *Das Stöhnen der Natur: Plädoyer für eine Schöpfungsspiritualität und Schöpfungsethik.* Düsseldorf.

Khalid, Fazlun, and Joanne O'Brian, eds. 1992. *Islam and Ecology.* London and New York.

Kinzelbach, Ragnar K. 1989. *Ökologie. Naturschutz. Umweltschutz.* Dimensionen der modernen Biologie 6. Darmstadt.

Kippenberg, Hans G., ed. 1977. *Seminar: Die Entstehung der antiken Klassengesellschaft.* Frankfurt am Main.

Kirsten, E. N. D. 1954. "Cappadocia." In *Reallexikon für Antike und Christentum*, 2:861-91. Stuttgart.

Klee, Paul. 1971 (1956). *Das bildnerische Denken: Schriften zur Form- und Gestaltungslehre.* Edited by Jürg Spiller. 3rd ed. Basel and Stuttgart.

Kolig, Erich. 1988. "Mission Not Accomplished: Christianity in the Kimberleys." In *Aboriginal Australians and Christian Missions: Ethnographic and Historical Studies*, edited by Tony Swain and Deborah Bird Rose, 377-90. Australian Association for the Study of Religions 6. Bedford Park, South Australia.

Kopecek, Thomas Alan. 1972. "Social/Historical Studies in the Cappadocian Fathers." Diss., Brown University.

Koyama, Kosuke. 1983. *Det svårhanterliga korset: en asiatisk meditation över den korsfästa själen.* Stockholm. In English, *No Handle on the Cross*, London, 1975.

Kreeb, Karl Heinz. 1979. *Ökologie und menschliche Umwelt.* Stuttgart.

Kretzenbacher, Leopold. 1977. *Das verletzte Kultbild: Voraussetzungen, Zeitschichten und*

Aussagewandel eines abendländischen Legendentypus. Part 1. Bayerische Akademie der Wissenschaften. Philosophisch-Historische Klasse: Sitzungsberichte. Munich.

Kyung, Chung Hyung. 1991. "Komm, Heiliger Geist — erneuere die ganze Schöpfung: Einführung in das theologische Thema der 7. Vollversammlung des Ökumenischen Rates der Kirchen vom 7.-20. Februar 1991 in Canberra." *Junge Kirche* 3: 130-37.

Labriolle, Pierre de. 1950. "Apatheia." In *Reallexikon für Antike und Christentum*, 1:484-87. Stuttgart.

LaCugna, Catherine Mowry. 1993 (1991). *God for Us: The Trinity and Christian Life.* New ed. San Francisco.

Lampe, G. W. H. 1976. *A Patristic Greek Lexicon.* 4th ed. Oxford.

Landels, John Gray. 1980. *Die Technik in der antiken Welt.* Munich. In English, *Engineering in the Ancient World,* London, 1978.

Lange, Ernst. 1981. *Kirche für die Welt: Aufsätze zur Theorie kirchlichen Handelns.* Munich.

Lepenies, Wolf. 1982. "Die Dynamisierung des Naturbegriffs an der Wende zur Neuzeit." In *Das Naturbild des Menschen,* edited by Jörg Zimmermann, 285-300. Munich.

Lessing, Eckhard. 1984. "Geist V, Dogmatisch und ethisch." In *Theologische Realenzyklopädie,* 12:218-3/. Berlin and New York.

Liedke, Gerhard. 1984 (1979). *Im Bauch des Fisches: Ökologische Theologie.* 4th ed. Stuttgart.

————. 1989. "Schöpfungsethik im Konflikt zwischen sozialer und ökologischer Verpflichtung." In *Ökologische Theologie: Perspektiven zur Orientierung,* edited by Günter Altner, 300-321. Stuttgart.

Lindbeck, George A. 1984. *The Nature of Doctrine: Religion and Theology in a Postliberal Age.* London.

Link, Christian. 1982. *Die Welt als Gleichnis: Studien zum Problem der natürlichen Theologie.* Beiträge zur evangelischen Theologie 73. Munich.

————. 1989. "Die Transparenz der Natur für das Geheimnis der Schöpfung." In *Ökologische Theologie: Perspektiven zur Orientierung,* edited by Günter Altner, 166-95. Stuttgart.

————. 1991. *Schöpfung: Schöpfungstheologie angesichts der Herausforderungen des 20. Jahrhunderts.* Handbuch Systematischer Theologie 7/2. Gütersloh.

Lossky, Vladimir. 1961. *Die mystische Theologie der morgenländischen Kirche.* Graz. In French, *Essai sur la Théologique Mystique de l'Eglise d'Orient,* Paris.

Lovelock, James E. 1979. *Gaja: A New Look at Life on Earth.* Oxford.

Luhmann, Niklas. 1990 (1986). *Ökologische Kommunikation: Kann die moderne Gesellschaft sich auf ökologische Gefährdungen einstellen?* 3rd ed. Opladen.

Luther, Martin. 1883. "Disputatio Heidelbergae habita. 1518." In Weimar Ausgabe, 1:353-74. Weimar.

MacKinnon, Mary Heather, and Moni McIntyre, eds. 1995. *Readings in Ecology and Feminist Theology.* Kansas City, Mo.

Marc, Franz. 1978. *Schriften.* Edited by Klaus Lankheit. Munich.

Maximus Confessor. 1860-65. *Ambiguorum Liber I.* In *Ambiguorum liber de variis difficilibus locis Sanctorum Dionysii Areopagitae et Gregorii Theologi*, pp. 1032-1417. PG 91.

———. *Zweiter Brief an Thomas*. In *Epistulae*, pp. 363-649. PG 91.

Maxwell, Nicholas. 1992. "What Kind of Inquiry Can Best Help Us Create a Good World?" *Science, Technology, and Human Values* 17, no. 2: 205-27.

May, John D'Arcy. 1990. *Christus Initiator: Theologie im Pazifik*. Theologie Interkulturell 4. Düsseldorf.

McAfee Brown, Robert. 1978. *Theology in a New Key*. Philadelphia.

McCagney, Nancy. 1998. *Religion and Ecology*. Oxford.

McDaniel, Jay B. 1990a. *Earth, Sky, Gods, and Mortals: Developing an Ecological Spirituality*. Mystic, Conn.

———. 1990b. "Revisioning God and the Self: Lessons from Buddhism." In *Liberating Life: Contemporary Approaches to Ecological Theology*, edited by Charles Birch, William Eakin, and Jay B. McDaniel, 228-58. New York.

McFague, Sallie. 1987. *Models of God: Theology for an Ecological, Nuclear Age*. Philadelphia.

———. 1993. *The Body of God: An Ecological Theology*. London.

———. 2001. *Life Abundant: Rethinking Theology and Economy for a Planet in Peril*. Minneapolis.

Mellor, Mary. 1998. *Feminism and Ecology*. New York.

Merchant, Carolyn. 1987. *Der Tod der Natur: Ökologie. Frauen und neuzeitliche Naturwissenschaft*. Munich. In English, *The Death of Nature*, 1980.

Metz, Johann Baptist. 1972. "Erinnerung des Leidens als Kritik eines teleologisch-technologischen Zukunftsbegriffs." *Evangelische Theologie* 32: 338-52.

Meyendorff, John. 1974. *St. Gregory Palamas and Orthodox Spirituality*. New York.

———. 1983. "Creation in the History of Orthodox Theology." *St. Vladimir's Theological Quarterly* 1: 27-37.

Meyer-Abich, Klaus Michael. 1979. "Zum Begriff einer Praktischen Philosophie der Natur." In *Frieden mit der Natur*, edited by Klaus Michael Meyer-Abich, 237-61. Freiburg im Breisgau.

———. 1988. *Wissenschaft für die Zukunft: Holistisches Denken in ökologischer und gesellschaftlicher Verantwortung*. Munich.

———. 1989a. "Eigenwert der natürlichen Mitwelt und Rechtsgemeinschaft der Natur." In *Ökologische Theologie: Perspektiven zur Orientierung*, edited by Günter Altner, 254-76. Stuttgart.

———. 1989b. "Der Holismus im 20. Jahrhundert." In *Klassiker der Naturphilosophie: Von den Vorsokratikern bis zur Kopenhagener Schule*, edited by Gernot Böhme, 313-29. Munich.

Michl, J. 1962. "Engel I-IX." In *Reallexikon für Antike und Christentum*, 5:54-258. Stuttgart.

Mick, Lawrence E. 1997. *Liturgy and Ecology in Dialogue*. Collegeville, Minn.

Mies, Maria, and Vandana Shiva. 1993. *Ecofeminism*. London, Halifax, and North Melbourne.

Mittelstrass, Jürgen. 1981. "Das Wirken der Natur: Materialien zur Geschichte des Naturbegriffs." In *Naturverständnis und Naturbeherrschung: Philosophie-*

geschichtliche Entwicklung und gegenwärtiger Kontext, edited by Friedrich Rapp, 36-69. Munich.

Moltmann, Jürgen. 1981. *The Trinity and the Kingdom of God: The Doctrine of God.* London. In German, *Trinität und Reich Gottes: Zur Gotteslehre,* Munich, 1980.

———. 1985. *God in Creation: An Ecological Doctrine of Creation.* Gifford Lectures, 1984-85. London. In German, *Gott in der Schöpfung: Ökologische Schöpfungslehre,* Munich, 1985.

———. 1989. *Creating a Just Future: The Politics of Peace and the Ethics of Creation in a Threatened World.* London. In German, *Gerechtigkeit schafft Zukunft: Friedenspolitik und Schöpfungsethik in einer bedrohten Welt,* Munich and Mainz, 1989.

———. 1990. *The Way of Jesus Christ: Christology in Messianic Dimensions.* London. In German, *Der Weg Jesu Christi: Christologie in messianischen Dimensionen,* Munich, 1989.

———. 1991a. *Der Geist des Lebens: Eine ganzheitliche Pneumatologie.* Munich.

———. 1991b. *In der Geschichte des dreieinigen Gottes: Beiträge zur trinitarischen Theologie.* Munich.

———. 1993. "Die Erde und die Menschen: Zum theologischen Verständnis der Gaia-Hypothese." *Evangelische Theologie* 53, no. 5: 420-38.

———. 1996. *The Coming of God: Christian Eschatology.* London. In German, *Das Kommen Gottes: Christliche Eschatologie,* Munich, 1995.

———. 2001a. *The Crucified God: The Cross of Christ as the Foundation and Criticism of Christian Theology.* London. In German, *Der gekreuzigte Gott,* Munich, 1972.

———. 2001b. *The Spirit of Life: A Universal Affirmation.* Minneapolis. In German, *Der Geist des Lebens: Eine ganzheitliche Pneumatologie,* Munich, 1991.

Moltmann, Jürgen, and Elisabeth Giesser. 1990. "Menschenrechte, Rechte der Menschheit und Rechte der Natur." In *Rechte künftiger Generationen. Rechte der Natur: Vorschlag zu einer Erweiterung der Allgemeinen Erklärung der Menschenrechte,* edited by Lukas Vischer, 15-25. Bern.

Moltmann-Wendel, Elisabeth. 1993. "Rückkehr zur Erde." *Evangelische Theologie* 53, no. 5: 406-20.

Momigliano, Arnoldo. 1963. "Christianity and the Decline of the Roman Empire." In *The Conflict between Paganism and Christianity in the Fourth Century,* edited by A. Momigliano, 1-16. Oxford.

Mossay, Justin. 1985. "Gregor von Nazianz." In *Theologische Realenzyklopädie,* 14:164-73. Berlin and New York.

Mösser, Andeheinz. 1976. *Das Problem der Bewegung bei Paul Klee.* Heidelberger Kunstgeschichtliche Abhandlungen, n.s., 12. Heidelberg.

Müller, A. M. K. 1978. *Wende der Wahrnehmung.* Munich.

Mynarek, Hubertus. 1986. *Ökologische Religion: Ein neues Verständnis der Natur.* Munich.

Næss, Arne. 1989. *Ecology, Community, and Lifestyle: Outline of an Ecosophy.* Cambridge. Shortened and revised edition of *Økologi. samfunn og livsstil: Utkast til en økosofi,* Oslo, 1976.

Nash, James A. 1991. *Loving Nature: Ecological Integrity and Christian Responsibility.* Nashville

Nelson, Leonard. 1974. "Über wissenschaftliche und ästhetische Naturbetrachtung." In *Gesammelte Schriften,* vol. 3, *Die kritische Methode in ihrer Bedeutung für die Wissenschaft,* 284-303. Hamburg. In English, "The Scientific and Esthetic Conception of Nature," in *Socratic Method and Critical Philosophy,* New Haven, 1949.

———. 1987. *Die sokratische Methode.* Kassel.

Nennen, Heinz-Ulrich. 1991. *Ökologie im Diskurs: Zu Grundfragen der Anthropologie und Ökologie und zur Ethik der Wissenschaften.* Opladen.

Nicholas of Cusa. 1937. *Idiota de mente.* Vol. 5, *Nicolai de Cusa: Opera omnia iussu et auctoritate Academiae litterarum Heidelbergensis ad codicum fidem ed.* Edited by Ludovicus Baur. Hamburg.

———. 1998a. *Nicholas of Cusa on Wisdom and Knowledge.* Edited by J. Hopkins. Minneapolis.

———. 1998b. *Metaphysical Speculations.* Edited by John Hopkins. Minneapolis.

Nissen, Johannes. 1993. "Helligånden sp12rænger grænser og sætter skel: om Helligåndsforståelsen i Canberra og i Ny Testamente." In *Du som går ud fra den levende Gud: Bibelteologiske og teologihistoriske overvejelser over helligånden,* edited by Hennig Thomsen, 13-54. Frederiksberg.

Norderval, Øyvind. 1988. "Keiser og kappadokier: Forståelsen av forholdet mellom kristendom og antikk kultur hos keiser Julian og Gregor av Nazianz." *Norsk Teologisk Tidsskrift* 89, no. 2: 93-113.

Norris, Frederick W. 1991. *Faith Gives Fullness to Reasoning: The Five Theological Orations of Gregory Nazianzen; Introduction and Commentary.* Translated by Lionel Wickham and Frederick Williams. Supplements to Vigiliae Christianae, vol. 13. Leiden.

Novalis. 1986. "Die Lehrlinge zu Sais." In *Mondbeglänzte Zaubernacht: Erzählungen der deutschen Romantik,* 79-109. Stuttgart and Munich.

Nozick, R. 1974. *Anarchy, State, and Utopia.* Oxford.

Origen. 1985 (1976). *De Principiis Libri IV, Vier Bücher von den Prinzipien.* Edited by, translated by, and with critical and explanatory notes furnished by Herwig Görgemanns and Heinrich Karpp. 2nd enlarged ed. Darmstadt. *(On First Principles.)*

Otis, Brooks. 1961. "The Throne and the Mountain: An Essay on St. Gregory Nazianzus." *Classical Journal* 56: 146-65.

Panikkar, Raimundo. 1993. *Trinität: Über das Zentrum menschlicher Erfahrung.* Munich. In English, *The Trinity and the Religious Experience of Man,* New York, 1973.

Panikkar, Raimundo, and W. Stolz, eds. 1985. *Buddhismus und Natur: Die Verantwortung des Menschen für eine bewohnbare Welt in Christentum, Hinduismus und Buddhismus.* Freiburg.

Pannenberg, Wolfhart. 1988. *Systematische Theologie.* Vol. 1. Göttingen.

———. 1994. *Systematic Theology.* Vol. 2. Edinburgh. In German, *Systematische Theologie,* vol. 2, Göttingen, 1991.

———. 1998. *Systematic Theology.* Vol. 3. Edinburgh. In German, *Systematische Theologie,* vol. 3, Göttingen, 1993.

Park, Chris C. 1994. *Sacred Worlds: An Introduction to Geography and Religion.* London and New York.

Peacocke, Arthur. 1990. *Theology for a Scientific Age: Being and Becoming — Natural and Divine.* Oxford.

Pelikan, Jaroslav. 1993. *Christianity and Classical Culture: The Metamorphosis of Natural Theology in the Christian Encounter with Hellenism.* New Haven and London.

Peterson, Erik. 1951. "Der Monotheismus als politisches Problem." In *Theologische Traktate,* 45-147. Munich.

Philo. 1968. "On the Giants." In *Philo,* edited by F. H. Colson and G. H. Whitaker, 446-79. London.

Picht, Georg. 1979. "Ist Humanökologie möglich?" In *Humanökologie und Frieden,* 14-123. Forschungen und Berichte der Fest 34. Edited by Constanze Eisenbart. Stuttgart.

————. 1989. *Der Begriff der Natur und seine Geschichte.* Stuttgart.

————. 1990a (1985). *Kants Religionsphilosophie.* 2nd ed. Stuttgart.

————. 1990b (1986). *Kunst und Mythos.* 3rd ed. Stuttgart.

Piepmeier, R. 1976. "Korrelation I." In *Historisches Wörterbuch der Philosophie,* 4:1139f. Basel and Stuttgart.

Pinault, Henri. 1925. *Le Platonisme de Saint Grégoire de Nazianze: Essai sur les relations du christianisme et de l'hellénisme dans son oeuvre théologique.* LaRoche-sur-Yon.

Plato. 1989. "Timaios." In *Sämtliche Werke,* edited by Ernesto Grassi with the collaboration of Walter Hess, 5:141-213. New ed. Hamburg. *Timaeus.*

Pohlenz, Max. 1948. *Die Stoa: Geschichte einer geistigen Bewegung.* 3rd ed. Göttingen.

Portmann, Franz Xaver. 1954. *Die göttliche Paidagogia bei Gregor von Nazianz.* St. Ottilien.

Prenter, Regin. 1944. *Spiritus Creator: Studier i Luthers Teologi.* Aarhus and Copenhagen.

Prigogine, Ilya, and Isabelle Stengers. 1985. *Ordning ur kaos: människans nya dialog med naturen.* Göteborg. In English, *Order out of Chaos,* New York, 1984.

Primavesi, Anne. 1991. *From Apocalypse to Genesis: Ecology, Feminism, and Christianity.* Tunbridge Wells.

————. 2000. *Sacred Gaia: Holistic Theology and Earth System Science.* London and New York.

Rahner, Karl. 1971. "Geist über alles Leben." In *Schriften zur Theologie VII,* 189-96. Einsiedeln, Zürich, and Cologne.

Rasmussen, Larry L. 1998. "Next Journey: Sustainability for Six Billion and More." In Daniel C. Maguire and Larry L. Rasmussen, *Ethics for a Small Planet: New Horizons on Population, Consumption, and Ecology,* 67-140. Albany, N.Y.

Régnon, Th. de. 1892. *Études de Théologie sur la Sainte Trinité.* Paris.

Reinhardt, Karl. 1926. *Kosmos und Sympathie: Neuere Untersuchungen über Poseidonios.* Munich.

Riley, Shamara Shantu. 1995. "Ecology Is a Sistah's Issue Too: The Politics of Emergent Afrocentric Ecowomanism." In *Readings in Ecology and Feminist Theology,* edited by Mary Heather MacKinnon and Moni McIntyre, 214-29. Kansas City, Mo.

Ritter, A. Martin. 1981. "Die Theologie des Basileios im Kontext der Reichskirche am Beispiel seines Charismaverständnisses." In *Basil of Caesarea: Christian, Human-*

ist, Ascetic; A Sixteen-Hundredth Anniversary Symposium, part 1, edited by Paul Jonathan Fedwick. Toronto.

———. 1988. "Dogman und Lehre in der alten Kirche." In *Handbuch der Dogmen- und Theologiegeschichte*, edited by Carl Andersen, 1:99-283. Göttingen.

Rockefeller, Steven C. 1997. "The Wisdom of Reverence for Life." In *The Greening of the Faith: God, the Environment, and the Good Life*, edited by John E. Carroll, Paul Brockelman, and Mary Westfal, 44-61. Hanover, N.H.

Rolston, Holmes, III. 1988. *Environmental Ethics: Duties to and Values in the Natural World*. Philadelphia.

Ropohl, Günter. 1987. "Neue Wege, die Technik zu verantworten." In *Technik und Ethik*, edited by Hans Lenk and Günter Ropohl, 149-76. Stuttgart.

Ruether, Rosemary Radford. 1969. *Gregory of Nazianzus: Rhetor and Philosopher*. Oxford.

———. 1992. *Gaia and God: An Ecofeminist Theology of Earth Healing*. New York.

———. [1993] 1994. "Ecofeminism: Symbolic and Social Connections of the Oppression of Women and the Domination of Nature." In *An Ecology of the Spirit: Religious Reflection and Environmental Consciousness*, edited by Michael Barnes. Annual Publication of the College Theology Society, vol. 36. Lanham, Md.

———, ed. 1996. *Women Healing Earth: Third World Women on Ecology, Feminism, and Religion*. Maryknoll, N.Y.

Russell, Colin A. 1994. *The Earth, Humanity, and God: The Templeton Lectures, Cambridge, 1993*. London.

Ryan, Judith. 1994. "En anderledes billdedverden: Australsk aboriginal kunst — fra ceremoni til galleri." In *Aratjara: Kunst af de oprindelige australiere*, 16-37. Exhibition catalogue. Copenhagen.

Sandström, Sven. 1993. "För fantasin står alla dörrar öppna: om förnuftets komplementaritet och kreativitet." In *Den barnsliga fantasin*, edited by Gunnar Berefelt, 85-119. Stockholm.

———. 1994. "Att tänka som en bild (en text om icke-semiotisk förståelse i det åskådliga)." In *Konstens metod som kunskapsväg*, edited by Maria Marklund and Robert Berg, 39-48. Centrum för didaktik vid Lunds universitet och Lärarhögskolan i Malmö 2/1994. Lund and Malmö.

Santmire, H. Paul. 1994. "Is Christianity Ecologically Bankrupt? The View from Asylum Hill." In *An Ecology of the Spirit: Religious Reflection and Environmental Consciousness*, edited by Michael Barnes, 11-25. Annual Publication of the College Theology Society, vol. 36. Lanham, Md.

Sauter, Gerhard. 1973. *Wissenschaftstheoretische Kritik der Theologie: Die Theologie und die neuere wissenschaftstheoretische Diskussion, Materialien, Analysen, Entwürfe*. Munich.

Savramis, Demosthenes. 1977. "Basileios der Grosse." In *Die Grossen: Leben und Leistung der 600 bedeutendsten Persönlichkeiten der Welt*, vol. II/2, edited by Jeremias Wolf, 610-21. Zürich.

Schäfer, Lothar. 1982. "Wandlungen des Naturbegriffs." In *Das Naturbild des Menschen*, edited by Jörg Zimmermann, 11-44. Munich.

Scharbert, Josef. 1990. "Leiden I, Altes Testament." In *Theologische Realenzyklopädie*, 20:670-72. Berlin and New York.

Scharper, Stephen Bede. 1997. *Redeeming the Time: A Political Theology of the Environment*. New York.

Schleiermacher, Friedrich. 1884. *Die christliche Sitte nach den Grundsätzen der evangelischen Kirche im Zusammenhange dargestellt.* In *Sämtliche Werke*, vol. 12, edited by L. Jonas. 2nd ed. Berlin.

Schluchter, Wolfgang, ed. 1985. *Max Webers Sicht des antiken Christentums*. Frankfurt am Main.

Schmidt, M. A. 1958. "Heiliger Geist, dogmengeschichtlich." In *Religion im Geschichte und Gegenwart*, 2:1279-83. 3rd ed. Tübingen.

Schopenhauer, Arthur. 1938. *Die Welt als Wille und Vorstellung II.5*. In *Sämtliche Werke*, edited by Arthur Hübscher, vol. 3. Wiesbaden. In English, *The World as Will and Idea*, 1896.

Schottroff, Luise. 1989. "Schöpfung im Neuen Testament." In *Ökologische Theologie: Perspektiven zur Orientierung*, edited by Günter Altner, 130-48. Stuttgart.

Schramm, Engelbert, ed. 1984. *Ökologie-Lesebuch: Ausgewählte Texte zur Entwicklung ökologischen Denkens*. Frankfurt am Main.

Schreiter, Robert J. 1985. *Constructing Local Theologies*. London.

————. 1997. *The New Catholicity: Theology between the Global and the Local*. Maryknoll, N.Y.

Schultze, Bernhard. 1973. "S. Bulgakovs 'Utesitel' und Gregor der Theologe über den Ausgang des Heiligen Geistes." *Orientalia Christiana Periodica* 39, no. 1: 162-90.

Schupp, Franz. 1990. *Schöpfung und Sünde: Von der Verheißung einer wahren und gerechten Welt, vom Versagen der Menschen und vom Widerstand gegen die Zerstörung*. Düsseldorf.

Schüssler Fiorenza, Elisabeth. 1995. *In Memory of Her: A Feminist Theological Reconstruction of Christian Origins*. 2nd ed. London.

Schüssler Fiorenza, Francis. 1991. "Systematic Theology: Task and Methods." In *Systematic Theology: Roman Catholic Perspectives*, vol. 1, edited by Francis Schüssler Fiorenza and John P. Galvin, 1-87. Minneapolis.

Seel, Martin. 1991. *Eine Ästhetik der Natur*. Frankfurt am Main.

Sheldrake, Rupert. 1988. *The Presence of the Past*. New York.

Shiva, Vandana. 1993. "Den biologiska mångfaldens kris." In *Den globala konflikten om miljön och framtiden*, edited by T. Björk and J. Wiklund, 32-41. Stockholm.

Simmel, Georg. 1918. *Lebensanschauung: Vier metaphysische Kapitel*. Munich and Leipzig.

Sindima, Harvey. 1990. "Community of Life: Ecological Theology in African Perspective." In *Liberating Life: Contemporary Approaches to Ecological Theology,* edited by Charles Birch, William Eakin, and Jay B. McDaniel, 137-47. New York.

Singer, Peter. 1990. *Praktisk etik*. Stockholm.

————. 1992. *Djurens frigörelse*. Stockholm.

Sittler, Joseph. 1961. *The Ecology of Faith: The New Situation in Preaching*. Philadelphia.

"Skapelsens förvandling — Ortodoxa perspektiv på skapelsen: Rapport från den inter-ortodoxa konsultationen i Sofia." 1987. In *Tiden är inne — ekumenisk teologi i uppbrott,* edited by Sigurd Bergmann and Gunborg Blomstrand, 75-92. KISA rapport 5. Uppsala. In English, "Orthodox Perspectives on Creation," in *Justice, Peace, and the Integrity of Creation: Insights from Orthodoxy,* edited by Gennadios Limouris, 1-15, Geneva.

Slenczka, Reinhard. 1988. "Dogma und Kircheneinheit." In *Handbuch der Dogmen- und Theologiegeschichte,* vol. 3, edited by Carl Andresen, 425-603. Göttingen.

Sobrino, Jon. 1988. *Spirituality of Liberation: Toward Political Holiness.* Maryknoll, N.Y. In Spanish, *Liberación con espíritu: Apuntes para una nueva espiritualidad,* Santander, 1985.

Sölle, Dorothee. 1975. *Suffering.* Philadelphia.

————. 1984. *To Work and to Love: A Theology of Creation.* Philadelphia.

————. 1990. *Thinking about God: An Introduction to Theology.* London.

Song, Choan-Seng. 1991. *Third-Eye Theology: Theology in Formation in Asian Settings.* Rev. ed. Maryknoll, N.Y.

Sörlin, Sverker. 1991. *Naturkontraktet: Om naturumgängets idéhistoria.* Stockholm.

Sparn, Walter. 1990. "Leiden IV, Historisch/Systematisch/Ethisch." In *Theologische Realenzyklopädie,* 20:688-707. Berlin and New York.

Spencer, Daniel T. 1996. *Gay and Gaia: Ethics, Ecology, and the Erotic.* Cleveland.

Spinoza, Baruch. 1989. *Etiken.* Translated by Dagmar Lagerberg. Stockholm.

Staniloae, Dumitru. 1984. *Orthodoxe Dogmatik.* Ökumenische Theologie 12. Zürich and Gütersloh.

Ste. Croix, G. E. M. 1981. *The Class Struggle in the Ancient Greek World from the Archaic Age to the Arab Conquests.* London.

Stendahl, Krister. 1990. *Energy for Life: Reflections on the Theme "Come, Holy Spirit — Renew the Whole Creation."* Geneva.

Stolz, Walter. 1992. "Natur und Naturphilosophie heute: Ein Literaturbericht zu Problemen und Perspektiven." *Herder Korrespondenz* 11: 514-20.

Stone, Christopher. 1992. "Should Trees Have a Standing? Toward Legal Rights for Natural Objects." *Southern California Law Review,* 1972.

Strey, Gernot. 1989. *Umweltethik und Evolution: Herkunft und Grenzen moralischen Verhaltens gegenüber der Natur.* Göttingen.

Sundermeier, Theo. 1987. "Jeder Teil dieser Erde ist meinem Volke heilig: Naturreligiöse Frömmigkeit." In *Frieden in der Schöpfung: Das Naturverständnis protestantischer Theologie,* edited by Gerhard Rau, A. Martin Ritter, and Hermann Timm, 20-34. Gütersloh.

————. 1988. *Nur gemeinsam können wir leben: Das Menschenbild schwarzafrikanischer Religionen.* Gütersloh.

Theiler, Willy. 1971. "Überblick über Plotins Philosophie und Lehrweise." In *Plotin Schriften: Text und deutsche Übersetzung von Richard Harder,* 4:103-78. Hamburg.

Thomson, George. 1985. "Demokratische Ideologie." In *Max Webers Sicht des antiken Christentums,* edited by Wolfgang Schluchter, 227-49. Frankfurt am Main.

Thunberg, Lars. 1974. *Mänsklighetstanken i äldre och nyare teologi.* Uppsala.

————. 1977. *"Det saliga bytet": Frälsningsschema och frälsarbild i teologihistorien.* Acta Universitatis Upsaliensis. Studia Doctrinae Christianae Upsaliensia 16. Uppsala.

————. 1979. "Guds förnuftige vicekonung på jorden." In *Människan i miljön — vårdare eller vandal?* edited by Göran Agrell, 48-65. Stockholm.

————. 1985. *Man and the Cosmos: The Vision of St. Maximus the Confessor.* New York.

————. 1986. "The Human Person as Image of God, I, Eastern Christianity." In *Christian Spirituality*, vol. 1, *Origins to the Twelfth Century*, edited by Bernard McGinn and John Meyendorff, 291-312. London.

————. 1988. "Ande och liv hos kyrkofäderna." In *På Åndens betingelser: Essays om sprog og spiritualitet*, edited by Lars Thunberg, 25-36. Aarhus.

————. 1993a. "Kristen helligåndsteologi i mødet med anderledes troende — nogle adspredte refleksioner." In *Du som går ud fra den levende Gud: Bibelteologiske og teologihistoriske overvejelser over helligånden*, edited by Hennig Thomsen, 98-120. Frederiksberg.

————. 1993b. "Troen på Helligånden i oldkirken." In *Du som går ud fra den levende Gud: Bibelteologiske og teologihistoriske overvejelser over helligånden*, edited by Hennig Thomsen, 198-213. Frederiksberg.

Tillich, Paul. 1951. *Systematic Theology.* Vol. 1. Chicago.

Track, Joachim. 1978. "Analogie." In *Theologische Realenzyklopädie*, 2:625-50. Berlin and New York.

Tracy, David. 1981 *The Analogical Imagination: Christian Theology and the Culture of Pluralism.* London.

————. 1985. "Theological Method." In *Christian Theology: An Introduction to Its Traditions and Tasks*, edited by Peter C. Hodgson and Robert King, 35-60. 2nd ed. Philadelphia.

————. 1986. "Abschliessende Gedanken zur Konferenz: Einigkeit mitten in Verschiedenheit und Konflikt." In *Das neue Paradigma von Theologie: Strukturen und Dimensionen*, edited by Hans Küng and David Tracy, 233-42. Ökumenische Theologie 13. Zürich and Gütersloh.

Trepl, Ludwig. 1987. *Geschichte der Ökologie: Vom 17. Jahrhundert bis zur Gegenwart.* Frankfurt am Main.

Treucker, Barnim. 1961. "Politische und sozialgeschichtliche Studien zu den Basilius-Briefen." Diss., Frankfurt University.

Trigo, Pedro. 1989. *Schöpfung und Geschichte.* Düsseldorf (Petrópolis, 1988).

Trombley, Frank R. 1993. *Hellenic Religion and Christianization, c. 370-529.* Vol. 1. Leiden, New York, and Cologne.

Tucker, Mary Evelyn, and John A. Grim, eds. 1994. *Worldviews and Ecology: Religion, Philosophy, and the Environment.* Maryknoll, N.Y.

Tutu, Desmond. 1985. *Hopp och lidande: predikningar och tal.* Stockholm.

Uexküll, Jakob von. 1982. "The Theory of Meaning." *Semiotica* 42, no. 1: 25-82. Translation of "Bedeutungslehre," in J. v. Uexküll and G. Kriszat, *Streifzüge durch die Umwelten von Tieren und Menschen, Bedeutungslehre*, 105-79, new ed., Frankfurt am Main.

Uexküll, Jakob von, and Georg Kriszat. 1983 (1970). *Streifzüge durch die Umwelten von Tieren und Menschen, Bedeutungslehre.* New ed. Frankfurt am Main.

Uexküll, Thure von. 1983. "Die Umweltforschung als subjekt- und objektumgreifende Naturforschung: Einleitung." In J. v. Uexküll und G. Kriszat, *Streifzüge durch die*

Umwelten von Tieren und Menschen, Bedeutungslehre, xxiii-xlviii. New ed. Frankfurt am Main.

————. 1989. "Organismus und Umgebung — Perspektiven einer neuen ökologischen Wissenschaft." In *Ökologische Theologie: Perspektiven zur Orientierung,* edited by Günter Altner, 392-408. Stuttgart.

Ullmann, C. 1867 (1825). *Gregorius von Nazianz der Theologe.* 2nd ed. Gotha.

Vischer, Lukas. 1953. *Basilius der Große: Untersuchungen zu einem Kirchenvater des vierten Jahrhunderts.* Basel.

————, ed. 1990. *Rechte künftiger Generationen. Rechte der Natur: Vorschlag zu einer Erweiterung der Allgemeinen Erklärung der Menschenrechte.* Bern. In English, *Rights of Future Generations: Rights of Nature; Proposal for Enlarging the Universal Declaration of Human Rights,* Studies from the World Alliance of Reformed Churches 19, Geneva.

Volf, Miroslav. 1998. *After Our Likeness: The Church as the Image of the Trinity.* Sacra Doctrina 1. Grand Rapids. In German, *Trinität und Gemeinschaft: Eine ökumenische Ekklesiologie,* Mainz and Neukirchen-Vluyn, 1996.

Wandén, Stig. 1992. *Etik och miljö: De svåra vägvalen i ny belysning.* Stockholm.

Ware, Timothy. 1985 (1963). *The Orthodox Church.* Harmondsworth.

Warren, Karen J., ed. 1996. *Ecological Feminist Philosophies.* Bloomington, Ind., and Indianapolis.

Warren, Karen J., and Nisvan Erkal, eds. 1997. *Ecofeminism: Women, Culture, Nature.* Bloomington, Ind., and Indianapolis.

Weber, Leonard. 1987. "Land Use Ethics: The Social Responsibility of Ownership." In *Theology of the Land,* edited by Bernard Evans and Gregory D. Cusack, 13-39. Collegeville, Minn.

Weizsäcker, Carl Friedrich von. 1976 (1964). *Die Tragweite der Wissenschaft.* Vol. 1, *Schöpfung und Weltenstehung, Die Geschichte zweier Begriffe.* 5th ed. Stuttgart.

Welker, Michael. 1988. *Universalität Gottes und Relativität der Welt: Theologische Kosmologie im Dialog mit dem amerikanischen Prozeßdenken nach Whitehead.* 2nd ed. Neukirchen-Vluyn.

————. 1994. *God the Spirit.* Minneapolis. In German, *Gottes Geist: Theologie des heiligen Geistes,* Neukirchen-Vluyn, 1992.

Wendebourg, Dorothea. 1980. *Geist oder Energie: Zur Frage der innergöttlichen Verankerung des christlichen Lebens in der byzantinischen Theologie.* Munich.

White, K. D. 1981. "Technik und Gewerbe im römischen Reich: Eine Untersuchung der Wechselbeziehungen zwischen Wissenschaft, Technik und Gewerbe im Römischen Reich." In *Sozial- und Wirtschaftsgeschichte der römischen Kaiserzeit,* edited by Helmuth Schneider, 109-27. Darmstadt.

White, Lynn, Jr. 1967. "The Historical Roots of Our Ecological Crisis." *Science* 155: 1203-7.

Whitehead, Alfred North. 1926. *Science and the Modern World.* New York.

————. 1933. *Adventures of Ideas.* New York.

Wiedenhofer, Siegfried. 1990. "Tradition." In *Geschichtliche Grundbegriffe: Historisches Lexikon zur politisch-sozialen Sprache in Deutschland,* 6:607-50. Stuttgart.

————. 1994. "Traditionsbrüche — Traditionsabbruch? Zur Identität des Glaubens." In

Traditionsabbruch — Ende des Christentums? edited by Michael von Brück and Jürgen Werbick, 55-76. Würzburg.

Wifstrand, Albert. 1976. "Medelpunkten." In A. Wifstrand, *Den gyllene kedjan och andra studier,* 38-49. Lund.

Wikander, Örjan. 1980. *Vattenmöllor och möllare i det romerska riket* (summary in English). Lund.

Wiman, Bo. 1991. "Implications of Environmental Complexity for Science and Policy: Contributions from Systems Theory." *Global Environmental Change,* June 1991, 235-47.

Wingren, Gustaf. 1983. *Människa och kristen: En bok om Irenaeus.* Stockholm.

World Council of Churches (WCC). 1983. *Gathered for Life: Official Report VI Assembly World Council of Churches, Vancouver, Canada, 24 July–10 August 1983.* Edited by D. Gill. Geneva and Grand Rapids.

————. 1990 (Seoul). "Slutdokumentet från världssammankomsten i Seoul i mars 1990." In *Skapelse, Fred, Rättvisa: en rapportbok från Svenska Ekumeniska Nämnden,* 157-244. Uppsala, 1991. In English, *Now Is the Time: The Final Document and Other Texts from the World Convocation on Justice, Peace, and the Integrity of Creation.* Seoul, 5-12 March 1990. Geneva, 1990.

————. 1991a. "World Council of Churches Seventh Assembly, Canberra, Australia, 7-20 February 1991." In *Kom, Heliga Ande! — Canberra 1991,* edited by E. Block and E. Ignestam, 67-110. Tro & Tanke 1991:9. Uppsala. In English, "Come, Holy Spirit — Renew the Whole Creation," in *Signs of the Spirit: Official Report of the Seventh Assembly, Canberra,* edited by Michael Kinnamon, Geneva and Grand Rapids, 1991.

————. 1991b. *Confessing One Faith: An Ecumenical Explication of the Apostolic Faith as It Is Confessed in the Nicene-Constantinopolitan Creed (381).* Geneva.

Worster, Donald. 1992 (1977). *Nature's Economy: A History of Ecological Ideas.* 8th ed. Cambridge.

Wuketis, Franz M. 1990. "Evolutionäre Erkenntnistheorie — Die neue Herausforderung." In *Die zweite Schöpfung: Geist und Ungeist in der Biologie des 20. Jahrhunderts,* edited by Jost Herbig and Rainer Hohlfeld, 205-20. Munich and Vienna.

Wyss, Bernhard. 1983. "Gregor von Nazianz." In *Reallexikon für Antike und Christentum,* 12:793-863. Stuttgart.

Yong-Bock, Kim. 1989. "Minjung-ekonomin: förbundet med de fattiga." In *Tiden är inne — ekumenisk teologi i uppbrott,* edited by Sigurd Bergmann and Gunborg Blomstrand, 29-37. KISA rapport 5. Uppsala.

Zimmermann, Jörg, ed. 1982. "Zur Geschichte des ästhetischen Naturbegriffs." In *Das Naturbild des Menschen,* edited by Jörg Zimmermann, 118-54. Munich.

Zizioulas, John D. 1985. *Being as Communion: Studies in Personhood and the Church.* New York.

————. 1995. "The Doctrine of the Holy Trinity: The Significance of the Cappadocian Contribution." In *Theology Today: Essays on Divine Being and Act,* edited by Christoph Schwöbel, 44-60. Edinburgh.

Index